PRAISE FOR THE MOST TALKED-ABOUT
BOOK ON WALL STREET

"Provides the closest loo' _____ o took the
fight to Philip J. Purcel _____ *York Times*

"In *Blue Blood and Muti* _____ ging narrative . . . [and] evokes _____ novel. . . .
Enlivened by accounts o. ___ groups behind-the-scenes maneuvering . . . this tale of subjugation has a certain Shakespearean quality, and in Ms. Beard's telling it also offers glimpses into the gilded lives of Wall Street kings."   —*Wall Street Journal*

"Beard brings impressive reportage to this chronicle of the rise and fall of Philip Purcell, the aloof outsider who ascended to the top of the storied investment banking firm. . . . Beard does a fine job assembling the cast of characters, tensions, issues, and backroom intrigues that color this saga. . . . [*Blue Blood and Mutiny*] plumb[s] the power intrigues of Wall Street and reveal[s] how the high and mighty are both made and laid low."   —*Portfolio*

"Hard to put down! *Blue Blood and Mutiny* is an excellent chronicle of an important event in the contemporary evolution of Wall Street. Patricia Beard writes as though she has spent her whole life on Wall Street."   —Samuel L. Hayes III, Jacob H. Schiff
Professor of Investment Banking, emeritus,
Harvard Business School

"The book that Philip Purcell didn't want you to read. . . . Beard knows the world of the blue bloods very well. . . . Bankers will find comfort in these pages, and those wondering what, exactly, they do for all that money will receive enlightenment." —Bloomberg News

"An unprecedented public battle. . . . Beard gained access to men who largely avoided the press even as they battled for a top-tier firm. The resulting portraits of these veteran bankers opens a window on a bygone age on Wall Street.   —*Boston Globe*

"Provides some strong clues as to why [Wall Street mergers fail]. The truth is that investment bankers are a pain to manage. They earn too much to fear the boss, and they regard themselves highly and other kinds of financial services workers not very highly at all. . . . [*Blue Blood and Mutiny*] gives a good idea of what Mr. Purcell was up against."   —*Financial Times*

"A wonderfully engrossing tale, skillfully and thoroughly told."
                              —Michael M. Thomas, *New York Observer*
                                                  columnist and novelist

"With Stan O'Neal [Merrill Lynch] and Chuck Prince [Citigroup] having been tipped over the precipice, this has been the ideal time to be reading *Blue Blood and Mutiny* by Patricia Beard. . . . We thoroughly enjoyed the book. . . . As there are relatively few books on Morgan Stanley, *Blue Blood and Mutiny* is already a collector's item. . . . A good read."   —*EuroWeek*

"At the heart of this fascinating and compelling saga is a remarkable and intense culture. The reader gains a keen insight into how it was formed, maintained, damaged, and finally saved, and how a board can be blinded by a CEO and stop listening to other important voices. When the eight elders determined that their beloved culture was in danger, they roared into action and fought and won back the firm's traditional values. It is heartening to see such business virtues rewarded."
                    —Paul Danos, dean, Tuck School of Business at Dartmouth

"Investment banks can seem like merciless places, but *Blue Blood and Mutiny* is an intriguing look at how eight renegade alumni at the venerable Wall Street financial services firm, including its former chairman, led a revolt to reinstall the traditional values they held dear, including fierce open debate, collegiality, and, yes, high profits. Journalist Patricia Beard does a good job of telling their story and recreating the resulting drama."   —*The Globe and Mail*

© Pamela Eberhard

About the Author

PATRICIA BEARD is the author of seven nonfiction books, including *After the Ball*, and hundreds of national magazine articles. She has been an editor at *Elle*, *Town & Country*, and *Mirabella*. Beard lives in upstate New York.

BLUE
BLOOD
AND
MUTINY

Also by PATRICIA BEARD

After the Ball
Good Daughters
Christie Whitman: Growing Up Republican

BLUE
BLOOD
AND
MUTINY

The Fight for the
Soul of Morgan Stanley

PATRICIA BEARD

HARPER ⬤ PERENNIAL

NEW YORK • LONDON • TORONTO • SYDNEY • NEW DELHI • AUCKLAND

HARPER ● PERENNIAL

A hardcover edition of this book was published in 2007 by William Morrow, an imprint of HarperCollins Publishers.

HarperCollins books may be purchased for educational, business, or sales promotional use. For information, please e-mail the Special Markets Departments at SPsales@harpercollins.com.

FIRST HARPER PERENNIAL EDITION PUBLISHED 2008.

Designed by Susan Walsh

The Library of Congress has catalogued the hardcover edition as follows:

Beard, Patricia.
　　　Blue blood and mutiny : the fight for the soul of Morgan Stanley / Patricia Beard.—1st ed.
　　　　　xii, 420 p., [16] p. of plates : ill. ; 24 cm.
　　　Includes bibliographical references (p. [369]–401) and index.
　　　ISBN: 978-0-06-088191-7
　　　ISBN-10: 0-06-088191-7
　　　1. Morgan Stanley (Firm). 2. Financial services industry—United States. 3. Investment banking—United States. 4. Securities industry—United States. I. Title.
　　　HG4910 .B355 2007
　　　332.63'270973 22　　　　　　　　　　　　　　　2008271907

ISBN 978-0-06-088192-4 (pbk.)

HB 12.12.2022

For David Jay Braga
and for the next generation,
Landry Hill Beard
Stella Ashley Schafer

The private banker is a member of a profession which has been practiced since the middle ages. In the process of time there has grown up a code of professional ethics and customs on the observance of which depend his reputation, his force and his usefulness to the community in which he works ... If in the exercise of his profession, the private banker disregards this code, which could never be expressed in any legislation, but has a force far greater than any law, he will sacrifice his credit. This credit is his most valuable possession; it is the result of years of faith and honorable dealing and while it may be quickly lost, once lost cannot be restored for a long time, if ever. *The banker must at all times conduct himself so as to justify the confidence of his clients in him and thus preserve it for his successors.*

If I may be permitted to speak of the firm, of which I have the honour to be the senior partner, *I should state that at all times the idea of doing only first class business, and that in a first class way, has been before our minds.*

—J. P. MORGAN JR., MAY 23, 1933

This is an excerpt from the statement that J. P. Morgan Jr. wrote out in pencil the night before he was to testify at the hearings held by a subcommittee of the Banking and Currency Committee of the U.S. Senate. Despite Morgan's sincerity and credibility, the hearings contributed to Depression-era sentiment in favor of creating legal restraints on the power of the banking industry. In 1933, the Glass-Steagall Act was passed, requiring banks to cease either their commercial or investment banking business. J. P. Morgan and Company chose to remain solely a commercial bank. Two years later, in 1935, a small group of Morgan partners founded a new investment bank, Morgan Stanley.

CONTENTS

PROLOGUE

New York, January 2005

On Sunday, January 16, 2005, seven men met at S. Parker Gilbert's Fifth Avenue apartment. They strode past the doormen, across the black-and-white-marble floor, glanced at a portrait of someone's eighteenth-century ancestor, and ascended quietly in the wood-paneled elevator.

Parker Gilbert, tall, reserved, and patrician, was the former chairman of Morgan Stanley, the most prestigious institutional securities firm in the history of American finance. That afternoon, as he walked down the hall to open the door, his gait was stiff: he was seventy-one years old and he had spent many mornings in damp duck blinds. His hips were due to be replaced, but that might have to wait until this business was sorted out. As the apartment filled, the Gilberts' clumber spaniel, Molly, stirred on her pillow under the front hall table, picked up a toy in her mouth, and padded off toward the bedrooms. Molly wasn't unfriendly, but she warmed up slowly. Like master, like dog.

Gilbert and the other two Morgan Stanley Advisory Directors who were there that afternoon were the initial members of the cadre of mutineers who would later be known as the Group of Eight, and also, sometimes derisively and sometimes with affection, as the "Grumpy Old Men." Robert C. Scott, fifty-nine, with his Edwardian beard and starched pastel shirts, had been president of the firm until 2003; Lewis W. Bernard, sixty-three, bald-domed, blue-eyed, pixie-faced, and brilliant, the youngest person outside of the Morgan family ever to be made partner, was Morgan Stanley's former Chief Administrative and Financial Officer.

Gilbert had asked four current leaders of the Institutional Securities division to come over for a chat. The firm's "old guard" took an active interest in the state of the business and in maintaining the culture of the firm and met with Morgan Stanley managing directors from time to time on an informal basis. They would stop by Morgan Stanley for lunch in the partners' dining room, or call people they knew with ideas or input on clients. An invitation to the Gilberts' for a late-afternoon visit wasn't a signal that anything was afoot—and at that point, nothing was.

Gilbert, Scott, and Bernard were looking for insight into what was going on at the firm. There were signs that something was seriously wrong. The stock was trading around $50, down from a high of $110 at the peak of the tech bubble, and while other firms had recovered, Morgan Stanley's stock price was stuck. That was one of the reasons that 2004 ended with a zinger from one of the most quoted analysts on Wall Street, Richard Bove of Punk Ziegel & Company. Bove wrote, "Management and the Board have failed to generate stockholder [value] for five years. This is rapidly emerging as the lost decade for Morgan Stanley." Just a week before, the *Wall Street Journal* had reported on a letter that hedge fund manager Scott Sipprelle, a large stockholder and a former Morgan Stanley managing director, had written to the board. Sipprelle proposed a drastic restructuring of the firm, and he sounded as though he was prepared to take action if changes weren't made.

On a more subtle, cultural level, a few days earlier, all of the men at Gilbert's that Sunday had attended the memorial service for their deeply admired and beloved former chairman, Richard B. Fisher. Although 1,500 people turned out to mourn his loss, not a single member of the board of directors was there. A couple of days later, at the next management committee meeting, an outraged John P. Havens, the Head of Equities, angrily asked why the directors hadn't been there. Whatever the reason, their absence was an unacceptable breach of etiquette and respect. As one senior Morgan Stanley executive remarked, "That kind of disrespect is unheard-of on Wall Street; it tells you how little the board understood our business, and our culture."

Gilbert's guests that afternoon were the intellectual Indian-born Vikram Pandit, Head of Institutional Securities, the Morgan Stanley division that accounted for between two-thirds and three-quarters of the firm's profits; Joseph R. Perella, the iconic Mergers and Acquisitions star who was Morgan Stanley's most famous face to the outside world; John Havens, a natural leader who patrolled the trading floor bellowing out his favorite refrain: "I wear Morgan Stanley blue *underwear*"; and Tarek F. Abdel-Meguid, Head of Investment Banking, a handsome, preppy banker of distinguished Egyptian descent, who combined social ease with an organized business style.

Every man there was a master of the calculated, intelligent risk, leaders of that class of men and women who make businesses great. Gilbert and his generation had built the firm. Most of the former executives who would soon make up the Group of Eight had joined Morgan Stanley before 1971, when it was still a private partnership, with 200 employees and $7.5 million in capital. It was now a $60 billion public company with 54,000 employees worldwide. Gilbert had been chairman when the firm went public in 1986, making himself and others far richer than they had ever expected to be. Now they were enjoying quasi-retirement, eased by wealth and invigorated by prodigious charitable endeavors and entrepreneurial enterprises—as well as by golf, fishing, shooting, skiing, and sailing, and in a couple of cases, new wives.

Except for Bob Scott, none of the Eight had been employed at Morgan Stanley in the twenty-first century. The title "Advisory Director" was granted to certain senior executives when they retired, earning them the eminence and pathos innate in such words as *emeritus*. Even the offices the firm provided for them in an innocuous Midtown building a few blocks from Morgan Stanley headquarters were known as "Jurassic Park," but they weren't finished yet.

The Eight were the epitome of the Morgan Stanley image: Ivy League or "little Ivy"–educated, socially conservative, nice-looking Eastern Establishment moneymen. Yet while Morgan Stanley was known as a "blue blood firm," Parker Gilbert correctly insisted that "Morgan Stanley blue" was not inherited through privilege, but earned by merit, and passed along from one generation of leaders to the next. Gilbert found the terms "blue blood" and "white shoe," which were so often used to describe Morgan Stanley executives, distasteful, but even so, he carried the DNA of the firm. His father, S. Parker Gilbert Sr., was a J. P. Morgan partner and was one of the six men present at the 1935 meeting when Morgan Stanley was founded. His godfather, Henry Morgan, the son of J. P. Morgan Jr. and grandson of J. Pierpont Morgan, was one of the named partners. After Parker Gilbert Sr. died at the age of forty-five when Parker was four years old, his mother married a widower, Harold Stanley, who was the other named partner. By Gilbert's legacy and his actions, he embodied the philosophy that J. P. Morgan Jr. read into the record at a 1933 U.S. Senate hearing: "At all times, the idea of doing only first class business, and that in a first class way, has been before our minds."

Some believed that the foundation of Morgan Stanley's culture was the conservation of the old, but in fact, the firm flourished because it fostered the willingness and courage to adapt and change—in a *first class* way. Beyond the history and the Morgan name, the business was built on the understanding that the most effective approach to solving difficult problems was to sit down together, look at the whole picture, and act in the best interests of the firm.

That Sunday afternoon in January, Parker Gilbert had invited the other six men to his apartment to learn more about what was now in the firm's best interest. They settled in his moss green library, among shelves filled with art books, a mysterious painting of a peasant woman holding a doll, by one of the nineteenth-century masters, that hung over the couch, and a little Russian Constructivist canvas that brightened the wall between windows overlooking Central Park. Arranging themselves around a burnished mahogany pedestal table with a silver tankard in the center, they started to talk.

"We weren't planning to do anything yet," Gilbert recalls. "It was before that—but we wanted to know what was going on. We were very clear at that meeting that we didn't know what, if anything, we were going to do, but we needed to get some intelligence.

"We wanted to make sure that should we do something—and we said we weren't going to tell them,"referring to Pandit, Perella, Havens, and Meguid,"for obvious reasons what, or when we might do anything, if at all—but we were prepared to stake our reputations. We needed to know if this was something that should be addressed, and whether the issues were real."

At the root of the "issues" was Philip J. Purcell, who became Morgan Stanley's chairman and CEO in 1997 by insisting that his midmarket brokerage, Dean Witter, would only merge with Morgan Stanley if he got the top position. A dedicated midwesterner—Chicago out of Salt Lake City—Purcell was six foot five, and loose limbed, with an understated all-American style. He had been a sort of boy genius—he was the youngest person ever to be made partner at the management consultant firm McKinsey & Company. Sears Roebuck hired him away and created the position of vice president for planning for him. When the new plans included acquiring a financial services firm, Sears bought Dean Witter and sent Purcell to New York to be its president, even though he had no financial services experience. He invented the Discover card, made it a success, and then spun off Dean Witter Discover in 1993, with Dean Witter as the lead underwriter, and Morgan Stanley as a co-manager of the IPO. That was when Purcell got to know Morgan Stanley's then-chairman, Dick Fisher, and the firm's president, John J. Mack, who was described as "charismatic" so regularly that it could have been part of his name. In 1997 Fisher and Mack had enough faith in Purcell, and believed their merger would create so much shareholder value, that they agreed that he could be chairman and CEO. For the first time someone who hadn't grown up at Morgan Stanley or on Wall Street was put in charge.

The day the deal was completed in 1997, Joe Perella, who had been at the table at hundreds of mergers and acquisitions, told his friends and colleagues at the firm, "John Mack has never dealt with a guy like this. Morgan Stanley people say Phil will be gone in six months, but you don't go from McKinsey to Sears, start Discover card, then get on a life raft called Dean Witter, and steer it down the river and negotiate to become CEO of Morgan Stanley, unless you know a lot about maneuvering. This guy plays a different game."

At sixty-three, Perella was lanky, elegant, and passionate, with long expressive hands and a Prince Albert beard that he stroked from time to time when he was listening intently. In 2004 alone he had more than four hundred face-to-face meetings with CEOs and senior executives of client companies. Too many clients and colleagues had been asking him what was going on with Purcell, and why the stock was in the doldrums. It wasn't just the outside shareholders who were affected; stock was 50 percent of most of the bankers' compensation. The executives in the Equity Division, which ranked number one in the league tables, had to wonder what more they could do, when their counterparts at lesser firms were holding stock worth considerably more.

As Head of Investment Banking, Terry Meguid was Perella's closest colleague, and they shared a gutsy, outspoken style. While Purcell did meet with clients, he did not do so nearly as often as prior leaders of Morgan Stanley or his successor, John Mack. So Perella and Meguid had to compensate for Purcell's absence when a CEO would have been expected to lend his presence and expertise to close a deal. When Purcell did agree to meet with clients, he was well prepared and personable, but he didn't do it nearly often enough, and he wasn't around like the CEOs of other major New York–based financial institutions, who were leaders in the city's civic or philanthropic life. Instead, he lived in a suburb of Chicago and traveled between his home and New York on a Gulfstream V the firm bought after he took over. The perception at the firm was that he arrived on Monday mornings and often left at the end of the week to return to Chicago. He was graceless enough to tell the New York State Comptroller, who managed $100 billion in state funds—of which $1 billion was invested with Morgan Stanley—that he couldn't wait to get back to the Midwest on the weekends. Purcell was viewed by many as a "commuting CEO," perhaps in part because he kept his visibility at the firm low.

Meguid and John Havens reported to Vikram Pandit, who had been considered to be Purcell's most likely successor. Purcell had asked Havens and Pandit to work on the current iteration of a strategy to integrate the old Dean Witter Retail and Asset Management Divisions with Morgan Stanley's Institutional Securities. The businesses were still on different platforms, had different standards, and their leaders remained antagonists eight years after the merger. The bankers had recently presented a nearly completed integration plan at a management committee meeting, but Purcell put them off.

The two of them were partners the way Perella and Meguid were. Another Morgan Stanley investment banker explains, "When Vikram endorsed an underwriting, he did it with John's explicit understanding that his sales force could sell it." Havens's office was a glass box on the trading floor, where he could survey the room, keep the traders' spirits up, and answer questions: trading is a high-tension job involving split-second decisions, with millions of dollars at risk on a single trade. When Dick Fisher was chairman he walked the floor too, even though navigating wasn't easy; he'd had polio as a child and used two canes. John Mack recalls a time "during a terrible market, Fisher goes down to the trading floor and lightens the mood by telling a joke. I saw how when people are stressed he could take the pressure off." Purcell, by contrast, was almost never seen on the floor. One of the questions that repeatedly emerged in 2005 was why Fisher, Mack, and Purcell all seem to have overlooked the innate differences in the relationship between a CEO and his executives in an institutional securities firm, by comparison to a retail business. Dean Witter and Morgan Stanley were both Wall Street firms, but in certain ways, leading Dean Witter had more in common with heading Sears, where policy decisions came down from the top, and no one expected the CEO to be readily available to salespeople, or participate in their sales efforts. Furthermore, it was no secret that, on Wall Street, the retail end of the securities business was generally regarded as lower in the pecking order than investment banking and M&A, both of which had a star system. The CEO was expected to be the brightest star, but while Purcell looked the part, he didn't play it the way his predecessors had.

Maybe these were "soft issues," as one of the directors later claimed—the commuting, the aloofness, the closed-door style—but the performance numbers told their own story. Purcell was presiding over a gradual diminution of Morgan Stanley's stature. The share price had failed to recover from the Internet collapse at the same rate as the competition, and the stock was trading at a discount, multiples behind chief rival Goldman Sachs. In 2004, Morgan Stanley's stock was down 8.2 percent for the year, and 20 percent since March. Some of the firm's rankings had been downgraded and the Retail and Asset Management divisions, which were Dean Witter's dowry and the chief reasons for the merger from Morgan Stanley's perspective, were seriously underperforming. The firm's 2004 revenue was $10 billion more than Goldman Sachs's, but profits were almost identical: $4.55 billion for Goldman and $4.15 billion for Morgan Stanley.

Yet the Morgan Stanley board gave Purcell a 46 percent raise at the end of 2004, bringing his compensation from $14 million in 2003 to $22 million. That year he also exercised an additional $18 million in stock options granted in prior years.

Performance wasn't the only problem; Morgan Stanley's reputation was sullied by run-ins with regulatory bodies and high-profile lawsuits.

Securities and Exchange Commission chairman William H. Donaldson publicly castigated Purcell for failing to take a recent settlement seriously enough. In the summer of 2004, only hours before a jury trial was to commence, the firm settled an Equal Opportunities Commission case brought by former convertibles trader Allison Schieffelin for $54 million, the second-largest sex discrimination settlement ever. And billionaire investor Ronald Perelman was currently suing Morgan Stanley for fraud, demanding billions in compensatory and punitive damages.

Purcell was now pursuing another merger, this time with a bigger but less prestigious bank, which could signal the end of the firm. Two of the names on the table were Wachovia and Bank of America. Whatever he proposed, he wasn't likely to get a lot of resistance from the Morgan Stanley board, which he had filled with retired CEOs of industrial companies, none of whom had financial services experience. Most of them lived near him in the Midwest; they played golf together and generally saw things his way. They favored a top-down hierarchical model that might work in a company that manufactured a product, but that kind of structure can be soul destroying at a firm whose assets are personal talent and reputation.

Former president Bob Scott confirmed that senior executives were calling to tell him they were spending a third of their time trying to talk their colleagues into staying.

Wall Street was whispering the kind of clichés that replace golf metaphors when the situation is dire: "The rats are deserting the ship," "The sharks are circling," and "The fish is rotting from the head"— that last, a reference to Purcell.

A *Fortune* magazine article had just appeared that ended by quoting Purcell: "Morgan Stanley doesn't have to do anything." Purcell was almost certainly answering a question about a possible merger or acquisition but the remark produced reactions of incredulity on Wall Street.

Parker Gilbert still hesitated to interfere. "The firm's performance results weren't all bad," he said, but he wanted to know "what was happening with the people?"

The three Advisory Directors, Gilbert, Scott, and Bernard, asked questions and listened to the executives for a couple of hours. It was getting dark outside when Gilbert thanked the men for coming and told them, "This is very helpful. I think we'll do something, but I don't know what it might be, and whatever it is, we're not going to tell you because we don't want to jeopardize your careers."

The four left without any sense of what, if anything, might happen.

When they were gone, Gilbert summed up the situation as he understood it: "There was no dialogue, no support, technical platforms needed to be fixed." He later said that it looked to him as though "the firm was not going forward, but was struggling like crazy to try and stand still, and in fact, was losing ground."

No one remembers who spoke up first, but one of the three Advisory Directors said to the others, "Phil has got to go." They nodded: Phil had to go.

And so it began.

The story of the eight renegade Morgan Stanley alumni, most of whom were old enough to collect Social Security, engaged the media and through them, the public, for months between the end of March 2005 and early July that year. When the Eight charged out of the shadows, they disrupted their lives, jeopardized their reputations, and spent millions of dollars of their own money—the final bill came to about $7.5 million over three months—and all for what? Because Phil Purcell didn't value the human harmonics that made Morgan Stanley great?

The fight raised fundamental questions about the character of investment banking, leadership, and Morgan Stanley itself. Purcell wasn't a crook, he didn't cook the books, bribe politicians, perjure himself under oath, or charge splashy parties to the company. The people in the Morgan Stanley saga seemed tame by comparison with the greed freaks and white-collar criminals in the news—"STOCKS AND BLONDES: BOOZE, BABES AND A DWARF!" the *Daily News* wrote, in a story about a bachelor party that Tyco's chief executive Denis Koszlowski gave for his future son-in-law shortly before Koszlowski was sentenced to twenty-five years in jail on twenty-two counts, including grand larceny and securities fraud. Bernard Ebbers, founder of WorldCom, was on trial for the largest accounting scandal in U.S. history, which caused the collapse of his company, $180 billion in losses to investors, and the extinction of 20,000 jobs. In 2000, when Ebbers was named number 16 in *Time* magazine's "digital 50," the magazine had labeled him "King of the WorldCom" and quoted him as claiming that God had a plan for him. Citing people who had "trusted this company with their money," he told *Time*, "And I have an awesome responsibility to those people . . ." (Ebbers was sentenced to twenty-five years in a Louisiana jail in March 2005.) Yet even with stories like those providing lubricious dramas, the "fight for the soul of Morgan Stanley" dominated the headlines.

In the era of centi-millionaires executing multibillion-dollar deals, the juxtaposition of *soul* with *money* attracted attention and some skepticism; cynics claimed the idea strained credibility. Some believed that the Eight were motivated by the stock price—cumulatively, they owned eleven million shares of Morgan Stanley stock, which meant they had lost half a billion dollars on paper in less than five years, since the stock traded at its high. Others agreed with Purcell, who painted the Eight as out-of-touch old men who didn't have enough to do and were indulging their nostalgia for a world that was long gone. Midwestern defensiveness versus Eastern Establishment "condescension" ran through the veins of the Morgan Stanley struggle. Suddenly Purcell's friend Orrin G. Hatch, the Republican senator from Utah, popped up, and declared, "It is time for the Skull-and-Bones Society types to stop controlling Wall Street," and called the Group of Eight "limp-wristed Ivy Leaguers." Hatch's comment also reflected the power of myth: Harold Stanley, Yale 1908, was the only senior partner, president, chairman, or member of the management committee of Morgan Stanley who had been a member of Skull and Bones at Yale.

When the betting opened, as it does when there is any kind of contest that interests Wall Street, the odds were terrible: the Eight heard that their peers gave them no more than a 5 percent chance of winning. Nevertheless as the fight rolled out many people came forward who believed that Morgan Stanley was more than just a reservoir of capital and a name that had once meant something; and they rallied to fight for a culture that had been the gold standard on Wall Street for three-quarters of a century.

PART ONE

Beginnings and Endings

1935–1990

One

A FIRST CLASS BUSINESS

The "Grumpy Old Men" of the 2005 battle were the Young Turks who came to Morgan Stanley between 1958 and 1977, entering a firm that was hardly bigger than it had been when it was founded in 1935. Those who called the Group of Eight conservative and accused its members of being stuck in the past forgot that the firm had remained preeminent because, while its executives were nimble, creative, and aggressive, they also kept certain underlying values alive. Chief among those were the emphasis on meritocracy, ethics, and an inclusive, debate-driven partnership.

As late as 1970, Morgan Stanley had only 34 general partners, 4 limited partners, and 165 employees, of whom 65 were professionals. It was meagerly capitalized—in 1964, former chairman Perry E. Hall declared that he didn't see the need for more than $10 million in capital. The business was dominated by "relationship banking," underwriting equity and debt for the blue chip companies of smokestack America. Its clients were so loyal that competitors didn't even try to solicit their business.

When the time came for the new, post–World War II generation to shake things up, it would take courage, strategic intelligence, and a willingness to smash icons to move forward without losing the firm's real capital: its name and all it had represented in the American and European financial markets for nearly one hundred years.

The first Morgan financier was Junius Morgan, a London-based American, who emerged as an international banker in the mid-nineteenth century. His most stunning accomplishment was to organize a 250-million-franc ($50 million) loan to the French during the Franco-Prussian War, an amount few bankers anywhere in the world could raise at that time. Yet despite an enormously successful career, he operated in an era when the United States was still a debtor, not a creditor nation, and the Industrial Revolution was yet to hit its peak. Junius would be overshadowed in the history of business and the development of nations by his only surviving son, J. Pierpont Morgan, who began his career when the great opportunities were American and industrial.

J. P. Morgan established himself in New York in 1857, founded the company that bore his name, and focusing on "industrial architecture on the Jurassic scale," he set the pattern for the enormous corporations that dominated global industry. When Morgan Stanley was founded in 1935, many of the great trusts and mergers J. P. Morgan put together— steel, farm equipment, railroads, communications—would become Morgan Stanley clients.

Morgan Stanley was born during the Great Depression, not because that was a propitious time to start a new business, but because the Senate Banking and Currency Committee hearings on Wall Street practices challenged the primacy of the great private banks, and the Glass-Steagall Banking Act of 1933 required them to separate their commercial and investment banking businesses.

In the early 1930s there weren't many companies that were looking to refinance, and J. P. Morgan & Co. decided to keep its commercial business and close down investment banking. Two years later, when interest rates were low and the economic climate was more favorable, a small group of J. P. Morgan partners got together to form a new firm, Morgan Stanley, to handle its clients' investment banking needs.

Morgan Stanley's first, and for many years its biggest, client was AT&T, a J. P. Morgan legacy; in 1906 Morgan had been part of a group that co-underwrote a $100 million bond issue to refinance American Telephone and Telegraph. From that time onward, J. P. Morgan was AT&T's principal banker, and when Morgan Stanley took over the investment banking functions, AT&T was a significant influence in the decision to found the new firm. Between 1936 and 1968 Morgan Stanley issued $4.85 billion of securities for AT&T.

Morgan's most famous trust, created in 1901, was United States

Steel, the world's first billion-dollar corporation. A merger of small and large steel companies, it was capitalized at $1.4 billion, more than 15 percent of the total market cap of all American manufacturing companies. Between 1938 and 1961, Morgan Stanley would issue more than $1 billion in equity and debt for U.S. Steel. In 1902, Morgan organized another great merger, creating International Harvester, which controlled 85 percent of the U.S. farm equipment business. In 1954, when International Harvester wanted to issue $34 million in secondary offerings of preferred and common stock, it brought the deal to Morgan Stanley. One of the oldest associations was with General Electric: J. P. Morgan's Philadelphia affiliate, Drexel Morgan, underwrote the first bond offering for the newly formed General Electric Company in 1892, and J. P. Morgan himself joined the GE board. In 1956, Morgan Stanley issued $300 million in GE debentures.

While Morgan Stanley inherited and then earned the respect and trust of industrial America, the firm was also bequeathed the responsibility and public attention that went with a great name. At a time when the United States had no central bank, the Morgans came to the rescue in times of economic crisis, earning the firm and its principals the awe and, often, the distrust of the general public.

The Morgans' most effective public interventions were the most controversial. In 1895, when U.S. gold reserves fell to $68 million, and the government vaults on Wall Street held only $9 million in gold, a $10 million draft against the gold was in the offing. J. P. Morgan traveled to Washington in a blizzard to meet with President Grover Cleveland, and as Morgan nervously crumbled his cigar, he proposed to lead a syndicate in partnership with the Rothschilds to raise $65 billion in gold bonds. The Morgan and Rothschild interests secured the bonds with a reserve of 3.5 million ounces of gold, which they assembled and held, stabilizing the price and the supply. The issue sold out, and J. P. Morgan turned a profit: the bonds were issued at 104½ but traded between 112¾ and 119, with the bankers earning 3¾ percent in interest. Massive political opposition to the gold standard, largely from farmers who wanted the cheaper silver-backed money to repay their loans, targeted Morgan as a profiteer and enemy of the people. Presidential candidate William Jennings Bryan claimed that the farmers had been crucified on Morgan's "cross of gold," but as historian Ron

Chernow wrote in *The House of Morgan*, the salvation of the gold standard was Morgan's "most dazzling feat." The British might have countered with another: J. P. Morgan and Company financed one-fifth of the cost of the Boer War for England. King Edward VII signaled his gratitude by inviting Morgan to dinner and seating him on his right.

Morgan was the chief banker for the railroad reorganizations during the 1893 to 1897 depression, when one-third of the nation's railroads were in default. That too was a profitable venture: by the turn of the century, he controlled one-sixth of the nation's rail lines. Then, in 1907, when the stock market was tumbling and trust companies, which backed loans with securities, were in danger of failing, there was a run on the banks. Depositors waited in line overnight to withdraw their funds, and mobs crowded outside Morgan headquarters on Wall Street as though they were huddling in the shelter of a fort—even though J. P. Morgan had no small individual depositors or clients. Morgan, who was seventy years old and largely retired, averted a national economic collapse by putting together a coalition of banks to pledge $25 million at 10 percent to cover the trust companies' calls. As the news circulated on the floor of the New York Stock Exchange across the street from Morgan's office, he could hear the brokers cheering him.

The 1907 crisis gave rise to the fear that a few bankers held too much power, and demonstrated the need for a national bank. In 1912 and 1913 the House Banking and Currency Committee held hearings to look into the alleged "money trust." The hearings were known as the Pujo investigation after the committee chairman, Louisiana congressman Arsène Pujo. Morgan was now seventy-six years old and in poor health, and resented what he considered unwarranted probing into the details of a business based on confidence and trust, but nevertheless, he was the star witness. In his hours of testimony, he made a statement that passed into the genetic code of the House of Morgan as a warning and a motto.

Pujo committee counsel Samuel Untermeyer, a leading lawyer with a specialty in trusts, asked Morgan whether he used money or property as the basis for deciding whether to make commercial capital available.

Morgan responded, "No, sir. The first thing is character."

Untermeyer asked again, "Before money, or property?"

Morgan insisted, "Before money or anything else. Money cannot buy it . . . Because a man I do not trust could not get money from me on all the bonds in Christendom."

The crowd in the hearing room applauded, and one Wall Street banker later claimed that a five- to ten-point jump in stock prices reflected renewed faith in the financial establishment. In 1914, when Jack Morgan laid the cornerstone of the firm's new building at 23 Wall Street, he placed a document bearing the "character statement" in a copper box in the stone.

Regardless of Morgan's personal code, it was time for the federal government to establish a financial safety net, and at the end of 1913 the government created the Federal Reserve Bank.

A year after the Pujo hearings, Jack Morgan was meeting privately with President Woodrow Wilson and told him, "The Pujo investigation, with Mr. Untermeyer in charge had been offered to us for $40,000 and that these offers were always made by underground channels, of course, but that we had never bought anybody yet and did not propose to begin with that sort of person."

J. P. Morgan was dead within months of the hearings, his death attended by transatlantic ceremonies. He died at the Grand Hotel in Rome, where the cable office was deluged by written condolences—3,698 on the first day, including one from the pope. A memorial service was held at Westminster Cathedral in London, where Morgan's affiliate firm, Morgan Grenfell, was located and where Morgan had a palatial town house. As his body was transported across the Atlantic the ships that had been part of his empire lowered their flags to half-mast. The New York Stock Exchange was closed on the day of his funeral, which was held at St. George's, known as "the Morgan church." Journalists who had accused Morgan of being the worst of President Theodore Roosevelt's "malefactors of great wealth" entered into a *de mortuis nil nisi bonum* mode. Morgan was compared to the merchant bankers of legend, kings, and emperors. No titan of the Gilded Age, saving John D. Rockefeller, was better known.

When Jack Morgan took over the firm, World War I was brewing. Shy and much in the shadow of his father, he found himself in a position of power and responsibility as the United States remained neutral, although many Americans favored the Allies. On July 1, 1914,

Jack Morgan went to the White House for a private talk with President Wilson, to discuss how the bank could provide extradiplomatic assistance. Over the next few years, J. P. Morgan and Company acted as the buying agent for the French and British governments, placing contracts for more than $3 billion in goods, about one-third of the purchases. In 1915, the firm took the lead in forming a syndicate to sell a $500 million bond issue for the Allies, on which J. P. Morgan and Company took no commission. When the United States finally entered the war, Morgan had been in the forefront of floating some $1.2 billion in bond issues. As a *New Yorker* profile noted, "The war helped Morgan & Company; and Morgan & Company, more than any other single financial force, saved the Allies."

After the war, Germany was staggering under the reparations payments to France and England imposed by the Treaty of Versailles. The French and English couldn't repay their loans, which hampered American postwar growth. Jack Morgan played a significant role in negotiating the Dawes Plan to get the money moving. It was then that the first Parker Gilbert entered the firm's orbit. Gilbert, who was undersecretary of the Treasury, was in his early thirties and already one of the leading men in government and finance. He was a prodigy, having graduated from grammar school at the age of eleven, from high school at fifteen, from Rutgers University at nineteen; he received his law degree cum laude from Harvard in 1915 whereupon he was hired at Cravath Henderson. In 1918 he joined the war loan staff of the Treasury Department, and in 1924, with the backing of J. P. Morgan partners, he was appointed agent-general for reparations payments in Germany. After six years, he returned to the United States and in 1932 was asked to become a partner at J. P. Morgan and Company. He died of heart disease attributed to overwork in 1938. By then he had been one of the small cadre of J. P. Morgan partners who were responsible for the establishment of Morgan Stanley. Nearly fifty years after Gilbert's death his son, S. Parker Gilbert Jr., would become chairman of the firm his father helped found.

When financial problems arose, the House of Morgan was a target. After the 1929 stock market crash, the mood of the country was dark, and Wall Street was blamed for the collapse of the economy.

Time magazine referred to bankers as "banksters," a reference to Chicago gangster Al Capone, who was convicted of tax evasion in 1931 on takings of some $100 million—tens of millions of dollars more than the estate J. P. Morgan left in 1913. In that environment of anger and mistrust, the Senate Banking and Currency Committee held two years of hearings to investigate Wall Street practices between 1932 and 1933. The hearings were known as "Pecora" for the committee counsel, Ferdinand Pecora, a former New York City assistant district attorney. Morgan, the name newspaper readers knew best, was targeted as the chief culprit, and Jack Morgan was the most famous witness.

The hearings had unpleasant echoes of the occasion more than twenty years earlier, when Jack Morgan accompanied his father to the Pujo hearings. Now it was his turn to be interrogated by a crusader against Wall Street, and this time, it was even worse: Pecora was a prosecutor, accustomed to going after criminals, not bankers. He operated as though he believed, as many did, that while the rest of the nation suffered, the "fat cats" were still raking off their take. Pecora unearthed the fact that certain of the Morgan partners hadn't paid taxes for the past few years, gliding over the fact that they had had negative income during that period; they were still rich, but they too were affected by the Depression.

Pecora reported that when Morgan arrived in the hearing room, "Public interest in his appearance was almost hysterically intense." As J. P. Morgan senior partner Thomas W. Lamont later noted in a private memorandum, "A mysterious sort of glamour . . . seemed to attach to the firm and possibly added to its influence." It was during those hearings that Jack Morgan read his statement about "doing a first class business in a first class way."

At the end, Pecora conceded that Morgan "manifested a pride in his firm and its works which was obvious and deeply genuine. And, in truth, the investigation of the Morgan firm elicited no such disclosures of glaring abuses." He added, "Mr. Morgan was undoubtedly wholly candid when he declared . . . 'I consider the private banker a national asset . . . any power which he has comes . . . from the confidence of the people in his character and credit . . . not financial credit, but that which comes from the respect and esteem of the community.'"

But once again, the hearings solidified public sentiment against

Wall Street, and Congress passed the Glass-Steagall Banking Act of 1933 that spring, radically changing the world of finance for the next sixty years: Glass-Steagall required banks to amputate one limb or the other, either investment or commercial banking.

After J. P. Morgan decided to sever its investment banking operations, Jack Morgan wrote one of his English partners, "We are not allowed to do any of the things to help people, by the doing of which . . . we have earned a very fine living and an unequalled reputation. Now we can do nothing more than any ordinary bank . . . I feel like the pictures of Gulliver, when the Lilliputians had tied him on his back on the ground with thousands of small threads . . . It is very annoying to be sane and honest, and be tied up in prison and a straitwaistcoat put on you besides."

Then, in 1935, interest rates dropped so low that some long-standing J. P. Morgan clients wanted to refinance. AT&T, in particular, planned to issue a public offering of Illinois Bell Telephone, but the Morgan bank was forbidden to prepare the registration statements or sell the issues. It was then that the leading Morgan partners decided to turn their liabilities into an asset; and the future entity code-named the "XYZ Corporation"—which would become Morgan Stanley—was conceived to unlace the straitjacket.

In August 1935, four J. P. Morgan bankers and their lawyer traveled north on the overnight train from Grand Central Station, away from the swelter of Wall Street at the dead center of the Great Depression. A car and chauffeur waited at the train station in Rockland, Maine, to drive them to the dock on Penobscot Bay, where they boarded Tom Lamont's seventy-five-foot motor launch *Reynard*, an impeccably maintained vessel with mahogany brightwork and fresh blue and white paint. The bankers were on their way to a top secret meeting at Lamont's summerhouse on North Haven Island. Residents of North Haven were careful to maintain their privacy, and it was a good place to hold confidential talks. Two years earlier, Charles and Ann Morrow Lindbergh had flown to the island to stay at the house of her late father, Dwight Morrow, a former J. P. Morgan partner, to escape the relentless media attention that followed the kidnapping and murder of their twenty-month-old son, Charles A. Lindbergh Jr.

The men who attended the "XYZ Corp" meeting were among the most distinguished bankers of the era, running J. P. Morgan and Company while the semiretired Jack Morgan spent half the year in England. They included J. P. Morgan partners George P. Whitney, Russell Leffingwell, S. Parker Gilbert, and Harold Stanley, and their lawyer, Lansing Reed of Davis Polk Wardwell Gardiner & Reed. The two names that would resonate down the decades at Morgan Stanley were Harold Stanley, one of the original named partners, and Parker Gilbert.

Tom Lamont's guests disembarked at his private dock and walked up a gentle slope to "Sky Farm," where the three-winged yellow clapboard farmhouse overlooked the bay and the Camden Hills. The house gave the impression that it had rambled into its current configuration over time, but in fact, a small original farmhouse had been relocated on the hill and sited by Frederick Law Olmsted, the designer of Central Park, and the wings were added later. Olmsted laid out the grounds to retain the sense of a farm, which it still was: to provision the Lamont larders there were thirty sheep, one hundred chickens, six cows, and extensive vegetable gardens.

A staff of twenty-five or thirty tended the livestock, the hayfields, and the grazing meadows and took care of the family and their guests. So many people came to see Tom and Frances Lamont—President Franklin Delano Roosevelt stopped by twice one summer on his way to Campobello—that the house was configured to accommodate hospitality at a high, if informal, level. The center wing, which had a large living room, dining room, and kitchen, housed guests, while the family lived in a more modest wing with the air of a small New England cottage, attached to the main section by a breezeway. On the other side of the guest quarters, a third wing housed staff. The house was big, but it wasn't grand. North Haven was a long way from Newport. Tom Lamont was rich, and in certain circles he was famous, but he preferred a quiet life. He had spent his first years in the dour, no-dancing parsonages provided for his father, an impecunious Methodist minister, until young Tom was awarded a scholarship to Phillips Exeter Academy and then to Harvard. Like most of the Morgan partners who came along after J. P. Morgan and Jack Morgan, Lamont was not inclined to ostentation.

Over the next couple of days, the partners met in the dining room, sitting on the hard Windsor chairs, or gathered outside overlooking the bay. What happened over those two days would be romantically called "the porch meeting," in reference to the Lamonts' hundred-foot-long porch, where partners in Adirondack chairs leaned in toward one another, oblivious to the view, and created a new firm.

At least one of them would have to leave J. P. Morgan and Company, with its capital of $340 million, to start an investment bank capitalized at $7.5 million, most of which would come from the Morgan and Lamont families. The man who agreed to take the job was fifty-year-old Harold Stanley, a college hero who went on to achieve great things, disproving the old saw that anyone who was outstandingly successful in college had already peaked. Stanley, whose father was the General Electric engineer who invented the Thermos bottle, was Class of 1908 at Yale, captain of its championship hockey team, played on the baseball team, was voted handsomest and most popular in his class, and was tapped for Skull and Bones. He became president of Guaranty Trust at the age of thirty-one, and joined J. P. Morgan as a partner in 1928 to run Investment Banking.

The Morgan in "Morgan Stanley" was one of Jack Morgan's sons, thirty-five-year-old Henry Morgan, called Harry. That August he was in Scotland for the grouse season and wouldn't return until September. When Morgan Stanley's Articles of Incorporation were written, they included a clause that if there was no Morgan in the business for a certain number of years, the firm would lose the right to use the family name. A third partner, William Ewing, came out of J. P. Morgan's Bond Department. Two others, Perry E. Hall and Edward H. York, would be seconded from Drexel and Co., J. P. Morgan's affiliated firm in Philadelphia.

At North Haven, the partners had dinner and spent the night, blessedly away from the city's August heat. They slept with the rich, damp Maine air puffing through their rooms, and after they had completed their plans, they embarked on the *Reynard* for the trip back to the mainland. On the way over, Lansing Reed remarked to Harold Stanley that he had made quite a sacrifice for the good of the House of Morgan.

On September 5, 1935, a parade of office boys pushed the former Morgan partners' rolltop desks down the block from J. P. Morgan headquarters, the famous "Corner" at 23 Wall Street, to Morgan Stanley's recently acquired offices at 2 Wall. There were eighteen original rolltops, and although copies were later made, the originals were distinguished by the call buttons that read BOY, referring to the office boy, GIRL—that was the switchboard operator—and SECRETARY. At 4 P.M. that day, Tom Lamont and Harold Stanley stood in front of the fireplace in the marble-floored 15,000-square-foot great hall at 23 Wall Street to announce the founding of the new firm. Morgan Stanley opened on September 16 with fewer than three dozen employees. Colleagues and competitors sent some two hundred floral arrangements. The office looked more like the site of a funeral than a birth, and there were elements of both in its beginning.

In three and a half months the Morgan Stanley partners raised $200 million in debt, and by the end of a year, the firm had handled more than $1 billion in underwritings, capturing one-quarter of the market. Over the next three years, they consistently managed 20 percent of the public offerings on Wall Street.

The Depression, followed by World War II, led Morgan Stanley partners to maintain a conservative stance in business, and the history of government intercession or intrusion discouraged them from taking too visible a public role. Only a year after the firm was founded, Senator Gerald P. Nye of North Dakota chaired a Senate munitions investigation that led to J. P. Morgan and Company being labeled "merchants of death." In order to prove that the firm had not been a war profiteer, Morgan had to exhume and submit twelve million documents—forty truckfuls. Jack Morgan declared at the hearings, "The fact that the Allies found us useful and valued our assistance in their task is the fact of which I am most proud in all my business life of more than forty-five years." He added, "Do you suppose that because business was good I wanted my son to go to war? He did though." The Nye Committee found nothing concrete to support Nye's allegations, but the phrase "merchants of death" was hard to outlive, not just for J. P. Morgan but also for any firm with the Morgan name attached to it.

Morgan Stanley had opened for business during the Depression, operated with a skeleton staff during World War II, and emerged into the 1950s under the leadership of partners who had lived through financial disaster and war. They were ready to go back to the business they had always known. For thirty-five years, from the day Morgan Stanley opened until 1970, the firm sailed a steady course, underwriting debt and equity for the same roster of blue chip clients.

Even in the late 1960s and early 1970s, the firm's conservative approach was reflected in the atmosphere at 2 Wall Street, and later at the firm's second location at 140 Broadway. The unprepossessing Morgan Stanley offices were very different from 23 Wall, where clients entered a vast templelike marble hall. Morgan Stanley was not a street-level operation, and the firm did not want to present a public face to the world. Harry Morgan and Harold Stanley had private offices, but they also had desks in the open partners' room, where the rolltops were lined up along two sides in order of seniority. The head of the line was known as "the platform," although the desks themselves were not elevated, except in the psyches of the young associates, who were in awe of their seniors. The management style still had Victorian overtones in the 1960s. The partners met every day; they spent hours discussing even the adjectives and punctuation in prospectuses to be sure they were perfect; and the office manager still took notes at the meetings on a yellow legal pad, stopped by the desk of any partner who missed a meeting, read him the minutes in a near whisper, then tore them up and threw them out. The secretaries were stashed in an office upstairs, but the head telephone operator, whose name was May, and who had served in the Marine Corps in World War II, sat within earshot; she knew everyone's friends, family, and business associates. Charles Morgan, a partner of the firm, who was one of Harry Morgan's sons, recalls that it wasn't unusual for May to answer the phone and call out, "Charlie! It's your mother." Charles Morgan was the last Morgan to join the firm under the original arrangement; after that the partnership agreement was amended, and it was no longer necessary for a Morgan to be working at Morgan Stanley for the firm to retain its name.

The sense of paternalism was pervasive, with Morgan as the paterfamilias. At Christmas, the employees gathered around, and Morgan stood on the platform and announced the bonuses, which were proportionally the same throughout the firm—usually one or two months' salary.

When some of the talented younger men couldn't afford to buy into the partnership, Morgan sometimes loaned them the money; and on occasion he offered to make funds available for more personal expenditures—he helped future chairman Dick Fisher buy a house in Park Slope, Brooklyn. Many years later, Fisher loaned his once-a-week cleaning lady the money for a deposit on a house for her family. She asked him why he had helped her, and Fisher said he hoped that if she or her children ever had the chance, they would do the same for someone else.

Certain aspects of the Morgan tradition were responsible for the firm's ability to grow and modernize when the time came for radical change. In a business where people were its only real assets, Morgan Stanley used its human capital to great effect. Even the most junior associates were encouraged to speak up in a meeting if they had something to add, and the interactions among partners were distinguished by fulsome debate. Charlie Morgan says that when he joined the firm, it was "the greatest twenty-two-man debating club in the world." The debates usually led to decisions most of the partners could support. That said, there were always rivalries, and one of the roles of senior partners was to enforce truces. Harry Morgan was "the sotto voce leader of the firm," says Frederick B. Whittemore, who joined the firm in 1958. "He was a peacekeeper, kept all these big egos from doing battle with each other. You'd have trouble having a dispute with Harry in the room. We all adored him."

The firm was intimate enough that there was room for the occasional raucous humor. One of the original partners, Allen Northey Jones, kept cherry bombs in his desk drawer and threw them out the windows during ticker tape parades, with a special salvo for General Charles de Gaulle. His high-pitched giggle could be heard as the cherry bombs exploded. On occasion he also tossed them inside the office. When Jones died, in 1958, the young associates were asked to clean out Northey Jones's desk drawers. They found a stash of fireworks, half a bottle of Scotch, and a handgun. The gun was a holdover from the kidnapping and murder of Charles Lindbergh Jr., grandson of J. P. Morgan partner Dwight Morrow. Fearful that other Morgan families were in danger, the bank hired 250 armed guards to protect the partners and their wives and children, and at one time Jack Morgan was guarded by men with machine guns—at the office. The partners were licensed to carry handguns, and at Morgan Stanley, as well as at J. P. Morgan, some of them kept the weapons in their desk drawers. As late as the 1950s, a police sergeant came by once a year to check that the guns were in working order.

Morgan Stanley inherited the public attention and rigorous oversight that accompanied a famous name. The firm's reputation depended on its most senior executives, who had to be prepared to defend its standards, cooperate with the government, and avoid treating public officials as hostile adversaries. Harold Stanley took that role in 1949, when the Department of Justice filed a civil suit known as *United States of America v. Henry S. Morgan, Harold Stanley et al.* against seventeen investment banking houses for "conspiracy and combination" in violation of the Sherman Act. Stanley devoted nearly all his efforts to defending the firm for the next three years, turning over much of the management to Perry Hall, who succeeded him as senior partner from 1951 to 1961.

In 1952, Judge Harold R. Medina ruled against the Justice Department, and followed the ruling with a book, *Wall Street and the Security Markets: Corrected Opinion of Harold R. Medina*. Medina wrote of Harold Stanley,

> Sensing from the outset the importance of his credibility as a witness, I followed with great care and attention . . . his deposition testimony . . . I checked every statement of fact with other parts of the record . . . in search for discrepancies or possible equivocations, or lack of frankness; and I submitted his statements, under oath and otherwise, to every one of those tests which an experienced judge applies in his every day search for the truth. As a result I became convinced that his testimony could be relied upon . . . The fact that Stanley denied the existence of any such conspiracy as charged . . . is one of the significant features of the case . . .
>
> It would be difficult to exaggerate the importance of invest-

ment banking to the national economy. The growth of the past fifty years has covered the United States with a vast network of manufacturing, processing, sales and distributing plants, the smooth functioning of which is vital to our welfare as a nation ... [A]dequate financing of their needs is the life blood without which many if not most of these parts of the great machine of business would cease to function in a healthy, normal fashion.

Harold Stanley's role in successfully defending Morgan Stanley from charges of conspiracy was his last major contribution to the firm. By the time the case was over, he was crippled by arthritis. When he came to the office in his alpaca coat and his blue serge suit, his chauffeur had to disengage him from a leather corset that laced up the back and held him upright.

The Medina judgment entered the pantheon, along with Jack Morgan's statement about "a first class business" and his father's comment about the importance of character. Well into the 1970s, when a young man joined Morgan Stanley, he was given a copy of *Wall Street and the Security Markets*, known inside the firm simply as "Medina," and instructed to read it.

I n the mid-1960s, most of the older partners still believed, or hoped, that Morgan Stanley could continue to succeed as a small, private firm. It was then that Perry Hall wrote the 1964 memo addressing the future, in which he declared that he was opposed to increasing capital beyond $10 million ("I see no need for more at this time"); entering the investment advisory business ("is there not a limit to the number of clients one can service ... if it is deemed wise to sell or buy —— stock, which clients do you advise first?"); and strongly advised against merging with another firm: "If we merge won't it look as though we needed to, felt weak, etc.?" he wrote. "WHAT IS WRONG WITH US NOW?"

What was wrong was that Morgan Stanley needed permanent capital: as the partners retired or died, and their capital was withdrawn, younger partners could not afford to replace the funds. As for expanding into new businesses, even as Hall was writing, it was none too soon to consider diversification, growth, and a more aggressive position in international finance. None of these new directions would be practical unless the business was managed more professionally. The time had come for a new generation to shake things up. The challenge was to translate the first class culture into a modern idiom.

Two

BUILDING THE BANK

1970–1990

The foundations of the 2005 mutiny were laid in the last quarter of the twentieth century amid dramatic changes in society, business, and scale that challenged and in some ways redefined the interpretation of doing only "a first class business in a first class way." The leaders who insured that Morgan Stanley survived and flourished included all the members of the Group of Eight; Dick Fisher, whose death in December 2004 was an emotional catalyst for the fight; mergers and acquisitions pioneer Robert F. Greenhill, whom the Eight would hire as their strategic advisor; and John J. Mack, who, in 2005, was finally appointed to the job many felt he should have had all along.

They were part of a relatively small cadre that built the modern Morgan Stanley in the shadow—or light—of their predecessors. Most of them were in their thirties when they were admitted to the partnership around 1970, and they were close enough to the original partners to accept that, whatever new ventures they embarked on, the absolute prerequisite was the excellence of character, drive, intelligence, and training that led to excellence of strategy and execution. There were times when they disappointed themselves and one another, but the goals and standards were always clear.

Building on a great name and reputation, but with a minimum of capital and a small group of partners, Parker Gilbert took the firm public, raising the capital for its enormous expansion; Dick Fisher built the Sales and Trading Division, despite the resistance of older partners who considered selling and trading to be beneath the firm's dignity. John Mack, who joined the firm as a bond salesman under Fisher, developed the Fixed Income Division and later became the firm's president. Richard A. Debs was the founding president of Morgan Stanley International and opened the Middle Eastern business at a time when the firm did not have a single non-American managing director. Anson M. Beard Jr. took over a small private wealth management department that was an appendage to investment banking, established the Equity Division, and built it into a $1-billion-a-year business. Bob Greenhill was the first Head of the Mergers and Acquisitions Division, creating a huge moneymaker out of a service the firm had once offered for free. Joseph A. Fogg III joined Greenhill, and they built the most feared and respected M & A division on Wall Street. Lewis Bernard revolutionized the firm's technology and systems, drew up its ten-year plan, and established the foreign exchange business, among his many accomplishments in nearly every Institutional Securities division. John H. T. Wilson, the first partner assigned to solicit new business, brought in significant new clients and maintained the high standard of relationships and banking advice with clients that had been with Morgan Stanley since the 1930s. As Head of Syndicate, Frederick B. Whittemore upheld and enhanced the firm's power and preeminence as the lead manager on the most profitable and prestigious deals of their era. Bob Scott was just young enough compared with most of the others that by the time he became a managing director in 1979 the big divisions had been formed, but over the next twenty-four years, he ran nearly every division in Institutional Securities and played a significant management role. There were many others who built the firm, but during the fight for the soul of Morgan Stanley those were the names that emerged. The Eight were the protagonists: Fisher was an inspiration; Greenhill was the battle-hardened strategist; and, in a grand finale, John Mack gave the firm a chance to revitalize the meritocracy.

The story of where they started, what they built, and how they handled power struggles, leadership transitions, and dramatic changes in the business climate does much to explain why they fought, what they fought for, and ultimately, why they won.

The first of the future Group of Eight went to work at Morgan Stanley in the late 1950s and early 1960s, when even the dress code was redolent of the past. Partners always wore hats—fedoras in winter and straw hats in summer. When Harry Morgan saw an associate going out bareheaded, he would say, "What's wrong, young man? Don't we pay you enough to buy a hat?" There were even hat rituals: after Labor Day, partners who lived in New Jersey and took the ferry to work ritually flung their Panamas into the Hudson River. Then Jack Kennedy made going hatless look modern, and along with hats, vests and watch chains also went out of fashion—even the Morgan tradition of having gold pocket watches specially crafted by a special Swiss maker for every partner died. Office language became more informal, and secretaries became "assistants" and started calling their bosses by their first names. Harold Stanley, who would ask a partner to leave a meeting if he said "damn," would have been shocked to hear the words the next generation routinely used in the office. This postwar generation looked and sounded different from their seniors, and they thought differently as well.

When most of the Eight joined Morgan in the early phases of its transformation, Frank A. Petito was the head of the firm. Petito, the son of an Italian immigrant who worked as a janitor, went to Princeton on scholarship and earned his spending money by tutoring other students. He was said to be such an autodidact that he tutored boys in subjects he had never taken. He joined the firm a year after it was founded, when he graduated, in 1936. He thought he had been hired on a one-year trial basis, and when the year was up and no one said anything about staying on, he went home and didn't come back. The partners tracked him down in New Jersey, where he had found a job—legend says he was pumping gas—and cleared up the misunderstanding. Petito was made partner in 1954 and was chairman from 1973 to 1979.

Parker Gilbert describes Petito as "a brilliant investment banker. Clients just loved him. He was demanding and he could be intimidating, because he was so smart and knew what he wanted, yet people absolutely wanted to work for him." Petito had another quality that was valued, although not always observed at Morgan Stanley: his personal modesty was legendary. During World War II he had commanded a tank that crossed the Rhine under General George Patton, attained the rank of colonel, and earned quite a collection of medals. When he came home, he put the medals in a drawer, and his colleagues didn't know how many decorations he had received until Petito and John Young, one of the original partners, were at a shop in

Paris that sold medals. Young, who had received the Legion of Merit, was looking for replacements. Fred Whittemore, who was Young's assistant, recalls, "Petito was picking up medals and saying 'I'll have two of those and one of these.' Young said, 'Frank, you can't take those.' Petito said, 'Oh, but I won them.'"

Petito was forward-looking, but the driver of structural change and expansion was his successor, the tough, kinetic, blue-eyed Robert H. B. Baldwin, whose efforts to secure the firm's future often irritated his partners. Baldwin was one of three Morgan Stanley chairmen who were Princeton graduates (the others were Petito and Dick Fisher). He was elected to Phi Beta Kappa as a junior, played on three varsity teams—football, basketball, and baseball—and was ranked first in the Economics Department. He graduated in 1942, joined the U.S. Navy, then went directly to Morgan Stanley after the war—some say Petito had his eye on him after he saw him play baseball at Princeton. Baldwin was made partner in 1958, but in 1965, frustrated by what he saw as a stubborn refusal to grow and modernize, he accepted an appointment as Undersecretary of the Navy. He returned in 1967 to a firm that still wasn't much bigger than it was when it was founded. With Baldwin pushing and pulling, Morgan Stanley underwent its first major internal culture clash.

Baldwin, whom *Fortune* reporter Wyndham Robertson described as "a man whose straightforward approach to everything seems to preclude even modesty," began by proposing that, in place of an inefficient system in which partners met to discuss even the smallest matters, the firm establish separate committees to oversee compensation and operations—and that he be appointed head of operations. The partners declined to give him that much power. In 1969, he organized a planning meeting, but "it was a goddamn disaster," he says. Nothing much happened, except that the meeting exacerbated long-standing rivalries among partners, which the quiet, courteous Harry Morgan had managed to keep mostly under control.

Then, in 1970, the firm admitted six partners whom Baldwin called "the irreverent six." They were between thirty-two and thirty-eight years old and all of them had MBAs, a rare accomplishment in the previous generation. Five, including Dick Fisher and Bob Greenhill, were graduates of Harvard Business School, and one was a graduate of the business school at Stanford.

Baldwin set up three committees, organized by age—older, middle, and younger partners—and they held a more successful planning meeting in 1971. On the subject of growth, Fred Whittemore recalls with a chuckle, "They were all wrong." The older partners estimated that the firm would need to rent another floor to accommodate inevitable expansion, at about 10 percent over the next few years. The group in the middle age range predicted the firm might become "several times bigger," while the younger partners believed that it would become ten times its current size. No one anticipated that by the end of the century Morgan Stanley would be one hundred times bigger than it was in 1971.

Until then, Morgan Stanley exclusively represented the users of capital—companies that needed to raise money through equity or debt. Now they agreed to represent the providers of capital as well. To finance the expansion, the firm incorporated part of its business in 1970, and the rest in 1971; under the corporate structure, partners no longer would withdraw their capital at the end of every year. Morgan Stanley had never had a president or CEO, but a corporation had to elect officers, and one of the senior partners, Samuel Payne, was persuaded to take the job—but only because someone had to do it. As Payne recalled at the Fiftieth Anniversary Dinner in 1985, "We were reluctant to give up our Morgan Stanley partnership to become part of a corporate organization. We believed that the unique atmosphere of our partnership was one of our greatest strengths. . . . By continuing to refer to each other as partners and by electing only one officer, a President, from among our Managing Directors, we endeavored to retain the spirit of our partnership." To emphasize the philosophy of "all for one, and one for all," the Articles of Incorporation specified that any partner could stop the firm from doing a piece of business if he put his veto in writing.

After the 1971 planning meeting, the partners launched a series of new enterprises. The firm entered the sales and trading, mergers and acquisitions, research, private wealth management and equities, and international businesses, all within the next five years. Sales and Trading was considered a lower form of business than investment banking, but in 1972, Baldwin and Petito put one of the young stars, thirty-six-year-old Dick Fisher, in as its head. By 1975, the department had fourteen salesmen and six position traders, plus support staff, and the partners had to admit it was a success. Morgan Stanley had historically been a big bond house, and Sales and Trading began by building the fixed income, or bond, business, but in a natural evolution, the firm expanded into higher margin businesses and began selling and trading equities.

Sales and Trading bred two of Morgan Stanley's future leaders, Dick Fisher and John Mack. They were both self-made, charismatic, and deeply ambitious. Fisher, who was beloved, was described by a journalist who covered Wall Street as "the nicest ruthless man you'll ever meet." Mack was called "the heart and soul of Morgan Stanley," but was also nicknamed "Mack the Knife." In 1997, the two of them would be the architects of the merger with Dean Witter, which they saw as the culmination of the growth led by their generation. Like Frank Petito, Fisher and Mack were self-made scholarship boys, each with his own kind of business genius, and each with his own hurdles to overcome.

Dick Fisher was eight years old, living in Philadelphia with his parents and baby brother in 1944, a bright, merry little boy who had upgraded from a scooter to a bike, and was riding around the neighborhood with his friends, when he fell ill with paralytic polio. Dick recovered, but his legs were paralyzed, and he needed braces and crutches to walk. When his parents tried to reenroll him in public school, the principal said they wouldn't take him back; if the building needed to be evacuated, they said, he wouldn't be able to get out fast enough and could endanger his own and others' lives. The school advised the Fishers to send Dick to a trade school where he could learn to work with his hands. Fisher's father, who was an adhesive salesman, couldn't afford to send him to private school, and Dick briefly did go to trade school until his doctor, the felicitously named Dr. Chance, intervened and introduced him to the private William Penn Charter School, where he was awarded a scholarship. He graduated at the age of sixteen, in 1953. President of the student body and the honor society, he also earned a varsity letter in wrestling and a gold medal for the highest score in gym. He couldn't run and still needed a cane to walk, but he could bat and throw and play pickup baseball.

He was admitted to Princeton on scholarship, where he majored in history, was elected to the exclusive Ivy Club, and was head of the Interclub Council. In his senior year, his class voted him "Best all-around man (including athletics)," and he received the first Harold Dodds Award, named for the retiring president of the university. It was "given to the senior who best embodies the high example set by Dr. Dodds, particularly in the qualities of clear thinking, moral courage, a patient and judicious regard for the opinion of others, and a thoroughgoing devotion to the welfare of the university and the life of the mind." From Princeton, Fisher went on to Harvard Business School, again on scholarship, while his wife, Emily, worked to support them. He graduated as a Baker Scholar, a distinction awarded to the top 5 percent of the class, and started at Morgan Stanley in 1962.

His first job was as a lowly "statistician" (a position later renamed "analyst"). One of his early assignments was to work on a restructuring of the massive Churchill Falls hydroelectric project in Canada. He was driving to Montreal with senior partner William Mulholland when a Canadian immigration officer at the border asked who was sitting in the back of the car.

Mulholland said, "No one."

The immigration officer asked, "Then who is that?"

"That's just a statistician," Mulholland reputedly said.

By the time Fisher was in his early thirties, he was no longer anonymous. After starting and building the hugely successful Sales and Trading Division, he was elected president of Morgan Stanley in 1984 and became chairman in 1991. He was in the forefront of the firm's long-term investment in international expansion, which gave Morgan Stanley its global reach; but his most spectacular accomplishment was the $10.2 billion Dean Witter merger when he was chairman, in 1997. In order to create the world's premier financial institution, he and John Mack gave the keys to the kingdom to Philip Purcell. That, as it turned out, was Fisher's one spectacular misjudgment. Their "merger of equals," known as "MOEs," was one of only two in the financial world in recent years that did not provide for clear changing of the guard from one CEO to the next. The other merger was Citibank and Travelers. In both instances the terms did not provide for finite timetables for the transfer of responsibility, and both firms would become mired in infighting and power struggles.

Like Dick Fisher, "Johnny" Mack began to take grown-up responsibilities when he was eight years old. That was when he began helping his father and five older brothers in the family grocery distribution business in Mooresville, North Carolina—population four thousand. During the school year, the boys went to the warehouse in the evenings and packed boxes for the next day's shipments. In the hot southern summers, they worked from sunup until two in the afternoon.

John's father was born Charles Makhoul in 1893 in Roum, Lebanon, and immigrated to the United States at the age of twelve to join his father. When Charles arrived, he learned that his last name was now Mack; the officials at Ellis Island in 1908 thought Makhoul sounded "too guttural." Neither father nor son spoke English, and they started as peddlers, carrying trunks on their backs from house to house, and farm to farm, selling small household goods, sometimes walking fifty miles before they had sold enough to start home again. They saved their money and opened a dry goods store, but the store was destroyed by fire in 1910. Two years later, they had repaid their debts and opened a clothing store on the main street.

Charles Mack expanded, starting an ice cream and candy business and a wholesale grocery distribution warehouse. He had four sons with his first wife and, after she died, married Alice Azouri, a Lebanese seamstress who immigrated to Cuba before World War I, then made her way to North Carolina. Charles and Alice were married in 1939. John Joseph, born in 1944, was their second child, the youngest, and last, of the six Mack boys. By then everyone in town knew the Macks.

As part of a tiny minority of Roman Catholics in a Baptist Bible Belt town, the Macks found a priest who would come to say mass at their house. More Catholics moved into the area after World War II, and the Macks led the drive to move an unused brick chapel from an army base to Mooresville and established St. Teresa's Church. Alice Mack, who added to the family income by using her skills as a seamstress to work as a decorator, donated time to cook for the sick and raised money to build the church, and for a school and orphanage. Mack aunts and uncles settled in Mooresville, and they held family gatherings on weekends at which twenty to fifty family members would gather for lunch and dinner.

At Mooresville High School, John joined the school band, playing the clarinet; and the football team, where he was voted most valuable lineman. He made All-Conference and was an All-State performer, while he maintained his grades and his popularity. In his senior year Johnny Mack, with his black hair and bright brown gaze, six feet tall and 195 pounds, was elected president of the student body as well as to the National Honor Society.

He went to Duke University on a football scholarship, signed up as premed, joined a fraternity and the YMCA, and earned spending money by buying snack foods wholesale from the family grocery warehouse and selling them from his dorm room. A Duke publication noted that, as a member of the football varsity, he "has possibilities." During summer vacations, he supervised the packing in the warehouse and set up a more efficient system so they could finish by 11 A.M. On some days the boys would go fishing in the 32,500-acre Lake Norman nearby, where the catfish could weigh as much as fifty pounds.

In John's sophomore year, his father died at the age of seventy-two; and when John was a junior, he cracked the vertebrae in his neck. His football career, and with it his scholarship, were over. Mack says, "I knew then I was on my own." He switched his major to history and took a part-time job as a clerk at a North Carolina securities firm, earning $325 a month. He attended classes during lunch breaks and made do the rest of the time by reading the assignments and studying for tests.

After he graduated from Duke in 1968, he got his first job, as a municipal bond salesman at Smith, Barney; then he went on to F. S. Smithers and Loeb Rhoades & Co. He found his professional home in 1972, when he was hired at Morgan Stanley as a bond salesman. Dick Fisher was his ultimate boss.

Mack was twenty-eight years old, he had worked for three other firms, and he felt right away that Morgan Stanley was different: "There was a patina about Morgan Stanley. The client list—Johnson & Johnson, IBM, GM—their stock buybacks paid for the entire overhead of the firm. Morgan Stanley priced a bond deal and the Street sold it for them." When he entered the firm, the staff had grown, but not much. There were about 350 employees and partners, "a close-knit collegial group," he says. A few days after he joined, "The firm was pricing a $100 million deal, a 7⅛ coupon for the phone company. Every partner came to the meetings, because it was their capital, and everyone in the firm stated their view." Mack was impressed that he was included, even though he was new and young.

It wasn't until after 1979, when he was made a managing director, that he and Dick Fisher got to know each other well, and Fisher, who was a decade older, became his mentor. Mack says, "I had a lot to learn about pace and patience. Dick was very calm. He would point out another way of doing something in situations with tremendous pressure. Other than performance, Dick relied on me for honesty." Mack admits he was quicker than Fisher to pull the trigger. "It took Dick longer to make a decision," he says, "but once he did, he was masterful."

Chas Phillips, who worked for Mack in the early 1980s, says, "You can't understand John Mack without knowing what Morgan Stanley was like in 1978. It was a very small place with long-standing corporate relationships, and the majority of bankers who, for legacy reasons, controlled the firm still looked at Sales and Trading as a lesser business. You can't imagine the skepticism."

Two changes in SEC regulations disrupted the firm's business model. On May 1, 1975, the SEC abolished fixed equity commissions, an event that U.S. Navy man Bob Baldwin called "Mayday," referring to disaster at sea. All over Wall Street firms lowered their commissions, undercutting one another and shrinking their profit margins; by early 1978 competitive commissions were halved. While price competition collapsed other firms, Morgan Stanley had begun to diversify, and money was streaming in from Sales and Trading. The other new regulation was SEC Rule 415, also known as "shelf registration," which permitted a company to file—or shelve—a prospectus for two years before making a public offering while waiting for a propitious market. Prior to Rule 415, offerings were priced the afternoon before they were issued, and sold by investment bankers through the syndicate system. With this new rule allowing for a long lead time, companies became more independent of their bankers, and the bankers had to compensate by offering other services and entering new businesses. Some could not do it, and so many seemingly impregnable firms went under that Bob Baldwin kept a "tombstone" ad that listed a couple of hundred members of a pre-1975 syndicate. As one after another closed their doors, he crossed the names off with a red pencil.

Mack became Head of Worldwide Taxable Fixed Income in 1985, and as Chas Phillips says, he "was willing to be direct in a culture run by a bunch of investment bankers who didn't take each other on. It was like a club, everyone was deferential, but John was willing to tell you what you had to do." He was instrumental in moving Morgan Stanley away from a singularly relationship culture to a performance culture, creating scorecards and helping people understand how they ought to be judged. In the past, compensation had often been decided by feel. Mack developed metrics for the high-yield bond business such as "how to judge performance, how much capital you were using, what kind of returns you were getting," Phillips says. "The other thing John did that was pretty remarkable, he picked people for key jobs based only on merit. John looked for insight and talent; he surrounded himself with people who were hungry. None of these guys were Ivy League old-school kind of guys."

In the 1970s, Morgan Stanley made another notable shift. Wall Street had largely been divided into Jewish and Christian firms, and Morgan Stanley had never had a Jewish partner. Then Frank Petito hired Lewis W. Bernard, who was his son's Princeton roommate. People who were at the meeting when Bernard was elected partner in 1969 recall the comment, "We're about to have a partner who is smarter than all of us put together." The remark smacked of stereotyping, but Bernard *was* brilliant, and his background was closer to the Morgan Stanley image than that of some of the other partners: he grew up on Park Avenue in Manhattan and went to prep school at Lawrenceville before Princeton. Bernard became one of the top officers of the firm. Over an almost thirty-year career, he was responsible for Administration, Finance, Operations, Technology and Strategic Planning, and served as Head of Corporate Finance, Investment Banking, and Fixed Income.

Baldwin and Petito led another controversial move: they decided to establish an expensive research department, even though some of the older partners considered research to be a frill. Baldwin remembers Perry Hall saying, "Bob, what are you getting into research for? We'll just go ask for the business." Baldwin told him, "That's old style, Perry. Won't work. It's who's producing ideas." Fred Whittemore remembers that Hall said, "How can we give General Motors advice if we have some fuzzy-headed person in the back saying don't buy GM?" By 1978, with the increasingly respected and well-known Yale graduate Barton Biggs as Chief Analyst, the firm was spending $4 million a year on research. It paid off: when Morgan Stanley priced a deal, it usually hit the market at the right level.

After Biggs was appointed Global Strategist, he asked Byron Wien, then a successful fifty-year-old money manager at another firm, if he would consider becoming the U.S. strategist. "Barton was a holy man by that time," Wien says. Over a six-month period Wien was interviewed by dozens of people in groups of about ten to make sure he could maintain the standard. That was somewhat extreme, but it wasn't unusual for Morgan Stanley to interview prospective employees again and again, to be sure they would be a good fit. When Wien joined the firm, he says, "I was coming up with ideas I didn't think I could have, and it was because the place was so supportive. They'd say, Go for it. Take a risk. If you fall from the bar, there's a net. We're holding the net because we want you to try. I thought, My God. Isn't that a terrific thing? That was the culture, that was what was making the place great." The analysts were the firm's most visible examples of the culture of debate, intellectual rigor, and creativity that was a natural evolution from the partnership mentality. When the Monday-morning meetings began to be televised on the in-house system, Biggs, who was eccentric and outspoken, and Wien, who was eccentric and humorous, were apt to face off and air their differences. Listening to them invigorated the whole firm.

The person who took his designation as one of the "irreverent six" further than anyone else was the feisty Bob Greenhill, the firm's first Head of Mergers and Acquisitions. Greenhill was a Yale graduate and Baker Scholar at Harvard Business School, and an extreme outdoorsman with a slight, muscular build, a big head of curly hair, and a wicked grin. He was famous for his endurance and his adventures. In the 1970s, he and his wife, Gayle, and their three children went to the Arctic with Jack Wadsworth, a handsome Kentuckian who worked at First Boston, and Wadsworth's family. They were flown in by seaplane and dropped off above the Arctic Circle to begin a monthlong canoe trip on the Back River—as in "watch your back," one of Greenhill's friends says—to the pickup point. They left their maps behind and guided themselves using the journals of earlier explorers. Among the outcomes of the trip was that Greenhill persuaded Wadsworth to come to work at Morgan Stanley. Wadsworth would become the head of Asia.

Greenhill was undiplomatic, impatient, and brilliant. Working at a demonic pace, he led Mergers & Acquisitions to become a major profit center and played a significant role in changing Morgan Stanley's reputation from the bastion of "gentlemen" to the headquarters of Wall Street's new "gentlemen killers," as one executive told a reporter. In the summer of 1974, Greenhill shocked Wall Street when Morgan Stanley represented INCO, International Nickel Company, Ltd., of Canada in a hostile bid for the Philadelphia-based battery-maker ESB (Electric Storage Battery). The more reputable investment banks had previously avoided representing the aggressor in a hostile takeover, but with the INCO deal, Morgan Stanley set the pace, and other firms followed.

By 1978, mergers and acquisitions was the most profitable area of the firm. It was staffed by twenty-three professionals and had sixty prospective deals in the pipeline. Baldwin says, "It was perfect for Greenie. It was a fast-moving, brash business." A magazine article enthused, "The atmosphere [in mergers and acquisitions] is tinged with a sense of high drama and extreme secrecy. Companies are referred to only by code names, locks are sometimes changed and Xerox machines sealed. 'We sweep this place every two weeks for electronic bugs,'" Greenhill said. Greenhill was unstoppable, but Bob Baldwin says, "Sometimes he drove me crazy—he'd start calling the chairman of the board [of a client] by his first name on the second day he was on the job. I'd say, 'Jesus Christ! Don't you ever call anybody mister?' He said, 'Uh-uh.' I said, 'What do you call your father?' He said, 'By his first name,' and I said, 'Dear God.'"

Keeping the "first-class business" motto in mind was a challenge, but pride, or perhaps arrogance, was a powerful motivation. Morgan Stanley people felt they were good enough to prevail by doing things the right way, and that other methods were beneath them. At times, when the pressure to accommodate a client was intense, the firm's mettle was challenged. Joe Fogg was a twenty-nine-year-old member of the Mergers & Acquisitions Division when Morgan Stanley was hired as the banker representing a small family-controlled oil company in California whose majority owners wanted to sell their stake. The company had a heavy oil deposit with billions of barrels of oil, but a tertiary recovery that required a lot of technology and expense. Fogg says, "We hired engineers and we did an evaluation, and it looked like it might be worth a couple hundred million dollars, a reasonable size business."

Morgan Stanley was preparing to hold an auction when the second oil shock caused the price of oil to skyrocket. "All of a sudden, it looked like this thing might actually be worth some very serious money," Fogg says. "All kinds of people were trying to climb on the train." Texaco and Mobil, both important Morgan Stanley clients, each owned about 18 percent of the company, and both companies tried to persuade Morgan Stanley not to hold the auction, so they could work out a deal with the family that owned the majority of the company.

Greenhill, Fogg, and the M & A team felt that staying with a sealed bid auction would give the majority owners the fairest deal, and Frank Petito backed them up. "Mobil and Texaco were threatening lawsuits, but we did what we felt was the right thing," Fogg says. "Shell bid $3.65 billion, with a substantial cover over the next bid, which happened to be from Mobil. We ended up awarding the deal to Shell over the objection of the other two companies. At the time, that was the largest deal in the history of Wall Street," Fogg recalls, although he adds, "every few years there's another 'largest deal.'" When it was over, Baldwin says, "I had a call from Mobil and a call from Texaco and they said as long as Bob Greenhill—which was Morgan Stanley—was around, they're not going to do business with us. I went to work on both companies and John Wilson went to work on Mobil, because he had a very good relationship there. Time went on and Texaco was being sued about the values of the reserves. They came to see me and said, 'Do you think you could get Bob Greenhill to do the testimony on this?' And I said, 'Certainly think so.' And I went to Bob and said, 'This is a testament to your abilities. I think you ought to do it and see what comes out of it.' He did a very, very good job."

As a more aggressive style overtook the old culture, one of the senior partners, William Black, played a significant role in maintaining balance and civility. Parker Gilbert says, "He was a great friend of all of us, in many ways the person that was the most sympathetic to people who had issues and problems, needed bolstering and encouragement." Ron Chernow takes an even stronger stand. In *The House of*

Morgan he writes, "Black held the firm together and prevented an outright split between bankers and traders."

The focus of the firm was still on the domestic arena, with little exposure in the international arena. Outside the United States, the firm had a one-man representative office in Tokyo and a joint venture with Morgan Guaranty in Paris, where two members of the future Group of Eight, Parker Gilbert and John Wilson, worked. The main objective of the foreign offices was to serve U.S. companies that wanted access to the Eurobond market by avoiding the strictures of the then-in-force 1963 Interest Equalization Tax, an obstacle to raising money abroad. In 1975, the firm concluded that it was time to develop a truly international business, and Frank Petito and Bob Baldwin recruited Richard A. Debs to undertake that mission.

Debs was the Chief Operating Officer of the Federal Reserve Bank of New York and had played a leading role in the Fed's international operations, particularly during the Petrodollar-energy crisis of the mid-1970s. He was the principal representative of the Federal Reserve System and the U.S. Treasury in the dialogue with the OPEC countries and the major central banks of Europe and Japan that were dealing with the acute financial problems of the time. He had been a Fulbright Scholar in Egypt, had studied Arabic at Princeton, where he earned a Ph.D. and was also a graduate of the Harvard Law School, where he later established an Islamic Law library. During the cooling-off period after leaving the Fed, he served as pro bono financial advisor to President Anwar Sadat of Egypt. With that background, he was well suited to develop the international business.

Within three years, Debs was personally active in bringing in a $4 billion equity portfolio from the government of Kuwait, at a time when Morgan Stanley's assets under management totaled less than $1 billion. He developed a relationship with the Saudi Arabian Monetary Agency (SAMA), the central bank of Saudi Arabia, through which Morgan Stanley clients were able to borrow about $1 billion a year in the form of private placements. When China permitted U.S. institutions to enter the country, Debs and Frank Petito traveled to China and opened relations; and Morgan Stanley was also awarded the lead manager role for the first Yankee bond issue for the United Kingdom.

In 1976, every one of the Morgan Stanley managing directors was

American. That quickly changed as the firm established an investment banking office in London, a liaison office in Cairo, built up its Tokyo office, and established an international division in New York to coordinate the firm's growing international businesses. At the time of the Dean Witter merger in 1997, Morgan Stanley had eighty-four offices abroad.

Private Wealth Management was another undeveloped area in 1977, when Morgan Stanley hired Anson M. Beard Jr., the COO of Donaldson, Lufkin & Jenrette Securities Company, to establish an in-house private wealth management unit. Dick Fisher announced that the firm "had decided to enter the retail business 'in an important way . . . seeking the substantial individual investor and the small investment manager,'" which provoked the *New York Times* to note, "The 'little guy,' of course, will not become a Morgan Stanley client. The firm is interested only in the 'substantial' individual, with a net worth of at least $500,000, or the small institution." In fact, there was no stated minimum account. Beard was made Head of Equities at the beginning of 1981 and built it into one of the firm's most successful businesses.

Underwriting was still the bedrock of the business, increasing 79 percent between 1974 and 1975. Parker Gilbert and John Wilson were two of the young partners who perpetuated the tradition of advising major clients and developing and nurturing long-standing relationships. Wilson's biggest client, the energy company Tenneco, billed more in some years than any other Morgan Stanley client. With Fred Whittemore as Head of Syndicate, the firm ranked number one as a syndicate manager, and issued more than $6 billion in public offerings in 1975, when Morgan Stanley represented six of the top ten, and eleven of the top twenty in *Fortune*'s list of the 500 largest industrial concerns. By 1977, the firm, which now employed more than seven hundred people, served as the investment banker to six of the ten largest industrial companies in the world, and fourteen of the twenty-five companies with the largest aggregate market value on the New York Stock Exchange.

The firm suffered a blow to its pride and its business when longtime client IBM, along with Salomon Brothers, challenged Morgan Stanley's sole manager policy. The firm had always insisted that its name be listed first, on the top left of the offering prospectuses and tombstone ads. It was both prestigious and profitable: Morgan Stanley priced the offerings, decided which other firms got to participate, oversaw the distribution, which was done by others, and reaped a larger percentage of the profits. In 1979 IBM was about to issue its first public debt offering, for $1 billion, and told Morgan Stanley it wanted Salomon to co-manage the issue. Morgan Stanley's inviolable arrangement that they would never share the lead manager position, which not only produced bigger fees but also appeared on the tombstone ads, was an indication of the pecking order to anyone who understood the business. The management committee was explosively divided about how to respond to IBM: Dick Fisher thought they should compromise; Baldwin and Whittemore said they weren't going to let a customer dictate to them, and they didn't think it was wise to share the lead. As Whittemore says, "Saying yes to Morgan Stanley was meant to be a habit, not a decision." Morgan Stanley refused to give up the lead, IBM gave Salomon the go-ahead, and after that every firm on Wall Street lined up to try to unseat Morgan Stanley from the preeminent position in future offerings.

IBM was the kind of client the firm had always represented, but Morgan Stanley was taking on companies outside the traditional mold. When the management of Wisconsin-based Oscar Mayer & Co. wanted to hire Morgan Stanley to issue a $50 million debenture, "the old man, Oscar Mayer, had never heard of Morgan Stanley," one former executive recalls. "His managers explained that Morgan Stanley is the best firm in the business. He said, 'I've got it. They're the Oscar Mayer of investment banking. Let's hire them.'" In July 1980, a *Wall Street Journal* reporter visiting Morgan Stanley happened upon a group of supposedly sedate investment bankers celebrating the Oscar Mayer debenture. They had hung a six-foot-long inflated hot dog from the ceiling, and the theme song, "I Wish I Were an Oscar Mayer Wiener," was blasting into the room. It wasn't the scene he had expected to see at Morgan Stanley.

In 1985, when the Mergers & Acquisitions Division was headed by Eric Gleacher, who had come in from Lehman Brothers Kuhn Loeb, the firm eagerly accepted another nontraditional client, Ronald O. Perelman, and represented him in the hostile takeover of Revlon Incorporated. Twenty years later, Perelman would be one of the most damaging clients, and potentially one of the most expensive, in the history of the firm.

In 1979, as the new businesses became more established, the firm appointed a six-man task force to create a ten-year strategy. Lewis Bernard was in charge of planning, and Anson Beard and William Kneisel, who would become Head of Worldwide Capital Markets, did the analysis. As Beard says, "It was the first time anybody had showed the partnership the full anatomy of the firm." The analysis led to more changes: in 1981 Greenhill and Bernard were named coheads of Investment Banking, overseeing corporate finance, M & A, the international and syndicate businesses, and energy and utilities finance. Joe Fogg took over Mergers & Acquisitions. Dick Fisher was in charge of Institutional Securities, which covered Sales and Trading, Research, arbitrage, and marketing.

With the syndicate system partly undermined by shelf registration, Salomon Brothers stepped up with "bought deals," which meant that Salomon would buy an entire deal and sell it, without including other firms. As Sanford Bernstein analyst Brad Hintz, who was formerly Morgan Stanley's treasurer, says, "Salomon was the ten-foot giant, coining money from the trading business. Morgan Stanley had never taken risk and had very little capital." Fred Whittemore explains, "In the old days, we needed each other to do deals, but after 1981 John Gutfreund [the then-chairman of Salomon] could produce hundreds of millions of dollars the same day. After that, we no longer had the same kind of built-in relations with other firms."

Bob Baldwin retired in 1985, leaving a tremendous legacy: the firm had added Mergers & Acquisitions, Sales and Trading, Research, and International businesses to its core Investment Banking. It employed 4,100 people, its capitalization had ballooned to $300 million, assets had risen to nearly $16 billion, it had set profit records six years in a row, and return on equity ranged from 35 to 43 percent. Revenues from investment banking were $159 million in 1981 and $423 million in 1985, and rose 58.7 percent between 1984 and 1985. Principal transactions were up from $45.48 million to $243 million, with revenues up 99.7 percent. In 1985, revenues were the highest in the firm's history, at $1.79 billion, an increase of 33.9 percent in the past year. About 60 percent of the earnings records were coming in from Mergers & Acquisitions. As Joe Fogg says, "We were the engine that produced the cash flow to build the other businesses."

For all the collegiality and the value placed on partnership, competition was always an element in the firm's life force. In 1985, the chief competitors were Bob Greenhill and Dick Fisher, who had been trying to outpace each other since they were in the same class at Harvard Business School. Now they both wanted to become chairman. If Baldwin chose either of them to succeed him, the other would leave. Instead, Baldwin selected the forty-nine-year-old Parker Gilbert as his successor.

Gilbert's historic connection with Morgan Stanley, his unimpeachable ethics, stature, and competence provided a comforting link between the distinguished past and the competitive present. He was, however, shy, and there was some question as to whether he would be assertive enough. As Fred Whittemore remarked, "Parker's way of working a party was to stand behind a potted palm." Baldwin went to see Gail Gilbert after he had talked to her husband about becoming chairman. "You know, Parker isn't going to be able to take the early train to Southampton on Friday anymore, nor will all the meetings start at ten o'clock," he warned her. "Great," she said. "He'll love it." Gilbert took office as chairman on January 1, 1984.

He turned out to be self-assured, straightforward, and unwilling to let politics interfere with business. He spoke quietly, sometimes with an undercurrent of amusement, but he was firm. Whittemore says, "Leadership requires a positive nature. Parker, who had been a conservative investment banker, learned to be positive." Gilbert appointed Dick Fisher president, in charge of Sales and Trading, and Greenhill head of Investment Banking. Joe Fogg reported to Greenhill, and Anson Beard and John Mack reported to Fisher.

Morgan Stanley celebrated its Fiftieth Anniversary in September 1985, and the firm took out a full-page newspaper ad announcing that the partners had agreed to dedicate themselves to remaining a private company and serving its clients; but before the end of the year, the management committee made the decision to go public. It was the boldest move since Parker Gilbert's father and stepfather helped form the firm half a century earlier. Morgan Stanley needed more than its current $300 million in capital if the firm was to continue to be a market leader, particularly in fixed income, securities, proprietary trading, and merchant banking. Other Institutional Securities firms had already gone public. Donaldson, Lufkin & Jenrette was the first, in 1970. A year later, Fred Whittemore sat on the pricing committee when Merrill Lynch went public with a market cap of $2 billion. Bear Stearns launched a successful $215 million public stock offering in the fall of 1985; Goldman Sachs had sold some of its ownership in a private placement to the Japanese company Sumimoto and was considering going public as well, but decided against it, until 1999. Morgan Stanley was not alone in worrying about exchanging privacy and long-term profits for capitalization and the more immediate compensation rewards of a public company. But as Brad Hintz says, "If all my businesses require capital investment, the worm can't get bigger than the apple." To grow the apple and feed more capital-intensive businesses, Morgan Stanley needed to raise money on the public market.

In the fall of 1985, Parker Gilbert stood before the managing directors and announced that for the first time in his recollection, rather than making a decision by consensus, the management committee had taken a vote. They had unanimously agreed that the firm should become a publicly owned company, and he was now asking the managing directors for their vote. A successful public offering would finance expansion and instantly and incrementally increase the personal wealth of everyone with a financial interest in the firm. The delicate question was how much richer each of the partners would become: older partners had more capital and time invested and were technically entitled to a larger number of shares, but the future rested with the young. The management committee considered possible formulas, and Gilbert took the lead in apportioning more stock to the younger group than they would have been entitled to if the only consideration had been their current investment of time and money. When he went back to the managing directors to tell them how the system would work there were enough cries of "not fair!" that the management committee agreed to review the plan. They decided that the original formula was the right one. At the next partners meeting, Gilbert said that the firm would buy out anyone who didn't want to participate—at par. As par was around $15, approximately $40 less than the likely opening price, he didn't have any takers, and the partners voted to issue an IPO. Anson Beard says, "Parker did a superb job of making it fair, a brilliant job. Everybody was equally unhappy."

On March 2, 1986, Morgan Stanley filed its registration with the Securities and Exchange Commission and issued 24,201,715 shares of common stock. An important ingredient of the arrangement was the owner-manager philosophy: 81 percent of the shares would be owned by the 112 managing directors and 145 principals, at an average price of $15.33 per share. The remaining shares would be sold to the public at an opening price of $56.50. Gilbert was allotted 772,133 shares, Fisher 729,574, Lewis Bernard 673,521, and Greenhill 710,275. The issue was priced at 56½ and closed just over 70. A managing director whose interest in Morgan Stanley was valued at $8 million on March 2 had a stake worth $25 million the next morning. As long as the firm was still private, the partners had owned preferred stock, much of which wouldn't be paid out until after they retired at age sixty, and even then, only in increments. Suddenly, their stock was locked up for only two years.

Until then, money was only part of the reward for working for the firm, or on Wall Street. Prior to 1986, Morgan Stanley partners could expect to become "respectably rich in a respectable way," as Fred Whittemore says, but not hugely—even excessively—rich.

Along with the multiplication of the ability to build personal wealth through stock ownership, deals got bigger, and managing directors were compensated at a much higher level. The firm segued into "prudent risk taking," and began to deal in junk bonds, equity derivatives, and leveraged buyouts. When the transactions became more complicated and the stakes got bigger, bankers needed a higher tolerance for risk than their predecessors. One explains, "You had to be able to contemplate the billion-dollar deal, the five-billion-dollar merger, and think 'those are just zeroes.' All the people in the room needed a deep experience at that heroic level." As the risk-reward equation was heightened, Wall Street attracted people who were less interested in the first class business than in the promise of mega-paydays.

In the early 1970s, investment banking still maintained a relatively even balance between job satisfaction and the accretion of wealth. The thirty-nine Morgan Stanley partners were paid $100,000 a year and considered that they were being well compensated. Parker Gilbert recalls commuting with a couple of colleagues when they were in their early thirties, and hearing someone say, "If we could only make $3 million, we could retire and play golf."

Anyone lucky enough to have inherited a million dollars in 1970 could buy an apartment on Park Avenue—four bedrooms, two maids' rooms, living room with wood-burning fireplace, dining room, kitchen, and library—for under $100,000. In 1971 corporate raider Saul Steinberg bought one of the most expensive apartments in the city, at 740 Park Avenue, for $250,000. One young partner bought a rambling house with a guest cottage in commutable Greenwich, Connecticut, at the top of the market for $207,000. A weekend house in the Hamptons cost even less; if it was one of the eighteen-room seaside monsters built in the 1920s, it was practically a giveaway. After paying for the apartment and the summerhouse in cash, there was three-quarters of a million dollars earning interest to cover the tuition for two children in private school, the salary of someone to take care of the children and someone else to clean the house, and the dues at city and country clubs. A $100,000 salary paid for everything else.

Less than twenty years later, massive inflation hit the rich. Upper-middle-level bankers owned stock in their companies and earned between $5 and $10 million a year. The top bankers were bringing home double and triple that. In the early twenty-first century, the former Steinberg apartment at 740 Park Avenue sold for more than $30 million, and it wasn't the most expensive apartment in town. Hedge fund managers paid tens of millions of dollars for 5,000-square-foot houses in Greenwich, where previous generations of successful bankers and corporate executives had brought up their children. They tore down the houses, built mansions the size of small schools, and bragged that they had spent $50 million. Club initiation fees that had been a couple of thousand dollars in the 1970s skyrocketed to $25,000, then $50,000, and instead of having to recruit members, the clubs had waiting lists. Wall Street golfers started their own clubs. John Mack helped build the membership of a new club, which was established by Japanese executives led by Masa Kasuga, who was in the Green Stamp and real estate business. The initiation fee began at $150,000, and rose to $175,000. By 2006, two golf clubs in the Hamptons were vying for which was the most expensive; one charged an initiation fee of $600,000, while the founder of the other bragged that his club was more expensive at $650,000.

As the numbers became surreal it was more important than ever for Morgan Stanley to emphasize the firm's culture and reputation, to keep the younger managing directors grounded. Understatement, which had always been part of the Morgan Stanley style, became another way of showing off. One small manifestation of the antiflash trend was the competition among certain Morgan Stanley executives to see who could find and wear the cheapest watch. (Lewis Bernard was the winner.)

Quality didn't always trump greed, but the leaders of the firm made a conscious effort to hold to a certain standard. William Kneisel, then based in London as Head of Corporate Finance, explained that an element of the firm's success was: "Clients like our long-term commitment. We don't feel we have to have all of our cake today."

The glory days of the 1980s were tested on "Black Monday," October 19, 1987, when the Dow Jones average lost 508 points, the largest single-day point drop in the history of the stock market. The market had been acting badly for a couple of weeks, Morgan Stanley had a couple of M & A deals fail, and a hurricane took down thousands of trees in London, impacting the valuation of an IPO for a British company the firm had priced the day before the storm. At 7:45 A.M. on October 19, Anson Beard held his daily Equities Division managers meeting and said, "This is the worst-looking market I've ever seen. We have some hiring requisitions out: cancel them. Long positions: I don't like them. We're going to run this business like there's a big storm out there. We're going to manage the business as if the market is going straight down from here."

Six hours later, the market had lost 22 percent.

At the 4:00 P.M. close, Beard held a meeting of all the equity traders to assess the size of their positions relative to the established limits, and approximate their gains and losses for the day. "We had a couple of secret weapons. One of our thoughtful traders, Peter Palmedo, had drawn an analogy in August between 1929 and this market, which led us to purchase a modest amount of out-of-the-market puts that showed a substantial profit by the close. We also had some excellent derivatives traders, who profited that day in the depreciating market. Clients trading in blocks and over the counter, of course, got killed. But on balance,"

Beard says, "it looked like we came through the day in pretty good shape."

Beard went to look for Dick Fisher, who was upstairs in the gym, changing for a black tie dinner. On the way to the gym, he walked through the cafeteria, which was empty except for a man he'd never seen before. "Can I help you with something?" Beard asked. The man told him that a week earlier, he'd put fifty cents in the ice cream machine and hadn't gotten either the ice cream or his fifty cents. He was trying to get the change the machine owed him. Beard told him, "You I can help," and gave him the fifty cents. "Then I went to see Dick to tell him we'd lost $10 million here and $5 million over there."

As Equities looked at their accounts, they singled out some that looked unstable; the chairman of a Swiss arbitrageur had borrowed money from Morgan Stanley, using his stock as security, and Beard says, "The stock was going down like a stone. It was going under water." Based on an opinion from a lawyer at Davis, Polk, Morgan Stanley sold the arbitrageur out. That led to one of the very few SEC investigations that took place when Beard was Head of Equities. (Morgan Stanley was exonerated.) Beard says, "Every one of our competitors had to pay big fines, or people went to jail, but on my watch, except for some small fines for time-stamping trades late, we had no problems with regulators."

The worst Street-wide fallout from the 1987 crash was the pending multi-billion-dollar British Petroleum deal. U.S. underwritings are usually priced within hours of registration with the SEC, and go to market the next day, but the British lead times were longer. The firm committed to a price in early October, and the issue hadn't gone to market when the stock market collapsed. An undersecretary of the Treasury called the firm to ask what the government could do to help Wall Street. Beard recommended that, to substantially reduce the supply of new issues on the overall market, the U.S. government could ask the British government to postpone the BP issue. When the British Chancellor of the Exchequer announced plans to go ahead with the issue, every firm in the underwriting lost at least $60 million; Morgan Stanley lost about $5 million less than the others because they were up all night hedging.

After the crash, John Mack recalls, "one of our best managers came to my office, he had tears in his eyes. He said, 'I'm going to lose every-thing.'" Mack asked him, "What did you start with?"

"Nothing."

Mack said, "It pays to start with nothing. We didn't come from a lot of money. We work hard. If we lose it, we'll make it back."

Parker Gilbert decided to retire in 1989, creating another opportu-nity for internal turbulence. Now that Morgan Stanley was a pub-lic company, its workings were more exposed, and the appearance of dissension could hurt the firm. Dick Fisher was president and Green-hill was vice chairman. As Gilbert recalls, "They were the two people the management committee would accept as one being chairman and one being president, but we all knew that Dick and Bob were both very strong personalities and had competed with each other for a long time. While they were fine in a Morgan Stanley business sense, they didn't get along particularly well. The danger was that they couldn't work together."

John Mack and Dick Fisher were friends as well as colleagues, and when Fisher talked to Mack about the succession, Mack recalls, "Dick said, 'I'm not running for class president. If they want me, they'll ask.'"

Mack says, "I hounded Dick. I said, 'What's wrong with you? Don't just wait to see what happens.'"

Gilbert discussed the issue with the management committee and the outside board. The consensus was that Fisher should be chairman and Greenhill president. Gilbert called them into his office and said, "I think this is what's right for the firm, but if you don't think you can work together productively and supportively, I will stay on and I'll ask one of you to leave"——Gilbert, who was only fifty-seven years old, didn't have to retire until the situation was resolved. A day later, they told him they had agreed that they could collaborate.

The firm chose not to establish the position of CEO; as Gilbert says, "That wasn't a designation I particularly liked. At a place like Morgan Stanley there is a consensus and there is a senior group. It's not like a corporation where there is a vertical structure. I was more or less the CEO, but we never took votes on anything, except going public. There was no question that Dick and Bob were the two most senior officers of the firm, and they had executive authority, and it just stayed that way."

When Dick Fisher and Bob Greenhill took over, Fisher told a reporter, "We have been working together for so long that there is not going to be something that can be characterized as a major change here." Greenhill added, "Going forward, the people here expect the two of us to lead the business." The most visible sign of the leadership transition was the change in the art in the chairman's office. At work, Gilbert preferred "birds and guns" art, and a painting of a ship on a raging sea. Fisher hung a large, colorful Frank Stella on one wall and a Roy Lichtenstein brushstroke on another.

Gilbert retired in 1990 but remained on the board. When he left, Morgan Stanley had more than $2 billion in equity and 6,800 employees, including a thousand people in Tokyo and even more in London. In the first quarter of 1990, the *New York Times* noted, "some firms were reporting gigantic losses, while Morgan Stanley was booking some $82 million in net income, up by $1 million from the first quarter of 1989." Morgan Stanley was described as "the most profitable" firm on Wall Street, and its 1990 earnings of $443 million on $2.5 billion in revenues set a record. The firm could afford to make some investments on its own account; as of 1990, Morgan Stanley had invested $250 million in merchant banking ventures.

In thirty years, the firm had been transformed, but it was still based on the principles and standards set by J. P. Morgan, Jack Morgan, Harry Morgan, and Harold Stanley: it was run by people of character doing a first class business in a first class way.

Morgan Stanley began with a silver-spoon reputation and never fully overcame the image, but the culture and the business at all three Morgan firms—J. P. Morgan, the private bank; Morgan Guaranty, the commercial bank; and Morgan Stanley, the investment bank—had always been enriched by such self-made Wall Street aristocrats as Tom Lamont and Frank Petito. When the firm was accused of social elitism, Bob Baldwin would announce that his grandfather had been a conductor on the Pennsylvania Railroad, and that he had worked his way through Princeton by running the college laundry—which, he might add, was the best-paying job on campus.

By the time Parker Gilbert retired, the firm was hiring talent from a wide range of sources. In 1990 only thirteen of twenty-four new managing directors were Ivy League graduates, while others came from the universities of Nebraska, Rochester, Dayton, Massachusetts, North Carolina, and New Hampshire. After 1970, Morgan Stanley was looking for the top business school graduates, regardless of where they'd grown up or gone to college. The goal was to hire as many Harvard Baker Scholars as could be enticed into banking—and to choose people who would adopt and, when necessary, adapt the long-standing mores of the firm.

Six future stars were in the classes of 1990 and 1991, and three of them would play significant roles in the events of 2005:

In the 1970s, when Vikram Pandit was an undergraduate engineering student at Columbia University, he lived in Queens, gave his home address as Nagpur, Northern Maharashtra, India, and wore a loud plaid jacket for his 1976 yearbook picture. The hopeful young man with a mustache and an innocent smile in the yearbook picture was hired at Morgan Stanley in 1983, after earning a master's degree in engineering, an MBA from Columbia University Business School, and a Ph.D. in finance from Columbia's Graduate School of Arts and Sciences. By 2005, Pandit was the clean-shaven, graying, and distinguished Head of Institutional Securities, the division that included Equities, Investment Banking, and Fixed Income. Institutional Securities was "the crown jewel of the business." He was also the front-runner to become the next CEO.

The first and only woman on Wall Street to head a Fixed Income division, Zoe Cruz was another member of the Class of 1990. Cruz grew up in Greece, but when she was in high school, her family lived in Boston for three years, where she went to public school. She was a sophomore at Radcliffe College when she met her husband, Ernesto Cruz, a Harvard junior. Cruz graduated in 1977, received her Harvard MBA in 1982, and was recruited by Morgan Stanley.

In 1990, Mayree C. Clark, an Oklahoma native, graduate of the University of Southern California, and a Stanford University MBA, was also named managing director. Clark would become Global Head of

Equity Research. She and Cruz brought the total number of female managing directors up to six, out of more than two hundred.

John Havens was a couple of years behind Cruz at Harvard; he graduated in 1979 and came to Morgan Stanley in 1986. Havens, who was the son of a prominent Philadelphia internist, was one of the few modern Morgan Stanley executives who fit the stereotype of the WASP banker. He was a five-club man—two city clubs, two country clubs, and one in Florida—but he was also the epitome of the "regular guy." A popular rumor was that Havens's real dream had been to be a white hunter in Africa. In 2005, he was Head of Equities, one of the divisions of Institutional Securities that reported to Pandit.

The fifth star in Morgan Stanley's Class of 1990, William M. Lewis Jr., was the firm's first African-American managing director. Lewis graduated from Harvard in 1978 and was awarded a Harvard MBA in 1982. He would serve as cohead of Mergers & Acquisitions, and Head of Corporate Finance. Lewis left in 2004, to become cochairman of Investment Banking at Lazard. In 2005 a friend said he'd later joked that he was part of the advance guard of top executives who left because they didn't want to work for Phil Purcell.

A year later, in 1991, Tarek F. Abdel-Meguid became a managing director. Meguid had been a premed graduate of McGill University in Canada until four days before he was to enter medical school, when he decided to enter investment banking instead. When Morgan Stanley considered hiring him, Dick Debs recognized that, with his background and experience, and his fluency in Arabic and understanding of the Middle East, he could make an important contribution to the firm. Meguid's father had been a Fulbright Fellow from Egypt studying economics at the University of Wisconsin. He was a member of a wealthy, philanthropic family with a long history in the civil service. Meguid's grandfather was in charge of all the ports in Egypt; his uncle, then the Egyptian Foreign Minister, was one of the signatories to the Camp David Agreement; and a cousin was a Deputy Prime Minister. Dr. Abdel-Meguid met and married an American sorority girl in Wisconsin, and they returned to Egypt with their first child, Tarek. Over the next nine years, they lived in Cairo and Khartoum, where Dr. Abdel-Meguid taught at the universities and Terry went to a Jesuit school. He was nine when his father joined the United Nations and the family moved to the United States.

When the 2005 fight began, Meguid had been Morgan Stanley's Head of Investment Banking for five years.

The diverse backgrounds of this small sampling of future leaders was an indication of Morgan Stanley's rapid evolution in twenty years: here were two women, one Greek, the other from Oklahoma; an African-American Harvard MBA; an Indian with a multiplicity of graduate degrees; a WASP; and the Arabic-speaking son of an important Middle Eastern family. Their commonality with the original partners were the quality of their education, their intelligence, and their affinity for the Morgan Stanley ethos.

I n 1992, soon after that year's new managing directors were chosen, the firm held a day of meetings for a couple hundred executives. John Mack had asked Byron Wien, "What do you think about writing a little skit? Anything you want." Over the weekend Wien mentioned the skit to his wife. "That's a bad idea," she said. "You can get yourself into trouble." The idea appealed to him, and after he had sketched out a few scenes, he told Fisher and Greenhill that he would write the skit, on three conditions: "First, nobody's going to read it before it's performed. If you want to fire me afterward, that's great." The second condition was that, as chairman and president, Fisher and Greenhill had to appear at the first rehearsal and "tell everybody how important the skit was to the culture of the firm, so they would be comfortable." He was casting the new managing directors as members of the management committee, and his final requirement was that the "actors should have complete immunity." Even so, he says, "the first guy I picked to play Greenhill wouldn't do it. He was afraid it would hurt his career." As for cost, "There were plays that came onto Broadway at a lower budget," Wien says, grinning.

The title of the skit was "The Return of Mr. Morgan"—played by Wien himself in glasses and a false nose, and a sort of porkpie hat that certainly didn't come from Mr. Morgan's closet. Wien stood behind a podium to the side of the stage and interrogated the "management committee" members, who were seated at a table, as though for a panel discussion. First onstage was a new managing director bravely playing Fisher, wearing a Princeton orange and black jersey, and Princeton Tiger baseball cap, and swinging across the stage on crutches—it took a certain mixture of guts and affection to make a joke of your crippled CEO. Next, "Greenhill" bounded in, wearing a version of the trademark dollar-sign suspenders that his daughter needlepointed for him, and a World War I aviator's helmet with the goggles pushed up. Greenhill had recently gotten his jet pilot's license, bought a plane, and in 1992 had logged 325 hours in the pilot's seat.

Bits of the dialogue presaged events that would culminate within a year. All the members of the management committee were caricatured, but the three actors to watch were those playing Fisher, Greenhill, and John Mack.

Fisher and Greenhill were running the firm, but Greenhill was flying around the country, visiting clients, usually in his Cessna Citation X, and he was acquiring other aircraft too. The Cessna flew at Mach 0.93, just short of the speed of sound. Greenhill said he could get to an appointment in London faster on his own plane than by taking the Concorde, if you included the time waiting for luggage and at customs. Zooming through the sky at 52,000 feet, Greenhill was the emperor of the air. As an associate remarked, "Greenie was great at getting business, but it's hard to run a company if you can't sit still." Increasingly often, Greenhill was out on business, and Fisher and John Mack, who had recently been made chairman of the Operating Committee, met without him.

It was against this background that "Greenhill" says to "Fisher," in the skit, "You promised if I let you become chairman I could make all the decisions. Let's keep it straight. You're the Queen of England. I'm the prime minister."

Wien's caricatures of the principals were good-humored, but on target. When, speaking as "Morgan," he asks Fisher if someone who is unhappy with his bonus ever asks for a meeting to discuss it, Fisher admits that occasionally happens, and Wien asks him how he handles it.

"Fisher": I listen sympathetically to what they have to say. I inform them that I am shocked, SHOCKED to learn of the injury done by some of our partners to others. I promise them exactly what they ask for. They leave my office smiling. I never follow through, of course. You know they call me "Dr. Feelgood." [Laughter and applause.]

Some of the other references were familiar a decade later, among them "Fisher's" mantra, which he interjects whenever he has a chance: the goals of the firm, he says, are "globalization, integration, planning, technology, and diversification." In fact, the real Fisher repeated the goal of "globalization, deregulation, and technology" so often in his speeches that his colleagues teased him about it.

The young managing director playing John Mack saunters on-stage wearing a Duke football uniform, pads, and helmet, and tossing a football. Mack, who was an irrepressible practical joker, was amused by this sort of thing. He played jokes on his friends and sometimes on his colleagues. On one memorable occasion, the firm had invested in a pig farm in Missouri where all the pigs contracted fatal swine influenza. As a Morgan Stanley executive says, "We had to admit we had a pig farm with no pigs; so all right, we did." Mack had one of the deceased pigs sent to a taxidermist and stuffed, and delivered to Dick Fisher's office as a Christmas present. As Mack recalls, "I think I thought it was funnier than he did."

Wien, in the role of Morgan, remarks to "Mack": "You have a reputation for being pretty tough."

The Mack character says, in a strong southern accent, "I am not tough. I am fair." (It sounds like, "Ah ay-um fay-ur.")

Wien says, "I hear you are very ambitious."

"Mack" counters: "I am not ambitious. I am realistic," as the actor punctuates the remark by tossing the football up and down.

Wien: "You mean you think you should run the firm?"

"Mack" says cheerfully, "I am the *only* person who can lead the firm into the twenty-first century . . . I'm the kind of person everyone in the firm wants to grow up to be . . . I'm tough. That's what counts these days."

Wien: "I thought the firm was an intellectual and compassionate place."

The managing director playing Mack must have been getting nervous as he delivered his last line: "The firm is a ree-turn on equity place. The way we increase return on equity is fear and bru-tal-ity!"

This was greeted with great hilarity and applause, and anyone with the courage to look saw that Mack was laughing along with everyone else. The skit was videotaped, and as the credits rolled, a voiceover repeated the exchange between Wien and "Mack."

Wien: "I thought the firm was an intellectual and compassionate place."

"Mack": "The firm is a return on equity place."

Wien's final message was aimed at the new managing directors. "We are engaged in a deadly serious business," he said, "but it should always be fun. Part of the way you achieve success is by not taking yourself too seriously." Thinking back on the skit years later, he says, "No other firm would have done anything like it."

Byron Wien wrote one more skit, in 2001. A managing director playing Philip Purcell, a man most of the 1992 audience had never heard of, would be on center stage; and the climate of fear would not be a joke anymore.

Morgan Stanley's 1992 profit was a record $510.5 million, but Fisher, Greenhill, and Mack took voluntary pay cuts of at least 50 percent that year. The decision reflected a decrease in stockholders' return on equity, from 21.4 percent to 17.6 percent. The situation was temporary: equity capital had grown at a faster rate than earnings. As one analyst commented about the reduction in compensation, "You don't see it very often. But it just shows that Morgan is very much focused on shareholder returns." That was one side of the story, but growth, the fluctuation of businesses, and personality conflicts were testing the culture of cooperation, and the issue of succession was heating up.

That year, John Mack says, "We decided we should have a planning off-site, with breakout sessions and facilitators. Either the crash shocked us, or, because we became a public company, we became very focused on quarterly earnings." The firm had slid from number one in the Equity Research tables to number eight or nine, and was down in other league tables as well. The head count, which had grown about 25 to 26 percent a year between 1981 and 1986, and grew 35 percent in 1986, dropped to less than 4 percent after 1987. The off-site meeting, Mack says, "was close to a revolution," and the managing directors made some structural changes, including establishing an operations committee, with John Mack as the chairman. Mack moved from the Head of Fixed Income into a more sweeping management role. "We started breaking down silos between Investment Banking and Sales and Trading, to become a 'one-firm firm.'"

No amount of reorganization could avert the inevitable clash at the top. Greenhill, as president, should have been one step away from the chairmanship, but Fisher and Mack had worked together in Sales and Trading, and Mack's Fixed Income Division was flourishing: between 1985 and the beginning of 1992, the firm's bond revenue grew five times, and the Fixed Income department expanded by 75 percent. "On Wall Street, if you're making the money, you get to decide. Boys' rules," one managing director says. "Girls' rules too, by the way." And although Morgan Stanley had a record year, ranking number one in investment advisory services, mergers and acquisitions on Wall Street were down by one-third, and Greenhill's division was reflecting the poor M & A market.

In February 1993, Greenhill was entertaining clients on a ski trip in Colorado when a few members of the management committee, including Anson Beard and John Mack, went to see Parker Gilbert to talk about the Greenhill situation. Gilbert listened but said he didn't want to intervene. He said, "You guys make the decision and I'm sure you'll make the right one." The informal consensus was that Greenhill would have to step down as president: Mack says he told the other members of the management committee that if they chose to stick with Greenhill, they couldn't count on him. The committee decided that Greenhill should cede the presidency to Mack. They would ask Greenhill to remain on the board of directors, keep his office, and continue to work with clients.

Greenhill returned on February 28 to find a message that Dick Fisher wanted to see him. When he heard what the group had decided, he asked to talk to the members of the inside board. A meeting was quickly arranged, and one by one, as they went around the room, the members confirmed their decision. On March 2, Morgan Stanley announced that John Mack would replace Bob Greenhill. As *Institutional Investor* later wrote, "Never before had Morgan Stanley deposed its president."

In April, Greenhill sold 456,000 shares of Morgan Stanley stock for $26.9 million but retained another 1.85 million shares at a value of $119.8 million. In June, when his term as president was officially over, he bought 750,000 shares of Primerica, the company Sanford Weill was putting together, and left Morgan Stanley to become chairman and CEO of Primerica's subsidiary, Smith Barney Shearson. The day before he made the announcement he called Fisher and Mack, who were both out of the country, and told them he was leaving. They asked him to postpone releasing the news until they came back. When he said he wasn't willing to wait, Morgan Stanley issued a three-line notice of his departure that became known as the "thirty words for thirty years" memo.

The following November, Dick Fisher and John Mack recruited fifty-five-year-old Joseph R. Perella, one of Wall Street's most dynamic deal makers, to join the firm as Head of Investment Banking. Perella and another mergers and acquisitions star, Bruce Wasserstein, had left First Boston Corp in the 1980s to start their own firm, Wasserstein Perella & Co., but the partnership had broken up earlier in 1993, and just as the "Greenhill gap" loomed, Perella was at large. When Perella joined Morgan Stanley, his appointment marked another cultural change: it was unusual to bring in a senior-level executive who hadn't been brought up at the firm. Looking back, Perella said the cross-pollination created a "hybrid vigor. We kept old values and opened our arms to people from other firms that embraced our values, but brought fresh insight."

The Young Turks—including every member of the future Group of Eight—were now the Old Guard. Greenhill was gone. Parker Gilbert retired in 1990. Dick Debs gave up the presidency of Morgan Stanley International in 1988, although his international connections were irreplaceable and he continued to be on contract to do business for the firm. Fred Whittemore retired as Head of Syndicate, and served as chairman of Morgan Stanley mutual funds with $3.5 billion under management from 1990 to 1997. Lewis Bernard stepped out in 1991, at the age of forty-nine. John Wilson retired in 1993. Anson Beard reached his goal of building a $1 billion business in 1994 and retired at the age of fifty-eight. Joe Fogg was named Head of Investment Banking in 1993 but wasn't appointed to the board, despite being the subject of a *BusinessWeek* cover story titled "Morgan Stanley's Main Merger Man," after he had completed two hundred deals worth more than $100 billion. Fogg resigned to start his own venture capital firm, Westbury Capital Partners, L.L.C., in 1994. He continued his involvement in Princes Gate Investors L.P., a $750 million private equity investment partnership that he had founded for Morgan Stanley. In 1994, seven of the members of the future Group of Eight were gone; only Bob Scott was still an active executive at the firm. He had been Head of Capital Market Services from 1985 to 1992, Head of Corporate Finance from 1992 to 1994, and he was now Head of Investment Banking. Scott, who was then forty-eight years old, was on the leading edge of the next group of Morgan Stanley leaders.

Three

PHILIP PURCELL AND "THE GREAT AMERICAN COMPANY"

1982–1993

In the late 1970s, when Morgan Stanley was still a private company and Bob Baldwin was its chairman, two men in Chicago were making their own plans to create a magnificent enterprise with international reach and deep American roots.

High up in the Sears Tower, the Sears Roebuck chairman, Edward Telling, and his new vice president for planning, Philip Purcell, were looking for ways to bolster Sears's flagging retail returns and at the same time create The Great American Company. One of the options they considered was to acquire a retail financial services firm. Sears had set a standard as a populist retail culture, providing good deals on everything from tires to diapers. They thought it seemed appropriate to give the Sears customer the opportunity to buy stocks and bonds through the company they had come to trust.

That idea would lead Purcell to Wall Street, and eventually to a challenge that was beyond his reach. Phil Purcell would spend more than two decades on Wall Street, but in all that time, he would remain so unknowable to most of his colleagues and to many in the financial services industry that a wide range of theories proliferated to explain his aloofness. In the often-provincial world of Wall Street, it was believed that he had emerged from obscure middle-American roots, and that, as a Roman Catholic who grew up in Salt Lake City, a town dominated by Mormons, he had been an outsider all his life. People who tried to parse his character guessed that he didn't feel he belonged in either camp. In fact, he was solidly rooted in both groups. If Phil Purcell carried himself with an air of awkward eagerness, alternating with impenetrable reserve—a man who didn't quite fit—it was his career trajectory, not his background, that was more likely to be the cause.

He began his career at the management consultant McKinsey & Company, and long after he had left the firm, he continued to be described as "a consultant," implying too much objectivity and the absence of emotional connection. But the culture that burned itself into his soul was Sears Roebuck, the McKinsey client that hired him to serve as its in-house planner. Purcell was given a unique position at Sears, charting its future during a turbulent transition. He was exposed to political infighting, dislocation born of change, bone-deep loyalties and enmities, and a mythology even more pervasive than the one he would encounter at Morgan Stanley. The aloofness of the consultant and the paranoia absorbed on an executive floor under siege became characteristics of his attitude as he climbed the corporate ladder toward a career on Wall Street he had never planned.

Purcell's early worldview was formed in two tightly knit societies, that of his mother, Shirley Sorensen Purcell, a member of a prominent Mormon family, and of his father, Philip Purcell Sr., who was a Roman Catholic graduate of Notre Dame and the successful second-generation owner of an insurance agency that wrote policies for Brigham Young University.

Philip Purcell Sr., known as "Phil," was a member of the Alta Club, founded in 1883 when Utah was still thirteen years away from becoming a state. Modeled on eastern men's clubs, which in turn were styled after upper-echelon London, the Alta Club was the unofficial headquarters of Utah ranchers, miners, and businessmen. They gathered in the dining room with its coffered ceiling, or around the fireplace in the bar, or in the billiards room, and ran the city and the state. Purcell was also a member of the Salt Lake Country Club, where the Wasatch Mountains ring the golf course.

Shirley Purcell's father, Erastus Daniel Sorensen, known as "E.D.," was a self-made Salt Lake businessman, whose history had a major influence on his grandson. E.D. was born in 1876 in the Utah town of Manti. Orphaned at fourteen, he quit high school and eventually went into the business of buying and building up farms. He bought the best house in Manti and became active in Republican politics. When the governor came through town, he would visit E.D., and they would sit out on the porch and talk. After Warren Harding was elected president, E.D. was named Utah's surveyor general and moved to Salt Lake City. He owned an Abstract and Title company, and in his forties enrolled in law school, where he earned his law degree, despite his lack of a high school diploma. E.D. was active in the Mormon church, but as one of his grandsons, Philip Purcell's first cousin Richard Sorensen, says fondly, "He could see a dollar coming from farther away than anyone in Salt Lake, and he didn't have a spiritual bone in his body."

Shirley Sorensen was a Chi Omega at the University of Utah and had a reputation as the nicest, prettiest girl in Salt Lake City. Although she did not convert to Catholicism to marry Philip Purcell, they had three children: Ann, Philip, born in 1943, and Paul. Shirley was diagnosed with Hodgkin's lymphoma when Philip was five. For the next three years, she was in and out of the hospital and undergoing treatments. The day Shirley Sorensen Purcell died, eight-year-old Philip had gone over to his cousin Richard Sorensen's house. The boys heard Richard's mother answer the phone and start to cry, and they went outside and shot hoops all afternoon.

Philip got special attention, but it wasn't just because he lost his mother; Richard Sorensen recalls he was "a wonderful kid. Everyone loved him. There was something very sweet and nice about him . . . He's a competitive guy, but he still has that same kindness." Sorensen was good in school and a fine athlete—he was a National Merit finalist, won a scholarship to Harvard, and was awarded a graduate degree from Oxford—but he says Philip was "bar none, the family favorite."

Judge Memorial High, the Roman Catholic parochial school Philip attended, was only a few blocks from E.D. Sorensen's house. He often stopped by after school and heard E.D.'s stories about the old West. He learned about adventure and possibility and toughness from his grandfather, while his father made sure he understood the value of hard work. Philip sold magazines over the phone when he was in junior high, and in high school worked at a dry cleaning store, pressing clothes. One summer, his father sent him off to build the I-80 highway in Wyoming, pouring tar in the summer sun.

Phil Purcell met Anne McNamara in high school, and Purcell

described his teenage years as "just playing basketball and chasing Annie." She was the daughter of an Irish immigrant, a good storyteller with a brogue, who worked at the rail yards in Salt Lake City. The Mormons had strictures against mining, and many Irish came to Utah to be miners. They also often ended up working on the railroads. Anne had black hair, rosy cheeks, and a creamy complexion with a few freckles; she was pretty and devout. Phil was fair-haired with light eyes and a winning smile, more than a head taller than Anne, even when she was wearing heels. She was a cheerleader; Phil played on the basketball team. It seemed that between Annie and basketball, he didn't have quite enough time for his studies, and he graduated twentieth in a class of eighty.

He started college at the College of the Holy Cross, founded by the Jesuits in 1843 on a beautifully landscaped campus in Worcester, Massachusetts, then transferred to his father's university, Notre Dame, which was headed by the great Father Ted Hesburgh, a leader in education and civil rights. Purcell didn't make the basketball varsity, but he played on an intramural team and worked hard, distinguishing himself academically. He says, those years "were some of the best in my life."

He and Anne were married before he graduated from Notre Dame. He was accepted at the University of Chicago Business School, and they moved to Chicago. The first of the Purcell's seven sons, David, was born that year. Purcell was outstanding enough that he was awarded a fellowship at the London School of Economics, where he and Anne and the baby lived for a year, before returning to the United States. Back in Chicago, Purcell completed his MBA at the University of Chicago Business School. Years later, when he could afford to be generous, Notre Dame and the Chicago Business School would benefit from his largesse.

Meanwhile, though, he had to find a job. He received at least three offers, each of which would have set him on a far different path. His father wanted him to come home to Salt Lake City, and become the third generation to run—and expand—the insurance business. That appealed to Anne: in three years, she had moved from Salt Lake to Chicago, had a baby, moved to London, and back to Chicago. Home sounded good. But Phil had other ideas. He was offered a job at Morgan

Stanley which he turned down, and at McKinsey & Company, which he accepted. At the age of twenty-seven, he became McKinsey's youngest principal director, and at thirty-two, he was the youngest managing director in the firm's history. At the beginning of 1976 he was assigned the Sears Roebuck account.

Sears had just hired McKinsey to evaluate the company, a daunting project. Sears had 440,000 employees and a five-territory structure that gave the territorial managers a unique level of independence. Purcell was one of two account executives on the project, which began as a two-month overview. After the other partner moved on, Purcell stayed, and for nearly two years he flew around the country on the Sears planes, interviewing employees and analyzing the business.

In the early 1970s, two-thirds of all American shoppers made a purchase at one of Sears's nearly nine hundred U.S. stores in any given three-month period. Sears's sales represented an astounding one percent of the American gross national product. Then, in the late 1970s, the Sears business began to decline drastically, and by the end of the decade, specialty catalogs cut into the profits from the iconic catalog, discount stores ate at the retail customer base, and outdated merchandise dulled the company's appeal.

Purcell admired the employees' fierce loyalty, and the credo that Sears was an example of American opportunity for employees to earn a good living and for customers to get a good deal. He recognized with some regret that the Sears model would have to be reorganized to compete in a changing environment. When he completed his study, Sears chairman Arthur Wood was getting ready to retire, and Purcell recommended that Wood select territorial manager Edward Telling as his successor, and that the company set up a new strategic planning office.

Telling was elected in November 1977 and suggested to Wood that they create the job of vice president for planning and offer Purcell the job. It was a radical move. According to Donald Katz, author of *The Big Store*, "An outsider hadn't ever been hired into the senior ranks of the seventeen thousand executives working at the time for Sears. Not one." Katz thought Telling's idea was "that if he could find someone with no history of a childhood within the company, no axes to grind, someone who could operate outside the insidious chains of family, regional, and departmental loyalties, that individual could serve as a powerful agent of change."

McKinsey prided itself on how many CEOs of major corporations were McKinsey alumni. As an investment banker who has dealt with many hundreds of CEOs remarked, "McKinsey people are expected to move on into leadership roles." Katz believes Purcell was attracted to what he imagined was "the real work of building a nation and raising the living standards of an entire people" by saving Sears. Telling persuaded Purcell that they "could break the spell of the past and cashier the company kings . . . and create something new." It was the beginning of Purcell's career as an outsider who was often treated as an interloper in organizations with deep traditions. While McKinsey consultants could be viewed as unwelcome intruders, their strong bond with their "home firm" gave them a sense of belonging. For Purcell, becoming a member of another organization didn't offer the same psychological protection.

In 1980, Sears's first quarter results were the worst since the Depression, showing a negative balance of $432 million, as compared with $67 million on the plus side the year before. Some of the directors were privately talking about unseating Telling. Instead, Telling replaced the president of Sears with a dedicated retailer, forty-six-year-old Edward Brennan, vice president of the southern territory. Brennan had worked all over the Sears empire, and Sears was a family affair. Brennan's grandfather, father, mother, brother, and two uncles all worked for the store. As Donald Katz wrote, "The Brennans ranked among those special families so bred in the romance of the place that it was hard to tell company and family apart." There were many examples of families with a couple of generations of "Searsmen." The tradition mixed loyalty and nepotism so seamlessly that it sometimes wasn't possible to figure out where one started and the other stopped. When Ed Brennan's mother left her husband and sons back in the Midwest, she worked for Sears in Mexico.

While Brennan focused on pulling the retail business out of the hole, Purcell and Telling turned their attention to acquiring new businesses. Purcell looked for companies that might be available at a good price and could balance or complement Sears. Candidates included the all-American farm equipment company, John Deere, which wasn't interested; and the all-American movie company, Disney, but Telling distrusted even Mickey Mouse–style Hollywood; the all-American oil company, Chevron; the all-American communications giant, AT&T, and the great American technology company, IBM. (Chevron, AT&T, and IBM, coincidentally, were all longtime Morgan Stanley clients.) Purcell called such a combination "a major investment in American greatness."

When those prospects didn't work out, Purcell and Telling focused on financial services, where another Sears strength, consumer trust, would be an asset. Telling's first choice was to acquire the all-American stockbroker, Merrill Lynch, whose founder, Charles Merrill, was a pioneer in making securities available to small investors. Sears already had one financial arm, Allstate, which the company started in 1931. It provided home and automobile insurance to twenty million people. Recently, bankers had been complaining that Sears was competing with them through its proprietary credit card and installment loans, which in some years exceeded even the big banks' lending to individuals.

Telling told his board he was looking to acquire a financial services company and got no objections. In 1980 Purcell was quoted in the *Wall Street Journal* as saying, "There is no reason why someone shouldn't go into a Sears store and buy a shirt and coat, and then maybe some stock." The company had twenty-five million active charge accounts, but while only 9 percent of the card holders had stock brokerage accounts, 76 percent of households with a net worth of $500,000 had Sears charge cards. Purcell and Telling thought they had found an untapped market. Telling was spending about 85 percent of his time planning the Great American Company with Purcell. If Telling had seemed remote before, he now spent so much time behind closed doors that people weren't sure he was even on the premises.

Purcell's team undertook a study of brokerage firms that was so confidential that they had the information sent to their homes. In 1981, after Purcell met with the top strategist at Merrill Lynch, Telling, Purcell, and the Merrill CEO met at Merrill's New York office. The deal never got much further than lunch, and Telling wouldn't consider a hostile takeover because he felt it would undermine the Sears image as a trusted family friend.

A couple of false starts later, Purcell focused his attention on Dean Witter. The firm had been founded by two brothers, Dean and Guy Witter, and their cousin Jean Witter in San Francisco in 1924. Jean Witter's son, CEO William M. Witter, took the firm public in 1972, and it merged with Reynolds Securities in 1978. It was the largest merger of securities companies in U.S. history and created the fifth largest brokerage firm in the United States, with $274.1 million in capital. Dean Witter had a strong Main Street profile, especially in the Midwest and western states, but it was headquartered in New York, and Telling and Purcell went back to Manhattan to have lunch with Dean Witter's CEO and president in another private corporate dining room. Purcell made the pitch. He came equipped with a packet of paperwork but never looked at it, reeling off information about Dean Witter that many at the firm itself didn't know.

The Dean Witter people were impressed with Purcell, but their reaction to a merger was lukewarm. Telling and Purcell were convinced that the Eastern Establishment discounted them because they flew in from the "second city." They retreated to Chicago and put aside the Dean Witter idea. As Donald Katz observed, "The Middle American chips balanced on . . . [their] shoulders . . . [were] keeping them from seeing that big business deals were . . . quite separate from emotions like resentment." In the meantime, a parallel transaction was coming to fruition: Sears bought Coldwell Banker, the huge international real estate broker.

When Dean Witter's chairman heard about the deal, he called Telling, who sent a Sears plane for him. They met on Telling's home turf in Chicago, and agreed that Sears would buy Dean Witter for $50 a share, or $607 million. Purcell and another Sears executive, along with their Goldman Sachs banker, negotiated with the Dean Witter lawyers in New York. Purcell was so disgusted when negotiations turned to big personal compensation packages for Dean Witter's chairman and president that he walked out of the meeting. He later told Telling that the lawyers "treated us like some lower form of life."

When the acquisition was completed, Telling appointed Purcell president of the Dean Witter division and sent him to New York to learn the business. The appointment appears to have been based on the assumption that a talented management consultant can learn anything quickly, that Purcell deserved the job because acquiring the brokerage was his idea, and that loyalty should be rewarded. If Purcell had still been at McKinsey, advising Sears about whom to put in as president of Dean Witter, it is unlikely that he would have recommended that they choose someone who didn't have experience in the field or contacts in the financial services world, and who would only be living in New York during the workweek.

Telling acted as though anyone with brains and discipline could run a brokerage firm, a reflection of his bitter scorn toward bankers. His father had been squeezed out of a small family bank, and it had broken him financially. Telling rarely missed a chance to express his scorn for bankers, and on the few occasions when he had to meet them he was curt. He was the man who answered a retail analyst at a conference who asked him to explain "how capital is allocated now in the corporation," with a brisk and final "No." Significantly, Telling encouraged Phil Purcell's predisposition to distrust New York, Wall Street, and bankers.

In 1983, two years after Sears acquired Dean Witter, and a year after Telling sent Purcell to Wall Street to learn how to run a brokerage house, Telling and his successor Edward Brennan reluctantly attended a conference at Morgan Stanley's headquarters in New York. The host, Morgan Stanley's retail analyst Walter Loeb, had recently written of Sears that "The Battleship Has Turned," and Telling agreed to make one of his rare appearances. Sears had signed supermodel Cheryl Tiegs to a multi-million-dollar contract for her own line of clothing; at the time, it was the biggest contract any model had ever been awarded. Anson Beard was the Head of Equities, and one of his brothers, the photographer Peter Beard, had recently married Tiegs. Anson Beard asked her to come to the meeting, and he held a contest: whoever did the biggest trade could get the buyer and seller on the phone with Tiegs. Before the meeting she put on a Morgan Stanley hat and went to the trading floor, with Peter Beard crouching and hopping, taking pictures. Anson Beard remembers that the size of the crowd "was only to be exceeded the day we went public, and again, during the crash of October 19, 1987."

When Telling finished his talk, delivered in a style Donald Katz describes as "disdain," he and his group left. As they descended in the Morgan Stanley elevator, the firm's employees got on at various floors, and the enormously tall Telling, who was standing in the back with his jacket slung over his shoulder, called out in "a booming rural voice . . .'Say there, fellas, jus' what is it this here Morgan and Stanley outfit makes, anyhow?'"

The bankers, who had been in elevators with lunatics before, continued to look at the doors silently as Telling rolled along. "Morgan an' Stanley . . . Morgan an' Stanley . . . Nah, I do bu-leeve that is a tool company . . . bench and power tools."

Addressing Brennan, who was laughing, he remarked, as though suddenly remembering where he'd heard the name, "Seems to me, if 'n ah'm not mistaken, they make a passable 'xample of a claw hammer, too!"

Telling, who was said to love Purcell like a son, was his first and lasting example of how a chief executive officer should act. He had a closed-door management style, and he remained aloof from his employees; he disliked and resented an entire section of the country and a class of business people; and he got away with avoiding the press. Some might have asked why that model would make Purcell a good leader for an investment bank in New York. The degree of separation from Sears that Dean Witter gave Purcell helped obscure the reality that he was trained on the executive floor of a mass-market retail company that was in a dysfunctional phase, and that he learned his management style from a chairman and CEO who lacked nearly every outward manifestation of leadership, at a time when a deep-seated corporate culture was at risk.

Purcell was thirty-eight years old when he went to New York to enter the brokerage business, as the president of a company with more than four thousand employees. He and Anne had settled in the Chicago suburb of Wilmette, and they already had six sons. They decided that the family was too big and the children too young for them to move without causing a major disruption. Purcell rationalized that he would have to travel so much it wouldn't matter where he was during the week, and the Dean Witter assignment might last only a couple of years. He might return to Chicago—he was still on the Sears corporate strategic planning committee, and he was still Telling's favorite.

Anne wasn't willing to relocate, and she wasn't sure he should take the job if he was going to be a weekend father and husband. They agreed that she and the boys would stay in Wilmette, while Purcell got an apartment in New York and flew back to Chicago on weekends—on commercial flights. That was the beginning of a pattern that would last even when nearly all their sons were grown and out of the house: Anne went to mass every morning, took care of the house and the children, and saw her husband Thursday through Sunday nights. The wives of other CEOs attended corporate functions and met their husband's colleagues, if only to show their appreciation to the people who made it possible for them to lead the lives of the superrich, but in the early days, Anne had the boys. Later, when she had the freedom to travel and a corporate jet to fly her from Chicago to New York, she had come to feel that it wasn't necessary for her to participate in her husband's business life, or know the people he worked with. When Purcell worked at Morgan Stanley, her absence was the cause of puzzlement and resentment. In the nearly eight years Purcell headed the firm, no one could remember ever meeting her or seeing her at a firm function.

When Purcell told the *Wall Street Journal* it was perfectly logical that someone would buy coats and shirts and stocks in the same store, he meant it. The Sears, Allstate, Coldwell Banker, Dean Witter combination was based on the concept that Sears customers would want to organize their lives under one roof. They could buy a house from Coldwell Banker, insurance from Allstate, a line of credit and investments from Dean Witter, and appliances from Sears.

In a move that was memorably labeled "socks and stocks," Purcell opened financial network centers in 308 Sears stores. Telling, elated at what he and his chief strategist had put together in only a couple of years, said the future looked promising: "128 million people—three out of four American adults—will visit our stores this year." Telling had been named one of the ten worst executives in the 1978 *Gallagher President's Report*. In 1981, he leapt to the top as one of the ten best managers of the year.

It was one thing to understand a business from a theoretical point of view. But it was another to be attuned to the nuances, the way people are who have worked in an industry all their lives. Purcell, who had run a small think tank at Sears, was now responsible for thousands of employees in offices all over the United States. At Dean Witter, he acquired a different kind of mentor, the personable Robert "Stretch" Gardiner, who had headed Reynolds Securities and became chairman and CEO of the Dean Witter Financial Services Group soon after Purcell arrived. Gardiner, who was distinguished by his height—he was six feet seven inches tall—and his shock of thick white hair, was patrician but approachable. He was a retailer and a superb salesman, areas in which the results were quantifiable, and Purcell liked him, despite his Princeton education and his Eastern Establishment lifestyle.

Purcell was sympathetic to the stockbrokers, who were generally from more middle-of-the-road backgrounds and who worked on commission, which tied their earnings to performance. He was less enthusiastic about the Dean Witter investment bankers; he thought they were elitist, and he questioned—and resented—the huge sums they earned. Being catapulted in as president without experience in financial services set him apart from both groups. Dean Witter was still unsettled after the merger with Reynolds Securities, and Purcell and Stretch Gardiner decided to focus on the retail business and set their sights on competing with Merrill Lynch, always the retail brokerage to beat. Until Sears acquired Dean Witter, it had a relatively robust investment banking business, ranking tenth as an underwriter of corporate debt and equity, but as Purcell emphasized individual investors and the retail business, some of the most productive bankers left. Investment banking shrank until it represented only 10 percent of the business.

Purcell had entered finance in a bull market. Dean Witter was expanding, hiring brokers, opening offices, and creating in-house financial products that were accessible to investors with more modest resources. As the brokerage booths settled into the stores, they attracted first-time investors: 60 percent of the new customers had never had a brokerage account. They might have benefited from expert advice, but most of the Sears booths were manned by brokers who were working on commission and needed to make sales, and many of them didn't know a lot about investments. Inexperienced brokers were cheaper—and Purcell was determined to keep costs down.

He was still learning the securities business when Telling gave him another mission. He wanted Purcell to find a banking entity to buy. Purcell was now doing two jobs: he was the president of Dean Witter and he was traveling all over the country, scouting bank candidates. The arrangement was impossible, and when Purcell failed to produce a bank, Telling turned the major responsibility over to another top Sears executive.

There was a lot of jockeying for power at Sears in those days; everyone was watching his back, and Telling's mysterious near-invisibility made people wonder who was in charge—and when Telling was planning to step aside. When he reached retirement age, a couple of articles mentioned that Purcell might be on a short list of possible successors, but Telling engineered an extension of his term. That gave the contenders for his job more time to play office politics.

In 1986 Stretch Gardiner retired from Dean Witter, and after only four years in the securities industry, Purcell was appointed chairman and CEO of the Sears Dean Witter Financial Services Group. The *Chicago Tribune* wrote that the quick trip up the ladder hadn't been easy: "Dean Witter's image had taken a beating on Wall Street following its acquisition by Sears in 1981, and Purcell has been the target of much of the criticism surrounding the firm's overall strategy." The article also noted that "his somewhat aloof management style, and the fact that he was from outside the securities industry," contributed to the tension. Purcell, already media shy, "declined to be interviewed" on his promotion. *BusinessWeek* later recalled that, for Purcell, "being the new kid on Wall Street was a brutal experience . . . and Purcell was ridiculed for his contrarian strategies." In 2001, the *Economist* interviewed a colleague from the Dean Witter days who recalled that Purcell's leadership style was " 'autocratic and bureaucratic.' "

"Socks and stocks" had gotten off to a good start, but the two businesses didn't fit, the brokerage booths weren't doing enough business to justify keeping them, and Purcell closed most of the locations in the stores. By then Sears's visibility in financial services had awakened resistance from regional financial institutions. Local banks and their trade associations mounted a heavy lobbying effort in Washington against the invasion of major banks in their territory. Sears, which was not licensed as a bank or a brokerage, was included as an unwelcome interloper. Congressman Tim Wirth of Colorado had proposed legislation that could force Sears out of financial services, and Paul Volker, chairman of the Federal Reserve Board, testified in a congressional hearing, "We don't want Sears Roebuck in the banking business." There was a danger that Sears might be forced to spin off its financial services businesses.

Telling and Purcell were called to Washington to testify before the Senate Banking Committee. As head of Sears Dean Witter Financial Services, Purcell was threatened by the sudden gathering of forces determined to undo his good work. He thought that Sears *should* be in the financial services business; he and Telling were still talking about giving American investors a square deal, although employing inexperienced brokers was arguably not the best way to do it.

When the Federal Home Loan Bank Board passed a ruling that could force Sears to divest itself of Dean Witter and limit Sears's ability to perform other financial services, Purcell broke his own rule and held a press conference to announce that Sears would sue the Federal Home Loan Bank Board. The move to push Sears out of financial services failed, but Dean Witter's business suffered in anticipation of possible restrictions. Business was bad all over Wall Street, and 1984 wasn't a good year to be hobbled. At the end of the second quarter Dean Witter was $23 million in the red.

The lobbying effort was run out of "Sears House" in Washington, where Christine Edwards was a young lawyer on the case. Edwards, who came from a military family, had received her law degree by attending night school at the University of Maryland in Baltimore while she worked as a clerk at Sears, receiving her J.D. in 1983. Though she was only a few years out of law school, Purcell liked the fact that she had put herself through school; that differentiated her in his mind from the Washington crowd, which he lumped together with bankers and New Yorkers as being self-important, privileged, and disconnected from "real" Americans. Edwards, who was thin, fit, with a wholesome, open face, a fresh smile and winged eyebrows, and wore her dark hair straight and shiny, was bright and eager. It was a great assignment to work with the chairman of Sears and the president of Dean Witter, and she plunged into the job with enthusiasm and thoroughness. After that, Purcell could count her as one of his loyalists.

Dean Witter remained part of Sears, but the close call taught Purcell that it was important to have a lawyer on his side who could maneuver successfully in Washington.

In 1986, Purcell became chairman of Dean Witter and introduced Discover, a midlevel credit card. The market was largely controlled by banks with VISA and MasterCard franchises, and it was a bold move, but Sears had an advantage: its sixty-million-household mailing list. Discover was an innovative product. Members could use the card to set up savings accounts, accumulate balances using a system in which they would get cash back, based on their purchases, and establish Individual Retirement Accounts at Dean Witter without a setup fee. Cash machines were relatively new, and the Discover card could be used to access instant cash. Sears invested more than $1 billion in the launch. By the fourth quarter of 1987, Discover was showing a profit of $6.7 million. Whatever else happened later in his business life, Discover would be Phil Purcell's most incontrovertible accomplishment.

Dean Witter's business took off in the early 1990s, largely because the firm was selling its own mutual funds, which provided a steady income stream. The practice set a successful model of selling in-house funds to clients. The brokers were a captive in-house sales force for the firm's mutual funds—a practice that would later be frowned on by regulators, who were particularly concerned about incentives firms offered brokers for selling their own funds.

Ed Brennan was now chairman of Sears. He tried a series of strategies to revive the retail business, but between 1984 and 1990, it was dragging overall corporate performance down to a crawl: Sears's total annual return was 0.7 percent. For a decade Sears had predicted that return on equity would be a solid 15 percent, and the company had not delivered once. In 1992, Dean Witter and Discover brought in $3.7 billion in revenues, with net income of $400 million, but Sears had $38 billion in debt and faced a $4 billion loss. In a survey of business leaders, *Fortune* magazine ranked Sears management at 487 out of 500. The same year a *Fortune* cover story focused on three "dinosaurs": General Motors, IBM, and Sears. Standard and Poors reduced its credit rating, and institutional investors publicly suggested it was time for a management change. *BusinessWeek* suggested that Purcell might be in line to replace Brennan.

As Brennan came under siege, he and Purcell drew closer. An executive who was at Sears at the time described their attitude as "we run this club; don't challenge us." Purcell supported Brennan, who became his sponsor, which put Purcell more firmly on the suspects' list for the chairmanship. Like many of the colleagues Purcell trusted throughout his career, Brennan was an Irish Catholic, a golfer, socially and politically conservative, and a man's man.

In 1991, corporate governance crusader Robert A. G. Monks mounted the first proxy fight to gain a seat on a corporate board, and he chose Sears as his target. At the time of the challenge, Brennan was CEO, head of the retail division, chairman of the board, and head of the nominating committee. As Monks wrote, "He gets to pick his own bosses ... The directors are selected by the CEO ... [who] determines the directors' pay, and the directors set the CEO's pay." Both directors' and CEO's compensation, Monks commented, "have skyrocketed ... at many times the rate of increase in pay for employees." Monks placed an ad in the *Wall Street Journal* titled "Unproductive Assets" and illustrated it with photographs of the Sears directors. Sears hired takeover defense lawyer Martin Lipton of Wachtell Lipton to advise the board, sued Monks, and dropped three board seats to make it impossible for him to win a directorship.

Monks lost, but Brennan was removed from the nominating committee, and in 1992 Sears hired Arthur Martinez, the personable and talented vice chairman of Saks Fifth Avenue, to come in as CEO of the Sears Merchandise Group. When Martinez didn't accept the job at first, Brennan asked Sears director Donald Rumsfeld to call him. Rumsfeld, Martinez says, "created a patriotic argument. He told me it was my job to help save this American institution. He said, 'You owe it to the country and to American business.'" Martinez recalls thinking, "The biggest retailer in America is in trouble and I'm being asked to fix it. Pretty heady stuff." Martinez transformed the retail division and served as chairman and CEO of Sears, Roebuck and Company from 1995 to 2000.

With retail in a more hopeful situation, the Sears board held a special meeting to discuss spinning off financial services and taking Dean Witter public. Purcell was visibly excited at the prospect of becoming CEO of a public company. He had a habit of laughing nervously, and it was particularly noticeable that day. A Sears executive reflected, "He had his McKinsey pedigree, a nice ticket to have punched along the way, but he was sort of geeky and lacking in stature to be running a business."

The Dean Witter Discover spinoff was uncharacteristically aggressive for the usually passive Sears board. In *The Big Store* Donald Katz refers to a senior Sears executive who "believed that the board of directors under Telling had become one of the least animated decision-making bodies imaginable . . . reports to the board were all checked over by [chief financial officer] Dick Jones, and scripts were so rigidly followed that no deviation from approved texts was tolerated." The executive continued, "The outsiders on the Sears board were by and large people who owned a few shares of Sears stock and who collected $40,000 a year for attending occasional meetings. What they knew of the company came largely from the company." Brennan's attitude about his board was based on Telling's example of choosing a board he thought wouldn't challenge him. Purcell would take the same approach when he had the chance. If anyone at Morgan Stanley who was involved in the future merger had read *The Big Store*, they might have thought twice about making a match with Phil Purcell.

Purcell brought three important lessons with him to Morgan Stanley: a pair of strategists working behind closed doors could change the face of a company; disagreement should be quelled by circling the wagons; and a pliable board would accept scripted reports from top executives, and would believe what the chairman and CEO told them.

Four

THE DEAL

1993–1997

The beginning of the relationship that culminated in the mutiny of 2005 was set in motion twelve years earlier, when Phil Purcell and Morgan Stanley worked together on the Dean Witter Discover public offering. It was then that these two very different institutions began to rub up against each other, without recognizing how very dissimilar they really were.

Morgan Stanley's Chicago office pitched the business to Sears to do the Dean Witter public offering. Morgan Stanley didn't handle every IPO that came its way, and Purcell brought Stretch Gardiner along as a kind of unofficial sponsor—Morgan Stanley people respected Gardiner, who had been the head of Reynolds Securities, which was a tonier firm than Dean Witter. The Morgan Stanley bankers who worked on the deal recall that they thought Purcell was smart, and they liked his low-key style. "Dick [Fisher] thought the world of Phil," John Mack says—so much so that Mack and Fisher told Purcell, "We're doing this IPO for you. Would you like to do a merger?" They weren't the only ones who suggested the idea; at one of the management committee meetings another executive said, "These guys are good. Why don't we buy them ourselves?" William J. Kneisel was the Head of Equity Capital Markets, the department that was responsible for the pricing of the IPO. "That was when Morgan Stanley really, for the first time, glimpsed inside Dean Witter and saw what an extremely well run operation it was," Kneisel says. "Phil had turned Dean Witter into a profitable business. When he had to get in front of audiences at our road show, he was extremely effective." Purcell seemed as though he would fit in at Morgan Stanley, and Dean Witter would bring in assets under management. But as Mack recalls, when he and Fisher brought up the subject of a merger, "Phil said no. He told me, we've been part of Sears. Now we want to be independent."

In 1993, Dean Witter was the lead underwriter of the $796.5 million IPO for Dean Witter Discover and Morgan Stanley acted as a co-manager and pricing agent. When the deal was completed, Brad Hintz, who was the treasurer of Morgan Stanley, says that Morgan Stanley management asked some of the top people at the firm "to go and speak to our respective counterparties at Dean Witter and teach them how the business worked as a public company. Fisher told us to help them out. Explain, you're a public company now, you have ratings, you're going to be running your own balance sheet, investor relations, you're dealing with your competitors—how do you deal with the fact that equity analysts [who work for competing firms] are to some extent like KGB agents?"

Hintz recalls that the Dean Witter people "weren't Morgan Stanley, but they weren't terrible. The issue was that the corporate culture was one of centralized control. All decisions were made at the top." But, as Bill Kneisel remarks, "Wall Street is nothing if it is not about tribes and tribal behavior, people who work well together. Running a nationwide wire house is different from running Morgan Stanley, a different set of people. They might all be fine in their own way, but they are not compatible." In that early encounter there were indications that the firms had different management styles, but that wasn't particularly relevant; Morgan Stanley had done well for its client and would move on.

Morgan Stanley was on what the *Wall Street Journal* called "an expansion spree"; the firm had opened eight international offices, part of an aggressive globalization program, which started in the Frank Petito era. It was well under way when Parker Gilbert retired, and Dick Fisher had accelerated the move to become more international. In 1994, Fisher and Mack entered into merger talks with the British investment bank S. G. Warburg, a potential combination that the *Wall Street Journal* called a "marriage of blue bloods." Morgan Stanley was the third-largest U.S. investment bank, and Warburg would bring in $2.3 billion in capital. Their parity in prestige in their own worlds was seen as a significant advantage.

S. G. Warburg and Morgan Stanley were established at almost the same time, but their initial businesses were radically different. S. G. Warburg's founder, Siegmund Warburg, was a member of an ancient German banking dynasty, M. M. Warburg, which began as money-lenders in Westphalia in the 1500s. In the twentieth century, Warburg was based in Hamburg, but Siegmund studied and worked in London and New York, and in 1934, as the Nazi Party passed laws squeezing Jews out of certain professions, he emigrated from Germany to England. Over the next two years, as German Jews lost their citizenship, were barred from marrying non-Jews, banned from professional jobs, and subjected to violence and killing, some of those who could get out fled to England. There, Warburg established a mutual aid society, the New Trading Company, which provided financing and other services to help German and Austrian refugees start over. It remained "a small, sheltered Jewish enclave, bound together by a philosophy of reciprocal support and an atmosphere of friendly, even familial, camaraderie: the members were known as the 'uncles,' and the company's internal language was German," according to one account.

After the war, the New Trading Company was renamed S. G. Warburg and engaged in merchant banking. Warburg was known to be entrepreneurial and daring; the firm mounted London's first hostile corporate takeover in 1958, and launched the Eurobond market in 1963 with a loan to an Italian company. Warburg, who was by then Sir Siegmund, died in 1982, leaving Sir David Scholey as head of the bank. Four years later, the British deregulated banking, allowing merchant banks to enter the brokerage and sales and trading businesses.

In 1994, S. G. Warburg was considered England's leading securities company; it had thirty offices in twenty-three countries, and represented fifty of the top one hundred firms in England. The London *Independent* described Warburg as "a standard bearer for the City and a model of sound, inspirational management and success." The firm was a dominant force in mergers and acquisitions, equity financing and underwriting and fixed income, but one of the bank's principal attractions for Morgan Stanley was Mercury Asset Management, in which Warburg held a 75 percent stake. Mercury had a thriving international investment management business, and Morgan Stanley wanted to build strength in that area.

Sir David Scholey, who was a friend of Bob Greenhill's and knew

Morgan Stanley, opened merger talks with Dick Fisher, which Mack and Warburg's president, Lord Cairns, continued. In September 1994, Mack and Lord Cairns met over lunch at Lord Cairns's house in England and left with the hope that they could form what an observer called "the first truly global investment bank." The combined firm would be number one worldwide in mergers and acquisitions, number one in issuing equities, number three in the Far East, and number four worldwide in issuing debt. Morgan Stanley would gain access to the blue chip European markets, while Warburg would expand its reach in the United States, Latin America, and Japan. On one of the rare occasions when Morgan Stanley was *not* described as elitist, *BusinessWeek* commented, "It's hard to find two banks more culturally different. Cairns inherited his title and wealth; went to Eton, Britain's most exclusive boys' school; and is a vegetarian. Mack, a Duke University grad who was born in a small North Carolina town, is a decisive, meat-eating former bond trader nicknamed 'Mack the Knife.' Warburg," the magazine observed, "is old-fashioned, slightly stuffy, and paternalistic, while Morgan is bold and opportunistic."

The deal began to flag when Mercury Asset Management wanted Morgan Stanley to buy the 25 percent of its stock that Warburg didn't already hold, at a price Fisher thought was too high. There was another problem: Morgan would have to cut way back on its London staff, and Warburg would have to do the same in New York. No one wanted to fire competent people or let talented people go, who would probably end up working for the competition. Then, during the negotiations, Warburg's business turned sour, and in October the firm issued a warning that third-quarter profits would be halved from the same period in 1993. That added to the question some of the financial world was asking: was Warburg negotiating a merger with Morgan Stanley because Warburg was weak, or for the stated reason that the combined firms would be the largest investment bank in the world?

At the end of 1994, Dick Fisher and John Mack sat down to price the deal with a Warburg representative, who told Fisher that his number, which was more than Morgan Stanley was prepared to pay, was nonnegotiable. According to Mack, Fisher said, "Okay," and after a few polite remarks, walked away from the table. When Mack asked him, "Why did you do that?" Fisher said, "He said it was nonnegotiable."

On a December Sunday Mack and Lord Cairns met in Manhattan, and were reported to be "glum." The deal fell through.

It was a missed opportunity for Morgan Stanley, but it was fatal for Warburg. The failure of the deal led to Lord Cairns's resignation as CEO; and Sir David Scholey, who had been about to retire as chairman, took over. The following May, Warburg announced that the Swiss Bank Corporation (SBC), Switzerland's third-largest bank, would buy Warburg—without Mercury Asset Management—for £870 million. SBC would later become Union Bank of Switzerland (UBS), and S. G. Warburg's name would virtually disappear into the maw of a large international bank.

The year Morgan Stanley was negotiating with Warburg, there was a severe market downturn, and according to Mack, the firm was "behind because of lack of head count growth, and resources." Competitors were laying people off, but Mack says Morgan Stanley looked ahead and "we hired right through the cycle." By the fourth quarter, the firm's head count was up 16 percent. Mack recalls, "The *Wall Street Journal* said, these guys are not being realistic. We asked ourselves, are we making a mistake?" They went to the outside board, which at the time, included Dick Cheney, and asked the directors what they thought. As Mack recalls, the directors said, "If you believe globalization, deregulation, and technology" are imminent, "stay the course." Then, Mack says, with a little smile, "the market turns in late December '94, and in '95 Morgan Stanley comes out of the box. We became the firm to be at."

As part of the decision to move forward despite market conditions, the firm elected to invest in a research initiative, and asked Mayree C. Clark, who had been working for Fisher and Mack, to lead the new efforts. She and the other managing directors in research launched their revitalization with a policy statement in December 1994, to clarify the role of research, and to emphasize the Morgan Stanley ethos and how it was applied. The four-page paper was simply titled "Equity Research at Morgan Stanley: What's Important."

In a disarmingly frank opening paragraph, the authors wrote, "This piece has been put together because it has seemed that many of us in research could no longer put our finger on the important goals our group is trying to achieve." Calling on all the managing directors and group leaders in the research department, and "fully vetting" the results with senior management and the Equity and Investment Banking Divisions, the paper describes the role of research. Toward the end, in a section titled "Measuring Success," the authors state, "Very few (perhaps none) of us are in this business for money alone. Curiosity, intellectual challenge, the thrill of correctly anticipating the future, influencing the shape of an industry: all of these are part of the attraction."

The bottom line, they wrote, is that "investor impact comes first. If we are not influential with investors, we cannot be commercially successful. It is not acceptable to become so focused on generating revenue in the near term that one loses his or her primary franchise with investors."

With the market and the firm moving ahead, in 1995 the management committee created "Project Edison" to study the business's strengths and weaknesses. Brad Hintz explains, "At Morgan Stanley in those days, they'd never bring in a McKinsey. They'd take a group of smart young managing directors and throw them on a project, tell them to take time off and come back with some answers. It was a consensus-run company." Project Edison concluded that Morgan Stanley should get into the mutual fund business because it was "sticky"—shorthand meaning that if investors bought a Fidelity mutual fund and didn't like the way it was performing, they were likely to buy another Fidelity fund, and the money would stay inside the firm. They also looked at high net worth retail brokerage and considered how to expand into that business. The report concluded that "significant mutual fund penetration will require that we partner with an existing company which has a track record and a distribution channel already in place. Discussions with several partners are currently under way, however pricing remains an issue."

The study confirmed what Fisher and Mack believed was the next step—to capture assets by acquiring a firm with a retail clientele. Glass-Steagall was being eroded, and bankers were already selling public issues and proprietary funds, and making bridge loans to gain underwriting business. Soon they might use their branch networks to sell securities. The great bull market of the late 1990s was beginning, and Morgan Stanley wanted to compete with Merrill Lynch and other full-service firms. As one outside analyst said, "You've got to have that distribution, distribution, distribution." James M. Allwin, who was head of

Morgan Stanley Realty, joined Barton Biggs and became COO of Morgan Stanley Asset Management. Allwin, whom a colleague describes fondly as "a tall drink of water," was one of the younger managing directors who was seen as an eventual candidate for one of the top jobs. He was calm, astute about people, and naturally empathetic, "able to deal with complexity in a gray universe," his colleague says.

Morgan Stanley made a number of passes at acquiring a money manager, but the candidates were too expensive, and many of the firms they approached didn't want to be subsumed by a big Wall Street bank. In 1996 Morgan Stanley paid $1.18 billion to acquire the Chicago-based Van Kampen American Capital, Inc., the fourth-largest mutual fund company in the United States. With $57 billion under management and two million investors, Van Kampen gave "Morgan Stanley . . . a useful consumer for many of its financial products, and an entree into the retail business." Barton Biggs, as chairman of Asset Management, commented, "Individual investors control a growing percentage of the world's capital." Americans had rediscovered that they didn't have to start out rich to make money on the stock market, and mutual funds looked like a relatively safe investment. But as the *Wall Street Journal* asked when the Van Kampen deal was closed, "What do you get when you cross a blue-blood investment bank with a run-of-the-mill mutual-fund company?" The writer added, "Does [Morgan Stanley] want its name invoked by armies of brokers interrupting dinner to pitch mutual funds?" Evidently, it did.

Downtown at Dean Witter's World Trade Center offices, Phil Purcell was also weighing the potential of growing through a merger or an acquisition, and he had set up an ongoing strategy committee to evaluate potential deals. Morgan Stanley, whose two top executives had already expressed interest in getting together with Dean Witter, was one of the possible partners. Purcell and Mack talked informally about creating a connection between their firms that would expand the scope of each, without sacrificing autonomy or culture. They both believed that in ten to twenty years, the business would be dominated by the firm with the best-integrated vertical model—from manufacturing financial products to distribution. A diversified firm might also be more resistant to swings in the market, and less vulnerable to downturns. As a retail broker, Dean Witter wasn't even nipping at the heels of Merrill Lynch in the two key measures used in the industry: assets under management per broker, and revenue per broker. With Morgan Stanley, they might have a chance.

One reason Morgan Stanley and Dean Witter looked as though they could complement each other was that Purcell had minimized the Dean Witter businesses that would have been competitive or redundant with Morgan Stanley. Before Purcell came in, as one analyst says, "Dean Witter was a highly respected broad-range player, but Phil dismantled all the risk, the potentially profitable, risk-taking aspects of the business, and left the firm with a mediocre retail division." In theory, Dean Witter's retail brokerage could be brought up to Morgan Stanley standards by getting rid of the underperforming brokers and hiring and training better ones. Dean Witter's Asset Management wasn't up to Morgan Stanley standards either, but it had substantial assets under management.

"We wanted to have more of a recurring revenue stream," Mack explains. "Thirty percent of Dean Witter's fixed costs were paid for by fees. The idea of the merger wasn't to distribute our IPOs, but to capture assets. Dick and I wanted to do this deal."

One of the people on the management committee at the time recalls, "John was the promoter and the architect behind the merger. It wouldn't have happened without him, although Dick agreed to it and was supportive of it. Most of the calls came from Mack. He had a code name, 'Mr. Lee.' Calls were coming in from Mr. Lee." One of Purcell's colleagues says, "Phil really liked John. To this day, he'll say he's the best salesman he's ever seen. He was friendly, he didn't push, and he was flexible, but he would say, 'Here's what you could do. I think this makes sense for you.'"

Purcell and Mack had common touchstones that may have made them think they were more alike than they turned out to be. Mack was one of six brothers; Purcell had seven sons. They were both Roman Catholics who grew up in societies dominated by another strong religion, Mack with the Baptists in Mooresville and Purcell as a half-Mormon in Salt Lake City. They weren't Ivy League graduates, but they were proud of their universities and served on their boards. In the 1990s they also had ski houses near each other in Utah. And Mack and

Purcell were both close friends of sports coaches who had effective team leadership skills. Mack was close to the Duke basketball coach Mike Krzyzewski (pronounced Sha-shef-ski), known as "Coach K," who was the subject of books with such titles as *How to Be Like Mike*, and *Leading with the Heart*. Coach K was famous for such sayings as, "A basketball team is like the five fingers on your hand. If you can get them all together, you have a fist."

Purcell's examplar was Jim Yerkovich, his classmate and basketball teammate at Judge Memorial High School. Yerkovich returned to Judge Memorial to coach and teach math after college, and he had developed the "WE" model. WE isn't an acronym; it's the synonym for "us." Instead of focusing on the "scoreboard world," which Yerkovich writes arose along with the "bottom line" business mentality, he pointed out that the best college basketball teams were rarely the ones with the highest individual scorers, but those "that fit together and have chemistry."

When Purcell felt the Dean Witter team needed to pull together better, he gave his vice presidents sweaters that read "WE," and when the coach wrote a book about the WE idea, Purcell wrote a blurb that read, "Coach Yerk understands, communicates, and teaches the life values that, if we are lucky, we learn from sports (or academics or home): The journey is more important than the destination; others are more important than ourselves; and, if we are successful, others make it happen." It is signed "Phil Purcell, Former High School Teammate of Jim Yerkovich, Chairman and Chief Executive Officer of Morgan Stanley, New York, NY."

Mack and Purcell seemed to be playing the same game by the same rules, and they appeared to "fit together and have chemistry," which, as Coach Yerk said, was a requirement for a good team.

Those were good days for John Mack. With most of the old guard gone, he was bringing along a younger group. There was a kind of largesse about him that showed in small gestures that turned into legends. People liked to tell the story of "John Mack and the pizza delivery man" (sometimes it was "the Chinese food delivery man"). Whichever kind of food was in the bag, or the box, the point was the same: John had heart.

The gist of the story, as usually recounted, is that Mack noticed that a man with a food delivery had been sitting in a Morgan Stanley reception area for half an hour. He asked who he was waiting for, then went back to the man's office, chewed him out for inconsideration, and told him never to keep someone who depends on tips waiting.

According to Mack, what actually happened was that, at some time in the 1990s, "at 8:00 in the morning, I'm walking down the hallway. I see a delivery boy waiting outside with a breakfast delivery. I come back 30 minutes later; he's still there. I asked him, 'Are you still waiting for the same pickup?' He said, 'Yes.' I said, 'Well, give me the phone number. Let me talk to the trader.' I got the trader out there, and I said, 'Look, this guy's trying to make a living like you. You can't keep him waiting 30 minutes. Never let it happen again.'" When someone wanted to explain that, though John Mack might be tough, he was also compassionate, that was one of the stories that was told.

Mack had now joined the generations of Morgan leaders who followed the charitable and civic examples set by J. P. Morgan and Jack Morgan. Generations after the mighty Steel Trust that J. P. Morgan had founded was rusting, and the railroads he saved at the turn of the last century had to be subsidized by the federal government, the philanthropic aspects of the Morgan legacy were flourishing. Parker Gilbert served as vice president of the Metropolitan Museum of Art, of which J. P. Morgan was the first president; and was president of the J. Pierpont Morgan Library. Lewis Bernard was chairman of the American Museum of Natural History, which J. P. Morgan and Theodore Roosevelt's father cofounded. New York Lying-In Hospital, which benefited from J. P. Morgan's $1 million legacy, had been folded into the merged hospital that became New York–Presbyterian Hospital. Mack was on the board of New York–Presbyterian and was elected chairman in 2001. His special project was to establish the Morgan Stanley Children's Hospital at New York–Presbyterian; he raised $65 million from the people of Morgan Stanley for the facility, which was soon ranked among the top five children's hospitals in the country.

At Dean Witter, performance continued to be strong, largely thanks to its proprietary mutual funds, and although Discover didn't match Morgan Stanley in terms of image, the division made money on a steady basis, which could reduce the volatility of overall earnings. In the tech euphoria of the 1980s and 1990s, it seemed possible that Discover could be the base for providing other financial services to its retail customers. Arguably, owning Discover could be like taking an option on forty million cardholders. Mack and Fisher were talking to Purcell behind the scenes, and in late 1995, Morgan Stanley's five-man inside board held a secret meeting in a suite in one of Manhattan's luxury hotels to hear a presentation about the economics of a merger with Dean Witter. One of the division heads who was there recalls, "John was the initiator. He is an emotional, intuitive man and a passionate one. He would say over and over again, 'Phil Purcell is my friend and I trust him. I believe him.'"

In December 1996, the talks became more serious, and the merger took on code names. Morgan Stanley called it Project Ranger after the New York hockey team, with Morgan Stanley as "Messier" for the Rangers' captain and Dean Witter as "Gretzky"—Dick Fisher was such a fanatical Rangers fan that for a while the code on the Fishers' home alarm system was "Rangers." Dean Witter picked "Dr Pepper" as its name and "7-Up" for Morgan Stanley. Perhaps "Coke" didn't sound quite right in the light of Wall Street's drug scandals of the 1980s.

For all the high hopes for a merger, Purcell's old firm, McKinsey and Company, estimated that "only 12 percent of merged corporations grow revenues at above the rate of other companies in the same industry, while up to 40 percent fail to achieve promised cost savings. In other words, they mostly might as well not have bothered." It was characteristic of Fisher, Mack, and Purcell to be confident that the enterprise they were embarking on would beat those numbers.

In preparation for a major move, Fisher announced on January 16 that Mack would be his successor and promoted some of the firm's top talent. Peter Karches moved from Head of Fixed Income to become Head of Institutional Securities, with Stephan Newhouse as his number two. Joe Perella, who was corporate finance chief, replaced Bob Scott as Head of Investment Banking, and Scott became CFO. James Allwin became president of Morgan Stanley Asset Management. The *Wall Street Journal* speculated that Karches and Allwin were both in line for the presidency when Mack became chairman. Vikram Pandit, Head of Equity Derivatives, moved up to Head of Equities, and Kenneth DeRegt, who worked for Karches, became Head of Fixed Income. Terry Meguid took over Perella's job as corporate finance chief. With an Institutional Securities team of that caliber in place, Fisher and Mack believed that Morgan Stanley had its house in order and was in a strong position to take the next step.

On a Sunday in February 1997, John Mack, Phil Purcell, and Dean Witter's chief financial officer, Thomas C. Schneider, arrived at Dick Fisher's for a meeting that would be nearly as historic as the one that took place at Tom Lamont's Sky Farm in 1935. When a momentous decision required absolute confidentiality, Morgan Stanley partners often met in one of their homes.

The meeting almost didn't take place. Earlier that week, Mack and Fisher were negotiating with Purcell and Schneider at Fisher's apartment. As Mack recalled, "We said, 'We'll do it at this price,' which included a slight premium for merging. They said, 'We'll think about it,' and they left. I said to Dick, 'They should have shaken hands on it right then. It's not going to happen.' I went into the office, met with some members of the management committee, and I said, 'We're not going to do the deal.' "

But Purcell did think about it. He and Mack got together again on Friday night for dinner in a private room at Manhattan's charming little Box Tree restaurant. At the end of the evening, they had agreed on the general terms of "the biggest-ever brokerage merger."

At Dick Fisher's that Sunday, Mack, Purcell, and Schneider stepped out of the elevator into a book-filled vestibule where an old-fashioned coatrack stood next to the open door. Fisher and Jeanne Donovan were getting married in a few months, and they had only bought the apartment recently, but it already felt settled and inviting. The walls were hung with paintings by Willem de Kooning, Milton Avery, Richard Diebenkorn, Wayne Thibault, and Robert Motherwell, which were distinguished by their quality and size: nothing was so big it overwhelmed the people or the rooms. Books were everywhere, even in the guest bathroom. A ledge under the windows looking out on the terrace was filled with photographs of Fisher and his grown children, and of Jeanne, with a sunlit smile. She was tall and trim, with light brown hair, and a face made unforgettable by its openness and warmth. In their bedroom, Fisher's rolltop desk, which had belonged to one of the original Morgan Stanley partners, was covered with more family photographs. Dick and Jeanne had both gotten divorced so they could be together, and their happiness shone throughout the house.

Fisher invited the others to settle around the table in a dining room furnished with an Arts and Crafts table and chairs and brightened by a lyrical watercolor by Arshile Gorky, and a brilliant blue and orange Robert Motherwell collage. Peter Waring, the Fishers' friendly British majordomo, was usually off on Sundays, but he came in specially that day. Fisher loved good food, and if there was ever an occasion that merited celebration by palate this was it, and the Fishers borrowed a friend's chef. Waring passed hors d'oeuvres, which included tuna tartare and quail eggs. The chef had prepared a lemon dessert, which failed on the first try, so he made another. The men drank coffee from the Fishers' special espresso machine, Fisher smoked a cigar, and they talked.

That afternoon, the $10.2 billion merger that would be referred to as "the handshake agreement" was finalized. Earlier, Fisher had advised Mack not to give up the CEO title, but Mack said, "It's not our firm"—meaning that Morgan Stanley belonged to the shareholders and employees, and that he thought the merger was best for the future of the firm. As for the handshake, Dick Fisher told colleagues, "Phil shook my hand." Fisher and Mack believed that Purcell had agreed to turn the jobs of chairman and CEO over to Mack after two or three years. As one of Mack's closest associates says, "Phil made it clear to John and everyone around him that he needed John, that everyone was totally equal, that they were partners, they were going to get paid the same amount, and Phil wasn't going to do this forever."

Another colleague explains, "John was used to doing business like that with Dick. They agreed on things and they happened. In retrospect, John admits it looks naive."

Purcell later claimed that he had agreed in principle that Mack was his logical successor, but they hadn't discussed details, or a date. A person familiar with the talks says, "I don't think there was ever a handshake or an oral agreement that within three years Mack would take over. Purcell and Schneider are very clear on that. But Mack wouldn't have made it up out of whole cloth."

When the meeting was over and Fisher's guests had left, he told Jeanne that all that remained was for the lawyers to refine the details. Fisher would be retiring sooner than he expected, with a historic accomplishment behind him and a new life with Jeanne ahead.

Agreeing to agree was the beginning of the next phase of negotiations, including executive officers, board positions, stock distribution, and governance. One of the attractions of the merger was that it didn't involve much redundancy. Dean Witter and Morgan Stanley were about the same size, but their businesses were different enough that neither would have to fire many people. The major personnel dislocations would take place at the top. Purcell and Mack developed a formula: the first person to choose got to pick one officer; the second got to pick two. Mack went first and selected Philip Duff as Executive Vice President and Chief Financial Officer; Purcell followed, choosing Thomas Schneider as Executive Vice President and Chief Strategic and Administrative Officer and Christine Edwards as Executive Vice President and Chief Legal Officer.

Morgan Stanley's general counsel, Jonathan Clark, had worked at Davis, Polk, and Wardwell, the law firm that had represented Morgan Stanley since it filed its original incorporation papers in 1935. Clark had been handling the firm's affairs for years at Davis Polk. By the time he moved to Morgan Stanley, he was steeped in the firm's philosophy: as many managing directors have said, "Morgan Stanley always felt it helped craft the law and the standards that shaped the law. We tried to follow the spirit of the law." That was a philosophy that would be increasingly out of favor under the new regime.

Christine Edwards, the woman Purcell had first worked with in Washington, had been Chief Legal Counsel at Dean Witter for the past eight years. Edwards's strengths were in retail brokerage, credit cards, and the related domestic regulatory laws governing both, but she lacked experience in institutional securities, mergers and acquisitions, and international transactions. Her appointment surprised Morgan Stanley senior executives, as well as outside lawyers who did business with the firm. She appeared under-qualified to take the lead position, especially considering the disruptions a merger was bound to cause. Many had expected the firm's most senior lawyer to be a Wall Street insider with a depth of experience in Morgan Stanley's legacy businesses.

While some at Morgan Stanley attributed Purcell's choice of Edwards to his close friendship with her, Brad Hintz expresses another perspective: "Phil understood how important it was to control the infrastructure," and he appointed people he could count on to be loyal to him. Jonathan Clark learned that he had been swapped out when his wife, Priscilla, brought him a fax that came in at home, listing the officers of the merged firm. "I think you're out of a job," she said. Clark returned to Davis, Polk.

Edwards was devastated when a major national publication expressed surprise that Clark, a Yale graduate with a degree from the University of Virginia Law School, was passed over for Edwards, who studied law at night at the University of Maryland in Baltimore.

On the Morgan Stanley side, the selection of senior executives seemed more important than controlling the infrastructure or the board. Morgan Stanley's confidence that the board wouldn't be a problem was partly a legacy of the original stock ownership structure. When the firm went public in 1986, the employees owned 81 percent of the shares, and a few senior people controlled about 30 percent of the stock. Voting results were modeled on the U.S. electoral college: even if the split was 51–49, all the votes would be counted as a block rather than on the "one-man-one-vote" principle. In the decade after the IPO, many of the partners had retired, or left and cashed in their stock to free up the capital for other investments, and by the mid-1990s, the balance of stock ownership had shifted. Morgan Stanley hadn't been giving enough stock to employees as part of their compensation, and the percentage of employee owners had dropped so substantially that the management committee appointed a task force to discuss how to increase employee holdings, and, thereby, control. One of the task force members recalls that they formed a plan to give "a boatload more stock" to employees, offer incentives to hold the shares, and vest it over time. Stock ownership encouraged an owner-manager attitude, but the more the big stick was whittled down, the less control the employees would have over the fate of the firm. The task force set a target of 40 percent inside ownership, which had been achieved by 1997. After the merger, Morgan Stanley employees would own 18 percent of the merged company, while Dean Witter employees would own 3.6 percent. A former Dean Witter investment banker commented, "Eighteen percent is a big voting block. Phil is going to have to listen to that insider group more than he probably listens to his own executives." That assumed that Morgan Stanley employees would vote together, rally to assert their influence, or mount a proxy fight. But in sixty years, the senior partners, the chairman, and the board had never been at odds with the employees.

Morgan Stanley and Dean Witter each had the opportunity to appoint half the directors. The perception that Morgan Stanley employees owned the controlling stock contributed to a seemingly nonchalant approach to the composition of the board; the catch was that once the firms were merged, and there was no longer a separate Dean Witter or Morgan Stanley, there would be no structural way to maintain that balance.

For the board of the merged company, Morgan Stanley chose Mack, Fisher, and five other directors who were already members of the Morgan Stanley board: Laura d'Andrea Tyson, who had recently left government as President Bill Clinton's National Economic Advisor and had been the first female chair of the White House Council of Economic Advisors; Robert P. Bauman, the nonexecutive chairman of British Aerospace, and former CEO of SmithKline Beecham; Diana D. Brooks, president and CEO of Sotheby's Holdings; Daniel B. Burke, the former CEO, president, and COO of Capital Cities/ABC; and Allen E. Murray, former chairman and CEO of Mobil joined Fisher and Mack to represent the Morgan Stanley "side." Purcell chose current Dean Witter director and former Sears chairman and CEO Ed Brennan; C. Robert Kidder, chairman and CEO of Borden; Miles L. Marsh, chairman and CEO of Fort James Corporation; Clarence B. Rogers Jr., chairman of the board and former CEO of Equifax Corp, who had become a Dean Witter director in 1996; and Michael A. Miles, former chairman and CEO of Philip Morris and an ex-McKinseyite. Tom Schneider, who became Executive Vice President and Chief Strategic and Administrative Officer, had not previously been a Dean Witter director, but he had been Executive Vice President and CFO.

Both firms would have to drop some directors to comply with the fifty-fifty board split; each of the old firms could only have two insiders, and Mack and Fisher were the two from Morgan Stanley. Purcell refused to name Parker Gilbert, the symbol of the firm's history and continuity, as an outside director. Fisher called Gilbert and told him, regretfully, that he could not be on the new board.

"They view you as an insider," Fisher explained.

"How about Ed Brennan?" Gilbert asked. "Isn't he an insider?" As the former chairman and CEO of Sears when it owned Dean Witter, Brennan had held a position that was comparable to Gilbert's former role at Morgan Stanley.

The decision nagged at Fisher, but Purcell said it was final. "Why would you want to change it now?" he asked.

Purcell had proposed a "supermajority" clause. In a meeting with several senior executives, Mack said, "Phil has one more thing to ask. He wants a 75 percent vote on the board to remove the CEO or the president." While this provision seemingly protected both Purcell and Mack equally, Purcell, as the CEO, could change Mack's responsibilities without board approval and make life so difficult for him that he would quit (as he eventually did) without any vote by the board. Furthermore, over time, Purcell would be able to replace the directors with people closer to him.

Dick Fisher said, "If that's what he wants, I wouldn't do the deal. That means he doesn't trust us."

Another executive at the meeting said, "That applies to me too."

Their objections were overbalanced by the apparent advantages of the deal, and Morgan Stanley agreed to the 75 percent rule.

Ironically, Purcell's mergers and acquisitions advisor was Bruce Wasserstein of Wasserstein Perella, the firm he cofounded with Joe Perella, who was on the Morgan Stanley M & A advisory team.

Despite any misgivings, the deal went through. Soon after the merger was completed, Purcell named Michael Miles chair of the nominating committee. Purcell would vet candidates for board positions before deciding whether to send them to Miles. Mike Miles had been chairman and CEO of Kraft Foods Inc. from 1989 to 1991, and chairman and CEO of Philip Morris until 1994, when he abruptly resigned after a "rancorous" board debate about his proposal to spin off the tobacco business, which owned such brands as Marlboro and Virginia Slims, from the Kraft and Miller Brewing divisions. After the board meeting about the spin-off, Miles submitted his resignation, which was accepted, effective immediately. A year later, he became a special limited partner at Forstmann Little & Company, a private buyout firm. Miles understood how important it was for a CEO to be able to count on his board to back him.

In contrast to prior practices at Morgan Stanley, Purcell limited communication between the board and Morgan Stanley executives, even the most senior among them, except for his direct reports. For the most part, such contacts involved only short presentations to the full board and invitations to more informal dinners the night before. Anyone, including division heads, who wanted to contact a director directly was instructed to check with Purcell first. Over the next seven years his control of the board's membership would gradually increase as Morgan Stanley–appointed directors retired and Purcell replaced them with people he had selected, and who would receive all their information from him. By 2005, the program read: Midwest 8, Brits 1, Germans 1, Expat 1, Home Team, zero. Of eleven directors, Laura Tyson would be the only one left from the Morgan Stanley board, while five, including Purcell, had been members of the Dean Witter board.

On February 5, 1997, Dick Fisher, Phil Purcell, and John Mack were seated at a long conference table with microphones in front of them. Flashbulbs glinted off their glasses as they announced a "merger of equals," even though Dean Witter was technically buying Morgan Stanley. To indicate that it was a "merger of equals," the firm would be called "Morgan Stanley, Dean Witter, Discover." Some at Morgan Stanley wondered why they agreed to such a mouthful, rather than using the name of the more prestigious firm. One theory was that they didn't want to put Morgan Stanley's full imprimatur on a second-rate broker. As it developed, the firm would go through three name changes in four years, dropping Discover first, and then Dean Witter, until by 2001, the firm would again be called Morgan Stanley. The new entity would have $12 billion in net revenues and a $21 billion market cap, and it would be the biggest securities firm on Wall Street, with Merrill Lynch dropping to second place.

In light of what happened later, and the pain both Mack and Purcell suffered, the photographs of them at the announcement of the merger evoke a certain sad nostalgia. In one picture in particular, the photographer captured a moment of spontaneous joy. The two men are sitting at a long table with microphones in front of them. Mack is holding up a Discover Card, his glasses are pushed down on his nose, his eyes are sparkling, and he's speaking and smiling at the same time. Purcell has a grin so broad his eyes are almost closed. They didn't look smug or "corporate"; they looked like team captains at prize night.

Purcell told the *New York Times*, "This may be a more gray and rainy day for some of our competitors." He reportedly also remarked, "This is a great day for Dean Witter shareholders and customers and a lousy day for Merrill Lynch." Morgan Stanley heads snapped up when they heard those remarks. That wasn't the way they were trained to talk about their competitors, at least not in public. The Merrill spokesman's comments sounded more like the old Morgan Stanley. He said that his company had been following the same strategy that Morgan Stanley had just adopted for more than twenty years. "They are two fine firms and we wish them well."

Newspapers ran charts showing the contribution each of the partners would make to the new company. Morgan Stanley's 1996 revenues were $13.1 billion as compared with $9.03 billion for Dean Witter, and their earnings were about the same, hovering around $1 billion. Dean Witter had many more mutual fund assets under management, 8,406 brokers, and a total of 30,799 employees; as compared with Morgan Stanley's 402 brokers and 9,725 employees. Morgan Stanley had by far the largest percentage of underwritings of common stock, debt, and initial public offerings: $90.56 billion, as compared with Dean Witter's $5.6 billion.

Morgan Stanley's stock rose 7⅞ on the merger announcement; Dean Witter was up two points. Other Wall Street firms saw their stocks jump on the speculation that Morgan Stanley had started a trend, and they might become targets for big banks or consolidations.

I f our two firms can't get this kind of thing right, it says something about our ability to help our clients," Dick Fisher announced. "This will be a superb partnership." A symbol of their "equality" was that Purcell and Mack would be paid the identical amount for 1997: $14.5 million each in cash and restricted stock, plus 126,000 options. It was quite a jump for Purcell, who earned $4.3 million in salary and bonuses at Dean Witter in 1996, while Mack was paid $10 million at Morgan Stanley.

The potential that they might clash was foreshadowed in some of the contrasting descriptions in the financial press. The *Wall Street Journal* called Purcell "a respected, low-profile chief executive," and "an enigmatic former management consultant." Another *Journal* story noted, "Despite Mr. Purcell's decade-long tenure as Dean Witter's chief executive, a number of chief executives at other Wall Street firms say they have met him only a handful of times," while Mack "is often seen on Morgan Stanley's trading floors." The New York *Daily News* called Mack "a take-no-prisoners manager" and "a shrewd boss who doesn't mind bloodying some noses and scraping elbows." A "Morgan Stanley source" said, "He is an extremely tough, talented, brutal manager. It's not a lot of fun, but he knows where he is going."

Purcell and Mack did seem as though they would complement each other. Purcell was a strategist with a cool management style; Mack was decisive, ardent, and reacted fast. Purcell was cautious; Mack was experienced at taking risk. Purcell shut down if he was challenged; Mack said, "I don't care what you say to me, but do it privately. Be forthright and honest, just do it behind closed doors, where you won't embarrass anyone."

As the merger was coming to fruition, one of Purcell's colleagues says, "he was almost worshipful in his praise of Mack. He would say, 'Because of Mack, we're going to get this done. He's a straight-shooter and sensitive to us.' He would say to people at both firms that he and

Mack would have 'the sort of partnership that Dick and John have.' What Purcell may not have taken into account is that Mack would still be running the biggest part of the business, even though Purcell was still CEO."

The merger evoked dramatic, if mixed, predictions and commentary. The *Daily News* wrote, "The deal stunned bankers, brokers and traders here by bringing the decade's merger mania right to their front doorstep." Calling it a "merger of opposites," the *News* reported that the biggest surprise was that two such different corporate cultures should attempt a marriage. In one Sears store the financial services booth was located next to the children's department and a broker reported that at Christmas when she called clients, they could hear the soundtrack of a Disney movie behind her voice. It "sounded like I was calling them from my house with the kids screaming in the background," she said. The contrast between that scene and even the loudest day on the Morgan Stanley trading floor was striking.

Bob Greenhill had started his own M & A advisory firm, and when he heard that Purcell and Mack had literally or symbolically "shaken hands" over the succession, he said he would never have let a client sign such a loose deal. Another well-known merger specialist explained, "In a 'merger of equals' you don't leave anything important to be fought over after the deal is done; and number one on the list is the succession plan."

Many people on Wall Street wondered why Morgan Stanley would choose Dean Witter. One former Morgan Stanley managing director told a friend inside the firm that he sold his Morgan Stanley stock the day the merger was announced. But most people figured that the Morgan Stanley executives were so smart they must know what they were doing, and that the Morgan Stanley contingent thought they could take back control whenever they wanted. Perhaps Mack felt the same way—he had prevailed over Bob Greenhill and other possible competitors—but above all, he was excited about the possibilities of building the new firm and accustomed to the Morgan Stanley partnership style of doing business. He believed it would work.

Bob Scott was given the responsibility of overseeing the transition, but in mid-February before he took on the challenge, he went on a brief Caribbean vacation with his wife, Karen, and his parents. Karen was reading on the beach when she looked up and saw Scott skim into shore on a sailboard and collapse at the edge of the sea. Scott, who was fifty-one years old, was having a massive heart attack. The firm sent a plane for him, but he was in such critical condition that the decision was made not to risk a longer flight, and he was flown to San Juan, Puerto Rico, for a quadruple bypass. Purcell was sympathetic and considerate about Scott's postponement of his new responsibilities, and in a strange way, the health crisis was a bond. Scott was back at work by the end of April.

On Saturday, May 31, the biggest combination of financial institutions in Wall Street history became official, and Dick Fisher stepped down as chairman of Morgan Stanley. At twelve-thirty that afternoon, he and Jeanne Donovan were married at their house in Westchester, New York.

Donovan had never known Dick Fisher in any role other than as president and chairman of the firm. She was usually described as "Dick's secretary," but that wasn't accurate—he already had a secretary, Patty Doyle—Donovan had been hired as his executive assistant, doing research and making arrangements. Donovan, who was a Brown University graduate, had been living in New York since 1981, first following what she had thought would be a career in photography, freelancing as an assistant to commercial photographers, and printing in a custom photo lab. Those jobs snuffed out any interest she had in being a professional photographer, and in the winter of 1986, she was editing a newsletter for a small economic research firm, where she began to get a sense of the markets and the players. One day when her boss had been exceedingly unpleasant to her, she turned to the "Help Wanted" pages in the newspaper and found an ad for a well-spoken Ivy League graduate with strong writing and communications skills. "It almost said 'pretty,' " she says. "It was just enough before political correctness that I understood they wanted a reasonably attractive young woman." Donovan was attractive, but her most immediately evident qualities were her spunk and optimism.

She answered the ad, and after half a dozen interviews with Morgan Stanley's human resources department, she learned that she was being considered to work for the president, and went upstairs to meet Fisher. She says she thinks he hired her because when she walked into his office, she noticed that a painting was hanging crookedly and went over and straightened it. On their second meeting, when Fisher was about to walk into the boardroom, she told him he had spinach in his teeth. She started at Morgan Stanley in the spring of 1986, soon after the IPO.

"Dick was an incredible boss. He expected you to be capable and smart. He treated people who worked for him with respect, and he was willing to give people a chance. Sure enough, a year into the job, I got asked to join the corporate communications department," Donovan says. "It was a quiet little area of the firm. Those were still the days when they thought, 'We're Morgan Stanley,' and the press could come to them, rather than the other way around, although that had begun to change after the IPO." Then Morgan Stanley's head of corporate communications left, and Donovan became acting director. After the firm had interviewed other candidates for six months, she says, "They gave me the job." Even with press and advertising as part of her responsibility, she only had two people working for her.

Donovan married her first husband in 1987; Fisher, his wife, Emily, and their daughter attended the wedding. In 1993 her marriage failed, and so did the Fishers'. By then she had left the firm and joined two partners who were starting a corporate public relations company. Eventually, when she and Fisher began dating openly and she was traveling with him, she couldn't give the public relations firm her full attention—Morgan Stanley didn't have a plane, and travel could be arduous for Fisher. They embarked on a series of philanthropic initiatives that engaged her skills and her training in art, finance, and communications, and the interests in film and theater and music that she and Dick shared. They had big plans in the philanthropic sphere, and as it would turn out, a very short time to get a lot done.

The wedding was held at the Fishers' weekend house, just north of Westchester, with about 150 guests seated on chairs on the lawn.

Dick and Jeanne stood on the porch and were married by a Baptist minister, the Reverend Gordon Smith. Dick wore white trousers, a light khaki jacket, blue shirt, and a light blue-and-white-striped tie that Jeanne had given him. He leaned on a cane with one hand and on the horn handle of a black umbrella with the other. The day was fine, but he often used an umbrella as a second stick, until Jeanne pointed out that he was giving mixed signals about the weather forecast. Jeanne wore a sleeveless white dress and jacket by Morgane LeFay and a delicate mesh straw hat that let the sun filter through on her face. After the ceremony, the guests drifted over the lawn toward a tent decorated in a relaxed Tuscan theme, with spring flowers and big chunks of Parmesan cheese on the tables. The dance floor was painted with martini glasses; Fisher was a connoisseur of exotic martinis.

Many of the guests were friends from Morgan Stanley—John Mack wore a white boutonniere, which signaled that he was an usher, although the atmosphere was so informal that there wasn't much ushering to do. As of that day, Fisher was officially no longer chairman of the firm, and Fred Whittemore joked, "It's very unusual to advise young partners to get married on the day they have lost their job." Some of the toasts celebrated the creation of a great global enterprise, but Fisher never mentioned the merger in the three pages of notes for his toast, which he wrote in his small, tidy hand.

Five

A CRISIS OF CONFIDENCE AND A CULTURE CLASH

1998–2000

I t didn't take long for people on both sides of the merger to feel that their new clothes didn't fit. At one of the first off-site meetings, about forty senior Dean Witter and Morgan Stanley people convened at the Hyatt Hotel in Greenwich, Connecticut. John Mack arrived with a black hat and a white hat, and told the group, "Around Morgan Stanley, I've always been the guy with the black hat and Dick [Fisher] has always been the guy with the white hat." And then he handed Purcell the white hat. Purcell set a different tone. He began by telling the group that when he graduated from the University of Chicago business school, he had been offered a job at Morgan Stanley, but decided to work for McKinsey instead. One of the Morgan Stanley executives recalls, "He was saying, 'I'm really better than you guys, and now here I am to tell you what to do.' "

Peter Karches, who used to say that he had learned about human nature in college when he worked as a waiter to earn money, unleashed a salvo in the direction of James F. Higgins, Dean Witter's Head of Retail. "Mack is a little like my old basketball coach that used to have a drill where you dribbled to the end," he said, referring to a training routine pitting two players against each other until one of them drops. The message was: "Get ready, guys, it's going to be one of the two of us." Higgins was a genial Irishman who was like some of the old guard at Sears: loyal and unthreatening, unless they were threatened, and Karches had set out the bait. Mack and his associates were accustomed to a kind of tough collegial playfulness that was unfamiliar to the Dean Witter people.

The new management committee, like the board, was meant to be split fifty-fifty, not including the chairman. Five of the members represented the old Morgan Stanley: Mack; Jim Allwin, Head of Institutional Investment Management; Peter Karches, Head of Institutional Securities (the title at the time was President and Chief Operating Officer, Morgan Stanley & Co., Inc.); Bob Scott, executive vice president and CFO; and Sir David A. Walker, Chairman of Morgan Stanley International. The six Dean Witter members were Purcell, Thomas R. Butler, president and COO of NOVUS Services, which was part of Discover; Richard M. DeMartini, president and COO of Individual Asset Management; Chris Edwards; Jim Higgins, president and COO of Dean Witter Securities; and Tom Schneider. For the most part, they were just names and new faces to the people in both camps, but from the beginning, it was clear that there *were* two camps and that it might not be easy to find their common ground.

Purcell didn't take long to make a geographical change that was an unambiguous indication of the power shift. He constructed a brand-new executive floor on thirty-nine, and moved the offices of the chairman and CEO and the president and their staffs downstairs, leaving Dick Fisher on the fortieth floor. Mack went along with the plan reluctantly; one of the senior executives called the move "a bad symbol and not practical." For one thing, the formal reception area on the fortieth floor had been designed as the main introduction to the firm. The walls were paneled in an exotic golden wood, with Charles Rennie Mackintosh–inspired black-framed doors and stair rail. Enormous windows commanded a view north and south over the Hudson River, and down toward the tip of Manhattan, where the Statue of Liberty was visible beyond the towers of the World Trade Center. A portrait of J. P. Morgan Jr. hung behind the receptionist's desk, and at the back of the room a dramatic double staircase led up to the executive dining rooms. That staircase could have been a stage set for a 1930s musical, with dancers dressed as bankers tapping up and down the steps. Portraits of Henry Morgan and Harold Stanley hung in the stairwell, a reminder of the genealogy of the firm. Their images bespoke an attention to principle and quality that should be possible even in the big corporation Morgan Stanley had become.

As a longtime senior executive said, "It was tacky at best, and gratu-itous at the least, to leave Dick on the fortieth floor. Purcell was disre-spectful to Dick. He attempted to get John to turn on him for a long time, but it didn't work." Eventually Purcell moved Fisher to "Jurassic Park," 1221 Avenue of the Americas, and subdivided Fisher's fortieth-floor office. Ultimately Philip Raskin, a Chicago advertising executive—the least inflammatory comment about Raskin from Morgan Stanley executives was that he was "Phil's lackey"—moved into one of these new offices.

For Fisher, there were advantages to being out of Purcell's immediate view; people stopped by Fisher's office to talk about what was happen-ing at the firm, and if they wanted more privacy, they went over to his apartment. Fisher would sit on the small red-and-white-striped bergère in the living room on Central Park West, lean his cane against the arm of the chair, and listen. The principal issues concerned people: Morgan Stanley's greatest strengths were the quality of its employees, its em-phasis on teamwork, and its culture of discussion and debate. The regu-larly repeated phrase "our assets go down in the elevators every night" was both an appreciation and a warning. Many of the senior executives Purcell brought in didn't meet Morgan Stanley's standards of excel-lence, and those who were first-rate, or had potential, were discouraged from developing the skills that honed ideas and built teams. The inte-gration of the firms wasn't moving along, the people weren't meshing, and there was a drift toward the median common denominator. The Advisory Directors never forgot the meeting when Purcell said, "At Dean Witter, if I told people to turn right, they turned. At Morgan Stanley they ask why." As a member of the Group of Eight who was at the meeting recalled, "He expected us to laugh."

By the end of Purcell's first year, Fisher had heard and observed enough to believe that the firm had a hole in the middle. If Morgan Stanley didn't emanate energy from the center, it wouldn't take long for it to become like a dead star. Fisher still believed the merger strategy was right, but he had concluded that Purcell was the wrong person to execute it. At some point in 1998, he made an appointment to go down to the chairman's office for a private conversation. Fisher was known for his kindness, but the stakes were high, and he was prepared to be blunt.

Fisher often made a few notes before he addressed a group, and some-times even when he was preparing to talk with a colleague, although he rarely referred to the notes during the meeting. Before he met with Purcell, he had neatly written some phrases in pencil on a small lined pad. He found Purcell in his office, at the special four-foot-high desk that Purcell had ordered so he could work standing up, to take pressure off his bad back. The desk accentuated his height, and visitors either stood and tried to talk to him, which almost always required looking up, or sat with their necks craned while he loomed. Purcell was a model for the finding that chairmen of major American corporations were taller than average.

Fisher began by telling Purcell that he was there as a friend, colleague, and director—and that he was speaking for himself—to be sure that Purcell did not think he was the advance guard of an insurrection. He said he was concerned that the firm was losing momentum and would continue to deteriorate, cited the people whom Purcell had brought in—"not a meritocracy," he wrote in his notes—and that the decision-making process was too cautious, took too long, and was hampered by "constant seeking outside."

"What you need to understand," he wrote—and presumably said—"is that you cannot fix it, or at least it is not the best use of talent." He observed sympathetically that Purcell was under stress, and that the effort was taking a toll. "John is better suited to provide leadership," Fisher concluded. "He will get more out of the DW senior people." Fisher proposed that Purcell "take the initiative" and "tell the board you believe you should focus on L.T. [long-term] strategy—stay as chairman—make John CEO." He noted that his own "responsibilities are clear because I feel that strongly. Unless you and John both ask me not to, I will begin to talk to directors."

When Fisher left the meeting, he was not optimistic that Purcell would consider his recommendations, and he was right. Purcell's reaction can only be imagined. After his experience in the conspiracy culture at Sears in the late 1970s and 1980s, he must have assumed that Fisher and Mack were colluding against him. In fact, Fisher was acting as an elder statesman. He had recently been diagnosed with prostate cancer, and his motivation was to secure Morgan Stanley's future. He regretted having conceded to Purcell's insistence on becoming chairman and CEO; it was at least worth trying to undo the damage.

In June 1998, Mack told Fisher he was going to propose to Purcell that they share the CEO position. Later, people who were close to Mack were surprised to hear about that conversation. As one senior banker said, "John didn't want to embroil others in the leadership problems." Fisher didn't have much faith in a co-CEO structure, but Mack went ahead and Purcell agreed to discuss it, although a definite no was the predictable answer. He did respond to two of Mack's major concerns. As a step toward consolidating the parallel elements of the firms, he moved the Dean Witter Fixed Income traders over to the Morgan Stanley Fixed Income Department. At close quarters the combination didn't necessarily bring out the best on either side. According to an April 1999 *Fortune* article, "One Morgan Stanley trader described the moment as bringing into his life 'guys named Vinnie in cheap suits.'"

Purcell did not agree to the co-CEO proposal, and the sense that Mack was breathing down his neck made him even more careful to watch his back, but he did expand the membership of the management committee, which after the merger had been constituted differently from other major Wall Street firms. Prior to the merger, it was known as the Operating Committee and included the managers of Morgan Stanley divisions that were bottom-line producers. Purcell took a more corporate approach. His management committee had only four heads of revenue-producing divisions: Jim Allwin, Peter Karches, Richard DeMartini, and Jim Higgins. The others were in staff positions: the chief financial officer, general counsel, chief administrative officer, and the head of the London office. With Mack's prodding, in September 1998, Purcell added Joe Perella, Head of Investment Banking; Stephan Newhouse, who was Karches's deputy in Institutional Securities; Kenneth DeRegt, Head of Fixed Income; and Vikram Pandit, Head of Institutional Equities.

He would tell close colleagues from Dean Witter that Morgan Stanley wasn't what he thought it was going to be. He hadn't quite anticipated the aggressiveness, the fierce internal competition, the fights, and the enormous egos. A *Wall Street Journal* reporter later noted, "Deepening turf battles were exacerbated by the very different personal styles of the two top men. Mr. Purcell, who reveled in his reputation as a strategic thinker, complained to others that Mr. Mack had a short attention span. Mr. Mack, meanwhile, moaned that Mr. Purcell couldn't make a decision." More fundamentally, "Mack had been reared in a consensus-driven partnership, where lively debate was encouraged, Mr. Purcell was more authoritarian."

Purcell knew what he wanted to accomplish. He believed the move toward consolidation in financial services would continue to accelerate, even cross-border, and that deregulation, privatization, and a new middle class in many regions of the world would create opportunities in consumer financial services as well as in the institutional business for firms with the scale and global reach to take advantage of the trends. A banker who was close to the situation says, "When John and Phil put this merger together, they shared a vision that this was the first of many parts of an assemblage that would lead to a giant Citibank-type financial services organization." The concept created tensions within the management committee, as some of the leaders in Institutional Securities didn't want "to sell out Morgan Stanley to some big organization," as one recalls, and when the possibilities were raised, tried to block them. Mack turned down deals, which was also a source of friction between him and Purcell. The banker says, "Phil was thinking as a strategist; he wasn't interested in being a manager of the business; it was just a chip in putting together something larger."

Whatever Purcell was considering for the long-term, he needed experienced and highly qualified people to build a global brand. Morgan Stanley executives had begun to recognize that in Purcell's hierarchy, loyalty—not to the firm, but to him—trumped competence and experience on a more complex playing field. When the bankers, who didn't think twice about jetting around the world on business, heard that some of the brokers got passports for the first time to go on trips sponsored by the firm for high producers, they were astonished by the low ratio of brokers to passports. It was more than a culture gap; it was disjunctive with the idea of building a global presence.

It wouldn't have been easy for anyone to make the combination work. The culture clash between institutional securities and retail brokerage was endemic in the industry. Institutional Securities was geographically centralized and team oriented, while the brokers were part of a network spread all over the United States. Brokers—or "financial advisers" as they were now called—were entrepreneurs, working for themselves under the corporate umbrella, and they needed more of a top-down structure to hold them together. Bankers tended to think of brokers as interchangeable spokes on the wheel of fortune who did penny-ante deals and had to sell hard because they were paid on commission. Brokers thought the Institutional Securities people were stuck-up and outrageously overpaid. The cultural divide was heightened by the relative standings of the two firms. The unborn "Morgan Stanley Warburg" would have been a very different creature from Morgan Stanley Dean Witter Discover. The gap between Dean Witter's and Morgan Stanley's reputations was so significant that the management committee even discussed whether to leave the Dean Witter name on the retail operation until it could be brought up to Morgan Stanley standards. As a product manager in an entirely different business remarked, Hidden Valley Ranch salad dressing is made by a division of the Clorox company, but if Clorox were on the label it would scare people and they would wonder why it was tangy.

A former Morgan Stanley managing director says, "The re-branding of Dean Witter as Morgan Stanley was a catastrophic mistake in terms of image." Nevertheless, the Dean Witter brokers got new business cards with the Morgan Stanley Dean Witter Discover logo. The association gained them an advantage in the marketplace and attracted people to work in the retail division who wanted to be associated with Morgan Stanley. The Morgan Stanley Institutional Securities people felt that their brand was being diminished by brokers "dialing for dollars," and Purcell's "socks and stocks" play at Sears tormented them.

Morgan Stanley gave up its autonomy and joined forces with Dean Witter to gain retail distribution and asset management, and John Mack took on oversight of those divisions, to master that side of the business. He proposed to Purcell that he move downtown to the Dean Witter offices in the World Trade Center, get to know the people, and be involved on a day-to-day basis. Purcell countered that the brokers would think he was looking over their shoulders. At close quarters, Jim Higgins and his lieutenants would see John Mack as a threat, and Purcell vetoed the idea.

Mack had energy and charisma and he could have developed a

more productive team-oriented culture in Retail. He was relentless about results, and people who worked for him quickly knew what he thought of their performance. If someone made a significant error, Mack would bring him into his office and take him apart, but as Chas Phillips says, "When it was over, it was over. He's the only person I've ever worked with who could give it to you between the eyes, tell you what was wrong, why it was wrong, and the next day you were back to a positive supportive relationship." Another managing director says that when she was promoted, Mack told her he had voted against her. "Show me I was wrong," he said. A year later, she went to see him and laid out her results. Mack admitted he had made a mistake. "After that, he was my mentor and protector," she says. "You couldn't have had any part of that conversation with Phil. John had enough appreciation of situation and subtlety that an apology can go a long way."

Although Mack was blocked from moving into the Dean Witter World Trade Center offices, he was determined to familiarize himself with the brokers, and he began to stop by branch offices when he was traveling on firm business. The casual drop-in wasn't part of the Dean Witter culture; managers were accustomed to having weeks to prepare for the occasional top-brass visits. Once when Mack arrived at a branch office near San Francisco, the manager was so flabbergasted he asked him for identification before he would let him walk around. Mack had a genuine small-town friendliness. He asked people about themselves and remembered what he'd heard, and most of them responded positively, but the manager was so upset that he called Jim Higgins in New York to report that Mack had disrupted business. After that, Higgins asked Mack to give him a heads-up before he went into the field. Mack continued to drop in unannounced at retail offices, Higgins complained, and Purcell told Mack to coordinate with Higgins. Mack stopped the visits.

Mack and Higgins clashed again over the way in which brokers were compensated. The Dean Witter brokers were paid on commission, a practice that had existed at Morgan Stanley for Fixed Income salespeople until Fisher stopped it because it created the potential for a conflict of interest between the firm and its clients. Mack proposed that the commission system be discontinued, but Higgins argued that other brokerage houses worked on commission and the best brokers would leave if they were paid any other way. Purcell agreed with Higgins, and the commission system remained in place.

The potential for conflict of interest was inherent in the ways Dean Witter compensated brokers for selling in-house mutual funds. Dean Witter offered brokers incentives to push its proprietary funds, but regulators were looking askance at the practice by the late 1990s. Morgan Stanley executives warned Purcell that the firm was asking for trouble, but as one of them says, Purcell told them to keep doing what worked. When it was proposed that Dean Witter integrate and invigorate its online trading, Higgins told Purcell that the low-cost option would cut into brokers' commissions, and they would quit. Purcell again gave in to Higgins.

Prior to the merger, Dean Witter analysts had also received incentive awards, a formulaic bonus when they worked on or brought in investment banking transactions. That system had been suggested from time to time at Morgan Stanley, but Research management insisted on a neutral compensation system to keep research objective. Unlike the situation with brokers selling in-house mutual funds, once Dean Witter merged with Morgan Stanley, its research analysts no longer received such formulaic bonuses.

Dean Witter's overall compensation formulas were meant to correlate pay and performance, but they were far from straightforward. Bob Scott, who was CFO, says, "These so-called analytical and objective systems were too complicated and hard to understand for the brokers to be motivated. Because of the complexity in the calculations, guys in that business figured out how to game the system: move costs and make the numbers work. You weren't trying to run the business better; you were trying to make the numbers work for you. The system was opaque."

Compensation was one of the issues that divided Purcell and the Institutional Securities executives. Back in the 1980s, when Purcell joined Dean Witter, he had made a point of saying that investment bankers were overpaid. His own compensation had jumped by millions when he took over at Morgan Stanley, but soon after the merger, a couple of managing directors who met him for the first time at an off-site meeting compared notes. They found that, after Purcell had had a couple of glasses of wine, he told them each separately that he did not understand how they could be paid more than he was.

The system for deciding bankers' compensation was loose because of the volatility of the business, and that drove Purcell crazy. One year, a banker might be hatching deals and have little to show for it; the next year, all the deals might come to fruition and he would earn a huge bonus. A formulaic approach would create too much instability from year to year, and the only way to keep the bankers on a relatively even keel was for managers who understood the business to decide on their compensation. As Bob Scott explained, "It was a mysterious process, but the bottom line was that the Morgan Stanley people were paid better, and Purcell couldn't justify why."

Management was another problem in Retail brokerage, and that too was driven by compensation, in this case Purcell's bias against spending money. As one managing director in the Retail division said, someone needed to have the authority to tell the brokers "you can't sell that product to our eighty-year-old customers." The managers were the logical controls, but Dean Witter paid them less than other firms did and gave them more work. Each of the eight divisions had one manager, who oversaw three or four dozen branch managers. The pay scale and the workload mitigated against getting the best people in the managerial slots, and the good managers often didn't have the time to oversee the salespeople.

Mack was frustrated by Purcell's insistence on sticking with business practices that weren't consonant with the Morgan Stanley culture of excellence, and he told Purcell he couldn't be in charge of Retail if Purcell let his old colleagues bypass him. Purcell said that he and Higgins had a long-standing relationship, and he could hardly tell him not to call him if he wanted to talk. Higgins called so often that even Purcell got irritated and complained that he was always being asked to referee between "Jimmy" and John.

Purcell finally asked for Higgins's resignation in June 2000, but he didn't consult with Mack or even notify him about the decision until an hour before he made the announcement. He later told Mack that he was afraid he would leak the news. An enraged Mack reputedly told Purcell, "Never refer to me as your partner again." It was more likely that Purcell left Mack out of the loop because he hated to admit that he had lost that round.

One of the significant differences between Purcell's attitude toward the business and the attitudes of the Morgan Stanley executives was their approach to risk. One of Morgan Stanley's top analysts explains, "If you haven't been responsible for losing $100 million at some point in your career in a senior role, you're not taking enough risk. That doesn't mean you want to lose $100 million, but it's inevitable if your goal is to earn $500 million or a billion." In 1998, one of the firm's emerging-markets hedge funds lost between $300 and $400 million in the Russian bond collapse. Purcell took that as evidence that John Mack and Jim Allwin, who was Head of Asset Management, had unnecessarily exposed the firm to loss. He took Asset Management away from Mack, put it under Richard Worley from Morgan Stanley, and later Mitch Merin, who had been with Dean Witter, and said, "I've been in the financial business for twenty years and I've never lost $400 million." Purcell fired Morgan Stanley people whom he held responsible, and there was a growing sense that he was using market problems to get rid of people, especially if he thought they were Mack supporters. Institutional Securities executives who had been savvy risk takers recognized that they would have to be more conservative. As the desire and willingness to take risk diminished, so did the returns.

To moderate the firm's exposure, Purcell imposed constraints on the Institutional Securities divisions. When John Mack ran Fixed Income, a trader explains, "Morgan Stanley had a decentralized risk culture. If you ran a business you were given capital. If you made good bets, you kept some of the capital; if you made bad bets, after a while you were fired." Purcell followed the model of other firms that were more centrally managed, and instituted a system in which the traders' positions were rolled up and stress-tested daily, in a risk-modeling system. "Money isn't made by the pusillanimous," the trader said. "Purcell's attitude was 'cut your losses and sell.' Mack would double."

Then, in 2000, Morgan Stanley's global high-yield bond department took a $1 billion hit on high-yield telecommunications bonds. Following the $400 million Russian bond debacle two years earlier, it was understandable that Purcell would insist that the firm take a more conservative stance. In 2000, the executive on the griddle was Dwight

Sipprelle, the forty-two-year-old cohead of the global high-yield bond department. Sipprelle had started the unit in 1984, and now managed an $8 billion portfolio, which included bank loans. In 1999, he was said to have brought in $500 million in fees, underwriting high-yield loans worth $12.5 billion, and Morgan Stanley was ranked globally as the number one high-yield underwriter.

Sipprelle, who was a son of diplomats who had served in a number of emerging-market countries, believed that the bond-underwriting business could have a dramatic, positive effect on shaping international policy and helping emerging markets grow. The concept of influencing international affairs had a strong resonance with the history of the House of Morgan—Junius, J. P. Morgan Sr., and Jack Morgan had all taken significant roles in financing foreign governments.

Forbes published an interview with Dwight Sipprelle titled "Master of the Planet" on July 24, 2000. The business was looking strong when the article appeared, but by the end of October, the junk bond market, and telecoms in particular, had crashed, Morgan Stanley had taken the $1 billion loss, the firm's stock had dropped more than 10 percent in a single day, and Sipprelle had left. Although Goldman Sachs, Merrill Lynch, Lehman Brothers, and many others had also been battered by the junk bond market, that did not ameliorate the situation from Purcell's point of view. As an executive in the Equities Division says, "Phil had had it with Morgan Stanley's big bets." The difference between Purcell's reaction and that at the competitor firms was that he imposed a firm-wide damper on risk, while other Wall Street executives went back to looking at the market with an eye to taking more aggressive advantage of opportunities. Purcell's aversion to risk would ultimately lead to the firm's performance slipping, particularly in contrast to its archrival, Goldman Sachs, but also in comparison to lesser firms.

One of the perceived advantages of the merger had been the possibility that the synergy between Morgan Stanley and Dean Witter could close the gap between Dean Witter and Merrill Lynch, which was the industry Retail leader. It was harder to define market share in Retail; unlike Equities, Debt, and M & A, there were no league tables in the brokerage business, which was measured by each financial advisor's assets under management and revenue per advisor. Instead, the gap was getting wider—in favor of Merrill Lynch. Purcell's tactic was to expand the sales force, rather than investing in improving performance or attracting better brokers. Turnover was high, and even though production was low, Purcell thought they could come out more or less even by adding brokers. Even if they produced less per head, the bottom line could be competitive.

The scheme sacrificed quality. Bob Scott says, "Dean Witter used to train four thousand brokers. Phil and I had several conversations and I told him that the training program wasn't working. He didn't agree, so we put together a team to do a financial analysis. After three months they produced a study that showed that the cost of training was too high for the results. To get one good broker, we had to train four. I showed him the report, but it didn't jibe with his view of the world, and he said, 'Your figures are wrong.'" Scott had to go back to the team that compiled the data and tell them that the chairman had dismissed their work as inaccurate.

The focus on more, rather than better, people affected the morale of the best brokers, who later complained that they were not being heard. When the Group of Eight emerged they would receive a flurry of confidential reports from managers and brokers in the Individual Investor Group, blaming Purcell for the lack of quality control, the failure to invest in technology, and the bureaucracy that overrode innovation. One angry vice president claimed that his division's relatively low profits were directly attributable to the discouragement of "creative thought . . . unnecessary layers of overhead and outdated technology."

A regional broker who had developed a strategy for combining high yield and prime bond funds to provide current income for elderly clients said that headquarters wasn't watching out for the interests of the small investor. He had attended four of the retail conferences known as "Insights" and "Horizons," and each time met with the portfolio manager to ask about the status of the fund. The manager assured him that it was solid, and the broker told his clients that everything was fine. The broker said that the prospectus had not made it clear that 70 percent of the fund was invested in telecommunications. The telecoms defaulted, and his elderly clients lost money.

Another broker reported that clients were "bailing" to external funds "in record numbers," and Dean Witter's American Opportunities

Fund, formerly known as American Value, dropped from $6 billion under management to $2.5 billion. In 2000 and 2001, the broker wrote, Morgan Stanley ads claimed that the firm had taken the lead in financial markets, but the brokers were told to push risky growth funds at a time when value and bond funds were safer and more profitable. The broker who was reporting on the loss of business in the proprietary funds wrote that he resented the Retail Division's reputation as a laggard. He said that Retail was "taking the shaft for corporate malfeasance at the highest levels."

At the end of 2004, Retail was still the worst performer in the firm. By comparison to its peers, the Individual Investor Group ranked fifth in revenues per financial advisor, and eighth out of eight in profits before taxes (PBT), although it was third in head count.

Yet many of the Dean Witter executives and top performers were sympathetic to Purcell. They thought that if there was a problem, it was on the Morgan Stanley side, and that the Institutional Securities people could not see that the two businesses should be run differently. When they felt Purcell was under attack, they rallied around him, and he repaid their loyalty.

Stretch Gardiner had started a "Chairman's Club" for the top-producing brokers. Chairman's Club members were invited to annual outings at glamorous locations, often abroad, and had a chance to spend some time with the chairman. The highlight of the trips was a dinner at which new members were solemnly inducted. As one banker says, "It was Phil's club, part of the way he controlled his people. Once you got up there, it was hard to fall back out. Phil kept changing the rules to keep the old guys in." A banker who attended one of the meetings said Purcell told the brokers, "You are the most important people in this firm." The banker's reaction was: "Are you kidding me? These people each generate $2 million of revenues and the bankers generate $60 million apiece."

Serving the "little guy" wasn't as profitable as it had seemed back in 1981 when Purcell and Ed Telling talked about giving the average investor a break. (In 2003, Purcell would institute a policy that brokers would not be paid commissions on accounts with balances under $35,000.) Even though a new Wealth Advisor training program was implemented in 2002, many executives of the former Morgan Stanley believed that too few of the brokers were effective in dealing with sophisticated financial issues, and that these brokers' dealings with clients hurt Morgan Stanley's reputation.

It was easy to overlook the weaknesses in Retail and Asset Management during the euphoria of the technology boom. As Morgan Stanley's investment banking teams took tech companies public, Private Wealth Management, which Purcell had put under Dean Witter, had a burst of activity from entrepreneurs who looked to the firm that had made money for them to manage their wealth. Then the tech bubble burst, the Private Wealth Management business fell off, and it never rebounded. Over ten years, eight different managers tried to run the division. Anson Beard, who was the head of High Net Worth in the 1980s, remarked, "You can't run Tiffany's inside Kmart. I thought they should leave PWM alone until the thing rolled over and died from broker attrition. It would be folly to try to integrate it."

The Individual Investor and Institutional Securities groups remained psychologically and philosophically at odds, the performance gap wasn't improving, and the divisions were structurally on different platforms. Bob Scott took on the challenge of coordinating the back offices, and proposed using the Morgan Stanley platform throughout the firm, but Dean Witter executives said the platform would cost too much. "The Dean Witter refrain was, 'You guys don't pay attention to expenses,'" Scott says. "It became a mantra: anything that's Morgan Stanley is more expensive. At Morgan Stanley you came to work every day thinking about how you can generate another dollar. Phil woke up and asked himself, How can we save more money?"

Scott asked the comptroller and the IT offices to analyze the costs of the two platforms. They reported that the cost of a trade on the Morgan Stanley platform was higher, but was coming down rapidly, would soon be cheaper, and was designed to handle more complex transactions. The Dean Witter platform was built for a low-tech securities business and could not process all the Morgan Stanley products. When Scott presented the results, Purcell told him there was something wrong with the analysis. "He was a man perpetually in search of the analysis that supported his view of the world," Scott says. "Phil thought that if there were only enough hours in the day he could do everyone's job better than they could do it."

The affection and loyalty Purcell commanded at Dean Witter was difficult for people in Institutional Securities to understand. The *Wall Street Journal* noted that he was "enigmatic" and had an unusually low visibility ratio. He did not walk the trading floor, and he rarely appeared, as Dick Fisher and John Mack had, on the in-house television system addressing the firm at the Monday-morning meetings. Major clients complained that he was not available to meet with them. One banker who had occasion to go to client meetings with him says, "If you wound him up, he was prepared and credible, but he didn't like meeting with clients." It wasn't just that the clients wanted to be courted; they were accustomed to swapping ideas and information with the heads of the big firms. Clients and investors commented on his apparent indifference, especially by comparison to the CEOs of such competing firms as Goldman Sachs, Lehman Brothers, Citigroup, and others. Purcell never called Stephen A. Schwarzman, cofounder of the investment firm Blackstone Group, until 2005, when Purcell was under siege. Schwarzman, whose office was seven blocks from Morgan Stanley headquarters, reportedly remarked that it was a little surprising that he hadn't ever heard from him in eight years.

Small but damaging missteps added to the sense that Purcell was not on the bankers' team. A top banker who worked with Dick Debs on international business told Debs that an important client called him one day and said, "That was a great affair you guys put on for us." The banker had no idea what he was talking about. "Turns out that Phil had invited this guy's clients to go down on the planes to play golf, and didn't tell him about it, ask his advice before he went, or brief him when he returned." As one of the investment bankers remarked, "He did that all the time. You pay a managing director $5 million a year, he talks to his client every week, and you shut him out? That's a CEO who is totally disconnected from his own company."

That kind of missed opportunity was at odds with Purcell's objective of emphasizing Morgan Stanley's strength as a relationship banker. After the 2000 crash, he proposed a strategy to revise the client/banker structure by assigning top people in institutional securities to specific clients and instructing them to make client connections across business lines. Vikram Pandit developed and oversaw the strategy, and Terry Meguid created the Strategic Investment Group, chaired by Joe Perella. The idea was to relieve top bankers of administrative burdens, and to create a SWAT team for clients. Over the next few years Meguid and John Havens made it work, which would lead to Morgan Stanley's ranking as number one in global equity underwriting in 2004. Yet for the most part Purcell didn't follow his own policy, at least in the sense that he spent far less time establishing or maintaining client relationships than his predecessors. The irony was that, as a number of investment bankers commented, when he did interact with clients whom he considered important, he was very good: focused, informed, and personable. He played a significant role in two of the biggest deals during his tenure at Morgan Stanley: the IPOs of Google, and Deutsche Post's banking division.

Harking back to his McKinsey training, when he did get involved, he reviewed the materials extensively before he went into meetings, an echo of the occasion when Sears was considering acquiring Dean Witter, and dazzled the Dean Witter top executives with the depth of his research, and his ability to roll out facts and figures without referring to his notes.

Nevertheless, the Morgan Stanley bankers had been accustomed to being able to access Fisher and Mack for client meetings more often, and more informally. When the bankers could produce the CEO as part of a pitch, or to close a deal, clients felt confident that they were important to Morgan Stanley, and that the CEO was on their team. The investment bankers and mergers and acquisitions executives regularly expressed their frustration that when they felt they needed Purcell to show up, their sense of what might be worth his time and his often didn't match.

The telecom loss, following the Russian bond collapse, gave Purcell the chance to do some housecleaning. Morgan Stanley wasn't alone in being slammed by both situations, but nevertheless, it was hardly unreasonable for Purcell to lose trust in executives who had cost the bank hundreds of millions of dollars. Peter Karches was a particular target. Members of the management committee couldn't ignore the fact that, as one of them said, "Peter Karches was very much in Phil's face all the time, and Phil wanted to get rid of him." "The person who punished

Phil every day was Karches," a senior executive says. "Purcell would ask Karches, 'What can I do to make John [Mack] happy?' and Karches would invariably give him the same answer: 'Just leave.'" Karches never let up. He challenged Purcell in management committee meetings, sometimes to get under his skin, but often on substantive matters. One committee member recalls a meeting in 2000 when Purcell criticized the Institutional Securities business, and Karches looked at him and said, "Name one thing we could do better, Phil."

Purcell said, "In technology."

Karches said, "Like what? Tell me. What?"

Purcell backed off, but he was waiting for Karches to stumble so he could get rid of him, and the telecom loss in the early fall of 2000 provided the opportunity. Purcell told Mack he was going to ask Karches to leave, and Mack went into action, speaking privately to individual directors. They said they liked Karches, but if Purcell wanted him gone, he should go. The board discussed Karches's fate, but a senior executive says that Mack didn't oppose the decision because he had already made his position clear and had lost the argument. He believed the board had wasted a talented member of the team and he was frustrated that he hadn't been able to protect him. Purcell was so anxious to get Karches out that he gave him $48 million in cash, and Karches left in September 2000. As one investment banker says, "That was really puzzling to the troops. Karches was having a record year, despite the telecom loss. Why fire him?" Karches's parting advice to Purcell was: "You don't have the game for this business." He told people Purcell's answer was: "Don't tell anyone." Karches told a reporter—for attribution—that Purcell "probably is the most incompetent executive in the history of financial services."

With hindsight, Peter Karches's departure may have been the last straw for Mack. The promotions that immediately followed seemed as though John Mack was preparing his own succession plan—as someone said, "writing his will," putting the strongest people in the coming generation in place to run Institutional Securities. Vikram Pandit and Steve Newhouse became coheads of Institutional Securities, and on September 25, 2000, Morgan Stanley promoted John Havens to Head of Equities, Terry Meguid to Head of Investment Banking, and Zoe Cruz to Head of Fixed Income. They were like the Three Musketeers, "all for

one and one for all," as they were heard to say, launching their partnership with enthusiasm, energy, and goodwill. They had dinners together,
held off-sites, made plans, and supported one another. It looked like a
hopeful beginning to a new phase of leadership.

W hatever was going on within the firm, Wall Street was having
a string of good years, and Morgan Stanley was at the top of the
action. As long as performance was still strong and the stock was trading at increasingly higher numbers, the difficulties of the merger es-
caped the attention of investors and shareholders. In 1999, the firm
ranked second in dollar amounts of IPOs—Goldman Sachs was technically first, but it had handled its own IPO, which skewed the numbers. The Morgan Stanley Mergers & Acquisitions group was in the
number two spot in the league tables, doing huge deals—Vodafone
bought Airtouch Communications for $65 billion; Viacom bought CBS
for $38 billion. But long after people forgot how well Morgan Stanley
stood in comparison to its competitors, they remembered that in the
last two years of the twentieth century, the firm was in the eye of the
scandal storm. So many personnel issues flared up that a reporter for
the *New York Observer,* the peach-tinted weekly newspaper known for
its spicy reporting style, published a story titled "Morgan Stanley's
Season in Hell." Kate Kelley, who wrote the piece, conceded that the
firm "might be the best investment bank on Wall Street," but that the
summer's headlines overrode the news that business was "booming"
and "made it sound like the place was full of sexists, sex fiends and rac-
ists, protected by inept lawyers and flacks."

The principal "flack" was Philip Raskin, the Chief Marketing Officer, who also advised Purcell on public relations and image. Raskin
framed a fake "employee of the month" flyer and hung it outside his office. Raskin—plump, self-satisfied, and unpopular—annoyed just about
everyone, but he was Purcell's confidant, and he was feeling his power.
Every afternoon employees on the fortieth floor would see a waiter from
the Morgan Stanley dining rooms come downstairs carrying a tray
with a plate of homemade chocolate cookies and a glass of milk for "Mr.
Raskin." It was a very small perk, but a visible symbol of his privileged
status. When he held meetings to show mock-ups for suggested ads, he
was apt to respond to negative comments with, "Fine. I quit. You do it."

One person who was usually at the meetings says, "He quit a hundred times. His appointment was irrational. He knew nothing about the business. He was self-pitying and a bully, but he had Phil's ear." John Mack didn't have much respect for Raskin's abilities, and he kept at Purcell to get rid of him, but Purcell continued to rely on Raskin, not only for advertising and public relations matters, but also as a sounding board for other issues. Raskin was Phil's guy.

One of their pet projects was to develop a logo for the firm. Morgan Stanley had never needed a symbol to distinguish itself. "Morgan Stanley blue"—the color of the type that was used on the firm's printed materials—was recognized wherever it mattered, and the name alone signified quality. Joe Fogg says wryly, "We *had* a logo. It was Ronaldson Slope, a rare and ancient typeface. When we went to a new printer we had to take the type with us. The use of that typeface, printed in blue, was our logo. It was a subtle thing."

Nevertheless, Raskin and Purcell huddled together, developing an emblem. Eventually they would come up with a cockeyed triangle that looked like a stunted dunce's cap, flipping off the end of the *n* in *Morgan* and heading up toward the right.

The dig at "inept lawyers" was a reference to general counsel Christine Edwards, who kept her distance and insisted on being called "Mrs. Edwards" in a first-names business. She seemed to believe that Dean Witter had to be protected from Morgan Stanley, and the Morgan Stanley lawyers found her hostile and defensive. That was the way it seemed when Morgan Stanley and Dean Witter were separately involved in a case in Orange County, California, along with other securities firms. The county had passed a law preventing local governments from raising property taxes, and a trader for the county was aggressively trying to generate income to make up for the shortfall. In 1994, interest rates rose, and he got caught on the wrong side of the market. The county sued a number of broker-dealers, including Morgan Stanley. Credit Suisse First Boston, which settled first, established a formula based on the volume of trades, and Morgan Stanley was compelled to follow the formula. The settlement was considerably larger for Morgan Stanley than for Dean Witter, but Edwards claimed that the lawyers on the "Morgan Stanley side" had crafted a formula that would hurt Dean Witter.

A former Morgan Stanley lawyer comments, "At Morgan Stanley, if you and your boss agreed on a course of action, you were in it together." But he adds, "The Dean Witter people were unable to make decisions, so they'd set you up to make the decisions, criticize you, and settle scores." The real damage, he claims, was that Edwards did not have the broad knowledge of the financial services industry necessary to run the legal department.

Many found Christine Edwards to be unfriendly and remote, and within the firm, at least on the Institutional Securities side, there was an increasing sense that she was "the strong arm of the chairman's office," as a former Morgan Stanley lawyer says. Edwards had been well regarded during her years as chief counsel at Dean Witter, but her time with Morgan Stanley after the merger was rockier, and she lasted only two years in that position. Ironically, the event that led to her departure from the firm had very little to do with her knowledge of the business, or her skill as a lawyer. In 1999, Edwards made a small, but symbolically significant, misjudgment that led her to leave the firm.

Christian Curry, a twenty-four-year-old junior analyst in the real estate department, was fired and sued the firm for bias. Curry was a graduate of Columbia University, an African-American son of a prominent surgeon. The firm had been investigating the expense vouchers he had submitted and for which he had been reimbursed. The operations officer in real estate who spot-checked the vouchers found one that read "Dinner at Cole Haan." He looked again: dinner in a shoe store? That led him to review Curry's other vouchers; he estimated that he had collected on 150 fraudulent claims, from the $300 Cole Haan shoes to car washes. A few days before the firm was preparing to fire Curry, an issue of *Playguy*, a gay porn magazine, appeared on the newsstands. Curry was featured in an eight-page story, modeling naked and aroused. (The photographs were taken before he was hired at Morgan Stanley.) Morgan Stanley fired him on April 22, 1998, a week after the pictures were published. The firm said he was terminated for padding his expense accounts, but Curry claimed he was the victim of racial discrimination. Some months earlier, a series of offensive "Black Sambo"–style e-mails had circulated within Morgan Stanley. The firm had punished the

people who circulated the e-mails, but sensitivity to issues of prejudice was high.

Even the *New York Observer*, which followed the Curry saga closely,
had trouble figuring out what happened next. A former friend of Curry's,
Charles Joseph Leuthke, twenty-nine, whom newspapers generally described as blond and blue-eyed to avoid saying that he wasn't African-
American, heard that Curry was suing Morgan Stanley and might get a
lot of money. Leuthke, who claimed that he had been in the U.S. Army
Special Forces, and made unsubstantiated assertions about other past
career experiences, got in touch with Curry, and they concocted a scheme
to plant racist messages in the Morgan Stanley computer system as a
way of providing false evidence that the firm encouraged racism.

Leuthke, evidently hoping to get a quick payoff, double-crossed
Curry by calling the Morgan Stanley legal department and a law firm
where one of the Morgan Stanley in-house counsels had worked,
to warn them of the plan. Morgan Stanley contacted the Manhattan
district attorney's office, and an undercover cop met with Curry and
Leuthke and took instructions about inserting the messages in Morgan
Stanley's internal e-mail system. Leuthke asked for a job at Morgan
Stanley as a reward for his assistance. When the firm told him that he
would have to apply through normal channels, he asked to be paid
$10,000 instead.

Christine Edwards was out of the office as the decision to pay
Leuthke was becoming firm, but it was generally understood within
the Morgan Stanley legal department that one of the department's
lawyers finally reached her before the payment was to be made and
she did not object. Later, the DA's office asked if the firm had been
the victim of extortion, and another Morgan Stanley lawyer said no,
and didn't mention the $10,000. The lawyer later said that the firm
had paid the money willingly, so that it was not viewed as extortion.
Curry was arrested and booked on five counts of felony but did not
drop his suit.

The case dragged on with a great deal of exposure in the newspapers, while Curry and Leuthke captured a little fame. On May 18,
1999, the district attorney dropped charges against Curry and opened
investigations into Morgan Stanley for not reporting the Leuthke

payment. The next day, Curry filed a wrongful termination suit for $1.35 billion.

The subject was discussed repeatedly at the management committee meetings, and before the media hype got even more out of control, Morgan Stanley settled with Curry. The settlement involved a $1 million contribution to the National Urban League, and Curry dropped his suit. Morgan Stanley claimed it didn't pay him anything, not even his legal fees, but he went on a spending spree and created the impression that he had come into a lot of money. Numbers like $54 million were tossed around, as he drove up to a stylish restaurant in a Ferrari and treated everyone in the place to Champagne. (As someone who was on the management committee at the time remarks, "Do you think you have to *buy* a Ferrari to drive one? C'mon, you can rent any car for a night.") Curry "bought" a newspaper, although it turned out that he only made a minimal down payment; he opened a nightclub in the Hamptons, which closed within a couple of months, before the summer was half over. Some years after the frenzy had died down, it came out that he had run up enormous debts, coasting on the inference that Morgan Stanley had secretly paid him millions. His parents sued him because he had used their house in the Hamptons as collateral for a loan.

Christine Edwards resigned on June 10, 1999, after two years at Morgan Stanley. She returned to Chicago and went to work for ABN AMRO, North America. After that, she was hired as executive vice president and chief legal officer of Bank One Corporation, with a five-hundred-person law department under her. In 2003, she became a partner at Winston & Strawn, a Chicago law firm.

In July 1999, the New York district attorney criticized Morgan Stanley for its "poor judgment" but determined that the firm had not broken any laws. Purcell replaced Edwards with Donald Kempf, senior partner of Kirkland and Ellis in Chicago. Kempf was so deeply admired at his firm that when he left to go to Morgan Stanley, his partners named a boardroom after him. A former Morgan Stanley lawyer says, "He brought the attitude of a very tough commercial litigator. Kirkland and Ellis is one of the titans of the Midwest bar. They try major cases, and actually go to trial. The New York bar, firms like Davis Polk or Cravath prefer to settle rather than risk a trial." Even though Kempf's aggressive advocacy was at times effective, many within the firm believed that his tactics led to unnecessary or protracted disputes with regulators. As an investment banker remarks, "Don became known by Morgan Stanley people as a general in search of a war."

The other discrimination case that blistered Morgan Stanley was brought by a former convertible bond salesperson, Allison K. Schieffelin, who filed a discrimination complaint with the U.S. Equal Opportunity Commission in 1998 on behalf of female employees at the firm. Schieffelin, who was earning about $1 million a year, claimed that she hadn't been promoted to managing director because of her gender. The EEOC took Morgan Stanley to court on September 10, 2001. (The EEOC's New York office was destroyed the next day in the attack on the World Trade Center, but the case was resumed in 2002.) As the complaint was pending, Schieffelin continued to work at Morgan Stanley, but people in her group complained that she was making life at the office "hell," as an executive who was on the management committee recalls. He speculates, "She thought she was untouchable because she was suing Morgan Stanley and she wanted to provoke the firm to fire her." The atmosphere had become so difficult that a group of her colleagues went to Human Resources and said if she didn't leave, they would all quit. After many difficult management committee sessions, at which the case was discussed, Schieffelin was fired in October 2000. The Schieffelin case was not concluded until July 2004, at the beginning of another "season in hell" for Purcell.

Later that summer, a California-based banking analyst forgot to take a list of his illegal trades out of the copying machine and was fired for insider trading. Then, in New York, another analyst followed Curry's example and filed a racial discrimination suit for $35 million.

Morgan Stanley hit the news again in September when an administrative assistant, Elena Drill, and a boyfriend were found dead in her apartment, in a murder-suicide. Drill, a Russian emigré and former model, had been having an office affair with Morgan Stanley managing director Robert Kitts, who had a notorious temper problem. The preceding winter he was at an informal Morgan Stanley dinner when he got into a fight with a subordinate and bit his ear. Morgan

Stanley censured Kitts for his behavior and insisted he apologize to his entire business unit and commit to end his affair with Drill—who, not incidentally, had made a marriage of convenience to a man on the trading floor to get a green card. When Kitts continued their relationship, the firm fired him and did not promote her. She told the Human Resources department that she had been sexually harassed. After her death, detectives came to the Morgan Stanley office and asked to see a picture of Kitts because the man who died with Drill had no identification; they looked at Kitts's photograph and said, "No, that's not him."

The problem wasn't that a firm with more than 50,000 employees neglected to screen out a few cases of human frailty, but that by failing to recognize and handle potentially embarrassing situations early, leadership had lost its focus on Morgan Stanley's most important asset: its people.

John Mack had been fighting the battle against Purcell on his own. One member of the management committee says, "John wanted to protect us from the shit storm," and for the most part, Mack and Purcell were able to mask the extent to which they were at odds. One of Mack's colleagues who rode to work with him most days did notice that while Mack was usually on the car phone, Purcell was rarely on the other end. As the leadership clash intensified, Mack's boiling point got lower. At one management committee meeting he began by saying, "This merger isn't working. We disagree on virtually everything. Maybe one of us should leave." Purcell broke the silence that followed by asking what the committee thought they should do. One member recalls that Joe Perella said, "You're asking us? The two of you have to work this out." Another member of the committee said, "John, *you* can't leave; it would be a disaster for the firm." People who were there recall the moment vividly; one of them says, "It was embarrassing. The tension was so thick you could cut it with a knife."

At another meeting, a management committee member recalls, "people began to express the view that Retail didn't have the standing in its space that other parts of our business did. It was a chance for Phil to tell us what he thought, and for us to find out what was in his head." Instead, two Dean Witter executives jumped in to defend Purcell. They "got belligerent, attacking the Morgan Stanley people, saying, 'How can you guys bring up these issues? You don't know anything about the retail business.' Voices were raised, people got tense and emotional, and the chance for a productive dialogue was lost. Morgan Stanley was run on the belief that it is better to debate an issue without resolving it than resolve an issue without debating it, but Purcell just didn't get it." There were other occasions when strife burst out in the management committee meetings. One member of the committee remembers a discussion when someone said, "We're obviously on different wavelengths about how we define success. There's something wrong if we can't resolve these differences of opinion on strategic aspirations: What do we want to be? How do we define success?" That too led to acrimony.

As the discord on the thirty-ninth floor became more obvious, the firm held a meeting for senior executives in Coral Gables, Florida. In one of the "games" organized to build relationships and improve communications, the group broke up into ten teams at tables of eight. Each team was given a flip chart and asked to make lists of things that didn't work at Morgan Stanley, and why. Purcell went off to make phone calls and returned in time to hear the results. All of the teams came to the same conclusion: there was a failure of leadership at every level, including the top. That evening, one of the executives remarked to Purcell that the exercise was "fascinating." Purcell's response was, "That was a terrible idea," and said he had been set up. "C'mon," the executive said. "Nobody gamed this. Ten teams are telling us something. The employees believe we have a crisis of leadership, and leadership is in denial."

Purcell's experience as a management consultant must have prepared him to expect that some clients will "welcome the bringers of change as white knights riding to the rescue; others will see McKinsey as an invading army to either flee or drive out ... As one former McKinsey-ite put it, 'It was a rare engagement when there wasn't at least one sector of the client organization that did not want us there, and did not want us to come up with a real answer.'" Yet, in the past, when there were difficult strategic and human transitions at Morgan Stanley, there was always a leader who stepped forward. Henry Morgan, Bill Black, Parker Gilbert, and Dick Fisher all had to moderate between factions and individuals. But until Purcell came along, every head of the firm for nearly three-quarters of a century had grown up in the Morgan culture.

Six

"AXE MAN"

2000–2003

In 2000, Phil Purcell was working on another plan to restructure the firm, an exercise that Bob Scott called an annual summer event. He had already taken Asset Management away from Mack; now he removed Retail from his purview, left him with Investment Banking, and added Discover to his responsibilities. Reportedly, Purcell's rationale was that Mack "needed to run a consumer business" before he took over as CEO.

Around that time, Mack says he came close to leaving. His dissatisfaction was so apparent that two of the directors, Dan Burke, who had been on the old Morgan Stanley board, and Michael Miles asked him to have lunch with them to discuss how to mend the situation. Before that happened, Purcell spoke to Mack about the succession issue, saying, "Let's change something. I know you're unhappy. I'll step down. Let's do it at such-and-such a date." When Mack went back to Purcell to talk about timing, Purcell claimed he'd said, "at some time."

The Institutional Securities team that Fisher and Mack had carefully put in place before the merger was being decimated. Kenneth deRegt, head of the bond business; Dwight Sipprelle, cohead of junk bonds; and James Allwin, Head of Asset Management, were gone. Alan Goldberg, Head of Private Equity, left, and Purcell ultimately off-loaded Private Equity. As one executive observed, "Some people left because they felt constrained by Phil's timidity about risk. And with the serial evolution of other people getting shot, there was more focus on not taking risk." One managing director said, "Phil probably really believed we were a bunch of cowboys. It was fine when you were making money, but he didn't understand how it was made"—or lost.

After Purcell denied that he had set a date with Mack to turn over the CEO job, Mack had been edging toward the exit. In late 2000, he took his two sons, who were in their early twenties, and a friend and former colleague, Thomas R. Nides, who was now working in Washington, D.C., to dinner in a restaurant. He told them he was seriously considering leaving the firm where he had worked for nearly three decades, which he had helped to build, and which had made him rich, powerful, and happy. But, as he said, "we did a merger and we didn't do a merger."

Nides remembers, "John asked each of the boys how they felt about his leaving Morgan Stanley. He really cared about what they said. I went home to my wife and said I hope when I make big personal decisions I have that kind of relationship with my kids. It was grueling. Very few people, and none that I know of, would have picked up their bags and left."

Mack told Purcell that he was planning to resign in January, and Purcell proposed that they decide on the terms quickly to expedite his departure. Dick Fisher was deeply distressed about the actual and public relations consequences of losing one of the most effective and best-known leaders on Wall Street, and of leaving the firm solely in Purcell's hands. Fisher went to see Purcell, warned him that losing Mack would damage the firm, and asked him to reconsider. Mack later believed that nobody except Fisher stood up for him, but other important figures in the firm also intervened on his behalf. As one of them said, "John always had people thinking about him, but he made it very clear that what was done was done. He wasn't out there saying to Dick, To hell with these guys, let's figure out a way to fight back."

Purcell was adamant about accepting Mack's resignation, and Fisher, who was undergoing treatments for cancer and was no longer a director, asked to talk to the board. As Fisher and others from the Morgan Stanley side had left the board, Purcell had replaced them with people who shared his management style and corporate philosophy. In addition to the four directors he brought with him from Dean Witter, he had added Charles F. Knight in 1999. Knight, the chairman emeritus of St. Louis–based Emerson (formerly Emerson Electric), which was a supplier to Sears, brought the Midwest contingent up to seven out of eleven. Knight had a tremendous résumé: he had been chairman of Emerson since 1974 and CEO from 1973 to 2000; the company had had forty-one consecutive years of increased earnings and forty-two consecutive years of increased dividends, twenty-seven of them under his stewardship. Like most of the directors Purcell chose, he was a suitable candidate for the board of a major public company, but like them, he was steeped in industrial corporate management and disregarded the differences between a manufacturing business and one that was entirely dependent on talent. Purcell's board was now dominated by confident, powerful individuals, who were out of touch with Morgan Stanley's core businesses. John W. Madigan, chairman, president, and CEO of the Chicago Tribune Company, had joined the board in 1999; Madigan was another Chicago powerhouse, and an Irish Catholic. The gradual rebalancing of directors had an effect that was like the frog-in-hot-water experiment, in which a frog is placed in a tank of room-temperature water that is gradually heated up, with the frog feeling incrementally more uncomfortable until he is finally boiled. Only two directors were left from the Morgan Stanley side: Robert Bauman, the former CEO of SmithKline Beecham, and Laura Tyson.

As the directors met to discuss Mack's fate, Fisher waited outside the boardroom on a chair in the hall; he decided to be on the spot, so no one could use the excuse that, weakened as he was from the cancer treatments, it was too difficult for him to make his way to the meeting. He wanted to be sure they realized that he wasn't just making a case for Mack out of personal loyalty, but that if Mack left, an element of charisma and morale would leave with him, and those qualities would be difficult to replace. These were qualities that Fisher honored and admired, and they were qualities that he felt had always been a part of the legacy of Morgan Stanley's leadership style.

Fisher was determined to wait it out, and he sat in the hall for some time, while, on the other side of the door, the directors were considering how to handle Mack's resignation. At last Purcell emerged and told him that the directors weren't willing to see him. When people at the firm heard that Fisher had been left to sit in the hall and was turned away, they saw it as a sign of such discourtesy, disrespect, and arrogance that it seemed surreal, and the story was repeated over and over. Purcell was either oblivious to the damage a gesture of such incivility did to morale—and to him—or he didn't care.

Later in 2001 John E. Jacob, the African-American executive vice president of global communications at Anheuser-Busch, was added to the board. Now seven of the nine independent directors (plus Purcell) were from the Midwest, and there still wasn't a single director with experience in the securities or financial services industry.

On January 24, 2001, as Mack was about to announce his resignation, Purcell went to see Bob Scott. Scott recalls, "He says, 'I need you to be president and you need to accept immediately.'

"I said, 'Where's John?'

"He said, 'John's already left and he's about to either hold a press conference or issue a press release. We have to be ready to respond right now.'" Scott understood Purcell to be implying "that John was about to do something really unfriendly to the firm.

"I said to Phil, 'Normally this would require some conversation, but if you're telling me that you and the board need to do something right this instant, I'll say okay.'

"He said, 'Good,' and then told me, 'I'm going to make Steve [Crawford] CFO.' Purcell just did it and people began shaking their heads. Usually decisions of that magnitude would be discussed before they were made."

Mack publicly announced that he was leaving Morgan Stanley that afternoon. He told the press, "There's no anger here . . . There's nothing better than doing what's right." That day, the stock traded down from $84.25 to $81.69, and it was understood that some big institutional investors sold when they heard he was leaving. Those who criticize John Mack say that he made two major mistakes: the first was handing Purcell the leadership of the firm; the other was leaving.

The firm issued a press release that night, announcing the Bob Scott appointment. Scott should have been a good number two for Purcell. He was well liked and easy to get along with, he knew the business inside out, and, as a banker who worked closely with him says, "Scotty leaves his ego at the door, and he listens." He and Purcell had similar backgrounds: they were both brought up as Roman Catholics, although Scott no longer practiced; neither was from the Eastern Establishment, and Scott had even caddied at a golf club near Chicago, where Purcell was now a member. But Scott's mentor was Dick Fisher, who was friendly to man and beast. It didn't make sense to him that even after he became president and moved to an office close to Purcell's, he couldn't just stand in his doorway and ask if he was free, but usually had to make an appointment to see him. Purcell gave him Retail and Discover to oversee, but Purcell continued to rely on "his" people. As Scott later said, he was never really in charge.

A top equity analyst recalls, "The first time I ever met Phil Purcell was the day that Mack was thrown out. Purcell calls an analysts' luncheon meeting, and all the analysts on Wall Street come. Phil is in the middle of the table, flanked by Vikram on one side and Bob Scott on the other. I'm sitting opposite Vikram. Phil says, 'John is gone and our focus going forward now is commitment to our clients,' implying that had never been part of the Morgan Stanley culture. I'm sitting there looking at Vikram, and as he's speaking, Vikram rolls his eyes. Purcell walks out first and I go next to Vikram and I say, 'Gee, Vikram, that was always something I worried about, that the Morgan Stanley group didn't care about its clients,' and he bumps me."

Purcell flew out to the Boulders in Arizona almost immediately, for a meeting of about seventy Morgan Stanley executives. He was elated and optimistic. People who worked for him had noticed that he didn't like to hear the firm compared to Goldman Sachs, and word went around that it would be better not to mention the other firm. Now Purcell told the group at the Boulders, "To me, a great company is defined by the fact that it is not compared to its peers," and cited Disney and IBM as among the incomparables.

His confidence was misplaced: Morgan Stanley's stock was trading 25 percent below competitors, and second-quarter earnings were expected to be down 37 percent, about 9 percentage points worse than rival firms. The only way Purcell could meet his goal of making Morgan Stanley so unique it wasn't compared to any other firm—especially Goldman Sachs—might be to buy a large commercial bank, which some believe had been the plan all along. Talk around the firm that he was looking for another merger partner had already intensified when Purcell was quoted as saying, "You either allocate enough capital to bank it yourself"—referring to the capacity to lend substantial funds to

corporate clients as part of the package to secure their public offerings—
"or you buy a bank." As bank robber Willie Sutton was reported to
have said when he was asked why he went after banks, "That's where
the money is."

Mack had not signed a noncompete agreement with Morgan Stanley, and in July, he was hired as chairman and CEO of Credit
Suisse First Boston (CSFB). He still owned five million shares of Morgan Stanley stock, worth some $500 million, and CSFB was a direct
competitor, but he was restricted to selling only two million shares,
which left him as one of Morgan Stanley's largest individual shareholders.

At CSFB he knowingly took on one of Wall Street's biggest challenges. Allen D. Wheat, who preceded him as chairman, had been
fired abruptly the day before Mack's appointment was announced. First
Boston was under federal and criminal investigations. One of the high-
profile CSFB bankers, Frank Quattrone, who had worked at Morgan
Stanley with Mack, was running the technology banking unit so independently that it was said to be "a firm within a firm." CSFB was in
the process of a major reorganization that involved combining business
units, in particular Donaldson, Lufkin, Jenrette, which the bank had
bought a year earlier for $12 billion, initiating a managerial bloodbath.
As Mack put it, "There is a lot of room for improvement."

In early 2001, coincident with the time when John Mack left, Morgan Stanley dropped Dean Witter from its corporate name, and in
April, the triangle logo was announced. As a brief article about the
new symbol remarked, "Never has one small triangle meant so much
to so many." A spokesperson for the firm explained that the three
points of the triangle represented "the firm's mission of connecting
people, capital and ideas . . . three groups of constituents: clients, employees and shareholders . . . [and] points up and to the right, which . . . is
where everything good financially is supposed to go." Donald Callahan, Head of Institutional Marketing, gamely pitched in, saying, "A
triangle is sometimes called a delta and is the symbol of change." As
one former executive recalls, "It was unveiled with all this fanfare
about rebranding. It felt so phony and disconnected. You know a firm is
in trouble when management has to sell the troops."

The new logo was presented to managing directors in what some puzzled Morgan Stanley executives called "a spin job." Stephan Newhouse, who coheaded Institutional Securities with Vikram Pandit, arrived at the meeting in a suit and tie. When the last slide, an image of the triangle, went up on the screen, Newhouse unbuttoned his shirt and pulled it open to show that he was wearing a T-shirt printed with the new logo. An executive who was there said, "Everyone laughed, but it was a little uneasy. There weren't many more moments like that."

Soon after the triangle was adopted, Byron Wien produced another skit, in which he parodied the design. The ghost of J. P. Morgan says, "I hear . . . you've moved to a modern typeface from slanted Roman. And . . . I see you've invented the triangle. Isn't that a geometric cliché?"

Stephen Roach, who played Purcell in the skit, wrote and delivered the response: "Well, we started out thinking about alliterative slogans like passion, profit, and personality and leadership, leverage, and levity, but . . . the triangle . . . not just any triangle is . . . symbolic and communicative . . . a classic symbol of the perfect form. If seen as a delta, it symbolizes change and our inclination to innovate. The triangle points to the northeast—the direction of success in global finance . . . It's also a symbol of gay pride . . ."

"Morgan," in the person of Byron Wien, asks, "What does that have to do with anything?"

Purcell, as played by Roach, answers, "Nothing, but the meaning of the triangle keeps the clients baffled and our success is dependent on the confusion of our clients."

The year 2001 marked the beginning of an exceedingly difficult period for Wall Street, John Mack, Phil Purcell—and the country. The anti-Purcell war drums began beating in February, when the *New York Post* ran a full-page article illustrated with a cartoon showing a big-headed Purcell, fist clenched and tie flying, kicking two executives out the door. The title of the piece was "MORGAN'S MACHIAVELLI: As the body count rises, Phil Purcell consolidates his power." The caption read: "AXE MAN: In a recent power struggle, Purcell ousted Morgan Stanley COO and president John Mack." The story began by citing Niccolò Machiavelli, who "concluded that for a leader, it is better to be feared than loved." The reporter, Kimberly Seals, described Purcell's management style as "take-no-prisoners" and commented, "the head of every major business line [at Morgan Stanley] has changed in the last two years." She noted the firm's lower earnings and stock price, and the fact that while Morgan Stanley's legacy business, the Institutional Securities Division, brought in 75 percent of the firm's net profits, the Retail and other divisions were in the dumps. The piece ended with another Machiavelli citation, "A leader should take pains not to be hated." As Seals remarked, commenting on in-house morale, "Perhaps Purcell didn't get to that part."

That month, Morgan Stanley held a High Yield conference for one thousand institutional investors in Boca Raton, Florida, and invited former president Bill Clinton to speak. It was Clinton's first speech since leaving office in January. The fee was about $100,000. Clinton was one of the most effective presidential speakers in a century, and most of the attendees were excited to have a chance to hear him. But according to a Morgan Stanley spokesperson, some people in the Retail Division, who had not been at the conference, called to say that their clients had read about Clinton making his first postpresidential speech, and they had "expressed outrage" that Morgan Stanley had invited him to address the conference. Some even threatened to withdraw their business. Only weeks before, Clinton had used the prerogative of the president to issue some controversial pardons. The one that Wall Street found most offensive was the pardon of exiled financier Marc Rich. The Monica Lewinsky sex scandal, an indication of poor judgment, at the least, was also recent.

Purcell broke his nearly unblemished record of ignoring criticism and sent an e-mail to clients, writing that the firm "clearly made a mistake," and that he understood their "unhappiness in light of 'Mr. Clinton's personal behavior as president.'" Purcell apologized, saying that the firm should have "thought twice" about extending the invitation. Managing director Michael L. Rankowitz, the forty-three-year-old head of Morgan Stanley's junk bond division, who had made the Clinton connection, announced on February 16 that he had resigned. That was taken to be a gesture of disgust at Purcell's pusillanimous behavior, but in fact Rankowitz had made the decision prior to the conference, when he got wind that John Mack was leaving.

With Mack gone, Purcell was on his own, just as the tech-driven bear market was looking like a Kodiak. First quarter results were down all over the Street: 30 percent for Morgan Stanley, 24 percent for Lehman Brothers. Net underwriting revenues at Goldman Sachs had plummeted 36 percent. Layoffs were up, and bonuses were down. Morgan Stanley's stock had dropped from 85⅝ at the last annual meeting to $54.64, a $31 loss.

On March 22 Purcell presided over his first stockholder meeting without the encumbrance—or assistance—of Mack. He looked proud and cool and, of course, taller than almost everyone in the room, but it was, understandably, a tough day. The *Wall Street Journal* picked that morning to run a devastating page-one story. The *New York Observer* described the *Journal* piece as "laying out in withering detail, Mr. Purcell's cold-as-ice boardroom emasculation of his rival to the throne. 'You fucked me,' the *Journal* reported Mr. Mack (himself an in-fighter of legendary repute) as saying to Mr. Purcell when he learned that his jig was up." The reporter who wrote the piece commented, "Yes, he pretty much did," and noted that the annual meeting "was the time to relax and enjoy it."

Byron Wien's second skit, "The Succession Procession: A Play in One Act," was performed a few months later, in the summer of 2001. It opened with the soundtrack from *Chariots of Fire*, setting the tone for a long, arduous race that demanded superhuman endurance and skill. The main characters, played by that year's new crop of managing directors, were Purcell and a raft of possible future successors, most in their late thirties and early forties. Wien made short work of the overfifties: it didn't look as though Purcell, then fifty-eight, would be retiring until 2008, when he turned sixty-five. By then, the younger group would be ready to take charge. In Wien's skit, no one from the Dean Witter side was even considered as a possible future leader of the firm.

Wien, speaking as J. P. Morgan, tells the audience, "Succession is a key factor in the success of any investment firm and that's why I'm here." Since the merger, "almost every member of the group I talked with nine years ago has left. So I thought I would come back and meet the new people running the place."

The first question pushed the hot button of Mack's recent departure:

Wien to "Purcell": "Two weeks ago John Mack became head of Credit Suisse First Boston. What do you make of that?"

"Purcell": "It's going to be tough. They have had a culture of rape, burn, and pillage over there, so John has a lot of raping, I mean work, to do, but he's a very talented guy."

Next, "Steve Newhouse" appears onstage, and "Purcell" tells the audience that Newhouse got his job because "he was indispensable to the previous head of the securities division, Peter Karches. I recorded everything that went on in Peter's office, so I'd be glad to show you a segment." (It was no wonder executives were worried their offices might be bugged in 2005; they had been thinking that way for years.)

Later in the skit, in a back-and-forth between investment bankers, one of them asks the others to "bring me some first-class business in a first-class way." A banker proposes making a $900 million bridge loan to Sunbeam and another says, "Now you're talking. Chainsaw Al Dunlap [Sunbeam's chairman and CEO] is our kind of guy. Smart and tough as nails. A real moneymaker. This is a deal I want to do." The Sunbeam deal involved Revlon, Inc., chairman, the billionaire investor Ronald Perelman, who made Sunbeam's "Chainsaw Al" look like a butter knife. No one could have predicted the impact the Sunbeam and Perelman relationships would have on the firm, but Wien suspected the combination would not be good—and he was right.

When the MDs playing the possible future leaders in "The Succession Procession" come in, Wien lets some air out of their egos. Among his targets are Vikram Pandit, President and Chief Operating Officer of Institutional Securities, who had developed Morgan Stanley's successful hedge fund and derivatives businesses; Zoe Cruz, now Head of Foreign Exchange and Fixed Income; John Havens, Head of Institutional Equity Sales and Trading; and Terry Meguid, Head of Investment Banking. Cruz, Meguid, and Havens, who reported to Pandit, were still the Three Musketeers.

Purcell had his eye on another candidate, Steven Crawford, whom Wien did not include in the skit. Crawford and Purcell had started to work together when Crawford was a talented, young commercial bank coverage officer who knew the financial services industry very well. Purcell had been relying on people who didn't know that side of the business and asked Joe Perella if he could suggest someone to work with him. "How about giving up Steve Crawford?" Purcell asked. Perella agreed that it was fine for Crawford to move out of the division. As someone remarked, "Phil formed a chemical bond with Steve Crawford. Crawford shined his boots."

Crawford had been on the management committee since 2000, and Purcell had appointed him CFO to replace Bob Scott when Mack left and Scott became president. Crawford, a Roman Catholic family man, was a younger version of the men Purcell usually felt most comfortable with. He was a graduate of the University of Virginia, where he had played on the lacrosse team, and he was a runner and a golfer, one of the few younger executives who played golf with Purcell. With his Jim Carrey dimples, and neat haircut with a dark lock falling boyishly on his forehead, Crawford looked as though he could have been the eighth of the Purcells' boys.

He and his wife and three children lived in Bronxville, an idyllic suburb only twenty-eight minutes by train from Grand Central Station. Joseph P. Kennedy moved his family there from Boston, and John F. Kennedy went to school in Bronxville before he was sent to boarding school at Choate. Bronxville was still an attractive choice for Wall Street executives and other professionals who worked in the city. The commute was easy, the schools were good, and there were two clubs where children learned to swim and play tennis. The Crawfords belonged to the golf club, Siwanoy. Houses in Bronxville were handsome and spacious, many in the 1920s Tudor revival style. The price of a nice house could easily hit seven figures, but the Crawford family lived in what a neighbor described as a "cute little Tudor."

A Morgan Stanley observer commented that Purcell had found someone he could mentor the way he had been mentored at Sears. A colleague says that when Crawford covered the banks, he was "capable and competent, competitive and thoughtful. But when Phil pulled him up to be CFO and moved him into strategy and relied on him for discussions on financial services," he wasn't ready. And although *Institutional Investor* named him number three on its Best CFOs in America list in the Brokers & Asset Managers category, he became so clearly Purcell's acolyte that many on the Institutional Securities side at Morgan Stanley began to doubt his leadership potential. "Morgan Stanley had a culture where the partners vote on the leaders," one of his colleagues says. "There's no way in hell the partners would have voted for Steve Crawford to be the CFO. He was viewed as a 'teacher's pet' who didn't earn it on his own." As a consequence, "He got picked on," and became defensive: "He could be pretty terse."

In the skit, when "Morgan" returns to the issue of succession, he tells "Purcell," "The firm was an autocracy in my day. It ought to be a democracy today."

"Purcell": "Great idea . . . We say we have three constituencies—our employees, our clients, and our shareholders. Why don't we have each of them vote on who should be the next CEO? We could give clients votes based on the amount of business they do, employees votes based on the amount of money they make, and shareholders votes based on the number of shares they own. Future CEOs would have to spend their time reaching out to these constituencies to win their support, and that's what we want them to do anyway."

Finally, Wien gets around to Retail, the division that remains well behind its targets. An MD playing the Head of Retail tells Purcell, "You really ought to get down to the World Trade Center to see the retail brokers."

"Purcell": "Well, is there a landing strip there?"

In the light of future events, it turned out to be a macabre line.

I n 1994, Morgan Stanley had bought a building a couple of blocks away from its Times Square headquarters for the bargain price of $90 million. After the merger, John Mack had the idea of creating the most technologically sophisticated financial services building in the city, and moving the Dean Witter operations uptown from the World Trade Center, creating a "campus" in the Times Square area. On September 11, 2001, the move was six months away. The Retail Securities and Asset Management divisions were still based in the World Trade Center, where Morgan Stanley was the biggest single tenant, with 3,700 employees spread over more than twenty-two floors in two buildings.

That morning Bob Scott kissed his wife, Karen, good-bye and told her he was going downtown to the hotel across the street from the World Trade Center to speak before several hundred members of the Association of Business Economists. He had just begun his presentation at 8:46 A.M. when there was a loud noise, the room shook, and the ceiling tiles started to fall. Scott thought a bomb had gone off. Hotel employees directed the audience into the service corridor, and Scott worked his way to the lobby, which was crowded with guests, some of them fresh out of the shower and wrapped in towels. He spotted his driver, who said, "Bob, we have to get out of here right now. Something terrible happened." Outside on the street people had been injured by falling debris, cars were burning, and the air smelled of jet fuel. When they were about fifty yards away from the hotel, Scott looked up and saw a slash in the angle at the top of the tower, black smoke and flames, and millions of pieces of white paper drifting down like ticker tape.

People were still saying, "It's a small airplane," but as Scott got into his car, he saw the second plane bank, line up, and hit the second tower. "Oh, my God, that's where our people are," he said.

After the first World Trade Center bombing in 1993, Dean Witter had put an effective disaster recovery plan in place, and on September 11, most of its people got off the high floors before the second plane struck. By 9:20 A.M. Morgan Stanley's operations staff had walked twenty blocks north to a backup site and activated the systems. As Scott headed uptown to headquarters to help plan the firm's efforts to deal with the crisis, fire trucks and ambulances were racing down both sides of the West Side Highway.

At 1585 Broadway, the management committee was meeting when somebody came into the room and handed John Schaefer a note. Schaefer was Head of Retail, and his people worked at the World Trade Center. He left the meeting, which continued, and then he came back. "Something's happened down at the World Trade Center," he said. "Some kind of accident." They still thought, as many people did, that a small plane had flown into the top of one of the buildings. "I think I'm going to go down there," he said. About three minutes later, he came back in. "They're telling me they don't want me to go down. Something's very wrong."

Purcell said, "I think we should adjourn." From Purcell's office, he had a direct view of the Towers. He stood by the window, where, he later recalled, he "could see flames shooting up the north side of the building." It was a particularly devastating sight for Purcell, who had worked in the World Trade Center. As he said, "That was my home for a long time." As a symbol of his affection for the Dean Witter days, he had framed his World Trade Center identification badge and it hung on the wall in his office at 1585 Broadway.

The management committee adjourned to their 750 Seventh Avenue training center to set up emergency headquarters on a low floor. Bob Scott reached his wife, Karen, and told her that he was okay, and went over to Seventh Avenue to start planning. By 1:00 P.M. that day teams were formed based on expertise, and fell into a rhythm of working together. As Scott says, "People in a firm like this are trained to solve problems. It's one of the strengths of the firm as a whole." It took four days for the Human Resources Department to find everyone who worked in the World Trade Center. With phones out all over the city, the firm turned a Discover call center in Phoenix into a toll-free emergency hotline. The number was already posted on national television at 11:00 A.M., and by 1:30 P.M. the center had received twenty-five hundred calls.

A Morgan Stanley tie line connected New York to Chicago via London, and a managing director in Chicago dialed out from there to Washington. Scott says, "That was his job all day; playing operator." (Merrill Lynch called through Buenos Aires.) Communicating with the Federal Reserve, the New York Stock Exchange, the U.S. Treasury Department, and the City in London was critical to insure liquidity in the face of disruptions of the flow of tens of billions of dollars. Treasury was pushing to open the markets as soon as possible as a show of strength, but Morgan Stanley resisted, feeling that if they opened too quickly, they could risk having to close, which would have a worse impact on confidence in the markets. In the event, they waited three days. The equity markets could have opened earlier, but the main Verizon switch that served lower Manhattan had been atop 7 World Trade Center, and the grid wasn't back in service until Monday, September 17.

The Morgan Stanley board authorized the firm to repurchase its shares, as needed. Bob Scott told *BusinessWeek*'s Emily Thornton, "We thought it was important to remind the market that we had the ability to do that. We had a very substantial authorization from our board that we could use, if, in our opinion, the market pushed our stock down below what we thought was fair value." Thornton asked if there was an element of patriotism in the decision, and Scott replied that, like many other companies, Morgan Stanley was "helping to give confidence to the markets that there would be liquidity . . . to tell people that this was traumatic, but basically, we still have the strongest economy in the world." He added that the firm also "made more capital available where the events created some sort of liquidity problem for clients."

On September 12, Purcell, Scott, and the heads of all the major divisions broadcast a message to the Morgan Stanley workforce and put out a portion of the webcast in a press release, with a video excerpt for the broadcast media. The message was, "This is a human tragedy, not a financial one." Scott later told an audience of one thousand at Harvard Business School, "Communication was the most important thing we did. People need specific information to make decisions and [to feel] safe and connected." The firm took out a full-page ad in the September 13 issue of the *Wall Street Journal*, reassuring clients that the business was stable.

Friday night, Karen Scott called Bob at the office and said, "Just come home. I'll cook dinner." He said, "Save the dinner. We're going to have dinner with Phil." They went to Craft, the successful restaurant Scott had invested in, and Purcell brought two of his sons. It was one of the few times anyone from the firm in New York had met part of Purcell's family. As Scott recalls, Purcell "said that September 11 marked the end of the merger between Morgan Stanley and Dean Witter. We were more of a single firm after having been in the foxhole together."

The following week, Morgan Stanley held a memorial service at St. Patrick's Cathedral for the thirteen individuals from the firm, seven employees and six outside contractors, who were killed in the attack. Most of them had died trying to help others get out of the building. All the employees were invited, and the service was held by a priest, a rabbi, and a Muslim cleric; and Purcell and several employees who survived the attack spoke.

Later, when Purcell met with the Advisory Directors, he told them that the merger issues were behind them, and that 9/11 had brought the nation and the firm together. As one Advisory Director recalls, Purcell said, "Some good comes out of everything. We worked together like we've never worked before; we have a new respect for each other. It's one firm now."

After September 11 the skyline seen from the offices at 1585 Broadway was noticeably missing the iconic World Trade Center buildings. It was a sight that very few could look on for long.

Within weeks of the terrorist attack, Purcell decided that it was not practical to concentrate so much talent and information in the same power grid. Lehman Brothers, one of Morgan Stanley's chief competitors, had lost its offices in the World Trade Center, and its executives were working out of their homes and hotels. Purcell offered to sell the new building to Lehman, which paid $650 million, at the time the record per-square-foot price for any office building in Manhattan. Lehman took over the electronic display Morgan Stanley had been planning and programmed it to spell out its name in type a couple of stories high, along with the motto "Where vision gets built." The images that followed—the sea, the mountains, a highway, a red sunset, a field of yellow flowers—symbolized the good life, and the silhouetted figures briskly walking along were meant to represent Lehman's busy bankers on their way to make their clients rich.

As one of Morgan Stanley's senior analysts asks, "Does this make sense—to sell the building? Let's give our asset, our pride and joy, and hand it over to our competitors?" The analyst says, "That was typical of the kind of decisions Phil made in functional isolation."

In 2003, the firm bought the old Texaco Building next to the Mastercard offices in Purchase, New York, about a forty-five-minute drive from Midtown. The Texaco building was a vast two-story structure that had the air of a suburban high school in Anywhere, U.S.A. It had long halls, big offices, showers—and an empty feeling. The location was hardly an attraction for bright young people who wanted to live in New York, where the energy and the clients were. The Purchase location, however, was convenient to Westchester Airport, and had Purcell wanted to, he could fly from the Palwaukee airport in Illinois to the office in Purchase. As for the $650 million, the analyst wonders, "How did we redeploy the capital from the sale?"

The sense of teamwork and shared humanity forged on September 11 did not last. At Morgan Stanley solidarity was traditionally maintained

through debate and disagreement. Constructive, but often heated arguments were a characteristic of the meetings of the Strategic Engagements Group, which Terry Meguid set up and Joe Perella chaired. A
senior banker, who says, "Debate drives better decisions," recalls that
one weekend, she was on a conference call with members of the Strategic
Engagements Group, and in the midst of a typically sharp discussion,
someone on the call said, "This group has never agreed on anything.
One thing Phil has done for us, he's given us something to be in violent
agreement about." The banker adds, "There was a sense that the way
you did well was to have a lot of people reporting to you, and say yes to
Phil." What Purcell saw as confrontation, others saw as a dialogue that
led to respect for different opinions, and often to a more fully-thought-
out approach. Purcell could not embrace the Morgan Stanley way, and he
viewed it as disruptive to the chain of command.

The market was in bad shape after the technology bust, and the
terrorist attack was likely to exacerbate the problems. Instead, the
market briefly recovered but took another major blow from the corporate and accounting scandals at Enron, Arthur Andersen, and World-
Com, which created an environment of distrust and caused investors to
back away. In 2000, Wall Street's securities firms showed $21 billion in
pretax profits; in 2001, it was down to $10.4 billion. The stock market
lost 23 percent of its value in 2001; investors in American stocks had
lost $6.5 trillion in value in one year.

Predictably, there was a backlash. The public responded to the technology crash by blaming Wall Street, echoing the allegations that had
led to the Pecora hearings during the Great Depression. At issue was
whether securities industry analysts had knowingly pumped up flimsy
tech stocks to boost business. Lawsuits began to proliferate; the most
disturbing for Morgan Stanley was an investors' suit against the firm
and analyst Mary Meeker, accusing her and the firm of hyping research to bring in business.

Meeker, who looked like a wholesome college girl with her short
stick-straight light brown hair, and straightforward manner, was a
Wall Street celebrity, known as the "Queen of the Net" because of her
early recognition of the potential of Internet connectivity and her record for picking companies that became hugely successful. Like Purcell, she was a midwesterner, born and brought up in Portland, Indiana

(population in 2000: 6,437). She graduated from DePauw University in 1981 with a degree in psychology, took a job as a stockbroker at Merrill Lynch, then went back to school and received her M.B.A. in finance from Cornell.

In 1989 Meeker joined Morgan Stanley as an analyst in the PC Software/Hardware and New Media field. She was the research analyst for the 1995 Netscape IPO, on which Morgan Stanley was the lead manager, and she and analyst Chris DePuy wrote the landmark *Internet Report*, published by Morgan Stanley. Among Meeker's picks were Microsoft, Amazon.com, Google, Yahoo, Intuit, and eBay. In 1999, Morgan Stanley's Equity Research Team was ranked number one by *Institutional Investor*, with Meeker herself in first place for Internet and new media; and number three for PC software. Over a thirteen-year period, between 1993 and 2005, her picks had an average annual return of 46 percent, and from 1993 to 1997, the average annual return was 67 percent. "Of course," Meeker says, "past performance is not a predictor of future results," and in 2000, her positive-rated stocks were down 53 percent—she had stuck with them for too long. When the SEC investigated alleged fraud after the tech bubble burst, Meeker was singled out. The low point of her career came in May 2001 when she was featured on the cover of *Fortune* magazine with the cover line "Can We Ever Trust Wall Street Again?"

That August, Meeker and Morgan Stanley were redeemed when Judge Milton Pollack of the Southern District of New York presided over a class action suit that alleged that Meeker and the firm had artificially hyped their research, and that investors had lost money because they bought stocks in companies about which she wrote positive reports. Judger Pollack, who was ninety-six years old, and had only stopped taking the subway to work a year earlier, was the third-oldest active judge on the federal bench. He cut his teeth as a lawyer in the securities industry during the 1929 Crash and had a keen sense of risk and responsibility. Pollack promptly dismissed the complaint in a tone reminiscent of Harold Medina's 1954 opinion. He wrote, "The Complaint is hopelessly redundant, argumentative, and has much irrelevancy and inflammatory material," and was "in grossly bad taste." Pollack told the *Wall Street Journal* that he didn't see why he should "sit around and wait for the motions. I don't waste any time." As for Meeker,

Pollack told a Reuters reporter, the investors "don't owe her any of their profits, [yet] now they want her to take their losses."

A few days before Christmas 2002, ten major Wall Street firms agreed to a settlement with the SEC, the NASD, the New York Stock Exchange, and the New York attorney general's office in regard to research practices and alleged conflicts of interest. Purcell made the unusual decision to attend a meeting at New York Attorney General Eliot Spitzer's office. He was the only chairman and CEO there; the other firms had sent their legal representatives. Spitzer delivered a twenty-minute lecture, in which he gave the firms the option of settling immediately or being indicted under the Martin Act, which permitted prosecution for a criminal act without intent. Two days later, ten firms, including Morgan Stanley, agreed to restructure their research departments and pay a cumulative fine of $1 billion. Morgan Stanley was included among the seven firms who paid $50 million each—the largest fine, $325 million, was paid by Citigroup. Due in part to Kempf's efforts, Morgan Stanley was one of two of the eight firms that was not charged with fraud and Meeker was exonerated; however, some within the firm believed settling was a mistake. As a former senior member of the Morgan Stanley research team remarks, "The firm reluctantly agreed to settle so the whole Street could move forward. Knowledgeable observers wondered if the firm would have settled if Purcell and Kempf had had more appreciation of the way research indirectly added to the bottom line. I think Dick Fisher would have been more willing to take a hard line about things we had conviction about."

The details of the settlement were announced at the end of April 2003. The next day, Purcell addressed a conference of institutional investors attended by the media, and told the group, "I don't see anything in the settlement that will concern the retail investor about Morgan Stanley. Not one thing." As a former Morgan Stanley lawyer comments, "Phil took a victory and turned it into defeat by directing the ire of the SEC to Morgan Stanley."

William H. Donaldson, one of the founding partners of Donaldson, Lufkin & Jenrette, was the newly appointed head of the SEC, and he responded immediately with a scathing letter to Purcell, which he released to the press. Donaldson wrote that he was "deeply troubled" by Purcell's remarks, which "evidence a troubling lack of contrition." They also evidenced a lack of understanding of the rules. Under basic SEC procedure, the parties in a settlement cannot say anything to disparage the settlement, or to suggest that they were innocent of the charges.

In Morgan Stanley's 2002 Annual Report, Purcell wrote, the "institutional securities business was challenged economically by significant, industry-wide declines in the volume of equity trading, equity underwriting and merger and acquisition activity for the third year in a row." But, he added, "The corporate debt underwriting market held up better." It was, he said, "one of the few industry bright spots in 2002." Purcell noted that another bright spot was that "Vikram Pandit foresaw the margin pressures that would result from the impact of technology and decimalization of stock prices. Rather than acquire other established firms at a premium, which several of our major competitors did, we made the decision to build our own capabilities and invested significantly in technology to automate the vast majority of our NASDAQ and options trading. As a result, we were able to offer our clients the best execution at the lowest cost through our steady investment in systems rather than through large commitments of risk capital. That technology had helped increase market share in equity trading."

When markets are bad, journalists, like everyone else who follows finance, want to know who has the next good idea about how to get out of the slump. And they are curious to see who will withstand the strain and who will buckle under. Two years before the Group of Eight fired off their first letter demanding Purcell's resignation, New York Times reporters were given a brief opportunity to watch Purcell in action during a "photo op" on the trading floor. The Times noted, "It's not every day that Philip J. Purcell, Morgan Stanley's chief executive, takes a spin around his firm's sprawling trading floor . . ." and remarked that he "didn't seem completely at his ease." The "spin" was staged for the new Treasury secretary John W. Snow, who was visiting Wall Street for the first time since being appointed. The article indicated that Snow picked Morgan Stanley because the firm had "the least tarnish" from the current Wall Street problems. Snow, as the story noted, was a midwesterner. Born in Toledo, Ohio, he had been the CEO of a railroad company, and he and Purcell were both members of Augusta National Golf Club.

A few days after the Snow visit, two Times reporters interviewed

Purcell at 1585 Broadway. Their article begins by describing the scene in Purcell's office, where he stretched "back in a swivel chair . . . not at all frazzled by the financial, legal and regulatory troubles that are plaguing Morgan Stanley." Purcell was "clearly annoyed" by the pressure from regulators and plaintiffs' lawyers, and the reporters commented that while the heads of other major firms had apologized or made significant efforts to reform their practices, he opposed regulatory reforms.

The stock price was down 66.5 percent from the September 2000 peak, net income was down 15 percent in 2002, and analysts who were pessimistic about the firm's direction warned that the brokerage operation was a losing proposition. Business was bad enough that the board cut Purcell's compensation by 27 percent for 2002 to $11 million, as compared with $15 million for 2001.

The authors of the *Times* story compared Purcell, who had never worked as a broker, trader, salesman, investment banker, or investment manager and rarely visited the trading floor, with John Mack. They called Jim Higgins, who had left the firm a year earlier, and Higgins rose to Purcell's defense. "Phil is different," he said. "He didn't claw his way up the Wall Street ladder." That was true; Ed Telling handed Purcell the Dean Witter job. It was up to others to decide whether he found his way to the top of Morgan Stanley by tooth, claw, or by some gentler manner.

The *Times* story notes that the internal strategic planning staff that Purcell established when Dean Witter went public in 1993 to look at merger and acquisition opportunities was still in force and there was speculation that two candidates were American Express and Bank One. With the firm's performance lagging, it appeared that Purcell was looking for a "Hail Mary pass" in the form of a major merger.

When the authors asked Purcell if he was thinking of retiring early, they wrote, he "remains unfazed, despite the investigations, all the pending lawsuits and the poor prospects for a rebound in Morgan Stanley's main businesses." The story ends as it began, with Purcell leaning back in his chair, "grinning."

Purcell did not seem worried about his job, but he couldn't ignore the fact that the businesses remained at odds, and Retail brokerage and Asset Management were still performing below Morgan

Stanley standards. He was overseeing the disintegration of areas where Morgan Stanley had broken new ground in the past. As one banker says, "We were the first group on Wall Street to have a financial sponsor group. Phil reduced the financial sponsor coverage team, when other firms were growing that business. Phil starved leveraged finance, when others were growing. We were the first in private equity; he threw people overboard who had been at Morgan Stanley forever and spun it out. We were always a place of innovation. In 1990, there were five funds with more than $1 billion, and Morgan Stanley was one of them, the only investment bank in the top five."

Purcell called in Lowell Bryan, a senior partner at McKinsey and Co. who had worked for Purcell in the past. In the summer of 2003, Bryan developed yet another plan to reorganize the firm. Bob Scott recalls his proposal had some "interesting conversation pieces about different ways of organizing business activities or cross-business functions. But it was abstract. How do you really do it? Got pretty convoluted." Late that summer, Purcell held a meeting to discuss the proposed reorganization, and just after Labor Day, he asked Scott to have dinner with him in one of the Morgan Stanley private dining rooms on the forty-first floor. Purcell told Scott that the firm needed to be more client focused and that he wanted to involve the most senior people in the effort. He proposed to create "client relationship managers," or CRMs, who could guide clients through the firm, make the right introductions, and be sure they had access to all the services the firm could provide.

"So he gets to the point of saying, 'This is something for you,'" Scott says. "'You're great with clients, and we need somebody at a very senior level to send out the message that this is very important, that there is just one silo. Now, the heads of silos see it as "their client" and they're not willing to cooperate. You should become the sponsor of this initiative.' The conversation got esoteric about vertical and horizontal forms—'consultant speak'—but 'Bottom line,' Phil says, 'you're the guy. You're the president of the firm. Somebody very senior has to lead this, or we won't get people to cooperate.'"

Scott said that was fine with him; the firm needed to integrate its businesses.

On the Monday before the September board meeting, Purcell came into Scott's office and showed him a three- or four-page color chart. "It shows this horizontal organization, and hanging off the left side: 'client initiative.' He kinda flipped it in front of me for a second and told me I was going to be the guy responsible for this and potentially some other horizontal area of the firm. Then he left. I look at the chart, and nobody but my secretary reports to me."

The directors met for dinner in a restaurant that night, and while they talked about the initiative, Scott says, "I let this thing sink in a little. I'm at the end of this organization chart and Phil has set it up so everyone reports to him." The next day he made an appointment to see Purcell before the board meeting. "The way this was presented, I've got huge problems. I'm not COO anymore," he said.

"Yeah, that's right," Purcell said.

"I said, I thought this was something I'd do on top of these other things. You didn't make it clear that wasn't what you had in mind. Phil, as I look at this chart, you're chopping me off at the knees. If that's what you want to do, why don't you say it?"

Purcell denied that was his intention, but Scott persisted. "As I look at this thing, I have been working at the firm for thirty-three years, and been president and COO and now you give me a staff job. That's not for me." A few days later, at a management committee meeting, Scott asked Purcell if he removed him as president "and made me a staff guy, why would people who run big businesses [within Morgan Stanley] listen to me? 'This is set up to fail. Phil, if you're trying to fire me, stop going through this subterfuge.'

"I arrange another meeting with Phil and I say, in order to move this conversation along, you've made a proposal. As proposed, I will not do that. And he, that quickly, snaps fast, 'I guess you're going to leave.'

"That isn't what I've been thinking about, but if you're telling me I should, I guess I'd better," Scott said.

That afternoon Scott was on his way to Rhode Island to speak at a conference. "Ten minutes after I get in the car, the telephone rings. It's Purcell. He said, 'I just want to make it clear here that you're going to resign.'" Scott wasn't alone in the car, he said yes and got off the phone.

According to people familiar with the situation, shortly after Purcell talked to Scott, he went to see Joe Perella. He told him, "I asked Bob Scott to do a new job." When he explained what it was, Perella said, "Scotty would never take that job."

Purcell said, "You're very prescient. He's leaving the firm."

Perella was reported to have shot back, "Well, Phil, there goes your succession plan. Why'd you do that? Scotty's highly respected, he never lets ego get in the way."

When Scott announced he was retiring after thirty-three years "to pursue other interests," a friend at the firm recalls, "it was totally bizarre. I called him and said, I want you to have lunch with me and tell me the truth. I don't understand. Why would you go quietly? Why wouldn't you leave blood on his tie?" Scott said, "It wouldn't be good for the firm, and it wouldn't work, anyway."

In late 2003 Scott became an Advisory Director and moved over to "Jurassic Park" at 1221 Avenue of the Americas. He was the last of the future Group of Eight to leave as an active executive.

The firm did not give a dinner for Dick Fisher when he retired, perhaps because of the focus on the merger at the time. That never felt right, and "Scotty's" friends and supporters wanted to be sure they didn't repeat the mistake. Word went around that Perella said if Morgan Stanley didn't host the dinner, he'd pay for it himself. That wasn't necessary; the firm held a dinner honoring Scott for about 150 guests in the magnificent glass pyramid of the Temple of Dendur in the Egyptian Wing of the Metropolitan Museum of Art. As one banker recalls, "It was one of the early events that was part of the sense of the old Morgan Stanley coming back together. There had never been a retirement evening for Dick, and when Dick got up to speak, everybody stood up. We wouldn't sit down. It felt like a ten-minute standing ovation. People were saying 'We love you, Dick.'" Jeanne Fisher recalls, "It went on and on. Dick was incredibly touched." One of the bankers who was there that night says that when Purcell followed Fisher, "he tried to be humorous, he said something about Scotty being the smartest guy and he always made you feel like he knew he was the smartest guy. That got a really chilly response. Then Bob got up and was in tears. A lot of us were." The guests looked at what they'd had, and what they were left with, and they couldn't understand how it had happened.

The year ended with another media slam for Purcell. Gretchen Morgenson, who wrote an annual wrap-up of the year's business screwups for the *New York Times*, awarded what she called the Augustus Melmotte Memorial Prizes, "named for the schemer at the heart of Anthony Trollope's brilliant Victorian novel *The Way We Live Now*. Mr. Melmotte, a financier who reached the heights of London society by standing on his wallet, crashed when he was discovered to be a swindler," Morgenson wrote. Not all of the 2003 "winners" were swindlers; some had just overreached. Purcell won two of the awards. The first was the "Mea Culpa Is Me Award," because he had to apologize twice in 2003, once to Bill Donaldson for commenting publicly that the SEC findings about research conflicts of interest weren't serious; and again when Morgan Stanley settled with regulators over compensating brokers for pushing mutual funds that paid them higher commissions. His second citation was for "The Will They Ever Get It Award," because Morgan Stanley was stonewalling the NASD, at a cost of $10,000 a day, failing to produce documents that related to an investor suit over mutual funds. Morgenson noted that Purcell may have stumbled, but he hadn't fallen. The board had awarded him $4.1 million in restricted stock, 35 percent more than he received for 2002.

It could have been worse; Morgenson awarded Donald J. Carty, former chairman of AMR, which owned American Airlines, the "Most Tone-Deaf Executive Award." AMR, which was struggling to keep the airline out of bankruptcy, was negotiating wage and benefit reductions for its employees, when it was revealed that the board had paid large retention bonuses to some senior executives and had "set aside $41 million to protect the pensions of forty-five executives, including Mr. Carty." Philip Purcell and Edward Brennan were members of the AMR board.

Purcell chose Stephan Newhouse to replace Bob Scott as president. Newhouse, fifty-six, was a graduate of Yale University and Harvard Business School and a twenty-six-year veteran of the firm. He was based in London, where he rode to work on a motorcycle when he wasn't going somewhere on a plane. Between 2000 and 2002, Newhouse visited more than twenty countries. He knew and was trusted by clients worldwide. In the 2002 Annual Report, Purcell described him as "instrumental in forging the renewed focus on relationship that has enabled us to lead transactions with clients such as China Telecom, Lukoil, Ericsson and HSBC." Newhouse's most important role was to do what Purcell was reluctant to do—travel the world for the firm. Purcell didn't want a copilot from the Morgan Stanley side seated in the cockpit with him, and Newhouse was not appointed to the board, a distinct change in policy. Before and after the merger, the president of the firm had always been a member of the Morgan Stanley board of directors. Newhouse had one strike against him: he had worked closely with Purcell's nemesis, Peter Karches, and he and Karches were good friends.

With Mack, Scott, and Karches gone, other talented bankers seeped out to competitors and hedge funds, money machines that were hard to resist. Morgan Stanley's stock was down from more than $110 a share at its height to the mid-50s, and had dipped into the 30s. The depressed stock price was a disincentive to stay at Morgan Stanley for executives who received part of their bonuses in stock or options. In particular, many in Institutional Securities who were doing well expected the value of their shares to reflect their efforts.

In the tough, competitive world of modern finance, a dawdling stock price made everyone look bad, and a Purcell appointee who worked for the firm believes that the stock was at the root of the 2005 mutiny. "The idea that people were fighting for the soul of Morgan Stanley is, quite simply, ridiculous," he says. "I don't doubt that some members of the Group of Eight believed it. They loved the idea of the old Morgan Stanley, perhaps because it was part of their concept of themselves—but it didn't exist."

Now that Purcell was on his third president, the board was beginning to focus on succession. As one director said, "It was a basic problem with the departure of John [Mack] and then Bob Scott. Vikram [Pandit] was the obvious successor, but not everyone on the board was in tune," and because of Purcell's insistence on maintaining

distance between the directors and the senior managers, most of the
board members had little or no contact with a possible successor. On
the rare occasions when the executives were invited to board meetings, they made closely edited presentations. But they weren't asked
to stay for questions, and they were expected to leave when they were
done. John Havens, as Head of Equities, was never invited to a board
meeting in five years. Terry Meguid, Head of Investment Banking,
was invited to make a presentation once; he called it "twenty minutes; twelve slides." When Mayree Clark, Global Head of Research,
was asked to make a presentation to the board, it was highly scripted
and preapproved by Donald Kempf. She says, "It was definitely a
managed situation." The directors didn't circulate in the world of finance and made no effort to interact with the heads of the firm's
business units. "Phil saw that there was no interaction, and they
didn't demand it," a division head says. "The directors were paid
$300,000 a year; they flew in to the meetings, went up and down in
the elevator, and never went to the trading floor, or talked to managers and asked them what they were doing and what they worried
about at night."

As Purcell continued to draw away from all but a few close advisors,
fear, paranoia, and disappointment dimmed the sense that the firm
was the home of the best and the brightest. Morgan Stanley without
attitude wouldn't be different from other major Wall Street firms. If
something didn't change, there would not be any particular reason for
the smartest investment bankers to work there, rather than at Goldman Sachs, Lehman Brothers, or Merrill Lynch. "The essence of the
situation was that Morgan Stanley no longer felt like a meritocracy,"
one senior analyst says. Purcell's regime became known as "the culture of NO."

On June 24, 2004, the Credit Suisse Group declined to renew John
Mack's contract as co-CEO, a position he shared with the bank's
Zurich-based Swiss executive, Oswald J. Grübel. When Mack joined
the bank in 2002, it had shown a $1.2 billion loss; it was now operating
in the black. The federal and regulatory investigations had been resolved; Mack had hired Gary Lynch, who had been head of enforcement at the SEC, and settled the claims against the bank for $100

million. Mack and the bank's Swiss officers parted ways when he indicated that he was interested in pursuing a merger, possibly with Deutsche Bank or Bank of America. Mack might take the summer off, but at sixty years old, he wasn't ready to retire.

Around the same time in 2004, Phil Purcell was again discussing selling Morgan Stanley to a big bank. He had less to sell than in the glory days of 2000 and 2001, when the stock was at its peak. The aspect of the business model that had worked for Dean Witter, selling proprietary mutual funds, had been undercut by regulatory oversight; Purcell had been loath to invest in developing new products; and the financial advisers were not trained well enough to sell sophisticated products to their retail clients. The firm had moved out of the merchant banking business, which Sanford Bernstein's Brad Hintz calls "an appalling decision," explaining, "For every dollar a typical investment bank puts into a merchant banking investment, it will return, on average, forty-one cents in fees over the life of that investment, and when it goes public, there are additional fees. But Purcell concluded it was a terrible business, put it under Asset Management, and got rid of the entire team." The firm had suffered some big losses: a pre-Purcell investment in an airplane leasing company led to a $2.5 billion pretax loss, and the junk bond losses amounted to nearly $2 billion more. As a senior investment banker says, "If you were a CEO with a consulting background, you'd say, shut that down."

Purcell still wanted to use Morgan Stanley as a vehicle for a bigger deal, but by the end of 2003, the banker says, "there was nobody to talk to except Wachovia, and nobody wanted to do a deal with Wachovia," a middle-market financial institution, more like Dean Witter than Morgan Stanley. "All that was left to do was to fix the business. But Phil's game was to put companies together, not manage them."

In the summer of 2004, the management committee met at the firm's Westchester headquarters. "Phil was back to pushing for a deal," one executive who was there says. "And it looked like it was Wachovia." When Purcell presented the idea to the committee, it seemed as though he was getting close to a decision. Someone remembers that Vikram Pandit said, "This reminds me of the way I deal with my children: you can have your milk in a blue glass or a red glass—but it's *still milk.*" Some of the group thought Morgan Stanley could be sold for as much as $200 a share, but not in a deal that would be "dumbing it down."

The meeting was difficult and adversarial. "Mud-slinging," one executive recalls. One member of the committee challenged Purcell's idea of a merger that would bring in more brokers. "We can't get our own brokers to improve their productivity," he said, "how are we going to take on another eight thousand?"

Purcell responded, "If we give John Schaefer another eight thousand brokers, we'll run circles around Merrill Lynch." But, as one executive later remarked, "That was like saying, he can't shoot a pistol, so let's give him a machine gun."

Defensively, Purcell said that the reason Discover and the brokerage division hadn't flourished like Institutional Securities was that the firm was way overinvested in Institutional Securities to the detriment of those other two businesses.

Someone who was there recalls that Terry Meguid said, "Are you saying if you could have done it all over again, you would not have made those investments?"

Purcell's answer was, "I didn't say that."

The tension was palpable; and it was obvious that Purcell viewed Institutional Securities as a block. "That was true," one member of the division said. "There was a lot of solidarity. It seemed as though we were steadfast." After that meeting, some of the executives on the Institutional Securities side were "really concerned," the banker said, and they talked among themselves about whether they could prevent Purcell from doing a deal they thought would be deleterious to the interests of the firm.

The firm had been close to settling the EEOC case against Morgan Stanley filed on behalf of Allison Schieffelin, in March 2003, but the talks had collapsed. Judge Richard Berman called Cari M. Dominguez, the head of the EEOC, and Purcell to court to warn them that they were perilously close to going to trial, which he felt would be a "mistake." Nevertheless, on July 12, 2004, the trial was about to start, the jury was already seated, the attorneys for the prosecution had a slide presentation ready to show in court, and if the accusations were

aired Morgan Stanley would be in the headlines for weeks. Then Judge
Berman came into court and announced that Morgan Stanley had
agreed to settle for $54 million. Purcell had negotiated the agreement
himself, taking over from general counsel Donald Kempf, and spending much of Sunday negotiating on the phone directly with Cari
Dominguez until midnight. The firm agreed to pay Schieffelin $12
million, and $40 million would be held for women who had worked
at the firm since 1995. Schieffelin was also eligible to file for part of
the $40 million, and her lawyer was talking about sums in the $33
million to $72 million range, to compensate for her claims of lost fu-
ture income.

At the end of that day in court, Don Kempf told reporters that "the
company did not think she should get any of the money. It was the
commission's decision to give $12 million to Ms. Schieffelin." He said,
"We had zero input."

It was the first case the EEOC had settled with a major securities
firm, and the second-largest settlement the EEOC had ever reached.

At the end of September, Terry Meguid, Head of Investment Banking, held a worldwide managing directors conference for three
hundred investment bankers at the Hotel Arts in Barcelona, Spain.
The Arts, which was part of the complex built for the 1992 Olympics,
was a luxuriously spare modern hotel set in gardens overlooking a blue
Mediterranean harbor and neatly docked rows of boats. The hotel had
fourteen meeting rooms, each named for a different Spanish artist,
musician, or architect, and two large ballrooms for presentations. In
addition to the breakout sessions and the talks, the firm chartered thirty-
five sailboats, chose teams, and held a race.

The first morning, everyone gathered in one of the large meeting
rooms for introductory presentations. A videotape made at the time
shows Purcell as tired, flat, and withdrawn, starting with a feeble joke
about being glad that Meguid hadn't invited "the wives." As some of
the bankers in the room were wives—or at least women—it was an
awkward beginning. Pandit is more engaging and engaged, pleasant
and substantive, but possibly nervous; he is wringing his hands as he
speaks. Meguid, who chaired the meeting, is relaxed, direct, and con-
vincing, combining quick punchy videos with a presentation about

improving performance in a tough market. Joe Perella, who shambles up to the front of the room, wearing a sweater draped around his shoulders, has the presence of a late-night talk show host delivering a serious message in an entertaining way.

Terry Meguid later said that the Barcelona conference was a turning point for the Investment Banking Division. "That conference was worth $500 million to us. People were so upbeat. We were humming."

Team-bonding games were a staple of these meetings, and one afternoon, while the bankers were running around on the lawn in color-coded team T-shirts, six members of the management committee went off to have a quiet lunch together in the hotel restaurant. They were Steve Newhouse, Vikram Pandit, John Havens, Joe Perella, Terry Meguid, and Zoe Cruz. At that point, Newhouse, Pandit, and Perella reported to Purcell; and Havens, Meguid, and Cruz reported to Pandit.

The group started by discussing Purcell's presentation, which they rated between "terrible" and "not that bad." Meguid reported that "our best bankers are dispirited." Cruz remarked, "There's nothing we can do about Phil; let's talk about our businesses." Newhouse agreed that piling on Purcell wasn't productive, but they were all concerned about the direction of the firm, in particular about Purcell's apparent eagerness to sell Morgan Stanley to a big, but not necessarily suitable, bank.

Pandit turned to Perella, the senior Mergers & Acquisitions executive, and, as it was described, said, "Joe, what do we do? Phil might try to sell us. You've got the most experience in this game. What do you think?"

"Six people can't do anything on their own," Perella was reported to have said. "He's the CEO. Only the board can make a decision about him. We work at the firm; we don't run it. The fiduciary responsibility is with the board of directors. They're his friends. They get all their information from him, and what they think of us, he tells them. My feeling, Phil's strategy for dealing with Morgan Stanley people, he's a divide-and-conquer guy. He will inevitably try and pick off someone in this group. We're the revenue-generating part of the firm. If we lock arms, there's nothing he can do."

By "locking arms," Perella was not talking about taking a stance, leading a mutiny, or approaching the board. He was advising them to avoid succumbing to any attempts Purcell might make to pit them against one another, or to split one or more of them off.

Perella was in his early sixties, but all of the others, except Newhouse, were still under fifty. "Time is on your side," he told them. "Let the clock play out. You're in the filet of your careers, in your forties; he'll retire in a couple of years." As he reminded them, there were only three ways to exercise their power as individuals: to speak up; to remain loyal to the firm and do their jobs and wait it out; or to leave. He told them to dismiss the idea that there would be a revolt. "People aren't that courageous. Sure, if you had two hundred and fifty of the top producers in the firm saying he's gotta go, the board would do it in a New York minute. Defend the fort," he said. "Don't let him divide us. He will try to drive a wedge between us and you'll have to say we're in it together for the good of the firm."

It would not be easy to hold the group together. Newhouse was based in London and traveled constantly; and while Pandit and Cruz were civil, their relationship was reaching a crisis point. Cruz claimed Pandit was too conservative about risk and was holding back her division's performance because he didn't let her put enough capital to work, during what she described as "the best credit cycle in my time." Pandit felt that if Cruz's division wasn't performing as well as she thought it could, she should take responsibility. An analyst who admired Pandit remarked, "The Vikram I know is a pretty smart risk taker, good at cross-checking. He became more conservative because he wanted to survive and be part of bringing back the old Morgan Stanley. He had two choices: take a stand against Phil that he was sure to lose, or try to do his best within the subpar constraints Phil had set."

Whatever the reason, Pandit and Cruz were at odds, and Purcell was not managing the situation. Some believed that he was pitting them against each other to maintain his own power. There had often been rivalries in the past, but someone at the head of the firm always maintained the balance. Now Purcell's entire management committee was in discord; the Dean Witter people didn't see things the way the Morgan Stanley people did; Don Kempf had his own views; Purcell and Crawford were invariably on the same team; and Cruz and Pandit were drawing further apart.

One close observer says, "If you drew a green line between people on the management committee who liked each other, and a red line between people who didn't, you'd get more red lines than green." In the early days of the merger, Morgan Stanley had developed a "vision and values" statement; 35,000 people went through a training program that was meant to impress on them that the five core values of the firm were integrity, excellence, entrepreneurial spirit, respect for individuals and cultures, and teamwork. Part of Purcell's job, one former executive says, "was to create and operate a management committee that exhibited the core values of the firm, and it was well known that wasn't working."

It was later rumored—and Purcell believed—that by late 2004 some members of the management committee were planning a mutiny, but there was no insiders' revolt. The "insurrection" of the "Inside Five"—or "Six," depending on who was speculating—never went further than some private conversations like the one in Barcelona. By believing that a group of insiders was plotting against him, Purcell would force everyone who was at lunch that day to make a choice.

Seven

THE SIEGE OF PHILIP PURCELL

October 2004–January 2005

The worst year of Phil Purcell's adult life began in the fall of 2004. Starting around Labor Day each year, the firm shifted gears, as the focus turned to evaluating people and performance and determining compensation. It was time-consuming, the stakes were high, and the atmosphere was taut. Each department head drew up a sheet nicknamed "a bedsheet," with the names of people on the left, the areas they worked in across the top, and their compensation in descending order, across from each name. The "bedsheets" were constantly being reviewed, to see how people compared with one another and how the allotted pie could be divided. Compensation at the most senior executive levels was particularly sensitive, because those figures would be published in the proxy statement.

During that tense time Purcell finally succumbed to the blandishments of *Fortune* magazine and agreed to be interviewed by reporter David Rynecki for a long piece. Purcell was so distrustful of the media that when Morgan Stanley's head of public relations suggested he might consider working with the financial reporters a little more, he said he did not talk to the press when he headed Dean Witter and he did not plan to talk to them now. She had pointed out that "nobody was interested in Dean Witter," but he dismissed the remark, and told her that the press should just work around him. He had gotten away with that when Morgan Stanley was doing well, but business had turned down, and reporters were demanding an explanation for the poor performance that was reflected in the stock price. By the time Purcell finally gave in, a "chorus of critics" wanted to know what he planned to do about the 21 percent drop in Morgan Stanley's stock since the previous March; the financial advisors in the Retail Division, who were only bringing in a little more than half of Merrill Lynch brokers' revenues; the Asset Management Division that was underperforming its peers; and of course, the profits, which were 30 percent below the high in 2000.

Rynecki was also interested in Morgan Stanley's violations of ethical and legal constraints. In 2003, the firm had been fined for giving out $1 million in "incentive" payments and gifts to its brokers to push in-house funds, and $50 million for improper mutual fund sales practices. *Registered Rep* magazine ranked Morgan Stanley the firm most likely to put pressure on brokers to sell in-house products. The $54 million EEOC fine was bad enough, but around the time the *Fortune* article appeared, a far worse legal situation had turned ugly. Ronald Perelman had filed suit against Morgan Stanley in 2003 for defrauding him when his Coleman Company bought the now-bankrupt Sunbeam Corporation, which was represented by Morgan Stanley. The suit took a disastrous turn in the fall of 2004. A week before discovery was scheduled to end, Morgan Stanley notified Perelman's counsel that some backup tapes had turned up, contravening the firm's sworn statement in June 2004 that it had searched all its backup tapes. "Some," in this case, consisted of eight thousand pages of e-mails. Judge Maass said she could hardly believe what she was hearing. Morgan Stanley was represented by Don Kempf's old firm. Judge Maass asked the Kirkland & Ellis lawyer, "Were the tapes in a corner? Was this with the dust bunnies, or where was it?"

Rynecki commented, "If Purcell has a grand strategy for fixing Morgan Stanley's woes, he continues to keep it a mystery." He added that according to one analyst, his failure to articulate a clear vision for the firm, and his inaccessibility, had "put an uncertainty discount on the stock."

Purcell met Rynecki in his office on the thirty-ninth floor at 1585 Broadway. On the bookcase were photographs of Anne Purcell, whom none of the Morgan Stanley people had ever met, seven sons, daughters-in-law, and multitudes of grandchildren. Purcell stood at his special four-foot-high desk with its Bloomberg terminal and fielded questions.

Speculation was rife that Morgan Stanley would have to merge with a large bank, that Bank of America had offered an insultingly low price, and that there were other possible candidates. American Express, which had tried to buy into Morgan Stanley in the 1970s when Harry Morgan told his partners the Morgan name wasn't for sale, was mentioned. J. P. Morgan Chase was the sentimental favorite. The idea of reuniting the House of Morgan had been broached before, in 1973, when representatives of Morgan Stanley, J. P. Morgan, Morgan Guaranty, and the British Morgan Grenfell held a top-secret meeting in Bermuda. The operation was code-named "Triangle" for the Bermuda Triangle, the mysterious funnel in the ocean into which airplanes and ships were said to disappear. The plan disappeared too. Putting the Morgan brethren together was the financial world's equivalent of the reunification of Germany, even though Morgan Stanley had always been an independent entity. But despite their shared values and history, a merger between the Morgan firms wasn't practical; there was too much duplication, which would require mass firings. When Rynecki asked Purcell about the rumors, he angrily denied them. (Rynecki wrote, "His eyes narrow, and he suddenly looks like Gary Cooper staring down a gunfighter in *High Noon*.")

To create a more relaxed atmosphere, or perhaps make the time pass more pleasantly, Purcell took Rynecki to the Winged Foot Golf Club in Westchester County. The handsome stone clubhouse reflected the taste and wealth of an earlier Wall Street, but its appeal was in its two championship courses, one of which was ranked number eight in *Golf* magazine's top one hundred. Before Purcell teed off, he and Rynecki sat outside the grille room, and Purcell pulled out folders, clippings, and e-mails, ignoring the standard rule that members and their guests are not to appear to be conducting business at a private club. The two men set out for a round of golf, with Rynecki jostling along in the cart, asking questions. Purcell, slightly loosened up by a beer, defended his strategy. (When Morgan Stanley executives read the *Fortune* story, they said, "Drinking beer on the golf course? That's not Morgan Stanley.") Purcell explained that after the 2000 crash, he had "changed" the way the Morgan Stanley investment bankers worked, and, as Rynecki wrote, "turned the deal makers into quasi-management consultants." Later, a top banker remarked, "that would have been a disaster—no, *two* disasters: first, if you think that's a good thing; and second, if you think you could actually do it."

By the end of the round, as Rynecki wrote, Purcell was understandably "tired of answering questions . . . Turning his back on the question of his future, he walked off toward the clubhouse." His parting comment, which would later be regularly repeated, was "Morgan Stanley doesn't have to do anything."

Richard Bove of Punk, Ziegel & Company reported that when his firm upgraded Morgan Stanley to a "Buy" in November, he was "a bit surprised by the intensively negative reaction to our changed rating," especially after the *Fortune* article. "Every investor we spoke with believed that this was a terrible upgrade. Not only were they incensed at the company but they were furious with its CEO, Phil Purcell." Bove commented that Purcell had failed to offer a "clear vision for the company," and that the investors believed "he had no vision." He speculated, "Purcell is vulnerable to the storm of protest that hit Mr. Eisner, the CEO of Disney."

Purcell's next public embarrassment was set in motion on November 27, 2004, the Saturday after Thanksgiving, when the University of Notre Dame's storied football team, the "Fighting Irish," lost 41–10 to Southern California, the top-ranked team in its league. On Tuesday, the university announced that it had dismissed its head coach, Tyrone Willingham, without finding a replacement. Willingham's overall record was 21–15, but his team had suffered some spectacular losses. In his three seasons, the team had lost five games by thirty-one points or more.

Willingham was one of three African-American head coaches in the 117-team Division 1-A. Notre Dame had hired him from Stanford, where he led a winning team at a time when Notre Dame had a sixteen-year run without a national title and had failed to finish in the top ten for a decade. Willingham had a 10–3 record in his first season at Notre Dame, winning eight straight games before losing to North Carolina State in the Gator Bowl. The next year, however, would be the worst season in Notre Dame's 115-year history, as the team finished 5–7, without a bowl appearance. In 2004, Notre Dame rebounded to 6–5, but the Southern California loss was disastrous. Reverend John I. Jenkins, president-elect of the university, called a meeting of seven of the trustees, including Purcell, who was chairman of the athletics committee, to discuss Willingham's future. On November 30, Willingham was dismissed. The *New York Times*, describing the job as "the most prestigious" in college football, noted that Notre Dame usually gave its head coaches longer to prove themselves.

On December 9, the *Times* ran a story headlined "Notre Dame's President Says He Opposed Firing Willingham." The Reverend Edward A. Malloy, speaking at a panel on intercollegiate athletics, said, "In my eighteen years there have only been two days that I have been embarrassed to be president of Notre Dame, Tuesday and Wednesday of last week." Citing "a strong presence of the board of trustees," he indicated that the board was acting opportunistically, creating an opening for a "messiah coach," reportedly Utah's Urban Meyer, to step into the position and save the program. (Meyer did not take the job.)

A week later, Father Jenkins told a local newspaper that he had not been pressured by the trustees and took responsibility for approving the firing, but few at Morgan Stanley saw the article, and the Willingham story rocketed around the office. As one executive says, "Another embarrassment. We thought, there he goes again."

The Notre Dame football program contributes $61 million to the university's coffers every year and is responsible for funding two thousand nonathletic scholarships, yet even so, the move was highhanded and disruptive. It is an unwritten law of governance in higher education that the trustees of a university will not intervene in administrative affairs—hiring and firing of coaches, provosts, and so on. Father Malloy, speaking of "the philosophical shift we are taking," said, "I'm not happy about it, and I do not assume responsibility for it. I think it was the wrong move." The crowd at the Intercollegiate Forum gave him a standing ovation. Gordon Gee, the chancellor of Vanderbilt, told the *Times* that Malloy's remarks were "one of the most courageous things I've heard in my twenty-four years as a university president ... What he basically said is that the value system of the university and the value system of the athletic department have been totally disrupted." Others added that the direct interference of trustees in matters of hiring and firing was an inappropriate trespass on the administration's autonomy.

Malloy didn't mention names, but the *Times* cited two trustees, the chairman of the board, and Philip Purcell.

The public chastisement by Father Malloy, leader of an institution Purcell revered, must have had a sting that the *Fortune* article couldn't match. To violate the values of Notre Dame was too close to violating the values of the church.

A round that time, employees received their reviews and were notified about their compensation. The top members of the management committee were paid so handsomely that it raised questions. Vikram Pandit received $8.1 million, as compared with his 2003 bonus of $6.8 million. Zoe Cruz was paid $7.7 million, about $150,000 less than in 2003. John Havens's bonus was $7.1 million, $1.207 million more than the preceding year's. Purcell's actual total included a 46 percent raise from $14 million to $22 million, and an additional $18 million for cashing in options granted in prior years.

While Morgan Stanley's profits were up 18 percent, that didn't compare well with its peers, and the stock was down 8.2 percent for the year, and 20 percent since March 2004. Later, when a Morgan Stanley spokesperson was queried about Purcell's pay, she asserted that his $22 million was less than the CEOs of Goldman Sachs, Bear Stearns, or Lehman Brothers received, and that Stanley O'Neal at Merrill Lynch was paid a total of $32 million.

Vikram Pandit was Zoe Cruz's evaluation director, and although each person's evaluation was compiled from comments by many employees, it was the evaluation director's responsibility to synthesize them, while protecting the confidentiality of the individuals who contributed to the total. As such reports usually did, Cruz's report included both praise and "opportunities for growth." Pandit showed her report to Purcell; after the EEOC settlement, the firm was sensitive to the possibility of creating any impression of bias. Purcell told Pandit to go ahead and show it to Cruz. When she read the criticisms she was outraged. Her Fixed Income Division had a record year in total revenues, more than double the 2002 total, reaching $6.4 billion in 2004. Cruz wrote a two-page rejoinder and sent it to Pandit. Purcell advised her to fly to London on business, and take her case to the only woman on the board, Dr. Laura Tyson, dean of the London Business School. She knew a number of senior Morgan Stanley executives, who attended some of the same conferences, in particular the prestigious World Economic Forum at Davos, Switzerland. Tyson had attended a couple of the firm's client dinners, but she and Cruz barely knew each other. The meeting gave Cruz the satisfaction of knowing that a director she believed would be fair had heard her side of the story.

The next major blow fell on December 10, 2004, when Purcell received a FedEx envelope from Scott Sipprelle, chairman of the $1 billion hedge fund Copper Arch Capital. The Copper Arch portfolio was deployed in large chunks, and during the fall of 2004, the fund had bought about one million shares of Morgan Stanley stock. Copper Arch was a client of Morgan Stanley's Prime Brokerage Division, channeling its trading relationships through the firm. Sipprelle's letter, which was sent to each member of the board, expressed his belief that the Morgan Stanley Dean Witter merger had failed, and should be dissolved.

Sipprelle had worked at Morgan Stanley for thirteen years and was head of U.S. Equity Capital Markets when he left in 1998 to start his own firm. At forty-two, he looked like a clean-cut undergraduate, casually dressed in a crewneck sweater, blue shirt, and gray flannel slacks. His Midtown Fifth Avenue office occupied two floors, connected by a broad internal staircase, a small-scale contemporary version of the investment banker's design idiom. The wood paneling was pale and fresh; the modern furniture was upholstered in quiet colors; light passed through glass walls to illuminate the offices.

Copper Arch invested in public companies that Sipprelle says have "lost their way," are undermanaged, or are pursuing an ill-founded strategy. A three- or four-person team would be assigned to identify the root causes of the company's underperformance, and determine if they thought those factors could be remedied. The team would prepare a detailed report that outlined how the firm could do a better job, maximize revenues, and gain market share. Sipprelle estimates that the same kind of report might cost $5 to $10 million if it were commissioned from a management consultant like McKinsey. If Copper Arch's findings looked promising, the firm would take a significant position in the stock, then send its report at no charge to the chairman and CEO.

In mid-2004, Sipprelle became convinced that Morgan Stanley's stock was trading at a discount, and Copper Arch prepared what Sipprelle describes as "a relatively straightforward plan for remedying the problem." The fund started buying Morgan Stanley shares in October. By early December, it held a position worth between $50 and $60 million. Sipprelle wrote a letter addressed to "Dear Phil and Directors of Morgan Stanley," informing them that Copper Arch had recently become a large shareholder. "Our investment is not predicated on a rosy view of the current structure and performance of the firm, but rather in spite of it . . . We are deeply troubled that the current stewards of the firm are blind to the root causes of this affliction," he wrote.

He proposed that the merger be unraveled, pointing out that the diversified product lines were intended to protect Morgan Stanley from hitting bottom if there was a severe dip in some of its businesses, but diversification hadn't saved the firm from suffering the pain of the market collapse during the technology crash, or helped it recover. The brokerage operation, another justification for the merger, showed only a 2 percent pretax margin in the last quarter, he added.

Sipprelle had reread the press clippings from 1997, and wrote that he was "struck by the giddiness over the scale of the business that had been created." The merger was touted as a " 'global powerhouse' with a market value vastly in excess of any other pure securities firm," and was said to have "created with the stroke of a pen the largest collection of assets under management of any securities business of the day." But seven years later, Sipprelle had concluded that scale was "the enemy of performance." The Discover card division was sailing against "competitive headwinds" and held "shrinking, sub-scale market share in a land of giants." Institutional Securities, Morgan Stanley's "crown jewel," with "the strongest brand position, the largest pool of profit potential, the best growth prospects, and the greatest opportunity for overall value creation [was] the key to Morgan Stanley's future, yet it was dragged down by ailing operations." He proposed that Morgan Stanley sell or spin off Discover and Investment Management, sell the retail brokerage business, and shrink the balance sheet. Sipprelle estimated that his prescription would increase return on equity in the core firm to a minimum of 20 percent.

He reminded the directors of the fiduciary responsibility to shareholders "that has been entrusted, temporarily" to their care, and finally warned, in bold type, "Should there be no constructive steps made toward addressing our concerns, we intend to oppose strongly the re-election of each of the Directors."

Three "Exhibits" were attached to the letter. The first showed Morgan Stanley's stock performance relative to its peers (Goldman Sachs, Merrill Lynch, J. P. Morgan, Lehman Brothers, and Bear Stearns). Since 2002, the firm had dropped to sixth out of six. The second exhibit tracked the stock performance of the diversified model relative to Goldman Sachs and Merrill Lynch. Morgan Stanley's bear market performance was −64 percent as compared with −45 percent for Goldman and −59 percent for Merrill, and its recovery had been far worse. Goldman was up 102 percent, Merrill was up 90 percent, while Morgan Stanley had recovered only 69 percent of its value. With the stock hovering in the 50s, Copper Arch estimated the breakup value at $73.65 per share.

Sipprelle would later say that he purposely avoided attacking Purcell directly. "I asked him to be the agent of change. He could have said, 'I brought part of this portfolio [Dean Witter] to the mix, and it isn't working.'" The tragedy of the events that unfolded, Sipprelle says, was the "paranoia" that his analysis set in motion. "Anybody who called the king into question was the enemy." Purcell suspected that Sipprelle, who was close to John Havens, was a stalking horse for an internal rebellion, but Sipprelle says, "I wrote the letter. It was my idea, and I was acting alone."

Sipprelle sent a copy of the letter via FedEx to each of the directors, but many of the letters were addressed in care of Morgan Stanley, and some of them were not forwarded. Sipprelle's phrase "Should there be no constructive steps made toward addressing our concerns, we intend to oppose strongly the re-election of each of the Directors" put Purcell on notice that a proxy fight could be in the offing.

On December 13, Morgan Stanley filed a notice with the SEC that Ed Brennan had rejoined the board. Brennan, soon to turn seventy-one, would only be eligible to serve for a year, as the directors' mandatory retirement age was seventy-two. Then, on December 16, Morgan Stanley disclosed in an SEC filing that it had moved up its annual meeting date to March 15, 2005. Whatever the intention, both actions would serve to support Purcell. Brennan, an old ally, could be relied upon in a fight and any proposals on policy and board nominations would have to be received by December 27, an impossible date to meet for anyone who wanted to challenge the power structure.

Purcell presented his defense of Sipprelle's criticisms at the next board meeting in early 2005. He argued that Copper Arch, as a hedge fund, was looking for share price movement in a relatively short window of time, and had a different perspective from that of the board, which looked out for the firm's long-term interests. Purcell's defense, however, did not fully address the underlying problems that led Sipprelle to take such a strong position, and certain directors saw that as a red flag.

The next blow came when Dick Fisher died, on December 16, at the age of sixty-eight, after a six-and-a-half-year battle with prostate cancer. An extraordinary number of people were genuinely grieved that he was gone. Fisher was called a modern-day Medici, a great businessman, philanthropist, and supporter of the arts. The comparisons to Purcell were inevitable; he had been described as "Morgan's Machiavelli."

The evening of Fisher's death, Purcell circulated a memo describing Fisher as "one of the legends of our industry," "a brilliant leader of our firm," and "a case study for how talent and sheer determination can yield a life of distinction." Fisher, Purcell wrote, "moved mountains by the power of his intellect rather than the force of his will." He wrote, "There are not words to adequately state Dick's importance to the success of Morgan Stanley." That might have been an opportunity to remind a dispirited organization of how far the firm had come since

Fisher became a partner in 1970. The market cap alone was impressive—from $7.5 million to $60 billion. But Purcell wasn't about to talk about the past. At that point, the history section of the Morgan Stanley Web site stated that the firm was founded in 1997, the year of the merger, and of Purcell's ascendance to the chairmanship. Other publicity materials stated that Purcell had been the chairman of Morgan Stanley for more than twenty years, rolling over Parker Gilbert and Dick Fisher, and rolling in his role at Dean Witter.

Advisory Director Dick Debs heard about Fisher's death later that morning. He and his wife, Barbara Knowles Debs, former president of Manhattanville College and of the New-York Historical Society, were holding their annual Christmas party that night at their apartment overlooking the East River. Many of their guests worked at Morgan Stanley, and others were friends of Fisher's. Debs considered calling the party off and made some phone calls, but the people he spoke to decided that they would like to be together.

Standing had been a physical strain on Fisher, and some years back he had settled himself on a couch at the Debs's Christmas party to greet whoever came over to say hello. It had come to seem natural to find him on the same couch every year. On the night he died, the couch remained empty. When most of the guests had left, many of the Morgan Stanley people stayed on, talking about the old days and the current regime, which some had begun to call "the Evil Empire." There were two other traditional Christmas parties that friends from Morgan Stanley attended each year; one at Bob and Karen Scott's and the other at Terry and Barbara Meguid's. In both of those apartments as well, Fisher had chosen a place to sit and greet friends, and at the Scotts' and Meguids' those seats too remained empty all night. Colleagues stayed late at each party, talking about Fisher and, inevitably, about Purcell.

The day after Fisher died Brad Hintz, the Sanford Bernstein analyst who had been Morgan Stanley's treasurer, sent an e-mail titled "*Ultimus Romanorum*" (the last Roman) to 1,200 clients. Hintz wrote about the afternoon Fisher died, when "ex-partners of Morgan Stanley, colleagues and competitors [called] to recount Dick Fisher stories and to mourn the passing of an era. The architect of Morgan Stanley was gone."

Fisher's death left open the position of "Wise Man." A couple of months earlier, a senior managing director went to see him to talk about putting together a group to sign a letter to the board protesting the unusual governance regulations that entrenched Purcell. She proposed that they ask the board to eliminate the 75 percent majority required to fire the CEO, and that there be greater employee representation on the board. It would have been difficult to resist a corporate governance move that had strong employee backing, but the petition never got off the ground. She says, "We could have given Phil a way to leave and maintain some dignity, privately." Fisher told her, "There must be a Morgan Stanley way of doing this." Fisher agreed they had to do something, but he was just too sick.

She considered reassuring signers of confidentiality by leaving their names off the petition and giving them to Fisher or Lewis Bernard to hold, but Fisher was only months away from death, and Bernard had his hands full. He was a director of Marsh & McLennan, the professional services company that was, among other things, the world's largest insurance broker. "Marsh Mac," as it was called, was the size of Morgan Stanley, with 55,000 employees, $12 billion in annual revenues, and its own investment division. The company had been sued in October 2004 by New York Attorney General Eliot Spitzer on allegations of price fixing, bid rigging, kickbacks, and hidden commissions. When Spitzer brought the suit, Marsh Mac's chief executive, Jeff Greenberg, resigned. Greenberg was a son of Maurice "Hank" Greenberg of AIG, whom Spitzer had also sued.

Dick Fisher died on the day that new managing directors were appointed. That evening, there was a cocktail reception to welcome them, and one of the division heads read from the introduction to a small book that the firm published in 1990, with photographs and brief bios of each of the partners, starting with Harold Stanley. The last paragraph read, "Each participant, no matter how long their involvement, has found Morgan Stanley to be a vital part of their business lives. Each individual has shared at some time the privilege and responsibility of enhancing the Firm's success. The tradition of Morgan Stanley is that the welfare and reputation of the Firm is more important than that of any of its individuals."

Jeanne Donovan Fisher had known that she might have to face this day since 1998, when Fisher's doctor called on their first anniversary and told her husband that he had prostate cancer. "He said it was 'the bad kind,' " Jeanne Fisher says. "Some bedside manner." Now she began to organize his memorial service. Purcell, who had been chairman of Morgan Stanley for nearly eight years, didn't contact Jeanne Fisher directly, but he let it be known that he would like to speak. She says, "I was determined that this not be a 'Morgan Stanley service.' It was for family and friends. I chose a friend who represented the Morgan Stanley part of Dick's life, not the firm." Bob Scott was the Morgan Stanley friend who would speak at the service.

Christmas passed, the New Year opened, and a month after Scott Sipprelle sent his letter, he still had not heard from Phil Purcell or the Morgan Stanley board. Usually, when Copper Arch sent analyses to firms in which it was interested, Sipprelle got at least an acknowledgment, and his reports often prompted action. On January 5, when he assumed that Purcell and the directors had had the letter for a month, Sipprelle, whose one million shares of MWD in his fund were trading within a couple of points of the average price at which he bought the stock, released his letter to the press.

When Purcell learned that the *Wall Street Journal* was running a story, he hastily called a management committee meeting. That was the first time the committee members had seen or heard about the letter. He asked them what they thought he should do about it. People who were there recall that Joe Perella said, "When people send a letter like this, it is usually not that they're just having a hissy fit, or getting something off their chest, then going on to something else. My view is that this is not going away." He advised Purcell to "get in the mode as though you're going into an unsolicited takeover bid. Decide who your inner council is going to be, and deal with it."

When the *Journal* article appeared, Sipprelle says, "my phone didn't stop ringing with calls from investors, journalists, and current and former employees of Morgan Stanley." He still did not receive any response from Purcell or the board.

In mid-January, Sipprelle sent out an investors' letter titled "There Is No Disinfectant Like Sunlight." Describing his "debate with the executive suite of Morgan Stanley as a David vs. Goliath kind of struggle" to persuade a "gargantuan blue chip member of the financial services elite" to change its business model, he explained why he thought the merger should be dismantled. The combination, he wrote, was born from the idea that "success flowed from mass, not from mastery," but the process "was somewhat akin to childbirth, easier to conceive than deliver."

He reminded his investors that the Morgan Stanley Retail Brokerage Division continued to underperform, the asset management business had lost market share, and the Discover card wasn't important enough in its field. Those divisions weighed down the successful securities business, which "became increasingly at risk of diminished focus, eroding morale, heightened turnover and franchise decay." The static stock price reflected that the "once-premium valuation relative to peers has collapsed to a discount."

He wrote that Copper Arch's "assessment at the time we first initiated this investment in our portfolios was that separating Morgan Stanley into its constituent pieces would not only increase value by up to 50 percent, but also deliver focus and mission clarity as each of these operations strived to address its unique challenges and opportunities." He explained that the Morgan Stanley investment wasn't an easy win, but "we feel justified in calling out hubris and misguided corporate strategy when we see it. We take seriously our role as guardians of your capital to seek fair play and efficiency in the capital markets. We have been flabbergasted, frankly, by the silence and passivity of the institutional investors who have watched this company stumble over many years without raising the alarm." Copper Arch released an eighteen-page report titled "Morgan Stanley: A Time for Change."

Sipprelle says, "A match had been touched against a pile of dry tinder." Soon after the report was released, he got a call from Steven Crawford, who was now chief strategic and administrative officer, reporting directly to Purcell.

"Steve said, 'We haven't been in touch for a while. Why don't you come over and let's talk.'"

Two other men were at the meeting; one of them was CFO David

Sidwell, an Englishman who had recently joined the firm from J. P. Morgan, and had become a member of Purcell's inner circle. They flipped through the Copper Arch presentation, and slid over the charts about return on investment, growth, restructuring, and divesting units. They barely paused, even when they reached the page of headlines that reflected the erosion of the firm's reputation for integrity: "Morgan Stanley Hit with Record $19 MM Fine by NYSE," "Morgan Stanley Pays $50 MM Fine for Pushing Certain Mutual Funds: Widening Scandal Stains Growing List of Firms and Dismays Customers," "Morgan Stanley Fined $2.2 MM for Late Reporting on Brokers," "Censured for Submitting Information Late 1,800 Times."

Crawford didn't become agitated until they got to the charts titled "Board Relationships" and "Board Experience." As of early 2005, five members of the eleven-person board were ex-McKinsey-ites: Purcell, Bob Kidder, Sir Howard Davies, Klaus Zumwinkel, and Miles Marsh. The former Sears contingent consisted of Purcell, Brennan, and Michael Miles. Brennan had been chairman of AMR, the parent company of American Airlines, and he was still on the AMR board with Purcell and Miles. Marsh and Miles had both been senior executives at Kraft, and Brennan was a former Kraft board member. Charles F. Knight and John E. Jacob were directors of Anheuser-Busch. Even the independent-minded Laura Tyson was on a board with another director; she and Knight were directors of SBC Communications, the parent company of AT&T.

With the exception of the British Sir Howard, the German Zumwinkel, and Tyson, they were also geographically and socially entwined. Brennan, Miles, and John Madigan were members of the Commercial Club of Chicago. Purcell, Brennan, and Knight were members of Augusta National Golf Club. Purcell and four of the directors were also members of another all-male golf club, Old Elm in a suburb of Chicago. At least six of the eleven were Roman Catholics. Even some of the more sophisticated members of the board made a point of saying that they didn't think much of Easterners and Wall Street. As one former Morgan Stanley executive says, "Turning this institution back to the Easterners was something they had no interest in doing." The board meetings were most often held in New York but were also held in other places. In 2005, when the pressure was on, the board would meet twenty-one times, as compared with fourteen in 2004, and a significant number of the 2005 meetings were in the Chicago area.

When Sipprelle left the meeting with Crawford he understood that, above all, Purcell didn't want his board to be awakened. He had said that his first priority was keeping the board happy. Getting a letter like Sipprelle's was guaranteed to annoy.

Eight

THE LAST GATHERING
OF THE EAGLES

The *Wall Street Journal* article about Scott Sipprelle's letter and his "No Disinfectant Like Sunlight" missive were only a few days old on the morning of January 12, 2005, when Phil Purcell and Steve Newhouse addressed a group of managing directors. Purcell began with his recitation about the Morgan Stanley triangle, which, as he had said so many times, pointed to the northeast, the direction of positive financial charts. He reported that Morgan Stanley was number one in the league tables in equity and equity-related underwriting, number one in IPOs and convertibles, number two in global debt underwriting, number two in completed M & A and number five in announced M & A, but he expected the firm to be number two by the end of the year. All of the divisions whose performance he praised were part of Institutional Securities.

Discover had just had a tremendous boost when the U.S. Supreme Court ruled that Visa couldn't prevent banks from issuing other credit cards, and Morgan Stanley had acquired the Pulse system to enable Discover to be used as a debit as well as a credit card. Discover had also signed an exclusive agreement with Sam's Club. The Individual Investors' Group—Retail and Asset Management—had "a tough year," but there was an increase in client assets toward the end of the year, and the firm had hired more financial advisors. On the client side, Purcell described business as "the most positive I've seen in the last seven years." For shareholders, revenues were up 14 percent, profits up 18 percent, dividends up 8 percent; and return on equity (ROE) was up 18 percent. But ROE was "middle of the pack." The goal was to do better in 2005, which Purcell predicted would be a record year for Morgan Stanley.

After the meeting, the managing directors made their way uptown by taxi, radio car, or subway, and in Purcell's case, by armored car, to Riverside Church, where 1,500 people were assembling to honor Dick Fisher. By 11:00 A.M., when the service was scheduled to start, the pews were overflowing. Senior executives and Advisory Directors who had been Fisher's closest friends—and who also knew New York and the worlds of finance, philanthropy, and the arts well enough to recognize people who should be escorted to the front of the church—served as ushers, wearing white boutonnieres to identify them. Among the guests was the nearly-ninety-year-old David Rockefeller, the former chairman of Chase Bank, whose father, John D. Rockefeller Jr., had been the benefactor of the church. Riverside was modeled on the thirteenth-century Gothic cathedral at Chartres, and its crowning glory was the seventy-four-bell Laura Spelman Rockefeller Memorial carillon, named for David Rockefeller's grandmother. Fred Whittemore escorted Mr. Rockefeller to the reserved section near the front, with some of the current titans of finance.

Purcell, who was dressed as usual in a loose-fitting suit, clunky shoes, and oversized glasses, found his way down into the front pew, where he sat alone until New York Mayor Michael Bloomberg joined him. A couple of rows back, Steve Newhouse, Vikram Pandit, John Havens, and Terry Meguid moved up to sit with Purcell and the mayor, as though to make the point that Purcell wasn't the only person who represented the firm. Less than four years earlier, when Morgan Stanley held the memorial service for its employees who were killed in the terrorist attack on the World Trade Center, the firm had set aside a special section in St. Patrick's Cathedral for the Advisory Directors, who included former chairmen and presidents of the firm. This time, the senior alumni sat wherever seats were available. Although most of them were together in the first few rows, they noticed the slight. The members of the board had been invited to the service weeks earlier, and at least a few might have been expected to attend, but none of them did. Their absence was such a violation of the courtesy Wall Street pays to its leaders that Morgan Stanley executives, past and present, looked around to see if they had missed someone, but it was later confirmed that not a single director was there.

John Mack had an appointment that day, to meet with Egyptian president Hosni Mubarak in Cairo, presumably to talk about a business project. Mack was famous for his willingness to fly anywhere, arrive full of energy and enthusiasm, and close a deal. Torn between obligation and opportunity, he put off Mubarak, and he and his wife, Christy, were in church to honor Mack's friend and mentor.

One of the senior executives who saw Scott Sipprelle at the service later remarked, "The article about his letter had just come out in the *Journal* and there was a sense that it was dangerous to be seen talking to him, although of course we did."

Purcell seemed particularly alone, and there was a poignant aspect to his contribution to the memorial program. He wrote, "We have lost something much more than an inspiration, even more than a friend. With his passing, we also lost a bit of our spirit." As one observer comments, "What he wrote was gracious, but the irony is that Dick Fisher would never have said we'd lost our spirit; it sounded like Phil couldn't handle the leadership going forward."

The ninety-minute service was dominated by interests other than business—family, education, the arts and music. The great organ rolled into Bach's "Come, Sweet Death, Come Blessed Rest" and "Jesú, Joy of Man's Desiring." The American Symphony Orchestra, the Concert Chorale of New York, and the Brooklyn Youth Chorus performed. Two of Fisher's most loved musical works were on the program, the 1824 Missa Solemnis by Beethoven, and his favorite, the Alto Rhapsody of Brahms, from 1869. Another selection, " 'Nimrod,' from Sir Edward Elgar's Enigma Variations, represents in music deep friendship," the program noted. In recognition that Fisher "was a connoisseur of poetry," there were readings from Dylan Thomas and Elizabeth Bishop. The final musical interlude was the closing chorus from Handel's 1739 setting of John Dryden's "A Song for St. Cecilia's Day."

Most of the encomia in the twenty-four-page program Jeanne Fisher produced were written by representatives of the nonprofit institutions the Fishers supported. Fisher had been chairman of the Brooklyn Academy of Music's Endowment Trust; a trustee of Princeton University, and chairman of the Princeton University Investment Trust; chairman of the board of Rockefeller University; and one of the five Trustees of the American Fund for the Tate Gallery in London, where he directed the investment portfolio. As chairman of the board of Bard College in Dutchess County, New York, he endowed the Fisher Studio Arts Building and the Frank Gehry—designed Richard B. Fisher Center for the Performing Arts, with its dinosaur-in-flight design and flawless acoustics.

The first spoken eulogy was delivered by his younger brother, David W. Fisher, a former managing director of J. P. Morgan and the first president of J. P. Morgan's Securities unit. He spoke of the accomplishments of Dick's youth, and talked about more recent Fisher holiday gatherings. "Dick always had a different game that we would all play. One year we went around the dinner table and answered the question 'What is the one thing you would like to do more than anything else in the world?' There were answers like play the piano, or sing beautifully.

"Dick said, 'I would like to run.'

"This extraordinary person has left us," David Fisher said. "This clear-thinking man of moral courage with a patient regard for the opinions of others is gone.

"But, you know what? I'll bet I know what he is doing right now.

"He is running."

Leon Botstein, the president of Bard College and the conductor and director of the American Symphony Orchestra, delivered a richly textured speech. Botstein, a polymath of almost limitless talents, enthusiasm, and discipline, and Fisher became friends when the Fishers' daughter attended Simon's Rock College of Bard, an innovative institution that admits students before they graduate from high school. One of the Fishers' sons received his MFA at Bard.

Botstein's moving eulogy accomplished the near impossible: he portrayed "the perfect man." It would be unfair to hold anyone to the standard Botstein described, but as he mentioned each of Fisher's attributes, a senior Morgan Stanley executive found himself glancing over at Purcell. He recalls, "Each one hung in the air as an indictment, enumerating all that Purcell so vividly was not."

"Dick tricked disaster out of victory," Botstein said. "Ambition is ordinary. But ambition coupled with tolerance and patience and an elegant talent for focusing attention on others is extraordinary . . . Ambition without arrogance and the involuntary encounter with his own limitations led Dick to a unique achievement: the capacity to resist the corruption of success, the deformation of character, intentions, and principles that wealth, power, and fame seem to bring."

Above all, Botstein praised Fisher's "public virtue . . . Dick returned to the public sphere the gift of his life more fully than anyone I have ever known."

Technology analyst Mary Meeker ruefully recalls, "I've never been to a memorial service where 90 percent of my time isn't focused on the person and the family," she said. "And here I am at this service, thinking about Morgan Stanley, how things had changed, the sagging stock price, and that what was so wonderful about Dick didn't exist anymore. I was a mess. I told myself, 'Mary! Think about Dick.' Based on my conversations, it seemed as though the same thoughts were running through the minds of the other Morgan Stanley folks."

A senior investment banker recalls, "When I saw all our former colleagues, the quality of those people, respected, revered icons, and thought about the collegiality and the quality, I said to myself, What happened? What did Phil do that hurt this firm? For one thing, he hired Don Kempf as general counsel and stuck with him, until every regulator and court hated us—so much resentment for a firm that prided itself on proper conduct. Don Kempf walked into the church and I thought, He has no right to be here."

When Bob Scott stood at the podium, he spoke of Fisher's "genius at listening to a group of experts, who couldn't listen to each other, and at the end of the discussion synthesizing the conversation into a coherent whole. It was awesome to behold."

He "was a great listener . . . who genuinely cared about hearing what others had to say, and that encouraged people to be candid and frank in a way which was very helpful to Dick."

The executive making the mental Purcell v. Fisher checklist shook his head, recalling occasions when Purcell was confronted with research that contradicted his point of view, and dismissed the information by saying, "The numbers must be wrong."

Scott spoke of Fisher's long-term vision and patience, in particular his contribution to the firm's overseas expansion that took, "an unfailing commitment of people, capital, and time—in some cases ten or more years." Morgan Stanley executives uprooted their lives and moved across the world, raising the firm's flag on the then barely mapped business shores of Asia, with the faith that Fisher would support them for as long as it took to attain mastery. Scott remarked that, as Lewis Bernard often commented, Fisher knew that "you can't keep pulling up the plant to check the roots. It's not good for the plant, and it demoralizes the gardener."

Fisher, Scott said, admitted and was accountable for his mistakes. "When transactions didn't work out, or our judgments were proven wrong, he taught us by his own example, to be straightforward and honest with our clients and each other."

He wound up with a typical Wall Street subject: golf. Fisher found a way to play the game, despite his physical limitations, and Scott moved out from behind the podium to demonstrate his technique. "He would drive his cart up to the ball, then get out with a club in one hand, and his cane in the other. He would line up his shot, drop the cane, and hit the ball," Scott said, taking a mock swing. "He would then pick up his cane by hooking it with the golf club and move on."

He flicked his wrist, as though to pop a cane up into his hand, then moved back to the podium and led to the finish.

Scott told the congregation about the night Fisher died, when a group of friends and colleagues were together at a Christmas party. "There were tears and hugs, but it was also comforting to be sharing these memories. I suddenly realized that even in death, Dick was doing what he always did. He was bringing us together, helping us find feelings that bind us together and make us a community. And I thought to myself," Scott said, and his voice caught—"we are going to be all right."

A friend of Scott's, who had spoken to him that morning about what he was planning to say at the service, noted, "Scotty was saying, 'We're *not* all right, but we will be, Dick, because we're going to do something about this situation."

Another of Fisher's former colleagues recalls, "Everybody had inhaled the fact that Phil wasn't all the things that Dick was. This stuff was percolating. After that, a lot of people were talking. People who'd been at Morgan Stanley were taking me out to lunch and dinner and saying, What can I do? Who can I call?"

As the saga unfolded later that winter and spring, people came to believe that the Group of Eight got together at Dick Fisher's memorial service, and that the decision to fight Purcell was born out of Fisher's death. In fact, a mutiny was already brewing, but the gathering to honor Fisher hardened the resolve of the Group of Eight that would soon coalesce. The aura of greatness lingered, influencing the decisions that dozens of Morgan Stanley people made about the firm and their careers over the coming months. Those who gathered for a last salute to Fisher mourned more than the loss of one much-loved man. As Bob Scott said, Dick Fisher's memorial service felt like "the last gathering of the eagles."

Four days later, on Sunday, January 16, Bob Scott, Parker Gilbert, and Lewis Bernard met at Parker Gilbert's apartment for the fateful "chat" with Vikram Pandit, Joe Perella, John Havens, and Terry Meguid. It was then that the three retired executives resolved that the eagles would gather again.

PART TWO

The Battle Is Joined

Nine

THE LETTER

Morgan Stanley retail branch managers from all over the United States came together for their annual meeting every winter, and in 2005 it was held on February 1 and 2, in Scottsdale, Arizona. The branch managers were Purcell's natural constituency, although, as he admitted when he addressed them that month, he had "missed almost all" their meetings in the last seven years. Now he stood onstage, with his name and title lit up in huge letters on a screen behind him, and everyone could see that "Philip Purcell Morgan Stanley Chairman and CEO" had come to praise and encourage them, and bring them up to date on the state of affairs as it appeared from the thirty-ninth floor at 1585 Broadway. Wearing a light-colored sport jacket and a tattersall shirt, with his left hand casually in his jacket pocket, using his right hand to gesture, palm up and thumb out, he paced back and forth on the stage, taking three steps one way, facing forward, then turning and pacing three steps in the other direction, speaking extemporaneously, rather than from notes, as he usually did.

This was not like the investment bankers' meeting in Barcelona, where he had to compete with the natural ease of Perella and Meguid; or with Vikram Pandit, the one-man brain trust. The branch managers were not making more money than he was; they did not act as though they thought they were smarter than he was; and they treated him with deference. They were a receptive audience, but not an enthusiastic one. Purcell spoke with a flat midwestern accent, and there was never a moment when the audience was cued to clap, even when he finished and asked for questions. He sounded a little breathless, as he walked back and forth over the same couple of yards and laid out the map of "the best year in the history of Morgan Stanley": the firm was first in global equity underwriting for the first time since 1982; first in IPOs; first in convertibles; number one in Equity trading; Discover had increased the merchants who took the card by one million, up from a previous high of 600,000. In Retail and Asset Management, the aspects of the business that directly impacted the branch managers, the numbers weren't as good, and he spoke of "improving," and of "a stronger branch system per person than four years ago."

He repeated the "solid numbers" he had presented to the management committee on the morning of Dick Fisher's memorial service. "The only problem," he admitted "is the stock price didn't go up." He attributed the static share price to the fact that the firm's return on equity was "middle of the pack."

It was when he spoke of the "synergy" between Retail Brokerage and Institutional Securities that he indicated the underlying reason for his presence that morning: to make his position clear about Scott Sipprelle's proposal that the merger should be unwound. "We are stronger together," he said, referring to Retail and Institutional Securities, and "the people who advertise that what we should do is separate Retail— it isn't going to happen as long as I am chairman. You can take that message back to all of your FAs [financial advisors] if any of them are reading the paper and getting concerned," he concluded sternly. Finally, he said, "I look at 2005 as a year of execution. A year for the stockholder." He had no idea how true that would be.

While Purcell was in Arizona, promising the brokers a record year, Parker Gilbert and Lewis Bernard were discussing strategies for unseating him, and others were independently coming to the same conclusion. One morning in February, when Anson Beard was in his office at 1221 Avenue of the Americas, he asked his executive assistant, Farah Santoro, to see if she could get Parker Gilbert on the phone. At that time of year, Gilbert was likely to be in South Carolina, but Santoro reached him in New York. Beard told Gilbert what he was hearing about performance and morale from senior members of the Equities team with whom he had worked, some of whom he had trained.

Recently John Havens had stopped by Bob Scott's office to talk with Scott and Beard, and told them how unhappy he was about the way Purcell was running the firm. Beard was disappointed that he wasn't more "fired up," but he recognized that Havens was worried about protecting his people and afraid that a mutiny would damage the business and jeopardize their jobs. And when Beard attended a retirement dinner for Robert Metzler, who succeeded him as Head of Equities, he could tell that none of the active executives were getting organized to force a change. The guests at the dinner dwelled on the good times of the past, but Beard said, "They seemed to have no energy to address the current problems, or the future." He told Gilbert, "I'm not sure they're on board if we go to war. Somebody's got to do something about the situation at the firm," Beard said, "and I think it's got to come from this floor," referring to the advisory directors' offices.

Gilbert told Beard he had just met with Lewis Bernard about "doing something" and asked him to come to a meeting at his apartment at 10:00 A.M. the next day.

By February 15 the Group of Eight was complete. Parker Gilbert, Bob Scott, Lewis Bernard, Anson Beard, Dick Debs, Joe Fogg, Fred Whittemore, and John Wilson had agreed to work as a team to rid the firm of Phil Purcell. It had become clear to them, although probably not to Purcell, that an internal rebellion was unlikely, and that talented executives would leave, rather than challenging Purcell. Institutional investors were unlikely to interfere, except to vote on a proxy. Large shareholders and hedge fund managers like Scott Sipprelle were more independent and had loud voices, but Sipprelle had spoken up and been treated dismissively. The analysts were idling in neutral; Purcell had assured Richard Bove that he was working on the problem areas, and Bove now recommended the Morgan Stanley stock, saying it was undervalued. Other analysts continued to be guardedly optimistic. It was hard to believe that a firm with Morgan Stanley's history wasn't just going through a rough patch.

There was an acceleration of the talk about a possible sale to a big bank that might take advantage of Morgan Stanley's weakness to get the firm at a good price, which could be the first step to seeing the firm swallowed, just as Morgan Stanley had absorbed, though not fully digested, Dean Witter. An acquisition could give Purcell a way out that would leave him covered in glory, and even richer. If Morgan Stanley was bought by a major bank, Purcell would have created the biggest financial firm in history—again.

The members of the Group of Eight were well positioned to mount a challenge, even one with an improbable outcome. They couldn't be fired, they could afford to spend their own money, and none of them was on someone else's payroll. They anticipated that they would be accused of trying to protect their stock, discounted as having more money than sense, too much time on their hands, or an unrealistic hankering for "the good old days," and they were risking the reputations for sagacity and integrity they had built over a combined two hundred years in the investment business. They could live with all of that. What they didn't expect was that Purcell would accuse them of trying to "take down" the firm.

The biggest danger they faced was that Morgan Stanley would sue them and tie them up in years of litigation. The disaster scenario was that they would precipitate events that could irreparably destabilize or destroy the firm. But what was "irreparable"? Lehman Brothers was adrift in the 1980s, and now it was back as one of the top competitors on the Street.

After Parker Gilbert, Lewis Bernard, and Bob Scott had had their Sunday-afternoon meeting with the four active managing directors at Gilbert's apartment in mid-January, Gilbert and Bernard suggested to Scott that he "take a crack" at writing a letter to the board, to be signed by a group of advisory directors. The message was simple. Parker Gilbert says, "Getting rid of Phil Purcell was a '10,' and getting the board reconstituted was a 9 on a scale of 10, because most of them were in his pocket."

The Scotts had just built a new house in Naples, Florida, and Scott flew back south, sat down with a yellow legal pad, and started to write. He still hadn't told Karen what was brewing. That was unusual. She had been his secretary at Morgan Stanley from 1989 to 1994, and she worked for Dick Fisher after that. She was natural and well liked, she still had a lot of friends at the firm, and she understood the politics.

When Scott asked Karen to type the letter calling for Purcell to resign, she said, "Whoa! This is big."

"Yes," he said. "It's big. And it's confidential."

Then, Karen said, Scott told her, "Honey, this is going to cost a lot of money." That was fine; she was behind him 100 percent.

The Scotts canceled a ski trip to Sun Valley they were planning and told anyone who asked that they couldn't go because Bob's back was acting up. Scott and Joe Fogg flew back to New York and brought the draft of the letter to Parker Gilbert's.

On February 15, the Eight sat around the table in the Gilberts' library and shared the stories that had brought them together.

Dick Debs, who traveled the world for Morgan Stanley, said, "All over the place, morale was just terrible. And people weren't quite sure what . . . but they knew it came from the top." When Debs was in London on firm business, he said, "These guys, younger people, there were three of them—poured it out. One of them said, 'What if we got forty or fifty managing directors to sign a letter, telling the board to get rid of Phil Purcell, or else we'll quit—either fire him or we'll all quit.'

"That showed you how bad things were. How desperate people were. I didn't think the idea was crazy, but I wasn't sure they could do it. I said, 'Not just sign? Would you be willing to quit?'

" 'Absolutely. If we had enough people.' "

That never happened, but if managing directors were even considering risking their jobs, the situation had to be serious.

Fogg, who had run Harvard Business School recruiting for Morgan Stanley, was getting calls from people he had hired and who had worked for him. "I was focused on the people," he says, "and they were in misery. Perella and Meguid and the department heads were doing their best to run their business and deal with their clients, and they were not only getting no support from the top, they were actually having to keep the guy out of the way and not get him involved in their business. He'd go into meetings unprepared. Or he'd keep talking about golf, or not be respectful to the clients. Just plain not effective. For a year and a half before we got together as a group I was hearing that he was damaging the business and these guys' careers. And finally I felt I had to do something about it."

Beard told the others about what he knew about the situation in the Equities Division; John Havens was one of his close friends. Like Fogg, Beard's primary motivation was "the people."

Fred Whittemore was a virtual switchboard for Wall Street. Everyone called him, and he was disgusted by the stories he was hearing about senior Morgan Stanley people being hired away, or looking for jobs elsewhere. Whittemore had spent nearly fifty years at the firm; he loved the place and the people, and he wasn't going to let his colleagues make Morgan Stanley history without him.

John Wilson's motivation was simple: "We wanted to save the culture we helped build."

They were all hearing variations on the same story: "We've got these challenges and Phil's no help. We don't know the guy, he doesn't know our people. There's no leadership. It's . . . you know . . . we're exasperated. It's horrible," as one of them explained.

Something ineffable bonded the Eight to the firm, and to each other, but they did not always agree about tactics. Most of the members of the group were hawks, but others were doves or diplomats. The issue that separated them most was whether they would be willing to mount a proxy fight to unseat Purcell and the board. The most consistent hawks were Parker Gilbert, Bob Scott, Anson Beard, Dick Debs, and Joe Fogg, but they were hawkish in different ways.

Gilbert had resigned from most of the corporate and charitable boards on which he served and was leading a highly satisfactory life. He shot birds on his plantation in South Carolina in the winter; he lived on Fifth Avenue and spent his summers in Southampton, as he had all his life, and where he was president of the National Links Club, which admitted its first woman member during his tenure. He was married to the attractive, wise, and wry Gail Auchincloss Gilbert, a descendant of one of the families her relative the author Louis Auchincloss calls "Old Brownstone New York." They had children and grandchildren. If Parker Gilbert was willing to emerge from a near-perfect retirement to protect his old firm, no one doubted that his reasons were based on principles of honor, character, and quality. It was inconceivable that he was interested in personal gain. His reputation for absolute probity gave the fight gravitas and credibility, and once he was committed, Gilbert never flagged. In that sense, he was a hawk.

Bob Scott was the member of the Group of Eight who had the most personal reason to want to eject Purcell, which put him in a delicate position. Any of the Eight could be accused of starting a fight because the depressed stock price had made them, if not poor, less rich, but only Scott could be singled out as a man who wanted to take down an enemy or get his job. Scott was involved in his expanding restaurant business, but his office at Jurassic Park didn't look like the headquarters of a man who was only dropping by on his way to have lunch at Craft. Parker Gilbert had bequeathed him his corner office because Gilbert never went down to 1221, and while most of the advisory directors' offices looked like temporary quarters even when the occupants had been using them for decades, Scott furnished his with antiques and art. The first painting a visitor saw was a Bellows-like oil of two collegiate-looking prizefighters in a ring. The next was a painting of two men fishing in a boat on a wilderness lake—Scott had begun fly-fishing after his divorce from his first wife, when he took two of his sons on a fishing trip. An Oriental rug, a black leather couch, and windowsills crowded with family photographs were the backdrop to the focal point of the room: one of the original rolltop desks passed down from one partner to the next since the early days of J. P. Morgan and Company. Scott's desk was stacked with papers, the computer screen was live, and the television monitor was tuned to CNBC. The office had the air of the headquarters of a government in exile. Scott was a hawk.

The third hawk was the competitive Anson Beard, who told a ballroom of people at his retirement dinner, "I don't like to lose. Ever." Beard's Morgan connection was even older than Gilbert's. His great-grandfather James J. Hill was the founder and president of the Great Northern Railway, and Hill and J. P. Morgan were the winners in the famous railroad market play when E. H. Harriman and Jacob Schiff, the senior partner of Kuhn, Loeb, tried to corner the Northern Pacific Railroad. Beard always had large framed photographs of Hill and Morgan hanging in his office, although he hadn't gotten around to knocking the nails into the walls at Jurassic Park, and the pictures were leaning against a bookcase, on the floor. He had been retired since 1994, but in the course of the 2005 fight he would contact dozens of institutional investors, who represented 270 million shares, 25 percent of the stock. They took his calls and the majors met with him and other members of the Eight. As threats against the Eight were lobbed out of Morgan Stanley, many senior employees worried that their phones might be tapped even though no one had evidence to support their concern. Beard remarked, "I hope they *are* tapping my phone. Every chance I get I tell people how incompetent and unqualified Phil Purcell and his board are to be leading this firm." When he called investors to rally support, bravado gave way to common sense, and he didn't call from the Morgan Stanley office.

The slight, bespectacled Joe Fogg was definitely a raptor. Fogg had been described as "brilliant, but irascible," and while he preferred the adjective "demanding," he didn't suffer fools. Fogg's specialty was take-over defense. His most famous deal was, at the time, the largest take-over ever, although as he says there's a new "largest something" every couple of years. That one was in 1988 when he advised Chevron in its friendly acquisition of Gulf Corp for $13.4 billion. The year of the Chevron deal, Fogg was Senator Robert Dole's national finance chairman for the presidential race, and the point man on two other Morgan Stanley M & A deals: he led the team that helped one client resist a hostile takeover and developed the "Pac-Man" strategy that would enable a firm to acquire a larger predator. In 1990, *BusinessWeek* ran a cover story titled "Morgan Stanley's Main Merger Man," and reported that Fogg had played a major role in more than two hundred deals worth $100 billion.

Fogg was the chairman of his own venture capital firm, served on the Yale University Development Board, and was a director of the Yale Art Gallery, but his favorite project was Camp Keewaydin in Canada, where he had gone as a boy. He and Lewis Lehrman, a former Morgan Stanley partner who ran for governor of New York in 1982, bought the camp and funded a nonprofit foundation to keep it going. Another Keewaydin alumnus, Disney's former chairman Michael Eisner, wrote a book about the camp that was published in 2005. The members of the Group of Eight were involved in hundreds of millions of dollars of philanthropic endeavors, but Joe Fogg's camp was the most personal.

Fogg's principal roles over the next months would be developing

strategy, drafting written materials, making presentations to investors, and moving things along aggressively. As he says, "I'm the M & A
guy. I knew we could always do a proxy fight. It would cost a lot of
money, legal exposure, and it could get very nasty. But we wouldn't
have to decide until December. The fault line was whether we'd be
willing to do it. Ultimately, I said, at the least we ought to hire lawyers
and a proxy firm."

Dick Debs was the member of the group with the most diplomatic
experience; he had handled delicate situations for most of his professional life. Debs was a Princeton Ph.D., he had a degree from Harvard
Law School, and he was a Fulbright Scholar and a Ford Foundation
Fellow. He was big and bushy-browed, straightforward and elegant,
with an unexpected, if mild, Brooklyn accent—his father, who was a
Lebanese immigrant, lost his small business during the Depression
and moved his family from Boston to Brooklyn to start over.

As Head of Morgan Stanley International, and an Arabic-speaker,
Debs had taken hundreds of trips to the Middle East. He was chairman of the American University in Beirut before, during, and after the
revolution, an experience that called for patience, diplomacy, and the
long view. Still indispensable to Morgan Stanley's international business, he knew people few others could get to, and he traveled for the
firm. His widespread outside connections led him to one of the principal roles he would play in 2005. In preparation for a possible proxy
fight, he set about contacting top-level people who would agree to be
on a slate of opposing directors, if the Eight had to put one together. He
spoke to people with recognized financial backgrounds, sterling reputations, and stature in the community. Nearly all of them were interested, and about half a dozen said the Eight could count on them to
run, if necessary. Debs's background at the Federal Reserve was another significant contribution; he knew how regulators thought, and
he knew the regulators. One of his important roles was quietly to keep
senior regulators apprised of what was going on.

It would be hard to imagine that the irrepressibly enthusiastic
Fred Whittemore was moderate about anything, but Whittemore
had an old New Englander's philosophical approach. The son of a
New Hampshire industrialist, and the descendant of the Puritan Elder Brewster, Whittemore graduated from Dartmouth College and

went to work at Morgan Stanley in 1958, when it was still at 140 Broadway. He was the first of the Eight to join the firm, at a time when many of the original partners were still there. Harry Morgan offered him the avuncular advice that he might want to wait a year or so to buy a summerhouse. "We like credit, not debt, here," Morgan told him.

When Whittemore was Head of Syndicate, from 1970 until 1989, he was the firm's "outside man," and he still knew an astonishing number of people on Wall Street and in philanthropy and the arts. In the winter of 2005, he was producing a new musical play, *In My Life*, the story of a boy with Tourette's syndrome who falls in love with a girl who has obsessive-compulsive disorder. It was not fated to be the kind of success some of his other productions had been. He still got checks from *Chicago*, he had produced the revival of *Guys and Dolls*, and a few years back, he had branched out into movies; his first success was the Academy Award–winning *Boys Don't Cry*. Whittemore usually had someone coming to see him in one of the conference rooms at 1221; he had been chairman of the board of Dartmouth's Amos Tuck School of Business, where he endowed the Whittemore Wing for Information Technology and made a seven-figure gift to build Whittemore Hall, a student residence; and he had been a major donor and board member of the Whittemore School of Business Administration, named for his father, at the University of New Hampshire. He was also the "Moderator," an antiquated Yankee term roughly equivalent to "mayor," of Watch Hill, Rhode Island, the seaside resort town where the Whittemores spent weekends and summers. Part of his job was to oversee the fire department.

A dry raconteur with a New England accent and a gravelly voice, Whittemore had a way of peering over his glasses, leaning back with one arm over the chair next to him, staring down his quarry, then leaning forward again, steepling his hands and tapping his fingers together, asking the provocative question. Purcell didn't like going to the semiannual Advisory Directors luncheon meetings, which he said were a waste of time, and he didn't want to hear about Morgan Stanley's history. But Whittemore was such a legend that the firm regularly asked him to talk to trainees and new associates. His talks were among the most popular events in the training program. It was satisfying for someone who had just joined the firm to feel that he or she was part of a distinguished continuum.

At the time of the mutiny, as one of the investment bankers recalls, "Phil had it on his agenda to end the Advisory Directors program. They might not be up to speed on the latest trading floor whatever, but they understood the essence of the culture, they were all sophisticated New Yorkers, and that didn't make him feel good."

John Wilson and Lewis Bernard were the doves. The media exposure in particular made them wince, as they struggled to balance their concern that their fight would harm the firm with their recognition that it was already wounded. They soldiered on, developing strategy and considering consequences, and putting out a restraining hand if they felt the group was considering a move they thought was too aggressive.

"Culture carrier" was a term that was fashionable that year, largely because of the Morgan Stanley fight, although it was said to have originated at Goldman Sachs. It referred to a person who represented the best values of the firm, and among the Eight, John Wilson was an acknowledged front-runner. Tall and thin, with deep smile lines in his long face, Wilson was the quiet man, well liked, perhaps in part because he never wanted the top jobs. He joined Morgan Stanley in 1960 out of Princeton and Harvard Business School. One of his Harvard professors told him that the firm had a reputation for hiring the smartest people, and if he went to Morgan Stanley, even if he decided to leave, his perceived IQ would be higher than when he started.

Wilson worked in Paris, and on his return was asked to become Head of New Business in Investment Banking. He was the banker for some of Morgan Stanley's most important clients—"a big hitter in covering clients," as one of his colleagues says—and had earned their absolute trust. One of his clients, Tenneco, a gas transmissions company based in Houston, Texas, brought in more income some years than any other client. After Wilson retired in 1993, his tact earned him the position of Head Advisory Director, which made him the liaison with Purcell. One-on-one, Wilson says, Purcell was friendly and smart. He should have been good with clients.

When people spoke of Lewis Bernard's role at the firm and as a member of the Group of Eight, they always remarked on his incisive mind. He was thirty-one when he was made partner, and he wrote the firm's ten-year plan, ran the administration, finance, technology, and strategic planning departments, and served as a director. Bernard moved over from investment banking to be responsible for Fixed Income and then all finance, administration, and operations. He was credited with establishing systems that made Morgan Stanley the lowest-cost producer on Wall Street.

In 2005, Bernard was the chairman of the American Museum of Natural History, and was a founder and chairman of Classroom, Inc., an innovative educational project that had reached more than 635,000 students in fifteen states since it was founded more than a dozen years earlier. John Wilson, John Havens, and formerly, Dick Fisher had all been on his board. Bernard hadn't been an active executive at Morgan Stanley since 1991, but he was loyal enough to fight to preserve its values, and conservative enough to keep reminding the Eight to be sure they weren't doing as much harm as good.

Bernard and Wilson were the most strongly opposed to mounting a proxy fight.

Whatever differences the Eight may have had about strategy and aggressiveness, they were single-minded about where to begin: they would contact the board as a group, present the evidence, and ask for Purcell's resignation and a meeting to discuss their concerns.

At 10:00 A.M. on February 15 they sat in Parker Gilbert's library, passed drafts of Bob Scott's letter around the table, and went over the text, line by line. Beard says, "We asked ourselves, What did we want out of the letter? We wanted a response. A dialogue on a private basis. We hoped even if we got a negative response, we'd have a meeting, or a series of meetings, to argue it out."

They had agreed that they would take every precaution to keep the letter private. Morgan Stanley partners did not publicly discuss the firm's problems, and even if they had wanted publicity, the timing was off. The annual meeting was only a month away, and they did not have enough time to talk to large institutional investors and rally the huge blocks of votes that would demonstrate serious opposition to Purcell's leadership. If the Eight challenged him, and he still got a substantial majority of the votes, the campaign would be over and they would have made things worse.

They discussed whether to propose an interim replacement for Purcell, on the theory that the board might feel that at least there would be continuity if he left. If the Eight had a viable contender, Purcell could be asked to resign, the board could announce his replacement, and there would be less disruption. Without a candidate, the board might replace Purcell with someone even less qualified.

If they did suggest someone, it couldn't be anyone who was employed at Morgan Stanley, because that person would be fired. Most of the outside candidates who had the appropriate stature were already heading big firms. John Mack now had a corner office at Pequot Capital, a $6.5 billion hedge fund, and he and the firm's founder, Art Samberg, were still discussing how much of a role he should take, but to invite him into the fray would look like a replay of the 2001 power struggle and change the focus to "the battle of the titans." The chances were nil that the same board that had accepted Mack's resignation would now agree that he should replace Purcell. And while some of the Eight thought Mack should have been CEO, others had not had particularly good relations with him when they worked together. There was also the indisputable fact that Mack had brought in Purcell, and after he left Morgan Stanley, he had been hired and fired as chairman and CEO of CSFB.

In any case, suggesting an alternative candidate would be an empty gesture, would almost automatically eliminate that person as a candidate in the eyes of the board, and would hurt the cause. Anyone they proposed would be the one person the board was least likely to appoint. If they proposed anyone to replace Purcell, the focus of the challenge would shift to their relative qualifications. The point was to get Purcell to leave, not to try to choose his replacement.

L ate in the morning of February 15, as the Eight discussed how to take the next step, they agreed that they needed a strong strategic advisor. Parker Gilbert says, "We didn't have a lawyer, or an accountant, or public relations, or a place to meet and make phone calls." It would be difficult to find an advisor who was willing to take on Morgan Stanley. If Purcell kept his job he would be sure that anyone associated with the Eight would be banned from doing business with the firm, and possibly with some of its more important clients.

"How about Greenhill?" Anson Beard said. "My bet is he'd do it."

"Yeah, Greenie!"

Greenhill was fearless.

When Bob Greenhill left Morgan Stanley, he went to Smith Barney, but that didn't work out, and in 1996, he started his own business, Greenhill & Co., a private mergers and acquisition advisory firm: no sales, no trading, no product, no conflict. Greenhill had recovered from two public and unplanned career changes, and his survival skills in other endeavors were well tested. A former partner told a reporter that the outdoor expeditions he organized with his children were "virtual death marches." The *Wall Street Journal* began a front-page article about his "comeback" at Greenhill & Co. by describing an incident when he was in his sixties and was taking a midwinter break at his no-electricity, no-phone camp in Maine, and snowmobiled out fifteen miles to cell-phone range so he could talk to a client about a $1 billion deal.

Some of the Group of Eight had been on the Morgan Stanley board or the management committee in 1993 when they decided to take the presidency away from Greenhill and award it to John Mack. But if you liked Greenie, it stuck. Anson Beard voted against him at Morgan Stanley, but they kept playing squash on Sunday mornings. Sanford Weill fired him from Smith Barney, and they remained friends. When Greenhill started his firm, some of his old partners invested with him. When he took it public, they invested some more.

A year after Greenhill & Co. opened, the firm had been the advisor on Hughes Electronics' acquisition of the satellite company Pan-AmSat for $3 billion and Compaq's acquisition of Tandy for $4 billion, one of $15 billion worth of acquisitions Greenhill did for Compaq. The U.S. Department of Justice hired Greenhill to devise a plan to split up Microsoft, in the eventuality that Justice prevailed in its antitrust suit against the company. (Microsoft won.) When Nestlé, SA, bought Ralston Purina for $11.8 billion, Nestlé was Greenhill's client.

In 2004, Greenhill & Co. hired Goldman Sachs to launch its own IPO. *Barrons* described the firm as "the only pure-play in the lucrative merger-advisory business," while cautioning readers that "Greenhill's IPO should be good for him—but not necessarily for you." The stock opened at $17.50; a year later it had doubled.

As the Group of Eight was about to launch, Greenhill & Co. was ranked eighteenth worldwide among M & A advisors, had a $1.1 billion valuation (about one-third owned by Greenhill and his family), and was trading at 32 times earnings, a higher price—earnings ratio than the biggest investment banks on Wall Street—Goldman Sachs was trading at 12.5 times earnings.

Parker Gilbert reached Greenhill on the phone and told him what they were planning. Greenhill's reaction was, "You want to do *what*?"

"Can you come up here for lunch?" Gilbert asked him.

Greenhill said he was out of town, but he would be back that night. "Come to my office tomorrow and we'll talk about it," he said.

When Greenhill got home that evening and told his wife, Gayle, about the call, she laughed and remarked, "This is ironic."

But even former partners who left Morgan Stanley on less than desirable terms often had a deeply ingrained affection for the firm as it was when they were young, eager, and idealistic. As Greenhill explained, "We're the people who built the thing up. We care about standards. It was an intolerable situation. This was a person who never opened the office door. People become very attached to leadership. It's like a platoon; you have to lead by personal example."

The next morning, a few members of the Eight met with Bob Greenhill and Greenhill & Co. copresident Scott Bok at Greenhill's office on Fiftieth Street to discuss what they wanted to accomplish. The assignment had common elements with a hostile takeover, but this would be more like a hostile intervention.

The first questions the Eight asked were, "Will you help us?" and "Do we have a chance?"

Bok, tall and thin, fingers always busy checking messages on his BlackBerry, with a mind capable of performing at least two tasks at once, had worked in mergers and acquisitions at Morgan Stanley until 1997. "Two of the overwhelming factors that contribute to the culture and greatness of investment banks," he says, "are 'How do you feel about your CEO?' and 'Where's your share price?' " The Eight had a good case against Purcell on both counts.

As one of the Eight commented, "The most important advice Greenhill gave us was to say this is unprecedented; I don't know how to handicap your odds of winning, but the cause is certainly a correct one. He said that if you start down this path, you have to be committed for the long term. You have no idea how long this will take. This will be an emotional roller coaster, there will be days when you think you've made great progress and you're getting someplace and days when you're frustrated and think nothing's going to happen. He certainly was right about that."

Greenhill agreed to advise the Eight for a retainer, plus a "success fee" of an undetermined amount. "Success" was never strictly defined, although the letter the Eight planned to send outlined much of what they wanted to accomplish. The Greenhill agreement was pretty loose, but as John Liu, Greenhill's CFO, the other major executive on the project, said, "Mergers and acquisitions advice at the most sophisticated levels is all about trust and respect. Do you have to like a person? It helps." When they discussed what to charge for their services, Bok said, "This was totally unlike anything we'd ever worked on. We said, 'Let's just get started.' We knew Parker Gilbert would do the right thing. You can totally trust these people."

Gilbert adjusted the portion of the retainer each member of the Eight was to pay, based on how many shares he had, but the average first-phase cost was about $250,000 each. It was an indication of his reputation for fairness that no one questioned the apportionment.

Greenhill thought the Eight had better put a team together before they sent the letter. From his office there would be Bok, Liu, and general counsel Ulrike Ekman. They would also need an outside legal advisor and a public relations expert with a specialty in financial strategic communications.

"At some point this is going to get some coverage," Greenhill said. "Have you thought how you're going to handle that?" "Coverage" was anathema; the point was to take care of business privately, but he was right.

He called around to some top financial PR people, but many of them predicted a low probability of success and did not want to take on

Morgan Stanley. The issues of shareholder rights, corporate governance, and CEO pay were in the air, but none of them were front and
center, especially in comparison to the kind of news that was coming
out about chairmen who ransacked companies under the noses of their
boards and would be spending their golden years behind iron bars. It
didn't seem likely that anything could come out of the Group of Eight,
or Morgan Stanley, that could compete for ink with that kind of material, if the Eight decided to tell their story.

Andrew Merrill was forty-two years old and had recently joined
Edelman, one of the world's largest full-service public relations firms,
as Global Managing Director Financial Communications. Merrill,
who had worked on Wall Street, was building a boutique financial
practice. When Greenhill called and asked if he would be interested in
working on the project, he warned him about the danger of alienating
Morgan Stanley forever. "He was very up-front about it," Merrill says.
"He said, 'Think about it.'"

Merrill met Gilbert and Scott at Greenhill's office, and they showed
him a copy of the proposed letter. Merrill says, "The opportunity to
work with Bob Greenhill and these individuals was fantastic. It's an
unusual dynamic to have people of their stature involved in a project
like this. I found them highly credible, I believed in their cause, and I
was impressed by their resolve." He also believed that they could win.
From a professional point of view, Merrill says, "The stakes were high
for me. If we succeeded, it would put our practice on the map. If we
failed, it would have been a stupid move."

The Eight signed a letter of engagement with Edelman that week.
Merrill was invited to meetings to discuss scenarios and refine the
Eight's letter, but his mandate was to remain dormant unless the story
was leaked, or if events forced the Eight to defend or attack.

Legal representation was another concern. The Morgan Stanley legal department was huge, but the firm outsourced legal work among a
number of top law firms. Some were preempted because of conflict;
others didn't want to alienate Morgan Stanley. When Eric Seiler, who
was "a spin-off" from Martin Lipton's firm, Wachtell, Lipton and
Rosen, agreed to advise them, it was a coup. Lipton was on retainer to
the Morgan Stanley board, and Seiler knew how he thought and operated. The lawyers wanted to be sure the Eight didn't do anything that

would lead to lawsuits or an SEC investigation on the suspicion that they were mounting a proxy fight without filing.

Finally, all the pieces were in place. On Thursday, March 3, the Eight met in Greenhill's conference room and signed their names to twelve copies of a three-page letter addressed to Purcell and the board. When Federal Express picked up the envelopes from Greenhill's office, his staff was already preparing a twenty-one-page "Analysis of Morgan Stanley's Recent Financial Performance," the backup for the meeting they expected to have with the directors.

The letter was addressed to "Dear Mr. Purcell," although all of the Eight called him "Phil" on the rare occasions when they saw him.

They wrote, "Morgan Stanley's performance and its reputation have declined to the point where we are greatly concerned about the Firm's ability to regain its position as the premier global financial services firm." They cited Morgan Stanley's own proxy materials, which showed that for five years, "the Firm's total return has trailed the S&P diversified Financial Index by nearly 40%, a stunning vote of no confidence."

As of February 9, 2005, Morgan Stanley's stock "was down 27 percent over the past four years, compared with a 4 percent gain for Goldman Sachs, an 18 percent gain for Lehman Brothers, and an 11 percent decline for Merrill Lynch."

They attributed "poor performance and price volatility" to "the failure to continue to earn a premium return on equity; the failure to maintain earnings growth relative to its peers; and the weak performance of the firm's retail and investment management businesses."

"More fundamentally," they wrote Purcell, "we believe that the overriding cause of the Firm's poor performance is a failure of leadership by you as the Firm's CEO."

Citing "a crisis of confidence in the Firm's leadership and governance not only in the market, but also, we fear, among employees of the Firm," they wrote, "We believe that you will not be able to inspire and lead the Firm back to its rightful position in the financial services industry." The "loss of morale . . . puts Morgan Stanley at great risk of losing more key professionals."

There was some disagreement among the Eight over whether to criticize the board; attack wasn't the best approach if they wanted to open a dialogue, but in the end they wrote, "There is very little financial experience among the independent directors ... and while the Firm is headquartered in New York, the financial capital of the world, neither the Chairman nor any members of the Board reside in the New York area." They recommended that the board add three new directors with financial experience in the institutional and retail arenas.

They asked the board to "act promptly to change the leadership and governance," and advised them to pick a chairman who was "experienced and well respected by the senior executive group," and to act "as soon as possible."

"We are fearful," they wrote, "that in reaction to this letter you may reassign or remove more of the senior executives from the Institutional Securities Group," the firm's most profitable division and the one on which its reputation was built. They warned that "such action would damage the Firm's reputation and, perhaps irretrievably, injure its ability to attract and retain talented professionals."

They closed by requesting a private meeting with the independent directors and a "constructive discussion" that could "result in mutual commitment to a plan which can allow the Firm to regain its position as the premier financial services firm."

The morning the letter was due to arrive, the group was sitting in Greenhill's office and decided they should call a couple of directors and alert them that it was coming. Gilbert called Michael Miles; Scott spoke to Laura Tyson and Sir Howard Davies, who as a former regulator would have a particular interest in governance issues; and called Bob Kidder. Scott says that Tyson was aware that there were problems and thought it was a positive development for there to be an agent from outside. Sir Howard said that he was new on the board and didn't have the insight to react in depth, but Scott says, "He said, 'You guys are sophisticated and if you think it's appropriate to send the letter," he would read it carefully. Davies, who was head of the prestigious London School of Economics, was already somewhat disenchanted; the firm did not send him the board materials until the night before the meetings; the materials were usually waiting for him at his hotel, when he came in from London, which did not give him much time to review them.

When Parker Gilbert reached Mike Miles, he was furious. "I suppose you're going to release the letter to the press," he said.

Gilbert said, "No. We want to have a meeting."

Scott left a message for Bob Kidder, who called him at home that evening. Scott told him, "There are many problems and here's a group of people ... we want to have a meeting." Kidder asked him, "When are you planning to release the letter to the press?"

Scott answered that they intended to keep it confidential and not to create a public spat, and Kidder said, "Okay, I'll look for the letter."

Most of the directors received the letter on Friday, in time to spend the weekend considering their next move.

MORGAN STANLEY was an offshoot of J. P. Morgan and Company, founded by the most famous financier of the Gilded Age. J. Pierpont Morgan, above, was deeply averse to publicity, as demonstrated in this famous image, circa 1910, in which he is hitting a photographer with his cane. His son, J. P. Morgan, Jr., was said to class "as enemies all agencies and agents of publicity," yet despite their efforts to maintain privacy, as a senior Morgan partner remarked, "A mysterious sort of glamour . . . seemed to attach to the firm and possibly added to its influence." When the Group of Eight used the media as a weapon in their fight to unseat Philip Purcell in 2005, it was a radical deviation from more than a century of tradition. *Library of Congress*

J. P. MORGAN, JR., was head of the firm founded by his father when the Glass-Steagall Act forced banks to narrow their focus. Glass-Steagall caused J. P. Morgan and Company to close its investment banking division, which eventually led to the founding of Morgan Stanley. Morgan's 1933 testimony before the Senate Banking and Currency Committee included the statement that became the motto of the Morgan firms: "At all times the idea of doing only first class business, and that in a first class way, has been before our minds." *Portrait courtesy of Morgan Stanley*

HENRY MORGAN, one of J. P. Morgan, Jr.'s sons, was chosen to represent the family at Morgan Stanley. A patriarchal leader, he sometimes loaned promising young men the money to become partners. Morgan was a peacekeeper in a partnership once described as "the greatest twenty-two-man debating society in the world." *Portrait courtesy of Morgan Stanley*

HAROLD STANLEY, the other named partner, was a college hero who went on to great achievements. In 1935, he was an investment banker at J. P. Morgan, with its $340 million in capital, when he left to become one of the founders of Morgan Stanley, capitalized at $7.5 million. Partly thanks to Stanley's reputation and relationships, Morgan Stanley managed 20 percent of the offerings on Wall Street in its first three years. *Portrait courtesy of Morgan Stanley*

THIS PICTURE OF MORGAN (LEFT) AND STANLEY on a fishing trip on Lake Erie may be the only photograph ever taken of them together, according to the accompanying letter from Harry Morgan. *Photograph and letter courtesy of Morgan Stanley Advisory Directors*

IN 1935 WHEN MORGAN STANLEY opened, the office boys wheeled the partners' rolltop desks down the block from J. P. Morgan and Company. In the original partners' room the rolltops were lined up on either side of a central aisle, with the senior partners at the head of the line on the "platform." *Courtesy of Morgan Stanley*

ROBERT H. B. BALDWIN, who retired as chairman in 1985, was the intrepid force behind the growth of Morgan Stanley from an elite investment bank that still had only $7.5 million in capital and 200 employees in 1970 into a major force in modern financial services. *Photograph by Bachrach*

THE FEISTY ROBERT GREENHILL founded Morgan Stanley's groundbreaking mergers and acquisitions division, and later served as the firm's president. His suspenders embroidered with dollar signs were a trademark. When the Group of Eight decided to send their first letter to the Morgan Stanley board in March 2005, Greenhill's M&A advisory firm had recently gone public. They hired him as their strategic advisor. *Photograph by Daniel Kramer, from Morgan Stanley 1985 Annual Report*

IN 1996, RICHARD B. FISHER (right) was chairman, John J. Mack (left) was president, and they were looking for a merger that could make Morgan Stanley the most important financial services firm in the world. *John Abbott Photography*

S. PARKER GILBERT was the chairman who led Morgan Stanley
when the firm went public in 1986. He carried Morgan
Stanley's DNA: his father, S. Parker Gilbert, Sr., was one of the
J. P. Morgan partners at the famous 1935 "porch meeting" in
Maine, when the firm was founded. His stepfather was Harold
Stanley, and Henry Morgan was his godfather. Gilbert, a highly
respected and deeply private man, was the flag bearer in the
2005 mutiny. *Photograph by Shawn Ehlers, 2004; courtesy of the
J. Pierpont Morgan Library*

DICK FISHER, JOHN MACK, AND PHILIP PURCELL (left to right) join hands to celebrate the merger between Morgan Stanley and Dean Witter. The other "handshake agreement" took place between Fisher and Purcell, and led Fisher and Mack to believe that Purcell had given his word that he would turn over the job as CEO to Mack after a couple of years. Within a year, Fisher privately advised Purcell to step down as CEO; instead Purcell tightened the reins, and Mack left the firm in early 2001. *James Leynse Photography*

PHILIP PURCELL'S strategic intelligence, reserve, and clean-cut all-American style inspired confidence. But in 1997 when Purcell became chairman and CEO of the merged firm, he had only limited experience in Morgan Stanley's core investment banking business. *Wagner International Photos*

DICK FISHER AND JEANNE DONOVAN were married on May 31, 1997, the day the Morgan Stanley Dean Witter merger became official. When they were photographed on their terrace overlooking Central Park, Fisher had retired from the Morgan Stanley board, and was being treated for prostate cancer. Fisher was one of Wall Street's most beloved and respected leaders; his memorial service on January 12, 2005, was an emotional catalyst for the mutiny that led to Purcell's ousting only months later. *Photo by Leslie Fratkin; courtesy of Jeanne Fisher*

AFTER JOHN MACK LEFT THE FIRM, Purcell appointed Robert C. Scott as president. Scott served from 2001–2003, until Purcell pushed him out too. Jeanne Fisher chose Scott to deliver the final eulogy at Dick Fisher's memorial service. Along with Parker Gilbert, Scott, as a former president, was the most visible member of the Group of Eight. *Courtesy of Robert and Karen Scott*

FREDERICK B. WHITTEMORE joined Morgan Stanley in 1958, and became the enormously powerful Head of Syndicate. Whittemore, who was Morgan Stanley's unofficial firm historian, helped close one chapter of the firm's history and opened another, as a member of the Group of Eight. *Courtesy of Frederick B. Whittemore*

JOSEPH A. FOGG III followed Bob Greenhill as Head of Mergers and Acquisitions, and was dubbed "Morgan's Main Merger Man." As a member of the Group of Eight, he strongly advised the Eight to hire a proxy firm—and to be willing to mount a proxy fight. *Courtesy of Joseph A. Fogg III*

THE COMPETITIVE ANSON M. BEARD, JR., who declared, "I don't like to lose. Ever," built Morgan Stanley's $1 billion Equities division. During the fight, he contacted institutional investors whose combined holdings added up to 25 percent of Morgan Stanley's stock, and made the case for replacing Purcell. *Courtesy of Wheaton College*

WALL STREET'S FIRST FEMALE Head of Fixed Income, and a member of the Morgan Stanley management committee, Zoe Cruz was the only leader of an Institutional Securities division who supported Purcell. He chose her as copresident in March 2005. When Purcell and Crawford left, Cruz became acting president, and in February 2006, John Mack appointed her copresident with Robert Scully. Cruz reorganized Institutional Securities but was forced out in November 2007 after multibillion-dollar trading losses were reported from a desk under her supervision. *Wagner International Photos*

STEVEN CRAWFORD was a young investment banker at Morgan Stanley when Purcell picked him as his liaison with Institutional Securities. They bonded and Crawford became chief financial officer and then strategic and administrative officer, reporting to Purcell. Although Crawford had never run a business, Purcell made him copresident with Zoe Cruz at the time of the massacre. Crawford left in July 2005 with a $32 million platinum parachute, after three months on the job. He became a partner in a boutique investment firm. *Wagner International Photos*

ĐURING THE 2005 CRISIS, Robert Scully was chairman of Global Capital Markets and Vice Chairman of Investment Banking. His office was on the trading floor, and he played a significant role in reassuring clients and retaining talent, assuring them that he wasn't leaving the firm and advising them to focus on the jobs at hand. John Mack appointed Scully copresident with Zoe Cruz in 2006. When Cruz left, Mack moved Scully into a client relationship position in the office of the chairman. *Wagner International Photos*

INTELLECTUAL AND WELL-LIKED, Institutional Securities head Vikram Pandit was the heir apparent to the Morgan Stanley chairman and CEO positions—until he told Purcell he was loyal to the firm, not to an individual. Pandit was the first victim of Purcell's March 28, 2005, Monday Masssacre. Along with other senior executives who left Morgan Stanley that spring, he and John Havens founded Old Lane Partners, raised some $4.5 billion in assets under management in less than 18 months, then sold Old Lane to Citigroup for an estimated $800 million in April 2007. Pandit was appointed Head of Citi's Alternative Investments Group and became Citi's CEO in the fall of 2007. *Wagner International Photos*

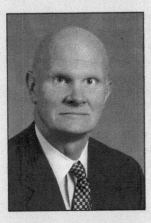

JOHN HAVENS WAS HEAD OF EQUITIES, reporting to Vikram Pandit, and was ousted by Purcell on the same day. Pandit and Havens were among Wall Street's top teams. When Purcell fired the enormously popular Havens, the Morgan Stanley trading floor erupted in a six-minute standing ovation to honor him, and some clients suspended trading with the firm in protest. As part of the Citigroup acquisition, Havens became president of Citi's Alternative Investments Group, then the head of Investment Banking. *Wagner International Photos*

LONDON-BASED STEPHEN NEWHOUSE was co-head of Institutional Securities and a highly regarded investment banker, trusted by clients worldwide when Purcell picked him to replace Bob Scott as president of the firm in 2003. When Purcell told Newhouse he was replacing him as president, the same day he fired Pandit and Havens, Purcell tried to persuade Newhouse to take on an "Ambassador with Portfolio" role, but Newhouse declined. *Wagner International Photos*

JOSEPH R. PERELLA (RIGHT), a Wall Street icon, was Morgan Stanley's most famous relationship banker. Two weeks after Vikram Pandit and John Havens were fired, Perella and Tarek M. Abdel-Meguid (center), Head of Investment Banking, quit in protest. By summer, Perella had independently completed the year's biggest M&A deal, the merger of MBNA, the credit card company, with the Bank of America; he was ranked ahead of Morgan Stanley and Lehman Brothers in Financial Services Industry deals; and *The Investment Dealers' Digest* named him "Banker of the Year." In June 2006, Perella and Meguid, along with Peter Weinberg (left), a former Goldman Sachs senior banker and member of Goldman's legendary Weinberg family, opened Perella Weinberg, an investment bank with a substantial asset management business. They raised $1.1 billion in startup capital from eleven investors from the United States, Europe, Asia, and the Middle East. By the end of 2007, they had $2.5 billion in assets under management, had five asset management businesses up and running and 135 professionals at work, and had done $80 billion in M&A deals. *Photographed during construction of their New York office by Tony Cenicola/The New York Times*

FORMER MORGAN STANLEY managing director Scott Sipprelle was the chairman of a $1 billion hedge fund, Copper Arch Capital, in December 2004 when his firm bought $100 million in Morgan Stanley stock and sent a letter to Purcell and the Morgan Stanley board criticizing the merger structure—and execution. The letter started a reaction that led to the Monday Massacre. *Courtesy of Scott Sipprelle*

RICHARD A. DEBS, the first president of Morgan Stanley International, was the member of the Eight who quietly kept regulators informed as the battle raged, and contacted potential candidates for a new board. Debs, who was president of the American University in Beirut, holds multiple graduate degrees; he is shown at AUB commencement in his academic robes. *Courtesy of Richard Debs*

QUIET AND BRILLIANT, Lewis W. Bernard ran nearly every division in Institutional Securities and played a significant role in developing the Group of Eight's strategy. Bernard and John H.T. Wilson were the "doves" among the Group of Eight. *Photograph by Daniel Kramer, 1985*

JOHN H. T. WILSON, the ultimate client-oriented investment banker, was Morgan Stanley's first Head of New Business, reversing the firm's tradition of not soliciting business. Wilson brought in, served, and retained some of the firm's biggest clients. *Courtesy of John H. T. Wilson*

In April 2005, Mary Meeker, Stephen Roach, Byron Wien, and Henry McVey wrote a private letter to Zoe Cruz and Steve Crawford that was the ultimate statement of the Morgan Stanley culture. "A value system based on integrity, trust, and respect for one another and a passion for the franchise," they wrote are "the hallmark of our culture." Their exceptional efforts to keep the letter private were an indication of the paranoia that infected the firm, and also of their interest in following the Morgan Stanley tradition of open—but private—internal debate and discussion.

MARY MEEKER, known as "Queen of the Net" and one of the most famous analysts on Wall Street, had an unmatched record of picking technology companies. Her name on the letter carried a significant impact.
Frank Veronsky

STEPHEN ROACH, Morgan Stanley's Chief Economist and Director of Global Economic Analysis, was once described as "Mr. Permabear," but he was persistently optimistic about the core values of Morgan Stanley. In April 2007, Roach was appointed the firm's Head of Asia.
Wagner International Photo

SENIOR ANALYST BYRON WIEN was the only Morgan Stanley executive included on a list of the sixteen most influential financial people in New York in 2006. He left to join Pequot Capital in 2005, but has continued in an advisory role at Morgan Stanley.
Wagner International Photos

HENRY MCVEY, Morgan Stanley's Chief U.S. Investment Strategist, represented the next generation at the firm. He said, "When you have a service-based organization and you do not have leadership that's reflective of the firm, you have to stand up and say that's not acceptable." *Wagner International Photos*

PHILIP PURCELL left Morgan Stanley in June 2005 with a retirement package worth some $113 million. Two months later, as he relaxed at home in Utah, he told a reporter, "If it were not for the articles and possible books, this would be a wonderful way to live the rest of your life." In the summer of 2006, he started a firm in Chicago to invest his own money in small financial services and growth firms. *George Frey/The New York Times/Redux*

JOHN MACK'S RETURN to Morgan Stanley as chairman and CEO in July 2005 would become one of Wall Street's legendary stories of revival, redemption, and—as some said—revenge. Eighteen months after Mack took office, the stock was trading in the low 80s, a rise of more than 60 percent since he took over. In 2006, Morgan Stanley had the best earnings and returns in its history. At one of the firmwide Town Meetings Mack instituted to reopen communications between the CEO and employees, he remarked, "Why did this firm come back so quickly? Because its DNA is excellence." *Photograph by Ken Korsh*

Ten

REACTION

Purcell received the letter on Thursday, March 3, and began to plan his defense strategy. He met with Don Kempf and Steve Crawford and started calling members of the management committee to inform them about the letter, to find out who else might be involved, and to take their temperature. People who were close to the events of those first few days say that he called John Havens and offered him the presidency, but that Havens put him off, saying he didn't know, and in any case that was a board decision.

A number of people heard that on Friday evening, Purcell called Joe Perella and reached him in Annapolis, Maryland, where he was about to go into a sports arena to watch the regional collegiate wrestling matches, in which his college, Lehigh University, was participating. Purcell told him about the letter and said he wanted to fax it to him. He read off the names of the signers and told Perella they claimed the firm was underperforming and that it was his fault.

As Perella later told his colleagues, he said, "Phil, that's not the kind of letter you should be sending to a hotel fax machine." Perella was going to California on Monday and would be at a secure Morgan Stanley site. He told Purcell to wait a couple of days and fax it to him there.

On Saturday, Purcell asked Vikram Pandit to come into the office around 6:00 P.M. He told Pandit that the board thought he was the ringleader of an internal mutiny, but that he could disabuse them of that notion if Pandit would walk arm in arm with him. The implication was that he would clear the path for Pandit to become president.

When Purcell asked both Havens and Pandit if he could count on them to be loyal to him, they gave the same answer: they were loyal to the firm.

Purcell decided not to fax the letter to Perella, and on Monday, he read it to him over the phone. Perella's response was, "For sure that ain't no Scott Sipprelle letter. This is serious." He said he wanted to put off commenting on the contents until he had time to reflect.

The only Institutional Securities division head who readily agreed to support Purcell was Zoe Cruz. Her rationale was that she had two choices: quit or stay, and if she stayed, she was going to support the sitting executive team. Throughout that spring, there would be people who criticized Cruz for "selling out." She called some of that on herself by her open antagonism to the Eight, by continuing to ride her antipathy to Pandit, and by expressing admiration for Purcell with more enthusiasm than seemed necessary.

The directors' reactions were hard to read. Over the next months, they would be described as monolithically behind Purcell, but it would be more accurate to say, as one person who attended board meetings did, "There were times when it was chaotic. Deer in the headlights."

The board did not have a permanent lead director, and the position was taken in rotation by different members. Chuck Knight happened to be in the seat when the letter arrived, and he took a hard line in defense of Purcell, and against anyone who challenged him. The directors were sure the letter would hit the press soon; their priorities were to find out which employees had been feeding the Eight, what their plans were, and to keep the Eight's allegations private until they had time to figure out what was going on. Believing that the Eight planned to leak the letter, as one director explains, they were particularly wary of talking to them, thinking that anything they said might find its way into print and they would have to fight a public battle for which they were unprepared. They needed to know if the Eight's views were shared within the firm, if the perceived problem was the strategy, as Sipprelle had claimed; the execution of the strategy; or Purcell. As one director said, "It initially looked like these were people who didn't like Purcell. What didn't show up in the numbers the board saw was the subtlety, the problems with the team, the allocation of capital across divisions. This seemed as though it might be an entirely personal attack."

After Purcell had shown the directors Scott Sipprelle's letter, Bob Kidder and Laura Tyson had discussed holding a nonexecutive session of the board, excluding Purcell, to discuss management, strategy, and performance. Now, with the letter from the Group of Eight hanging over their heads, it was too late for that plan. They had to find a way to catch up, and the threat of exposure was a constant worry.

They had just agreed to pay Purcell a whopping amount of money. Even without the Group of Eight calling attention to the firm's performance, the compensation package attracted notice. In addition, the directors modified their compensation, increasing their fees and direct stock awards and eliminating their stock options.

CEOs were now making more money than professional athletes, and more reliably than movie stars, and a backlash was brewing. In an *MSN* story titled "Extravagant CEO Pay Is Back," the writer, Michael Brush, focused on five companies "that were extraordinarily generous to their chiefs." Brush picked Purcell as the example of egregiously high pay on Wall Street. He calculated that Purcell made about half as much as nearly all of the top U.S. government officials combined: the president of the United States, the vice president, the 535 members of Congress, and the nine justices of the Supreme Court.

A shareholder proposal to cap CEO pay was coming up at the Morgan Stanley annual meeting on March 15. The board recommended against it, but the directors passed a new rule: no incentive pay in the future, unless return on equity was 10 percent or more.

It would not look good for the board if they had given the CEO a big jump in pay just months before a respected group of alumni, possibly backed by a cadre of senior executives, called for his resignation.

One of the first calls Purcell made was to Martin Lipton, the seventy-four-year-old partner of Wachtell, Lipton, Rosen & Katz. Lipton was on retainer as an advisor to the board on governance, and Purcell asked him to step up his involvement. Over the next months, he would be a major player. A galactic takeover lawyer whose tactics were described as "brass-knuckle," Lipton was a specialist in defending beleaguered CEOs and directors. He was credited as the inventor of a powerful defense against hostile takeovers known as the "poison pill." That involved increasing the debt of the target company to make it less attractive, and passing a provision that would permit current shareholders to sell their shares at a highly inflated price, sometimes as much as 100 percent more than current value, if a potential acquirer bought more than a certain percentage of the shares. Lipton had worked for Kraft when Mike Miles was its CEO in 1988, trying to protect it from a hostile take-over by Philip Morris. Kraft lost, but Lipton, who worked on the case for two weeks, was paid a $20 million fee. He had been the lawyer for Sears when Ed Brennan was chairman and CEO and Robert Monks threatened a proxy fight. Brennan had been demoted after the Monks episode; and Miles had been ousted six years after Lipton's expensive, but unsuccessful, defense of Kraft, but both of them were ready to listen to his advice again.

Lipton was involved in a high-profile case that was getting ugly when the Morgan Stanley problems erupted. As the lawyer for the board of the New York Stock Exchange, he had advised the NYSE compensation committee that CEO Richard A. Grasso should be allowed to withdraw the $140 million in his pension fund early. More informally, Lipton had told Grasso that the plan was defensible. The members of the NYSE compensation committee who agreed to the $140 million included the CEOs of Bear Stearns, Merrill Lynch, Time Warner, and BlackRock, and Henry Paulson, chairman of Goldman Sachs, who would be named secretary of the Treasury in 2006. The logic attending the payout was: the NYSE was gasping for air when Grasso took over, and he resuscitated it; the top executives at the NYSE member companies were taking away that kind of money, so why shouldn't Grasso? And Grasso had been mentioned as a candidate for Treasury and might leave the NYSE if he didn't get what he wanted.

One member of the NYSE board, H. Carl McCall, former New York State comptroller and the Democratic candidate for governor in 2002, thought the connections between the compensation committee and member firms appeared inappropriately cozy. McCall, who was not on the committee when it decided on Grasso's compensation, spearheaded a new policy restricting compensation committee membership, so that directors of companies regulated by the exchange would not be in a position to determine the chairman's pay. The NYSE promptly appointed McCall as the new compensation committee chair. Lipton called McCall from vacation in Italy to assure him that Grasso's pay package was "okay," before the committee signed off.

Purcell, who was a member of the NYSE board, but was not on the compensation committee, spoke up to say that he was concerned that paying the chief executive of a not-for-profit organization at that level would set off a public protest. When the information was released and the anticipated furor broke out, Purcell called Paulson at his Illinois farm, and they discussed the threat to the credibility of the Exchange. Purcell's reaction was reminiscent of his behavior during the 1983 negotiations between Sears and Dean Witter, when he left the room because he found the top executives' compensation demands excessive—in contrast to the attitude he had developed in regard to his own pay at Morgan Stanley. It was as though one side of him said, "This is outrageous," and the other countered, "Okay, but if everyone else is doing it, why not me?" The board voted thirteen to seven to ask for Grasso's resignation. Grasso subsequently filed suit against McCall, claiming that he had not properly informed him of the board's disapproval of the package. McCall countered that Lipton had counseled him that the pay was appropriate. During depositions, Lipton assumed responsibility for having given the board his approval, and the case was dismissed.

Lipton and Purcell decided to avoid direct engagement with the Eight; they wouldn't answer the letter, and they would wait them out. It seemed as though they expected that summer would come, and the dissidents would go off to their houses in Southampton or Sun Valley, or off for a month to a villa in Tuscany, and lose interest. It was just a matter of hanging on and ignoring them. The irascible Lipton called the Eight "Grumpy Old Men," but he was older than all but two of them.

The directors were not willing to discuss the Eight's allegations with them, but they were concerned enough about secrecy to make a couple more phone calls. Kidder called Parker Gilbert and warned him not to leak the letter. Gilbert repeated that they didn't plan to talk to anyone except the board, and hoped they could meet soon. Bob Scott got a couple of calls with the same message.

Gilbert was on vacation in the Caribbean when he got another call, this time from Chuck Knight. "We're convinced you're going to leak it," he said. Gilbert reaffirmed that the letter was private, and Knight asked him, "Well, why did you put that stuff in about the board . . . you know, being all from the Midwest and not versed in financial services?"

"Because it's true, and it's wrong," Gilbert said.

"Then there was that wonderful remark Mike Miles made," Gilbert recalls. "He told me, 'You don't have to be a locomotive engineer to be on the board of the Burlington Northern.' That basically says it all." The Burlington Northern had been one of Gilbert's clients, and it sounded as though Miles was saying that Gilbert didn't know how to run a train, but he could advise a railroad.

Gilbert recalls that later, when a reporter asked Miles why the board didn't respond to the Eight's letter, Miles remarked that if a group of retired GE union leaders who had worked on the factory floor had sent CEO Jack Welch a letter, Welch wouldn't have met with them. Gilbert couldn't get over the idea that any Morgan Stanley director could understand the industry so little that he would equate the Advisory Directors' understanding of the business they built with the knowledge of someone working on an assembly line. Of all the remarks Gilbert heard during the fight, the ones about the Burlington Northern and GE kept echoing in his head.

The Eight never understood why they didn't get an official answer from the board, but the personal nature of the attack raised the hackles of directors who had been CEOs themselves, and the Eight's aggressive approach reduced the possibility of a civil dialogue. They were operating on the theory that if you want to unseat the king, you have to kill him.

It was understandable that the directors were afraid of a leak; within a week, many people had either seen or heard about the letter—from Purcell, who was trying to find out who was with him and who was against him, and to rally support. By March 11, he had his own letter in hand, ready to release if it became necessary. Five former Dean Witter executives, including Stretch Gardiner and Jim Higgins, wrote claiming that the Group of Eight was using "selective and unrepresentative data to wage a 'sound bite' campaign with the board and with the press."

That last referred to a media campaign that hadn't started. When the letter was written, the Eight were not going near the press.

The annual meeting was held on March 15 in Riverwoods, Illinois, hardly the center of the financial world, or convenient for most shareholders. Two years earlier, when the meeting was held in Riverwoods, none of the independent directors attended. Even Miles Marsh, who was chairman and CEO of Fort James Corporation, the manufacturer of paper products, including Dixie Cups, and who was headquartered in Deerfield, Illinois, wasn't there. A well-known shareholder gadfly stood up and told Purcell that the absence of the directors was "outrageous," and asked him if he had instructed them not to come. His answer was, "I was trying to be efficient" with their time. As a reporter noted, the annual meeting was "the only opportunity for investors to question the people who are supposed to be their representatives."

The recently passed Sarbanes-Oxley legislation required independent directors to take more responsibility, and for 2004, Morgan Stanley adopted a new policy that directors were "expected to attend" the annual meeting. In 2004 the meeting was held at Morgan Stanley's Westchester, New York, location, but in 2005 they were back in Riverwoods. Four directors were up for reelection; three of them were opposed by 17 percent of the voting shares, and the fourth had 8.7 percent against. The Associated Press noted that it was "the slimmest election margin since the merger."

When the directors convened in Chicago the day before the annual meeting, Purcell and Lipton told them that they were dividing them into teams, to conduct a battery of virtually simultaneous phone calls to members of the management committee. There would be two or three directors on each call, who were meant "to ascertain what they [the executives] were really feeling." As one director said, "It was very orchestrated." Neither the directors nor the executives who received the calls had any advance notice of the plan. As one director said, "They didn't know we were calling them, but we didn't know, either." One director asked for assurance that whatever they heard on the calls would be absolutely confidential and could not be used to the detriment of the executives they spoke to. The director said, "We're pulling some of them out of bed in the middle of the night and saying, 'Don't worry; this is confidential. Be as honest as you can be.'"

That day, the directors reached every member of the management committee except John Havens, who was in meetings and either didn't get the message or didn't return the call. Terry Meguid was in Hong Kong and Steve Newhouse was in Beijing; their calls came in at 11:30 P.M. When Meguid returned, he told colleagues that when the directors reached him, they said, "Oh, where are you?"

Many of the responses were thoughtful, and no one attacked Purcell personally. A number of the managing directors said that they liked him, despite their criticisms and the serious problems at the firm. For the most part, they said they were sympathetic with the contents of the Group of Eight's letter, in regard to performance.

Marty Lipton was on some of the calls, which was intimidating, and the people they talked to were cautious, but no one assured them that everything was fine.

Joe Perella was hosting a conference in Cabo San Lucas, and according to associates to whom he talked when he returned, he was in the middle of a meeting with sixty clients when Purcell's assistant, Lisa Luca, called to summon him to the phone to talk to Ed Brennan, Miles Marsh, and Sir Howard Davies. There was something strangely off-hand about the rush to talk to him, but he went upstairs to his room and took the call.

As Perella's colleagues recall his account of the conversation, it went like this.

Perella: Where are you calling from?
Directors: We're in Chicago.
Perella: Anyone in the room with you?
Directors: No. Have you read the letter?
Perella: The letter was read to me by Phil.
Directors: What do you think of the company's strategy? [Meaning the merger.]
Perella: I don't have any problem with the strategy. I have a problem with the execution of the strategy. But before we go on, would you like to know what I do at Morgan Stanley, so you have some background?

Perella told them that he had been an M & A banker his entire career, that he'd been at Morgan Stanley for thirteen years, and had run Investment Banking and Corporate Finance, and was on the management committee. He explained that, in 2000, when Terry Meguid was ready, he'd turned over Investment Banking to him, and Perella had become the senior client person in the firm. In 2004, Perella said, he had some four hundred meetings with more than two hundred clients, and he was almost always accompanied by other Morgan Stanley executives. Perella believed he knew more about what employees and clients were thinking than nearly anyone in the firm.

Directors: How about the leadership?

Perella: I reluctantly have to tell you that I agree with the letter. I like Phil, but he is a failure as a leader. He's not a member of the community. It's not that he lives in Chicago, but as the CEO of Morgan Stanley he hasn't gotten involved as a leader in one charitable, educational, arts, or health endeavor in New York. He's virtually unknown to our clients, and to most of our employees he's a name in the annual report. If the letter were published on our intranet, the roar from the troops would be deafening. I speak for hundreds, if not thousands, of our people.

Marsh: But Joe, these are all soft issues.

Perella: Do you guys have to be reminded what business we're in? We don't make widgets. We're in a service business. We compete with Stan O'Neal, Dick Fuld, Hank Paulson, and Sandy Weill.

Most of the other management committee members the directors spoke to weren't as outspoken as Perella, but the directors must have realized that there was, at the least, a distinct lack of direct support for Purcell. Only one senior person in Institutional Securities was firmly behind the CEO. Zoe Cruz didn't criticize Purcell, but she said to the directors who called her, "We're punching below our weight in all divisions."

After the shareholders' meeting, the independent directors met to report on what they'd learned in their interviews with members of the management committee. It was an awkward discussion, because Purcell and Lipton were both there. After they had heard one another out, they agreed to think about their impressions overnight, and reconvene the next day. Some of the directors were still convinced that Purcell was a fine leader and were angry at the dissidents. Others thought the lukewarm or negative responses of many members of the management committee revealed weakness in leadership that couldn't be ignored.

The next day, Purcell did not attend the meeting. Mike Miles asked who wanted to comment first, and Laura Tyson offered to start. She told the other directors that the problem was serious, that the board couldn't pretend it didn't exist, and that they needed to tell Purcell that he couldn't solve it simply by moving people around.

Chuck Knight was furious; he told Tyson she was disloyal, but she was not the only one who wanted some answers. The directors decided to instruct Purcell to present a plan that would deal with the succession and other issues that Scott Sipprelle and the Group of Eight had raised. They asked Purcell to call each of them for further discussion, but some of them never heard from him.

Marty Lipton told the board that what they had to do was confirm Purcell as CEO. As one director said, "It was unsolicited advice. Very powerful. For those of us who didn't know the history of Marty and Phil and Sears, we thought, Okay, that's what we have to do." The Eight knew that the board had met, but they didn't know if their letter had had any effect, and they still didn't get an answer.

The board could not decide whether the Eight were actually dangerous. Geography is power, and the sense that the Advisory Directors were honored, but impotent, exiles from the country they had once ruled counted against them. The Morgan Stanley building in Times Square was at the center of the agora, the marketplace of the world, while the Advisory Directors were warehoused at 1221 Avenue of the Americas, and no one had to run into them in the halls of Morgan Stanley. The dissidents, in their dowdy offices a few blocks away, must have seemed as threatening as old philosophers sitting in the sun outside the Roman Forum, critiquing the senators. The Group of Eight were among the few who expected that when they marched into the Senate and insisted that Caesar step down, they could prevail. Nevertheless, Phil Purcell wasn't taking any chances, and after the annual meeting and the reports of the directors' conversations with the members of the management committee, he moved swiftly to clean house.

A few directors were concerned that Purcell might respond to the threat by mounting an executive upheaval, shifting personnel around, or pushing out respected Institutional Securities people, as the Eight had warned he might. A couple of board members called and e-mailed him, urging him not to make disruptive changes. As one of them told him, "If you move these people, I think you will regret it and the firm will regret it."

He ignored the warnings, put together a plan, and discussed it with the directors whom he could count on to agree with him. His targets were the people he thought were plotting to overthrow him.

He prepared to oust Vikram Pandit, John Havens, and Steve Newhouse, ironically, three of the people who were responsible for the performance in Institutional Securities that he had been citing all winter as marks of the firm's success. He would change the executive structure and appoint Zoe Cruz and Steve Crawford as copresidents in place of Newhouse. Purcell was doing Crawford and the firm a disservice by elevating him. As one of his colleagues said, Crawford "was set up. He was a staff guy, who had never run a business." He had one advantage; as CFO he went to board meetings to give financial reports, so he was one of the few executives the directors knew.

When Purcell asked Cruz if she would consider becoming copresident, she agreed. She would no longer be reporting to Pandit, and she would become the first woman president of a major financial services firm. It was irresistible.

Cruz was at a conference in Canada when Purcell sent a Morgan Stanley plane to pick her up and fly her to meet a couple of the directors, then to New York to meet with Marty Lipton. She was in Aspen, Colorado, on vacation with her husband and children when Purcell sent a plane out again and flew her back to New York. Between March 21 and March 27, Purcell, Cruz, and Crawford worked on their strategy.

The plan was based on a reorganization of the firm to achieve full integration of the disparate divisions, and at the same time sweep out potentially dissident elements. All the divisions would report to co-presidents Cruz and Crawford. Purcell would not have to fire Pandit, who would never report to Cruz, and it would be obvious that he was no longer in line for the succession. If Pandit left, so would Havens. The copresident structure left Newhouse out, but he was such an important client representative for the firm that Purcell thought he might agree to stay on in a different role. Maybe Purcell believed he was responding to the directors' instructions to come up with a succession plan and an approach to improving the underperforming businesses. As most of them knew only what he told them, they were likely to go along.

Purcell called the last of the independent directors to notify them of his decisions on Good Friday, three days before what came to be known to some as "The Monday Massacre," and to others as "The Easter Monday Massacre." At least one of the directors warned him that he was jeopardizing the firm's stability, but he said he had made an assessment of who he thought would leave, and he thought the damage would be limited. Anyway, he said, "we're going to do it Monday. Everybody agrees."

Purcell spent Easter weekend with his family, then flew back east. By this time, he had all the accoutrements of an Imperial CEO, including three G-5s. The Gulfstream 5 was among the most expensive private planes, but Purcell said it was convenient to have duplicates; if they needed spare parts, they could cannibalize one to fix another. The planes were viewed as "Phil's fleet," partly because he had a hangar specially built to house them at the Palwaukee, Illinois, airport near his home and the Discover headquarters. Initially, the planes had been parked in easy range of Morgan Stanley's New York headquarters, and executives could fly in and out of Westchester and Teterboro airports, each about half an hour from the city. Purcell explained the location of the hangar by saying that the fuel cost less in Chicago.

The air force was a convenience, but there was open resentment at the way Purcell used the planes. Morgan Stanley executives never became accustomed to his flights back and forth to Chicago, or the sense of favoritism about who rode with him; people still talked about these things, whether or not they were true, and about the occasion when a group of managing directors was waiting for a bus to take them to the airport to board commercial flights to New York after an off-site meeting, and Purcell and Steve Crawford climbed into a limousine and rode off to board a Morgan Stanley G-5. It later developed that they were making a stop at Augusta to play a round of golf before returning to the office. One executive who sometimes flew into Palwaukee with Purcell remarked that when they disembarked, Purcell's driver was waiting for him, and was ready to go. But as the banker said, "If he had been doing a good job, no one would have cared about the planes."

Byron Wien announced in a small meeting that Purcell hadn't attended that the "air force" was undermining the firm's culture, and he offered to give up a million dollars of his own compensation if Purcell would sell the aircraft. As they left the meeting, Vikram Pandit remarked, "Your million dollars is safe. He'll never get rid of those planes."

The corporate jets were another point of contrast with Dick Fisher, who usually flew commercial and did not always sit in first class. Brad Hintz remembers a trip when he and some other relatively junior colleagues were traveling with Fisher on business, and Hintz and the younger group were seated in coach. Hintz says, "Fisher walks back—with two canes—and says to the guy in the seat next to me, 'Go take my seat in first class. I want to be with my guys.' "

On Easter Monday, March 28, Purcell followed his usual morning routine, arrived at the New York office, and braced himself for the purge he hoped would expunge the poison from his system.

He called Vikram Pandit, asked him to come to his office, and told Pandit that, effective immediately, he was no longer Head of Institutional Securities.

Pandit asked if that meant he was firing him. Purcell said, "I have too much respect for you to fire you." Pandit said that he hadn't resigned, and he wasn't going to make it easy for Purcell by pretending that he had. Purcell told Pandit he was also replacing John Havens as Head of Equities. Havens was in a pitch meeting with prospective clients, and Pandit called him out to give him the news. Havens phoned Purcell, who confirmed that he no longer had a role in the firm. Havens went back and asked to be excused: something had come up.

Stephan Newhouse, who was in Spain on business, went to bed in Madrid assuming that his job was secure. Somewhere between 3:00 and 4:00 A.M. on the twenty-ninth the phone in his hotel room rang; Purcell was calling to tell him that he had been replaced. Purcell asked Newhouse to consider staying on in some role, but Newhouse, who was dazed and still half-asleep, had the presence of mind to say he wouldn't discuss it until he got back to New York. The media had already been notified that Morgan Stanley had two new copresidents. Newhouse could have read about it on the *New York Times* and *Wall Street Journal* Web sites around the time that he got Purcell's call.

John Havens's number two, Jerker Johansson, was on vacation at the Lyford Cay Club in the Bahamas when Zoe Cruz called him, also around 4:00 or 5:00 A.M. on the twenty-ninth. Cruz told him that Havens was moving on, and asked if he would take the position as Head of Institutional Equities. Johansson said he'd like to think about it and wanted to talk to Havens first.

He reached Havens, who told him that they'd been preparing him for that role and that somebody had to look after the people who were left; he reminded Johansson that they didn't work for Purcell, they worked for the people underneath them, and they had an obligation to protect them. Johansson took the job, but like Newhouse, he was based in London, out of the direct line of fire.

On the afternoon of March twenty-eighth, before Newhouse or Johansson knew how their lives were about to change, and when Pandit and Havens had quietly left the office, members of the Group of Eight were assembling to discuss the lack of response to their letter and the rumors Bob Scott had heard from confidential sources who called him over Easter weekend to alert him that some kind of shake-up was imminent.

The Scotts had been in Florida, where his parents and one of his grown children were spending the holiday with them. Scott made an excuse and left Monday morning, and he and Joe Fogg flew up to New York via NetJet. Anson Beard had had a quiet weekend with his children and grandchildren. He had gotten engaged at the beginning of February and planned to spend his sixty-ninth birthday the weekend after Easter with his fiancée. Energized by romance and natural competitiveness, he was ready to go to battle. John Wilson, who had an Easter-egg-hunt kind of day with his family, also came in from Greenwich, and Fred Whittemore drove down from Watch Hill. Dick Debs, who was working on the arrangements that would lead to the opening of Morgan Stanley's new Middle East full-service office, in Dubai, was abroad. Debs asked Scott to keep him informed of any developments while he was away.

That afternoon, most of the group were relieved to see that the landscape outside Parker Gilbert's windows had been restored to the usual hopeful condition typical of the verge of April—daffodils in bloom and trees in bud. When they began getting together a month earlier, they were looking out at *The Gates, Central Park, New York, 1979–2005*, a swarm of 7,500 sixteen-foot-high saffron-hued banners installed by the artists Christo and Jeanne-Claude. *The Gates* redefined twenty-three miles of paths, copses, and lawns with more than one million square feet of orange rip-stop fabric, suspended between structures that might have been goal posts or gallows. From the Gilberts' apartment it looked like a fire was sweeping through the park. It had been an unsettling, if appropriate, backdrop to a winter like none other for the men in the room.

The mutineers took off their jackets and hung them over the backs of their chairs, and leaned their elbows on the mahogany pedestal table, and sat there in their crisp blue, or striped, or white shirts and their conservative silk ties, and admitted to themselves that they were stuck. They had sent their letter and they had been ignored.

Dick Debs had said at the last meeting, "The silence is killing us. What do we have to do next?"

Now Anson Beard said, "It looks like we're gonna have to go to the mattresses." In case someone didn't understand the reference, he explained, "Mafia term. *The Godfather.*"

It was then that the phone near the couch rang. Gilbert got up to answer it, and the others heard him ask, "Are you sure?" and "When did it happen?" and "Where are they now?"

The caller was Greenhill & Co.'s copresident, Scott Bok. When

Gilbert hung up he turned back to the others. "Phil did what we were afraid he'd do," he said. "He fired Vikram and Havens."

"Anyone know where they are?" someone asked.

Scott later recalled, "We got to somebody's assistant. She said, 'You didn't hear it from me, but I think I know where you can find them.'"

Gilbert reached them and put them on the speakerphone. They confirmed that their jobs no longer existed and that Zoe Cruz and Steve Crawford had been promoted.

"What happened to Newhouse?" someone asked.

Pandit and Havens had the impression that Purcell might offer him some kind of "minister without portfolio" position.

"Hey!" Bob Scott said. "That's what he did to me." Later, he recalled, "In our hearts we were expecting something like this."

The "What do we do next?" question was answering itself. If the Group of Eight wanted the directors of Morgan Stanley to understand how serious the problem was, they would have to go public.

Andrew Merrill was in his office at Edelman when he got a call from Greenhill's office saying, "You need to get up to Parker's apartment. There are changes afoot. We may have to reconsider our position."

Merrill says, "I got the call and I went. In our corner of the PR world, what makes this job fun, you're used to getting that call, coming into a room that's full of people, usually fairly senior important ones, having to get up to speed quickly and have a strong strategic point of view. That's what you live for. I was excited."

When Greenhill brought Merrill in, he had instructed him that his role was not to get publicity for the Eight, but to be prepared to handle unwanted media attention. Merrill says, "They had no interest in having a big public row. They wanted a confidential meeting. It was never about, these guys want to get a ton of press, that was not the objective. One of the great 'conspiracy theories' they tried to advance at the Morgan Stanley offices was that we had an army of people, a full frontal PR campaign, but nothing could be further from the truth." The "PR army" consisted of Merrill, one other account executive, and a secretary.

Merrill had not heard much from his new clients since they sent the March 3 letter, and he says, "I wasn't on any kind of high alert. That call was the first sense I had that we had a fire drill on our hands." He hailed a cab and started north.

When he reached Parker Gilbert's he found that the group was making the decision that would propel them into the headlines for the next three months. Seeking publicity was an unfamiliar situation, and they turned to Merrill for advice about what their next step should be. He said, "If you want to act, and you're prepared and ready to go public and assume all the burdens and responsibilities, there's no turning back. And if that's the case, do it now." He expected Morgan Stanley to release the information about the reorganization at a carefully calibrated time, in order to get coverage from the most important media outlets. If Purcell were allowed to tell his version of the story first, he would control the message about why the firm was restructuring, why the leadership succession was normal, and why this was the right time to do it.

"You want to seize the advantage and put them back on their heels in a reactive mode, the mode we don't want to be in," Merrill said. "You're never going to have a better opportunity to tell your story. Let's make sure they're getting some inbound phone calls from the media asking if they have any comment. Force this out."

The dissidents instructed Merrill to get in touch with his media contacts and make the text of their March 3 letter available. Purcell would always describe that as "a leak," but it was a deliberate release of information.

Seeking publicity was a countercultural move for executives steeped in the privacy-conscious ethos of the firm. While the Mergers & Acquisitions bankers were often in the newspapers because of the nature of their deals, and had regular contact with business reporters, the leaders of the firm were scrupulous about maintaining privacy, when possible. Morgan partners had always had good reasons to keep a low profile. During a century of prominence, they had been subjected to bombings, kidnap, and death threats, vilification and ridicule. One of the most famous photographs of J. P. Morgan shows him striking a photographer with his cane. Morgan's former chauffeur told a *New Yorker* reporter that his house on Madison Avenue had "six or seven exits and

Morgan never used the same one two days running." The chauffeur said that while his boss wasn't afraid of anything, he wasn't looking to get assassinated any more than the next guy. J. P. Morgan Jr. had been attacked and shot twice in the groin in his home on Long Island by a German-American who objected to his raising money for the Allies in World War I. One of the few times Jack Morgan enjoyed being recognized was the day he returned to the office after the attack, and was hailed by a small cheering crowd. At J. P. Morgan & Co. headquarters at 23 Wall Street, more than three-quarters of a century after the bank was bombed by anarchists in 1920, killing two Morgan employees, there were still gouges in the stone.

Intense press attention had also affected the business of the House of Morgan, not least of all the interest in the Pecora hearings, which contributed to popular support for the Glass-Steagall Act, and led to the founding of Morgan Stanley. As a *New York Herald* reporter wrote, "The men of the house of Morgan keep in the background as far as possible. They shun the limelight as they would a plague." In the 1930s, another journalist noted that if the Morgans had "not practiced a highly publicized ritual of privacy—had they borne in mind the elder [Pierpont] Morgan's warning that 'the time is coming when all business will have to be done with glass pockets,'" they "would have attracted less interest and suffered far less embarrassment."

J. P. Morgan's Tom Lamont was steaming across the Atlantic on an ocean liner not long after the Pecora hearings when he wrote his partners that while "as private merchants there is no theoretical reason why we should have public relations . . . practically we have such relations and they are inevitable and proper because of the nature and importance of the firm's transactions." Lamont hired a public relations man, but to the extent possible, the Morgan firms kept faith with Jack Morgan who, according to the *New Yorker*, "classes as enemies all agencies and agents of publicity."

At Morgan Stanley as late as 1964, Perry Hall proposed that his partners "reconsider our policy of not advertising . . . Everybody else seems to be soliciting everybody's business." Yet when historian Ron Chernow wrote *The House of Morgan*, which was published in 1990 and which won the National Book Award, he acknowledged the cooperation of only "two of the three Morgan banks," J. P. Morgan & Co and Morgan

Grenfell in London. "Alone among the Morgan banks, Morgan Stanley refused cooperation and wouldn't consent to a single interview," he wrote, describing the attitude as "adversarial." Parker Gilbert was chairman of the firm at the time.

When Gilbert and his cohorts broke the tradition of silence and used the media as a weapon in their fight to overthrow Phil Purcell, it was a deviation from type and tradition. The irony was that Purcell was even more disinclined to talk to the media than his predecessors had been, and his unwillingness to have "glass pockets" did not end up serving his interests or the interests of the firm.

The session at Parker Gilbert's on the night of March 28 went on until 9:00 or 10:00 P.M. Gail Gilbert came into the library from time to time, offering coffee and something to eat. They talked about strategy, and Merrill called reporters.

He began by calling the *Wall Street Journal*, the *New York Times*, and *CNBC*. Randall Smith, Ann Davis, and Suzanne Craig broke the story at the *Journal*; the three of them would work as a team to cover Morgan Stanley over the next months. At the *Times*, Landon Thomas Jr. had worked at Morgan Stanley at the beginning of his career, and the firm was an important part of his beat. The story came in so late that the *Times* only managed to squeeze it into the bottom of the far-right column on the first "Business Day" page the next morning. The headline "Morgan Stanley Promotes Two to President" downplayed the drama until he was able to get more information.

People who had built tremendous careers and reputations at Morgan Stanley heard the news and seriously considered resigning, and by no means all of them worked with Havens and Pandit.

A senior executive who was in Asia received a call from the New York office late at night asking, "Do you want to be on the call when Phil explains what he's done?" She said no and went back to sleep, thinking, "I am going to resign. I don't want to work at this place anymore." The next day, she woke up with a different attitude: "I like Vikram, I like Havens, this is too bad, but in another way it's a good thing. The fever broke, this place has been too unsettled for too long. One of three things is going to happen: either Phil's going to leave, or Zoe and Steve will pull this off and it will work better, or we'll get sold to a global financial institution like HSFB for $72 a share, and I can live with all those out-comes. There's going to be action of some sort. From that day forward, by virtue of the calamity and the magnitude of the event, things were go-ing to end up being better," she says.

Others had similar reactions. Stephen Roach, Morgan Stanley's Chief Economist and Director of Global Economic Analysis, says the shock of the March 28 shake-up "paralyzed the firm. It had the biggest impact on people who had been here for a long time, who have Morgan Stanley values and spirit coursing through their veins. I was so upset and angry, I made up my mind that I didn't want to continue to be associated with Morgan Stanley." That didn't last either. On Friday morning, he held his weekly global conference calls for teams of economists. "Those teams I built were looking to me," he says. "And I thought, Not only am I not go-ing to leave, I'm not going to sit there" and do nothing. Roach took the view that it was up to the people who worked at the firm to "take it back," he says. "*We* are Morgan Stanley."

Joe Perella wasn't quitting either. On Tuesday he went into Purcell's office and told him that he didn't agree with what he was doing, that he had a big problem with his decision, and he didn't know how he could live with it, but if he did decide to leave, Purcell would be the first to know about it. Perella was sure Purcell expected him to walk out, but he was a master strategist. If he quit, he wanted to do it on his timetable, to be sure it would count for something.

Terry Meguid was on an island in the Caribbean with his family on his children's spring break when Purcell called to tell him that Pandit and Havens were leaving, and that the story had hit the newspapers. Ac-cording to people who saw him in the office the next day, Meguid said he'd see him when he returned at the end of the week. Half an hour later, Purcell called back to say that he was sending one of the firm's G-5s to pick up Meguid and his family at the nearest airport that could take a large jet, which was on another island, and for them to be packed and ready to go at eleven the next morning. The Meguids flew into New Jersey's Teterboro Airport, and he went to the office without changing his clothes. The story of his hasty return went the rounds because he ar-rived wearing an aqua T-shirt, khakis, and Top-Siders.

John Havens came back to the office to pick up his things and was greeted with a six-minute standing ovation on the trading floor. In protest against Havens's and Pandit's firing, some clients temporarily suspended trading with Morgan Stanley; and TIAA-CREF sold one million shares of Morgan Stanley stock.

That evening, around a quarter to four, Perella was in his office on the thirty-first floor when he got a call from Purcell saying that he was holding a firm meeting to introduce Zoe and Steve, and asking him to come down to the sixth-floor auditorium. Purcell held up the meeting until Perella got there, and when he walked in, hundreds of people were waiting. Purcell, Crawford, and Cruz were sitting together at the long conference table at the head of the room.

Purcell said, "Oh, here's Joe. Come on up and sit with us."

Perella took a seat, but left a gap between himself and the others.

Purcell began by announcing Crawford's and Cruz's new positions. Each of them spoke briefly, then Purcell asked Perella, "Well, Joe, is there anything you want to say?"

Perella later told friends that, as soon as he walked into the room, he knew he was going to have to speak. If he had stood up and said, "I think this is a travesty and I hereby resign," it would have been "good for Hollywood," but terrible for the firm. Instead, he began by congratulating Cruz, recognizing that she had achieved the highest position of any woman on Wall Street. He went on to say that this was a very difficult day for him, and that Pandit and Havens were his "blood brothers," but that he loved the firm. "I came to Morgan Stanley because I wanted to work with winners, and all of you are winners," he said, and the audience finally broke into applause. He never mentioned Purcell or Crawford.

Privately, some of the senior bankers who decided to stay agreed that the situation could not fester indefinitely. The competition would pick off good people, at some point the board would have to see that they were losing their assets, and Purcell would go down. As Byron Wien says, "Up until March 28 there was hope, and after March 28 there was no hope. People in Morgan Stanley fell into one of two categories, those who were planning to leave immediately and those who were planning to leave at year-end." Wien smiles, and says, "Obviously that wasn't really the case, but I tend to polarize things in the extreme."

Earlier that day, Purcell granted one of the few interviews he would give over the next months. He and a *New York Times* reporter talked in the chairman's private conference room, against a backdrop of signed photographs from dignitaries and sports stars—President George W. Bush, Tiger Woods, and Arnold Palmer. Purcell said that the firm was not divided and that morale was "fine."

By Wednesday, the story had zipped to the top of page one.

The *Times* headline read: "Intrigue Engulfs Morgan Stanley: 2 Executives Out, Chief Is Facing a Revolt. Turmoil Reflects Dispute over Direction of the Investment House." The piece was seeded with such phrases as "bitter power struggle," "long-simmering dispute," "public brawl," "palace intrigue," "long-standing divisions," "power grabs and abrupt firings."

Purcell said, "I'm disappointed that anybody who benefited by a career at this great company would take action and hurt the value of the brand and share price. We are trying to satisfy our clients, shareholder[s] and employees, not eight people who wrote a letter." The statement reflected the difficulty Purcell had in sounding like a leader who could stand above the fray when he was under attack.

The reporter reminded readers that the Morgan Stanley board was "dominated by directors who either hail from Dean Witter or have been picked by Mr. Purcell," that Purcell was "aloof and distant," didn't "schmooze with clients," and that he commuted to Chicago, an unfathomable concept to most New York readers.

The day the Group of Eight went public, reporters began to mention John Mack, "the heart and soul" of the firm, as a possible replacement for Purcell. Mack declined all comment, and maintained near-total public silence on the subject for the next three months.

As soon as the news broke, the challengers began to be called "Eight Grumpy Old Men," and Purcell characterized them as "senior citizens." They didn't like the appellations, but there is a point when it is too late to claim middle age. The spectacle of a group of elders stepping back in to save a company from their successors was rare enough to enliven the news, and the image of the old guard standing up to fight for the "good" Wall Street, for capitalism with honor, evoked images of the aging heroes of legend. Few reporters believed the Eight could succeed, but they treated them with a sort of puzzled respect. One seasoned financial reporter said that the only reason he thought they had a chance was that they had hired Bob Greenhill, who would never say, "Oh, well, we've given it our best shot, let's give up." Greenhill was persistent, tough—and expensive. If the Eight had engaged him, they were serious, and they were in the fight to stay.

At 7:04 A.M. on Wednesday, March 30, David Faber began the day on CNBC by describing the sudden flare-up as "a brawl. They're gonna continue to fight. It's gonna be fun," he said, adding that the Eight presented arguments against Purcell's leadership "beyond the stock price," which was down 28 percent since its high in 2000, while its competitors were up nearly 40 percent. Those figures would be regularly repeated all spring. Faber interviewed the representative of a large fund, who agreed that the company had "underperformed on every benchmark," compared with its peers. The fund manager said, "Either they turn this ship around, or it's a very attractive franchise and they sell or break it up."

CNBC ran the headline "Executive Scuffle" an hour later, calling the crisis "a huge management shake-up, an all-out battle."

"It's a failed coup," the CNBC commentator said, "and Philip Purcell, the CEO, is going and finding anyone who might have been involved in that failed coup and getting rid of them."

Later that morning, CNBC interviewed Scott Sipprelle, who remarked, in regard to the implication that the Eight were so old they might not be in full control of their faculties, that he was forty-two years old, and he had also warned the board about the firm's performance and leadership.

Melissa Lee, the young CNBC reporter who would be assigned to stand outside Morgan Stanley headquarters at 1585 Broadway for the next few months, announced, "This is where the battle is being fought. If you're a rival, then you're licking your chops."

Andy Merrill got a call from CNBC, inviting representatives of the Group of Eight to appear on Ron Insana's show. The dissidents were seated around the conference table at Bob Greenhill's, and as Merrill recalls, "there was a fair amount of debate whether going on TV was the right thing to do. It had tactical value; Ron Insana is a heavyweight serious business personality, and we felt if we were going to talk to anybody he'd be a good person. And CNBC goes to every institutional trading floor in the country, and every floor at 1585 Broadway.

It was the best way to reach the vast majority of investors and Morgan Stanley employees. Going on TV would put a face on the Grumpy Old Men. For one thing, people would see that they were not old, and that this wasn't a flight of fancy."

They agreed to accept the invitation, but when Merrill asked, "Who wants to go?" some people were willing, others were absolutely not. There was no way Lewis Bernard or John Wilson was going to appear on TV. The logical choices were Parker Gilbert and Bob Scott, who had held the top two jobs at the firm. Joe Fogg wanted to cheer them on and didn't want to miss the action, and said he'd come along. They called a car, and with Merrill as their guide, they set off for CNBC's New Jersey studios.

As they drove into the parking lot, Gilbert leaned over from the backseat and said to Merrill, "I probably should have told you this sooner, but I've never been on TV before." This was the first time anything was important enough to compel him to sit in the makeup chair and subject himself to an application of Pan-Cake makeup, while a stranger checked the top of his head to be sure the part in his thinning hair was straight.

And so it was that at 2:00 P.M., the pleasant-faced balding CNBC reporter Ron Insana sat at a smallish round blond wood table that made grown men look as though they were at school for a child's report, and introduced Parker Gilbert and Bob Scott.

On every trading desk with a computer monitor, and in every Wall Street office where the televisions were tuned to CNBC all day, in conference rooms and chairman's suites, and business school classrooms where students take notes on their computers and keep a pop-up screen open to CNBC, hundreds of thousands of people turned up the volume to hear the former chairman and president of Morgan Stanley patiently explaining why eight Morgan Stanley Advisory Directors were calling for their chairman and CEO to pack up and return to Chicago. No one at Morgan Stanley wanted to go anywhere near the chairman's office, but everyone wondered how he was reacting.

Gilbert was wearing a burgundy tie and a white button-down shirt, his legs were crossed at the ankles, and his hands were tucked between his knees until he found a more comfortable position and crossed his arms, hugging his chest. Making an evident effort to look at Insana, rather than down at the table where two white Styrofoam coffee cups sat untouched through the interview, Gilbert told Insana about the strictly private letter the Group of Eight had written a month earlier, expressing their concerns about the firm and asking that Purcell resign.

Gilbert said, "We wrote the letter as shareholders, as retired executives, people who have really dedicated their life to Morgan Stanley and care deeply about it. We asked for a private meeting with the board, which they absolutely refused and we never had a response from them ... [until] Monday evening and Tuesday," when Pandit and Havens were forced out.

A senior Morgan Stanley investment banker recalls that when he and his colleagues heard that the Advisory Directors had sent the board a letter and hadn't gotten any response, they "were outraged. The arrogance, that Advisory Directors weren't able to speak to the board—we were furious."

Insana noted that the morning's *Wall Street Journal* suggested that the Group of Eight was setting itself up as a new board of directors. Gilbert gave a little shrug, a mannerism that emerged as a response to being televised. "I'd like to see a new board," he said in a raspy voice, and smiled. "We are very much in touch, but we are certainly not a board of directors."

Insana asked Bob Scott, "What if you get a 'just say no' defense?"

Scott, whom Phil Purcell thought he had neutralized when he pushed him out of the presidency in 2003, blinked once. "We're not going away," Scott said, "and 'just say no' is unacceptable, a complete failure of fiduciary responsibility of the directors. We will keep applying the pressure. We did not go public with our letter, we didn't want this to be a public debate, but when Phil started shooting people Monday night, we didn't have a choice."

As Scott Sipprelle said earlier in the day, "The management changes that were made yesterday were the latest in a pattern of very troubling, if not scandalous behavior ... To be sent to the gulag for questioning strategy," as he believed Pandit, Havens, and Newhouse were, "is not the way capitalism is supposed to work."

Looking across the table at Insana, Gilbert summed up the challengers' position about the behavior of Morgan Stanley's leadership: "It's just wrong," he said.

Although control of a $60 billion company was at stake, most journalists understood that the fight was about more than money. As one former *Wall Street Journal* reporter said, "You saw naked self-interest. Bad guys and good guys. Colluders, who were eventually beheaded, and people who just wanted to do the right thing."

CNBC followed the interview with an "instant but hardly scientific" informal poll on its Web site. Of 1,500 voters, 84 percent were in favor of Purcell's resignation.

On Thursday, the Group of Eight incurred their first major expense: they ran a full-page ad in the *Wall Street Journal* at a cost of $250,000. Titled "A Letter to the Morgan Stanley Board of Directors," it began, "We regret that we must resort to another letter, but given your refusal to meet with us . . .

> The issues that are foremost in our minds as we call for a new CEO are at the heart of your responsibilities in the areas of business performance and governance. A common proxy for measuring performance is share price. Morgan Stanley's stock has dramatically underperformed the relevant market indices and its peers over the last five years. The Firm's growth in earnings per share has been negative versus positive growth for our peer companies. Morgan Stanley's premium return on equity has been eroded to where it is actually below that of our peer companies.
>
> When you begin to look at performance by business segment, the reason for our stock's decline becomes clearer. In retail securities, we have experienced negative growth in revenues and our pre-tax margins are unacceptably low. The key to profitability in the asset management business is growth in assets under management, and our performance since 1998 has been mediocre at best.
>
> The performance scorecard above summarizes Mr. Purcell's record since the merger. It is a failing report card.

The final straw was "the manner in which the Board brought this matter to a conclusion this week," the Eight wrote in their letter. "The loss of several key executives who were very important contributors to the success of the highly profitable institutional securities business— because they were unwilling to swear loyalty to an ineffective CEO—

is an outrage . . . We view the Board's actions, including its apparent support of this 'reorganization,' as a failure of corporate governance, a failure to fulfill its fiduciary duties and a failure to act in the best interests of the Morgan Stanley shareholders."

The letter cited Morgan Stanley's poor relationship with regulators and the blemish on the firm's reputations by "ill-handled court cases," and noted in particular "the Perelman/Sunbeam case in Florida."

Palm Beach County Circuit Court Judge Elizabeth T. Maass had just instructed the jury to set aside "presumption of innocence until proven guilty." She said that Morgan Stanley had shown "willful and gross abuse of its discovery obligations," and "a reasonable jury could conclude that the evidence of misconduct demonstrates consciousness of guilt." The firm added $100 million to its reserves for the case, which were now up to $360 million. The news came out on Monday, April 4. On Tuesday, Scott Sipprelle issued a press release announcing that Copper Arch Capital would "Pursue Breach of Duty Claim Against Members of Morgan Stanley Board of Directors," over the Perelman case, which Sipprelle described as a "fiasco."

The accusations directed toward the board were a real threat. The implication was that the directors might be subject to legal action by shareholders or government agencies.

For Purcell and Ed Brennan, the "open letter" had echoes of Bob Monks's advertisement in 1991 that showed the faces of the Sears directors under the headline "Non-producing assets."

The media dove into the story. Morgan Stanley's retail advertising was unpopular with many at the firm who felt it did not reflect the firm's financial expertise and sophistication in world markets. One print ad showed three shiny-haired girls who looked like debutantes, lounging on a sofa, with the tag lines: "Three car payments. Three private colleges. Three weddings. I think I am having chest pains. How are we going to pay for all this? Invest? Invest in What? The market is more unpredictable than our daughters." The broadcast ads featured a character called "my Morgan Stanley guy," who is humorously mistaken for a family member.

The *Saturday Night Live* skit inverted the snobbish tone. This time the girl was blond and tattooed, wearing a short skirt and a pink baby-doll top, accompanied by a boy dressed in complementary style. A clean-cut man in a suit, who appears to be her father, picks them up at school to drive them home.

This is an excerpt from the dialogue:

Man: You've really done it this time, Ashley. Smoking pot at school? That's gonna look great on the college application. That is gonna put you in the top earnings bracket for the rest of your life. (*Looks at boy*) Who's this? Your dealer? . . . If you don't get into a decent college, you know I'll empty out your college fund, so help me—I'll . . . buy a boat!

Girl: Fine!

Man: Fine! Get in here (*points to car*). You dress like a total whore, by the way.

Girl: I hate you.

Man: Well, I hate stupidity . . . And you're going to be paying credit card interest on that streetwalker outfit till you're too fat and old to wear it anymore.

. . .

Boy to
girl, in
undertone: Your dad's kind of a dork.

Girl: That's not my dad. *That's our Morgan Stanley guy.*

. . .

Voice-over: Morgan Stanley. Committed to your family's goals. Maybe even more than you are.

The skit was e-mailed around Wall Street from one firm to the next, to the amusement of the competition.

Retail brokers in distant markets got the news of the challenge and were at a loss as to what to say when their clients asked what was going on in New York. The *Fort Wayne Journal Gazette* in Indiana, the *Charlotte* (North Carolina) *Observer*, the Biloxi *Sun Herald* in Mississippi, and the *Deseret Morning News* in Purcell's hometown of Salt Lake City were among the dozens of papers that featured stories about what the AP's Michael Martinez told them might be "the biggest shareholder coup in history."

James J. Cramer, a former Goldman Sachs partner, columnist, author, television personality, and cofounder of TheStreet.com, later would write, "Purcell was hated for his intense arrogance by almost everyone who worked for him. His lack of people skills, Wall Street gibberish for 'he thought he was better than everyone else,' ate him alive." Cramer, who had $30 million invested in Morgan Stanley, had his own issues with Purcell, who never met with him, giving Cramer the impression that, to Purcell, he was "small fry."

Ron Chernow, author of *The House of Morgan*, said, "It was a merger of patricians and plebeians, and the final irony was that the plebeians outwitted the patricians. There is a feeling that Purcell desecrated the Morgan Stanley name. It's emotional for them and it goes beyond money: they gave Phil a Cadillac and got a Chevy in return."

The fight was closely followed in the British newspapers, which took a sharp tone. Peter Thal Larsen in the *Financial Times* wrote, "These days investment bankers are generally seen as egocentric mercenaries whose only loyalty is to their next bonus. So it was somewhat heartwarming last week to see eight former executives of Morgan Stanley . . . launch a public campaign to defend their former employer's 'reputation for integrity and excellence,'" and make the point that "at Morgan Stanley . . . history matters."

The "pox on both their houses" feeling was reflected in the stock price. On Tuesday, April 5, Morgan Stanley closed down 3.2 percent at $56.45.

Michael Thomas, the acerbic author and columnist who once worked at Lehman Brothers, where his father was the senior partner, compared the merger to the ravages of the French vineyards, when American vines, grafted onto the healthy stock, passed on a destructive pest known as phylloxera and nearly wiped out the wine industry in France.

At Morgan Stanley, Thomas wrote, "a so-so credit-card and retail-finance business has been grafted onto the powerful, premium rootstock of a first-class investment banking firm ... and is on the way to spoiling those vines.

"[T]he phylloxeric personality is Philip Purcell, a former management consultant who came with the Dean Witter merger into Morgan Stanley, rather like the parasitic louse that arrived in France on a shipment of American vines around 1860 and nearly wiped out the French wine industry."

Describing Morgan Stanley as the bluest chip on Wall Street, and the best "proof that money could be earned in great, gleaming sums by combining absolute professionalism with at least the appearance of absolute probity," Thomas wrote that under Parker Gilbert, the firm "represented the absolute zenith in team play, closed ranks, all for one and one for all." Now, he said, the firm "seemed to be drifting toward mediocrity and a 'dog-eat-dog' internal dissension." It was a considerable contrast to the motto, "Honor and optimism," that he attributed to the fictitious firm he wrote about in his novel *Hanover Square*, a firm that in its early days bore some resemblance to the traditional Morgan Stanley.

Eleven

"WHERE'S OUR $30 BILLION?"
AND OTHER QUESTIONS

April 4–April 20, 2005

Purcell didn't waste time. In the first four days of the public fight, Purcell, Zoe Cruz, Steve Crawford, and Jerker Johansson saw ten major institutional investors and clients. On the morning of April 1, they flew to Boston to visit State Street, the firm's largest investor, which held 7.41 percent of the stock; and Fidelity Management and Research Group, which owned 5.53 percent. Word had gotten out that they were coming, and a reporter and cameraman were waiting for them outside one of their appointments.

It did not make sense to the clients that Morgan Stanley had let Vikram Pandit and John Havens go; they were two of the most effective people on Wall Street, and the investors had long and fruitful relationships with them. Purcell couldn't restrain himself from attacking the Group of Eight and the media, but what the investors wanted to know was whether he was committed to the integrated strategy, or, as they had heard, was considering spinning off Discover, or the Retail Division, or both. Purcell assured them that rumors of a spin-off were false and that the shape of the firm would not change in the foreseeable future.

That afternoon, Purcell and the others flew back to address employees at the firm's Westchester headquarters. The atmosphere in the Times Square office was supercharged, and a large, if mostly silent, cadre of employees was rooting for the Eight. One executive recalls that many of her colleagues were saying, "You go, guys! This is great! Just keep it stirred up." In Westchester, the mood was calmer and more supportive. Purcell began by talking about what a difficult week it had been, and quickly segued into comments about the Group of Eight and their advisor. "Bob Greenhill's tried to spin this firm apart in the past," Purcell said. "He failed and he will fail again this time." He defended the stock price, saying that the Eight "conveniently pick a five-year period" and that in 2000 the stock was trading well above the usual price-to-earnings ratio, so its decline seemed more precipitous than it was. He accused "the eight retired executives" of "tearing the firm down," called them "disloyal," and asked rhetorically, "Should a firm be governed by a board of independent directors, or by seven people who made an immense amount of money by taking public a company in which they happened to be partners?" (He excluded Bob Scott, apparently because when Morgan Stanley went public, Scott wasn't senior enough to be awarded the same amount of stock as the others.)

One of the executives asked, "Why aren't we pushing back a little harder?" and wanted to know if the firm had plans to go on TV or take out its own full-page ads. Purcell answered that he expected that the Eight would learn "that usually [when] somebody is shadowboxing, you get tired of watching them and go home. Two people get in a fight, everyone watches, and everyone stays. We are not going to get into an unseemly public fight with the Eight. We will keep our dignity. We will keep our pride, and we'll win the debate by enhancing the franchise, although they are trying to tear it down."

Cruz was outraged and wounded by the Eight's attack. Purcell had introduced her as "the most successful woman in our business," her office was so full of flowers sent by well-wishers that she said, "it looks like a funeral home," yet instead of being able to rejoice in her new position, she was defending the firm in an environment she described as filled with "paroxysms of emotion." Cruz offered that it "would be inhuman not to expect sadness in the Equity Division" on the departures of Pandit, Havens, and another senior banker, Guru Ramakrishnan, who had also announced that he was leaving, but the response to Johansson's appointment was extremely positive. She said it was "unfathomable how journalists are allowing this circus to go on," but it was "enheartening" to see how many people within Morgan Stanley chose to stay "and fight for the firm in its hour of greatest need."

"This train has left the station," she said. "Let's just focus on killing the competition." She added that after "eight long years" the new structure had established "the United States of Morgan Stanley" and that it would be "no more them versus us," referring to the Retail and Institutional Securities divisions.

P urcell organized a dinner of his new management committee members, at which they discussed writing a letter to a publication, or taking out an ad that all the management committee members would sign, asking the Group of Eight to stop their attacks on management, and saying that they were united and determined to move on. Some of the people at the meeting felt that would create the impression that they unilaterally supported Purcell or that they took the Group of Eight's attempt to unseat him as an attack on them as well. Joe Perella was in London on business, and Terry Meguid used his absence as a reason to urge the group to hold off. He said he didn't think it would serve them to get in a "public pissing contest" with icons of Wall Street. When the meeting was over, many left with the understanding that they had decided not to send a letter to the media.

The next afternoon, the *Wall Street Journal*'s Randall Smith called sources at the firm, following up on a tip about a "loyalty letter." A management committee member who returned the call told Smith he didn't know of any such letter, but wondered if someone had leaked the conversation from dinner the night before. Around 5:00 P.M. Zoe Cruz stopped by Terry Meguid's office to show him a copy of a letter for the management committee members to send to the Group of Eight. According to people who spoke to Meguid that day, he told her he thought they had decided not to respond, but Cruz said the letter was strictly private.

The second page contained signature blocks for members of the management committee, but Joe Perella was not among them and Meguid asked Cruz why his name was missing. People who were there that day understood that Cruz told Meguid they wanted to get the letter out to the Eight that evening. Meguid later told people he had tried to lighten the atmosphere by saying something like, "What's the hurry? It's nearly their bedtime," referring to the "Grumpy Old Men" designation. At that point Ray O'Rourke, the director of public relations, showed up looking for the letter. It appeared that there had indeed been a leak and that O'Rourke was trying to respond to Randy

Smith's query in time to make Smith's deadline for the morning paper. Meguid said he wouldn't sign without talking to Perella, and he and Cruz went downstairs to see Steve Crawford, who had previously worked for Meguid. It seems that Meguid talked Crawford out of signing. Without Perella, Meguid, or Crawford, the letter would not have much meaning and it never went out. Rather than showing that the management committee was united, the failure to get the letter out underlined that, even in the absence of Pandit, Havens, and Newhouse, the committee remained divided.

During the course of that spring, and long after, unsubstantiated rumors continued to surface about a "loyalty oath" that hundreds of people were asked to sign. Nobody ever produced a copy or a draft; the aborted "unity letter" from the management committee is the most likely source of the rumors.

That weekend, Purcell flew home to Chicago, where the board held a special meeting and voted to sell Discover. Purcell announced the plan on Monday, after the market close. Some, if not all, of the directors who voted on the spin-off were unaware that he had just assured two of the firm's largest shareholders that the Discover connection was solid.

Purcell said Discover was "more properly valued as a stand-alone entity . . . [and the spin-off] makes it very clear that the remaining Morgan Stanley is in the asset management business. Hopefully, it ends any conversations that we are not in the retail or asset management business." The remark was a little odd, as no one had claimed that the firm wasn't in those businesses, only that the divisions were underperforming.

People on the analysts' call were puzzled that Purcell couldn't answer questions about such subjects as the tax implications of the spin-off, although Discover was the only Morgan Stanley division that reported directly to him. That made it evident that the decision had been taken at the last minute as a quick fix, although the board had, in fact, been discussing the idea for months. Journalist Roderick Boyd reported in the *New York Sun*, "Some analysts see this as fighting to save his job by offering to spin off units in the hope of appeasing former executives."

Scott Sipprelle told an interviewer, "If the board is suggesting getting rid of Discover and including the CEO in that divestment, I would support that." Speaking for the Group of Eight, Andy Merrill said, "Phil Purcell has a major people problem, not a major problem with the operating units."

David Hendler, an analyst at CreditSights said, "The stock investors hate the drama and defections this will cause, and the bond guys hate the sale of steady, cash flow positive units." Hendler expected Purcell to leave, possibly after the Discover sale. "He's already admitted defeat by offering to break up the financial conglomerate model he pitched the Dean Witter merger on." Christopher Atayan, a former Morgan Stanley banker, said that the Morgan Stanley directors, "do not understand that investors have no loyalty to anything but return. This will simply create more desire for spin-offs and sales." Atayan suggested that Purcell and the directors were fighting in the wrong weight class; some of the Group of Eight and Greenhill "more or less invented corporate takeover and defense. They know all the tricks."

Sanford Bernstein's Brad Hintz later explained that the valuation of Discover was based on the assumption that a third-rank card company would be able to borrow money at the same low interest rates as the first-rank Morgan Stanley. "On its own," Hintz says, "Discover would drop to the lower rating, money would cost it more and the bottom line would be negatively affected."

On Monday, April 4, Purcell and his team went to London. Although the public fight had been going on for less than a week, he already looked older and wound up. In London, Purcell, Cruz, Crawford, and Johansson met with a large group of managing directors at the Morgan Stanley office. Purcell told them, "We have visited ten institutions in four days. They're looking for premium ROE and growth," and said that if they achieved those goals, "the stock price will take care of itself." He referred to the Eight in boxing terms again, perhaps a holdover from his father's college sport: "Let these fellows punch themselves out," he said. "What these guys want is a fight. Let 'em shadowbox. That's about as boring as anything you've ever seen ... They're doing absolutely nothing except harming the franchise. The board is not going to change CEOs and not going to meet with the Grumpy Old Men.

There's no purpose [to their challenge] except self-aggrandizement."
He advised the Eight to "stop the circus of holding meetings with investors. They're up in Boston trying to tear us down."

Purcell was never a comfortable public speaker, but as the fight wore
on, he repeated the same statistics, continually attacked the Eight for
their "disloyalty," remarked bitterly on their attempts "to tear down the
firm," and blamed the media for his troubles. When someone at the
London meeting asked him about a Bloomberg article, he remarked
cattily that it was "probably by Margaret Popper [a well-respected financial reporter] and she writes lots of things that are fiction."

The angrier he got, the less confident he seemed. In high school, he
had played center on the basketball varsity, and he was known to be
"tough under the boards and a decent shooter." Now, he was more like
a player who dribbles around the court and can't make himself pass
the ball, or shoot the winning basket.

Cruz was as angry as Purcell, but she was energized. As for Crawford, with the little lock of hair falling over his forehead, he looked
more like a 1950s movie actor than a banker, and he never seemed
fully engaged.

Someone at the meeting in London remarked that Pope John Paul
II had died that week, and Purcell's name had been in the newspapers
almost as much as the pope's. Purcell's response: "Being compared to
the pope in newspapers . . . I don't know. He may have had a better
week than I did." That evoked laughter, but it was a strange remark.
Was Purcell saying he would rather be *dead* than attacked by a group
he called "old men"? Another managing director who was in London
at the same time fielded questions about what was going on at the firm
with another papal reference; she said, "If Morgan Stanley was the
Vatican, you'd be seeing a burst of black smoke now, but don't worry;
we'll get to the white smoke."

The *Financial Times* persuaded Purcell to give an interview, which
was published on Friday, April 8. Claiming "that clients had been
'overwhelmingly supportive,'" he declared, "it's over with the board in
terms of strategy [referring to the decision to sell Discover] and it's
over in terms of leadership. We are moving on." Later that week, Jack
Welch, the celebrity former chairman of General Electric Co., echoed
Purcell's remarks. In a CNBC interview, Welch commented, "It's over.

The board is with him." Purcell got a welcome pat on the back from David Komansky, Merrill Lynch's former chairman and CEO. Komansky, who left Merrill in 2003, told the *FT*, "Phil was a tough competitor and from what I could see, a good executive. I didn't see Morgan Stanley missing much when I was running Merrill Lynch."

In a background story, the *FT* described the scenario as "a complex mix of performance, personality and long-standing rivalries together with a pinch of peculiarly American snobbery." As *FT* columnist Michael Skapinker wrote, when the G-8 pointed out to the board that they had "very little financial experience," that was hardly likely to encourage the directors to listen. "Morgan Stanley, at present, sounds a miserable place to work," he wrote. "But someone should have told the eight to identify whom they needed to win around—and then remember not to call them idiots."

Purcell continued to take the "it's over" stance, even as events marched relentlessly forward.

The day the *FT* stories appeared, a couple of high-level executives quit. Managing director Brian Leach, the firm's senior risk management officer who came out of Fixed Income, left; and Vikram Gandhi, cohead of the financial institutions group, announced he was leaving to become head of the Global Financial Institutions Group at Credit Suisse First Boston. Gandhi, who had been at Morgan Stanley for sixteen years, appeared to have a good relationship with Purcell. The two of them had worked together in developing one of Purcell's pet projects, the Relationship Management Program in Institutional Securities. On another front, Gandhi and his wife, Meera, were well-known, glamorous New Yorkers. They had bought and restored a town house that once belonged to Eleanor Roosevelt (it was decorated "according to Vaastu principles"), and Meera Gandhi served on a number of important charitable boards.

The departures of Pandit, Gandhi, and Guru Ramakrishnan gave rise to a typical Wall Street quip: "Morgan Stanley? All chiefs and no Indians."

Purcell continued on to Portugal, where some one hundred top retail salesmen had convened for the Chairman's Club outing. He was surrounded by his allies, some of whom were angry to the point of tears. Mitchell Merin, president of the Morgan Stanley Investment Management division, spoke to a Morningstar.com reporter who reached him in Lisbon, and went after Bob Scott, saying, "He's blindly shooting at anybody who ever had Dean Witter on his nameplate." Merin was a bone-deep Purcell loyalist. A Morgan Stanley executive recalls attending one of the first "Insights" meetings for retail brokers after the merger, when Merin opened his remarks by showing a picture on the screen of himself, standing at a filling station, wearing a mechanic's jumpsuit. He told the audience, "This is what I was before Phil Purcell discovered me. Make no mistake: I owe everything I am to Phil Purcell." (Actually, Merin had been working in a planning department at Sears when Purcell "discovered" him.)

Morgan Stanley employees had three communications to deal with on Monday and Tuesday, April 4 and 5. Purcell had sent a letter by e-mail that weekend, and it was released to the newspapers on Monday. The board wrote its own letter; and the G-8 took out another ad in the *Wall Street Journal*.

Purcell wrote a memo "To my colleagues at Morgan Stanley" in which he conceded that this had been "a tough week for us all." Referring to "the disagreement with some of the decisions the Board and I have made in planning for our future," he expressed respect for Havens and Pandit and remarked, "Reasonable people can reasonably disagree." He assured the employees that he would have explained his thinking and strategies to them so the changes wouldn't have come as such a shock, but "unfortunately, the press has made that difficult. Our ability to lay out our thinking in making these changes has been hampered by leaks and an outside media campaign.

"I would not have chosen this debate to be so publicly aired. I do not believe it is in the custom of Morgan Stanley for any member of this firm—current or past—to risk a course of action that would damage our franchise. I cannot—and I will not—similarly respond in ways that ultimately harm our franchise."

He explained, "We are spending a good deal of time—as we should—meeting with as many of you, our clients and institutional investors, as possible."

He asserted that the board "made the right choice" in their stra-

tegic plans and the selection of Zoe Cruz and Steve Crawford as co-
presidents. To underscore the support for them, they were both
appointed to the board that week. Purcell made Joe Perella vice
chairman—without a board appointment. As one managing director
comments, "That was a critical error. Joe was much more senior than
Zoe or Steve."

The board issued its own "Message to Employees" on Monday. Receiving one of these epistles was alarming enough; two coming at
once created the impression that Purcell and the board were acknowledging a crisis but casting the blame as far away from themselves as
they could. The board letter described the criticism as "gratuitous, unfair and alarmist." It claimed that the directors had met to discuss the
G-8 letter, that they had "set out to gather facts as quickly as possible,"
and on the day before the annual meeting had talked "privately and
individually to all but one member of the Management Committee."
(Havens was the missing member.) They wrote that they believed the
management committee was in "substantial agreement on the existing strategy . . . despite some dissenting viewpoints and disagreement
about implementation."

The *Wall Street Journal* described the Group of Eight as "united as
if they were back on a deal team." The *Journal* had it right; it felt like
the old days. Over the next three months, they would meet fifty times
at Bob Greenhill's Park Avenue offices. Sometimes they convened in
the small conference room, where the walls were hung with 1943 U.S.
Navy photographs of World War II Vought Corsairs and Wildcats on
bombing missions, peeling off after dropping their loads. From the
west-facing windows there was a view of the steeple of St. Patrick's
Cathedral. On evenings when meetings ran late, the lights shone from
the windows of the surrounding buildings, and the city glowed. When
the whole group assembled with their advisors, they used a larger conference room where Bob Greenhill's wife, Gayle, who was chairman of
the International Center of Photography, hung a rotating exhibition of
dramatic, large-scale photographs. A large-screen TV was tuned to
CNBC. Meetings started with reports of who had heard what, and
what each of them had accomplished.

Beard, Fogg, Gilbert, and Scott were calling institutional investors and hedge funds. Everyone wanted to talk to them. The media coverage gave them currency; and people wanted to know the inside story. Few industries outside of the news business are as avid for the latest information as financial services, where it can be expensive to be the last to get wind of a change, and profitable to be among the first.

Andy Merrill swapped information with his media contacts. He updated them, and they asked him to confirm or deny what they'd heard, which kept him in the loop about what the other side was saying. He relayed requests for interviews or information to the Eight, and they discussed who, if anyone, should speak for the group.

Every day was different, and few days were planned. They were making it up as they went along, grimly entertained by the reports that Purcell believed they were conducting a highly orchestrated campaign.

They weren't all at every meeting, although Gilbert, Scott, and Beard hardly missed one. They usually took the same seats, like family at a dinner table. The chief strategists were Gilbert, Scott, Beard, and Fogg. Wilson and Bernard were the "governors," heading them off when they thought the group was going too far. Gilbert usually had the final word.

The Eight's ad, titled "A Message to Morgan Stanley Employees," was a response to reports that the fight was "really ripping the place up inside," as one of them admitted. The dissidents urged the employees to "remain focused" and not to "lose hope," and wrote that they understood that they were upset and felt powerless, due to "the atmosphere of intimidation and fear at the Firm in which you may feel that you cannot express your views without fear of retaliation."

The ad read: "We want all of you to benefit from an environment like the one we knew: where a commitment to excellence is a core value and where healthy debate can make us all better people." They had created a Web site, www.futureofms.com, and encouraged employees and anyone else who had a comment to use it to convey their opinions.

Letters and e-mails began to come in immediately, and a surprising number of them were from senior people in the Retail Division. On April 6, a letter arrived from a vice president in the Individual Investors' group, "in support of efforts to remove Philip Purcell as CEO of Morgan Stanley, a view shared by many other employees of the individual investor group—the former Dean Witter."

Citing the "common perceptions in that division," the writer mentioned that Purcell had reneged on his "handshake agreement" with John Mack, which was in direct contravention of "the foundation of our business . . . the long lasting legacy of verbal contracts evidenced by thousands of trades done every day." The "handshake agreement" had become a legend, even though Mack himself said that he and Purcell hadn't literally shaken hands. The angry broker mentioned the $250,000 fine levied by the NASD and paid by Bruce Alonzo, who was head of the Morgan Stanley branch offices nationwide, for his improper use of sales contests to market and promote mutual funds. Alonzo, who was believed to have taken the fall for his bosses—Jim Higgins and Purcell—was still working at Morgan Stanley.

The broker described the culture of the Retail Division as "extremely political," and said that employees were "reluctant to ask serious questions . . . suggest ideas or improvements for fear of clever retributions."

Individual shareholders with large stock positions wrote letters too. One writer, who addressed his letter to the Board of Directors, owned 60,000 shares of Morgan Stanley stock worth $3.3 million, down from $6 million in 2000. He wrote, "Instead of increasing Mr. Purcell's compensation by approximately $20 million and rewarding him for poor performance, I would recommend that he be replaced with a new CEO that would be able to manage with shareholder value in mind."

Another shareholder wrote each of the directors individually, enclosing a copy of a letter he had written in 2001, expressing concerns about Purcell's leadership. That shareholder owned 300,000 shares of Morgan Stanley stock, worth $16.5 million, down from more than $30 million at the market high. A shareholder with 80,000 shares wrote, "Please do not let the Firm fall apart and continue to disintegrate . . . remember what Dick Fisher always used to say, 'the value of Morgan Stanley lies in the employees of the Firm and they leave every evening.'"

The representative of an institutional stockholder with 1.7 million shares wrote, fully supporting the G-8. Daniel Strickler, the owner of 3.8 million shares, who had a twenty-five-year career at Morgan Stanley and was a former managing director, wrote a three-page indictment of

Purcell to the G-8 and copied the twelve largest shareholders of the firm, starting with State Street, Barclay's Bank, and Fidelity. He wrote, "Here is Purcell's workweek. On Monday, he flies in to New York from Chicago on his Gulfstream G-5, arriving at Morgan Stanley's offices between 9–10 A.M. He heads straight to his office. One top executive has never—over eight years—seen Purcell on the banking floors of the Firm. He rarely participants [sic] in client or industry evening events and it is very difficult to schedule a client meeting with him during the day. He leaves his office at 4 P.M. on Thursday and flies back to Chicago. On Friday, he works out of the Discover Card offices in Chicago. Is this how you run a major investment bank? I think not." (Strickler's comments were based on widely held perceptions that were likely exaggerated.) Strickler notes that Goldman Sachs's CEO, Henry Paulson, "schedules hundreds of client meetings every year. In the hotly contested arena competing for major assignments, Morgan Stanley has lost countless deals because it could not produce its CEO as the closer."

He adds, "I caution the Directors against relying on random contacts within Morgan Stanley for the purpose of assessing morale. Particularly in the climate Purcell has created, straying from his party line can put a manager's job at risk."

Strickler hit the ball out of the park, concluding, "What do you say about a CEO who has delivered the worst stock market results in the securities industry? What do you say about a CEO who does not enjoy the respect and confidence of his employees? What do you say about a CEO who spends more time on the greens at Augusta than on the trading floors of his own firm? And what do you say about a Board of Directors that refuses to recognize and deal with these issues?"

A Morgan Stanley employee wrote Chuck Knight that in two years when Purcell received bonuses of $11 million and $13 million, salaries were frozen, profit-sharing plans eliminated, promotions were not accompanied with pay raises, and cash awards in 401K plans were replaced with Morgan Stanley stock "whose sagging performance is jeopardizing the growth of retirement accounts." The employee wrote, "A true leader would walk the halls of this company and feel the sense of low morale, the insult of Purcell's compensation and the lack of vision and leadership."

Judson Reis, chairman of Sire Management, and a former Morgan

Stanley managing director, wrote the board, "I want to avoid the emotional issues that now seem to be attached to Morgan Stanley and share three concerns with you." Among them were the departure of top talent and the instability of leadership. "I cannot think of any market leading company that has had five presidents in four years. Most of you are or have been chief executives . . . I doubt if any of you went through this many number two's in such a short period." Reis enclosed a stock price study, which showed the performance of leading investment banks since Goldman Sachs went public in May 1999. He wrote, "I am confident if the people managing your corporate pension funds or your personal investment underperformed their peers for six years as badly as Morgan Stanley's stock has underperformed its peers, you would have already replaced them . . . I hope you heed the call."

Reis's chart showed that between May 3, 1999, and March 29, 2005, Morgan Stanley's stock was up 9 percent; Goldman Sachs was up 54.1 percent, Merrill Lynch up 38.6 percent, Lehman Brothers up 250.7 percent, and Bear Stearns up 128.3 percent.

The letters kept coming, written on personal or corporate stationery, or by e-mail. "Purcell has worn out his welcome. His track record is second-rate at best. His tenure is littered with the wreckage of an impoverished strategic plan . . . If the comedy is allowed to continue, Morgan Stanley shareholder value will be irreparably squandered."

The Eight were encouraged by the support, but many executives at the firm were upset by the public fight. Anticipating that their business would go down the drain, or downtown to Goldman Sachs while the G-8 and Purcell fought it out, some of them called members of the Eight to express their alarm. Bob Scott got some calls from people saying, "What do you guys think you're doing? You're killing us." Andy Merrill got a voice mail from a man who was "not happy," Merrill says. The message was: "He's screwed. You're screwed. You're just as big of a prick as he is. I'm a big shareholder. Just move on."

Anson Beard, Joe Fogg, and Bob Scott were the most active callers, and they reported that while many of the investors they spoke to understood that the firm was undergoing a leadership crisis, they weren't willing to intervene until the Eight could come up with an alternative plan. As Lehman Brothers analyst Mark Constant said,

"People who hold [Morgan Stanley] shares are going to want something concrete before they give up their votes."

The Eight and Greenhill's team analyzed the business, developed their ideas about what could be done to revive it, and came out with a plan. That brought them back to the tricky question of whether they should propose someone to replace Purcell, even though anyone whose name they put forward would never be approved by the board.

They looked around the conference table and turned to Scott. "It's gotta be you, Scotty," was followed by "but if you want to call Karen . . . ?" Scott didn't have to call; he knew what Karen would say. He said, "Okay."

The Eight released the plan on Monday, April 4. They proposed Scott as CEO, with a nonexecutive chairman who had financial services experience. The plan included asking Havens, Pandit, and Newhouse to return to fill an "office of the president," and set a priority of revitalizing the Retail and Asset Management businesses.

The decision to answer the question "If not Purcell, then who?" made this the most problematic part of the campaign. Even if Dick Fisher had been alive and well and had agreed to step in as the interim CEO, skeptics would have called it a power grab. As it was, given Scott's history with Purcell, some felt he was putting himself forward as cock of the walk; but as Dick Debs said, "Scotty was our sacrificial lamb."

Morgan Stanley's response was dismissive: "The Board is well acquainted with Mr. Scott and his record running our individual investor group and Discover card businesses and can only reiterate what it said yesterday in its message to our employees. The board is fully behind Phil Purcell and the firm's management team."

Scott responded that the lackluster numbers reflected the general market collapse, and in any case, Purcell had never let go of the reins of the Retail or Discover divisions.

Cruz and Crawford increasingly felt that the attack was directed as much at them as at Purcell. Cruz wanted to get back on track and pull up the performance numbers of the Institutional Securities Division, which was now reporting to her.

The debate over the qualifications of Scott versus Purcell diverted the board's attention. Merrill Lynch analyst Guy Moszkowski acknowledged the distraction by remarking, "It's an edifying spectacle. Some clients are going to feel like they'd like a little more discretion from their investment bank, and would prefer to do business with a place that seems to be in more internal harmony."

Gilbert and Scott went on CNBC again to explain their plan. They were in the greenroom, waiting to be interviewed by Ron Insana, when reporter David Faber stopped by. Faber said he didn't see how they were going to pull off the coup. They didn't know either, but as Scott said in response to the board's letter to the employees, "We're not going away." Andy Merrill recalls, "Everyone's initial reaction was, 'This is novel. Everyone respects you, but nobody thinks you're going to succeed.'"

The Advisory Directors were feeling vulnerable. John Wilson said, "Every day, we were sure we would come into the office and find that we were locked out." They worried that their assistants, most of whom had worked for them for many years, would be fired or reassigned to jobs that were uncongenial enough that they would be forced to quit. A couple of the Eight asked their assistants to call Maintenance and ask for big trash bins and packing boxes to be sent upstairs. They cleaned out their offices, threw out some papers, and brought others home. Some of the Group of Eight stopped using the office at 1221 entirely. Dick Debs says he and Bob Scott did "quite the contrary. We didn't want it to look like we were abandoning ship." The assistants and the other Advisory Directors who had offices on the same floor soldiered on.

The Eight still worried that their phones might be tapped, as did many people at 1585 Broadway who were in no way involved in the fight, except as onlookers. Paranoia was rampant. More and more Morgan Stanley executives were going outside the building, around the corner, and out of sight and making calls on their cell phones. Often, they were trying to respond to worried people who worked for them, and clients who were anxious about the situation at the firm. And, of course, in some cases, they were returning headhunters' calls.

Shortly after the Eight announced their new plan, Bob Greenhill called Brad Hintz at Sanford Bernstein. According to Hintz, Greenhill said, "I need help. We can't get anyone to host a meeting." Morgan

Stanley controlled so many underwritings that many firms would be afraid that if they gave the Eight a forum, they would be cut out of future deals. But Sanford Bernstein doesn't do underwritings; Hintz told Greenhill, "I think we can do something." On the morning of April 6, Hintz's salespeople called institutional investors and invited them to a meeting that evening. "Everybody wanted to come," Hintz says. "By noon we had filled the room beyond capacity."

On the evening of Wednesday, April 6, CNBC was outside the Sanford Bernstein offices, filming members of the Group of Eight as they made their way through a crowd of reporters and cameramen. Beard gave a thumbs-up sign; John Wilson looked as though he wished he were anywhere else. Scott, who was slated to take the brunt of the attention as CEO-in-waiting, looked locked and loaded.

People who talk about that meeting often mention that Jeanne Fisher was there, sitting in the front, as Bob Greenhill, Parker Gilbert, and Bob Scott spoke. Her presence, only months after her husband's death, was a confirmation that she believed Dick Fisher would have supported the plan to unseat Purcell. Jeanne Fisher says, "Dick never spoke badly of the firm, but he was fed up, disappointed and let down. I felt strongly that, given everything we knew had come to pass, Dick would have signed the letter, and it would have been a Group of Nine."

A standing-room-only crowd of about one hundred institutional investors listened to a thirty-minute exegesis of the curricula vitae of members of the Group of Eight. Reminding the audience of their experience may have helped their credibility, but it was also a sign that the investors had to be reminded of who they were.

Scott took center stage with a presentation that had been developed in a series of discussions around Greenhill's conference table. His plan was hung on the tag line "Where's Our $30 Billion?"

The merger had been based on the understanding that Dean Witter and Morgan Stanley would each provide approximately half the value of the new firm, but eight years later, the portion of the current firm that came out of the old Morgan Stanley was valued at $45 billion of the $60 billion market cap. According to Scott's logic, if the Dean Witter components had kept up, the market cap of the combined firm should be $90 billion.

Analysts were estimating the stand-alone value of Discover at $14 billion. If Discover was added to Morgan Stanley's $45 billion, that came to nearly $60 billion. Scott extrapolated that the "market is valuing Retail and Asset Management at very little." (Later, when the G-8 expanded their proposal, they estimated that the combined spin-off value of Dean Witter and Discover was between $28 and $32 billion, which valued Dean Witter alone in the $14 to $16 billion range.)

Scott's presentation focused on strategy, not personalities. He began with Retail, an area he knew well from the frustrating period when the division was nominally under his control. He proposed cleaning house and getting rid of low producers, becoming more competitive in products where Merrill Lynch had an edge, including deposits, mortgages, and consumer loans; and adding Alternative Asset and Fixed Income products, and further deemphasizing proprietary funds.

While competing firms invested in products and technology, Scott said, Morgan Stanley cut costs. Purcell hadn't been willing to invest in a platform to support High Net Worth, and didn't want to pay the executives as much as they could earn at other firms. Compliance, technology, operations, and regulatory relations were seriously underinvested, and the expectation that the Morgan Stanley brand would have a positive impact on Retail was never met. Instead, Retail had a negative impact on the Morgan Stanley name.

Scott estimated that the firm could add $1 billion in net income by increasing client assets by 25 percent, revenues from higher margin products by 30 percent, thereby increasing operating margins to 20 percent.

In Asset Management, Scott said that Morgan Stanley had missed out on building Alternative Investments, shut down private equity, and while Goldman Sachs was building value in Alternatives, and BlackRock in fixed income, Morgan Stanley was still focusing on money markets and traditional mutual funds, which were under margin pressure and were not as responsive to client needs.

As Scott noted, Asset Management is a "business of talent," traditionally one of Morgan Stanley's long suits, but Purcell was more interested in keeping costs down. "Current management refers to MSIM [Morgan Stanley Investment Management] as a factory," Scott said.

"Managers have been told they are not proprietary assets. They only stay if they get a percentage of fees generated."

Scott recommended that the firm restore the culture in Investment Management (MSIM), reward excellence, and tailor a series of High Net Worth products. Along with better management of mutual funds, he estimated there was an opportunity to add another $1 billion of net income in Asset Management.

So far, he had accounted for a hoped-for $2 billion pop in net income.

In the Institutional Business, Scott saw the opportunity to reevaluate the amount of capital supporting the business and the ways in which the capital was employed. The Institutional Division needed to invest in an updated risk framework and address an inefficient structure, multiple broker dealers, redundant operations, and outdated technology. After eight years, and despite efforts by John Mack and Scott to integrate the Morgan Stanley Dean Witter interface, Dean Witter was still on the old broker-dealer platform.

Scott added another $1 billion for net impact from strategic improvements in the Institutional business, and estimated cost savings of $1 to $2 billion.

On the "soft issues," Scott referred to the firm's relationship with regulators, which he said had become so adversarial that "we start out with two strikes against us in every regulatory encounter. Culprits are Kempf and Purcell." Just that day the firm had received another Wells notice that the SEC was investigating Morgan Stanley's e-mail retention policies, and the Perelman case was only getting worse.

Scott reminded the audience that the institutional business is a "people/talent business based on trust, commitment to excellence, unblemished reputation, pride of belonging, belief in meritocracy, and respect for unique talents."

"What do we have now?" he asked rhetorically.

"No trust of CEO and new management. Breakdown of meritocracy—if you want to succeed, be a friend of Phil." In the Morgan Stanley tradition, he said, competence came second only to integrity. Under Purcell, "Loyalty is valued above competence . . . People no longer believe excellence is a core value."

Describing the anticipated results of his proposed improvements as "low hanging fruit," Scott estimated that the firm could increase net income by $2 to $4 billion. At twelve times price-earnings ratio, that would equal an increase of $30 billion in market cap.

He exhorted the audience to contact the board "with a letter—you won't get a phone call returned. Better yet, do it publicly. Tell them you want your $30 billion. You want it now. You want a new management team that can get the job done. Eight years is enough time for the old team."

Within hours, a Morgan Stanley spokeswoman issued a response in the now-predictable tone: "We understand that today's presentation was long on bios and short on specifics."

It was easier to criticize the messenger than the message. As the *Financial Times* commented, "The rebels ... did their cause no favours" by putting Scott forward. "That only fuelled suspicions that part of the motivation behind their campaign is a personal clash between Mr. Scott and the man who ousted him from Morgan Stanley."

The meeting was a base hit, but it was far from a home run. For one thing, many of the people who attended represented hedge funds, which were more interested in the short-term fluctuation of stock prices than in the long-term picture.

For the Eight to make an impact, they had to persuade major institutional investors, who owned more than 63 percent of Morgan Stanley's stock, of the merits of their case. The day after the Bernstein meeting, as Andy Merrill says, they "took the show on the road." The next phase of the "air war" began when Greenhill flew Scott, Gilbert, and Fogg to Boston in his Cessna Citation X to visit State Street and Fidelity. As Scott describes the experience, "To fly with Greenie at the wheel? Are you kidding me? It's great. We get out there to Westchester. Plane is on the tarmac, steps down, professional pilot, everything through the checklist. Greenie sits in the pilot's seat, engines running, take off, land, do our meetings, come back to the general aviation terminal at Logan Field. Same routing. Greenie's always in a hurry."

Parker Gilbert recalls that at Fidelity, "they agreed with a lot we had to say. Phil had not made a favorable impression, but they said the difficulty in moving forward was what to do about it, short of mounting a proxy fight." Morgan Stanley's governance did not allow for a special meeting to be called. At State Street, the senior executive who met with them expressed support for their views, but much of the Morgan Stanley stock State Street held was custodial, which limited their options. In Boston the dissidents learned that Purcell had told the investors that he was committed to the integrated model and didn't intend to sell Discover, only three days before he announced the Discover spin-off plan. It looked as though he and the board were running scared. Still, though the dissidents got a hearing, the investors did not make a commitment to support a change in leadership, get actively involved, or make phone calls to the directors.

When Joe Perella returned from England, he told his colleagues that he had a voice mail message from Mike Miles and Ed Brennan, who were calling to say how pleased they were that he was going to stay at the firm. Perella said he was more convinced than ever that the board did not understand what was going on.

On Saturday, one of the most respected younger people at the firm called Perella and told him that a couple of them had come into the office and decided they wanted to express their views to the board. He asked if Perella could get them a meeting. Perella said he would try and called Mike Miles, to whom he owed a phone call. According to people Perella talked to later, he explained that the situation was graver than the board realized, and that a group of investment bankers were getting together to "save the firm" and asked him to organize a meeting for three or four of their generation to express their concern. Miles's response was, "If the purpose of that meeting is to tell us to get rid of Phil, that isn't going to be a very productive meeting." Miles told him, "If I were you, I'd be trying to put the genie back in the bottle."

Perella reiterated to Miles that the situation was serious, and that telling the bankers to "shut up and go back to work" was not the way the story was going to play out. Miles said they'd been on the phone for forty-five minutes, which was long enough. He would think about getting some directors together to talk to the bankers, but Perella never got a call back on the request for a meeting.

Miles called Perella again on Sunday. He had heard that another group was in the office, writing a letter to the board, and he was enraged.

As someone who spoke to Perella at the time recalled, Perella said, "Weren't you listening to me yesterday? I told you the state they're in. I have nothing to do with any letter, but I wouldn't worry about it if I were you. They'll never send it. They've seen what happened to the people who agreed with the last letter."

When he got off the phone, Perella later told friends that he thought, "All is lost. This is not going to have a happy ending. They don't understand what's going on. This guy sounds like he'd rather burn down the building than get rid of Phil."

On Monday, April 11, the Council of Institutional Investors (CII), the trade association that represented 140 pension funds with $3 trillion under management, convened its spring meeting in Washington, D.C. The CII was a leader in the shareholder activist movement; recently, the group had displayed its influence through headline-gathering support of the Disney directors by backing chairman and CEO Michael Eisner against Roy Disney. This year, Morgan Stanley was the hot topic. Members cumulatively had billions of dollars invested in Morgan Stanley stock, and they wanted to know what was going on.

Orin Kramer, the head of the $79 billion New Jersey State Investment Council, which owned four million shares of Morgan Stanley stock, had spoken up even before the meeting began. On Friday, he criticized Purcell for abrogating power to himself and disregarding shareholders' interests, criticized the board for refusing to meet with the Eight, and announced that he planned to bring the matter up the next week at the CII conference. Although he didn't view the Morgan Stanley situation as "one of the great corporate debacles"—and in the context of Enron, WorldCom, and Tyco, that was true—"I'm not sure if mediocrity and suboptimal performance ought to be sufficient." Kramer said, "Corporate governance is about creating shareholder value and a regime presiding over the slow vaporization of shareholder value is the antithesis of good corporate governance."

A representative of the California Public Employees' Retirement Fund (CALPERS), with $182 billion in managed assets and 5.9 million shares of Morgan Stanley, stated that the fund's managers were "concerned" about Morgan Stanley's leadership and performance. CALPERS' chief investment officer, Mark Anson, said, "I'd like to see a bit more communication from the board and Phil Purcell about the company's game plan and vision." Richard Ferlauto, director of pension and benefit policy for the American Federation of State, County and Municipal Employees, called for a meeting between CII representatives and Morgan Stanley.

A spokesperson for the firm replied blandly, "We are always willing to listen and be responsive to the concerns of our shareholders." But when pressed, the Morgan Stanley spokesperson explained that CII would have to wait for a while, as the firm was entering a "quiet period," prior to releasing quarterly results.

The Eight responded to the missives from Purcell and the board by writing another "Open Letter to the Board" and bought another $250,000 full page in the *Wall Street Journal*.

The letter read:

Last week, in an open letter to Morgan Stanley's employees, in which he discussed recent criticisms of his performance and calls for his replacement, your CEO, Philip Purcell wrote: "I would not have chosen this debate to be so publicly aired." We agree and demonstrated as much when we wrote to you in advance of the Company's annual meeting in March, to express our concerns and to request a private meeting with you to discuss them. You have stated that you believe there is no "fair and compelling case" to replace Mr. Purcell, yet you have not spoken to us and have so far declined our repeated requests to meet with you. You have chosen instead to react to our concerns and those of others by announcing a radical restructuring that has cost the firm some of its most talented professionals and further entrenched and insulated Mr. Purcell. Additionally in an abrupt and poorly explained about-face in corporate strategy, you have decided to spin off Discover.

In his carefully crafted press statements in London last week, Mr. Purcell declared victory and announced that the debate about his performance and leadership was "over." This is not a game of winning and losing. There are already too many losers among Morgan Stanley's employees, shareholders and clients. This is about corporate governance, executive leadership and creating value for shareholders.

The Eight asked the board to answer fourteen questions.

They asked if the board had approved the decisions to relieve New-house, Pandit, and Havens of their responsibilities, and if their departures had benefited the franchise and enhanced shareholder value.

They inquired as to whether the board had approved "retention" payments to key employees after the massacre. It was highly unusual to use money to retain people in the financial services industry, unless another firm was bidding for them. In light of the atmosphere at the firm, agreeing to take the money to stay was tantamount to taking Purcell's side.

Another issue the Eight raised was that, at the March 15 annual meeting, the stockholders had voted to eliminate staggered directors' terms, and reduced all of the terms of nonexecutive directors to one year. Yet, within a month of that meeting, the board had appointed Crawford to a three-year term. The Eight asked if that was appropriate.

Other questions dealt with Morgan Stanley's regulatory and legal problems. The Eight asked why the board hadn't disclosed to share-holders before the annual meeting that the SEC's Division of Enforcement had sent the firm a "Wells notice" in January 2005, in regard to enforcement action over retention of e-mails. (Another Wells notice had come in just that week, as Bob Scott had mentioned in the Bernstein meeting.) The Eight wanted to know what kind of investigation the board had conducted in the wake of the Florida court's finding in the Sunbeam/Perelman litigation that "contrary to Federal law" the company failed to preserve e-mails and willfully disobeyed the court's order. Was the board aware (as reported in the *Wall Street Journal* on April 8) that the Perelman claim could have been settled for $20 million in 2003?

They asked what happened over the weekend of April 2 and 3 to cause the board to depart from the publicly stated strategy that Dis-cover was an integral part of the company's asset base, and if the

Discover spin-off had been in the works for months, why the CFO couldn't answer basic questions on the analysts' call.

Finally, they wrote, "Since Mr. Purcell declared 'I would not have chosen this debate to be so publicly aired,' did he recommend that the board meet with us, and how did the Board determine that our concerns were groundless without even speaking with us?"

A day later, they got the only written answer they would ever receive.

Karen Scott was about to enter the Scotts' East Side apartment building when she ran into Bobby Holden, a former New York State trooper who had been Dick Fisher's driver and now drove for Purcell. Karen says, "I had a nice conversation with Bobby," and he handed her an envelope. It was a letter to her husband from the board, written on Morgan Stanley letterhead.

The letter, which was released to the media, included the home addresses of each of the Eight at the top of the page. While the directors knew that the firm was sending the Eight a letter on their behalf, they were not aware that it was publishing their home addresses.

The text read in its entirety:

Gentlemen:

The Board of Directors has considered each of your communications. We have full confidence in Phil Purcell and the strategy that management is pursuing. We are carefully monitoring the performance of Morgan Stanley. It is clear to us that your ill-considered, professionally-directed attacks on Morgan Stanley and our people are damaging the firm and our shareholders. We ask you to desist.

Very truly yours

The signature space was left blank, but at the bottom of the letter were the names of the ten nonexecutive members of the board—everyone except Purcell, Cruz, and Crawford.

The assertion that the attacks were "damaging the firm and our shareholders" implied the threat of a lawsuit. Greenhill & Co. was small by comparison to Morgan Stanley, but the firm was a competitor, and as London's *Independent* wrote, Morgan Stanley's independent directors "are considering whether the group's advisor Robert Greenhill has in particular been acting illegally by giving advice to the dissidents."

The Eight continued to convene every morning at Greenhill's office, and stayed to make phone calls and set up meetings. Greenhill made his telephones, offices, and conference rooms available, and the Eight became as familiar to the staff as the executives who worked there. In the mornings, a long table was set up outside one of the conference rooms with tea and coffee and fruit and pastries; at midday, one of the secretaries came by to take lunch orders—after a couple of days, she didn't have to ask Parker Gilbert what he wanted; it was nearly always a BLT. They began the day by watching the news on CNBC and passing around letters that were usually, but not always, from supporters, and newspaper and magazine articles. As many as twenty core reporters were covering the story. Some of them talked to Andy Merrill four or five times a day.

Through back channels, the Eight heard that the members of the board were getting selective press clippings from the firm, and agreed that they needed to put together more complete binders of clips. It was corporate policy to send all communications to the directors through the firm, and Andy Merrill later heard that "the directors may not have ever seen those clip books."

The media attention was keeping the campaign alive. The biggest threat to the Eight's chances of success was that the press would lose interest, but the story heated up again during the week of April 11.

In Florida, Judge Elizabeth Maass refused Morgan Stanley's request that she recuse herself from the Perelman case, "because of actual or perceived bias toward the plaintiff for an extended period of time." Maas said, "In all honesty, I've had this problem throughout the case, I am not relying on any assertion by Morgan Stanley unless you cite to me the record that establishes it."

In order to stem the talent drain before it got any worse, the board earmarked $200 million in "retention bonuses," and Purcell made a list of twenty-five senior Investment Banking executives who would be offered bonuses in the form of stock, in exchange for their agreement to stay at the firm until the stock vested. Purcell offered the bonuses to the first nine or ten people on the list, and all of them agreed to the terms; then one executive went home, slept on it, and the next day came in and rescinded his acceptance. Before Purcell got any further down the list, the *New York Post* published an unconfirmed rumor about the "stay bonuses," and other reporters started to hone in on the story. Employees who saw the payments as bribes and an insult to the ethos of the firm, and referred to them as "blood money," put pressure on those who had accepted to renege, and the firm immediately shut down the plan. The firm told reporters who inquired that it was not offering retention payments, which was, by then, literally true—although it would have been more accurate to say that the firm wasn't offering them *anymore*. A number of people who were privy to the process reported that the firm now advised the people who had accepted that "it would be in their long-term career interests" to tear up the agreements, another way of saying that they had been revoked.

The crisis worsened on April 13, when Joe Perella and Terry Meguid announced that they were resigning. While this was later taken to have been a simultaneous decision, Meguid had already resigned once, six days earlier. Purcell had said he wouldn't accept his resignation, and Meguid agreed to reconsider. Then one evening, Barbara Meguid told her husband, "You have to decide which Morgan Stanley you work for." He knew the answer. The next day, Meguid submitted his resignation to Purcell, then went downstairs to tell Joe Perella what he'd done.

Perella returned from lunch at San Pietro to find an urgent message to call Purcell. Terry Meguid was waiting to give him the news. Perella and Meguid shook hands tearfully, and Perella said, "I guess I'm going to go up and resign now," and walked to the elevator to ride up to the thirty-ninth floor.

He was in Purcell's office for about an hour, discussing how to minimize the damage. As it evolved, he and Meguid agreed to stay on until May 20, while Perella completed two major deals, and they both agreed to do whatever they could to provide an orderly transition, and to encourage other employees not to follow them out the door.

Eric Gleacher, formerly one of Morgan Stanley's top M & A bankers, and now the head of his own firm, described the departures of Perella and Meguid as "a staggering loss for Morgan Stanley in a business where stature and reputation count for a lot." Perella had just completed Federated Department Stores' takeover of the May Department Stores for $11 billion. He agreed to stay at the firm without further compensation until he finished two other big pending deals, the sale of Hylsamex in Mexico to Techint of Argentina, and the sale of Bavaria to S.A.B. Miller. Almost immediately after he left the firm, Perella, operating as an independent advisor, advised MBNA on its sale to Bank of America for $35.8 billion. In July, *Forbes* magazine ranked him fourteenth in Global Mergers and Acquisitions, with 5.2 percent market share; Thomson Financial reported that he was sixth on the Financial Institutions Group league tables at the end of 2005, ranked higher than Morgan Stanley, or Lehman Brothers. In 2005, *Investment Dealers' Digest* featured him in a cover story as "Banker of the Year."

Earlier that month, a posting on the Yahoo Morgan Stanley chat room advised readers that Perella was "the canary in the coal mine," the early-warning system that would signal the departure of other major executives; and indeed, others took heed. His resignation was followed by the departures of Jamie Greenwald, the managing director who was Head of Global Product Innovation; managing director Linda Riefler; William Kourakos, Head of the High-Yield Bond Division; and James O'Brien from Fixed Income. Thomas Jueterbock, former Head of U.S. Government Bond Trading and Head of Proprietary Trading, left on April 20. A team of eight institutional sales traders went off en masse to Deutsche Bank that week, and executive director Jim Vore went over to Barclay Capital. Purcell said that some attrition was normal, but that was not very persuasive.

Perella told the media that he had left because "I found myself uncomfortable at the firm. I was in a position where I couldn't publicly criticize the actions of Phil Purcell and the board. By not doing so and remaining there, I was tacitly embracing what Phil had done." Others said, "Joe was endeavoring to force change" and resigned when he realized he couldn't make any headway. Perella was among the first of the departing senior managers to negotiate a severance agreement. He was paid $6.4 million, pro rata compensation for the time he had worked that year. He agreed not to talk about the firm for thirty-six months, which was a standard clause in the so-called nondisparagement agreements that appeared in all contracts. He also agreed to help retain other executives who were thinking of leaving; and not to consort with any member of the Group of Eight. Those strictures were unique to the current situation. In a scathing *Bloomberg* essay, author and commentator Michael Lewis asked, "How Much Is Joe Perella's Silence Worth?" Perella was wounded: he said he was simply being paid for the number of days he had worked that year, based on his 2004 compensation. Between them, he and Meguid had some $50 million in unexercised stock options that the firm could rescind if they didn't sign the agreements. As the terms were being worked out, Perella was in Italy and Meguid was in Abu Dhabi, both on firm business.

With Perella's and Meguid's resignations, the fourteen-person management committee had lost five of its most important members in two weeks—the firm's president, the Head of Institutional Securities, the Head of Equities, Head of Investment Banking, and the firm's senior relationship banker—all from Institutional Securities, the "old" Morgan Stanley and the most successful area of the firm. That was a turning point for some of the directors. They decided to interview managing directors, principally from Institutional Securities and Private Wealth Management, and ask for their candid assessments of the situation, and Purcell gave the directors lists of people to meet. As one director says, "Those meetings were very important to changing the outlook of the board."

When the meetings were held at 1585 Broadway, they often took place in the chairman's conference room outside Purcell's office. Sometimes Steve Crawford would wait at the elevator to greet the managing director who was coming to the meeting and would usher the person in, past Purcell's door. If Purcell was working at his standup desk he would look up and say hello. Then Crawford would introduce the banker to the directors and leave. The door to the small room stayed open, and the executives being interviewed could look up and see Purcell across the space where his secretary, Lisa Luca, sat. As one investment banker who was interviewed under those circumstances says dryly, it was "not a very comfortable setting," but the meetings were relatively frank. Most of the people being interviewed had been at Morgan Stanley long enough that they remembered the days of open dialogue and discussion.

The net effect of the interviews was that fewer directors were telling themselves, "It's just a power struggle—get over it." More of them were considering whether Purcell could, or should, survive the onslaught.

Purcell also invited some of the Institutional Securities executives to talk with him one-on-one. One banker says she told him, "Morgan Stanley never gets an 'F' in anything and we had an 'F'" from a prestigious corporate governance rating service. "This isn't going away. When you've gone this far to one extreme, you have to do something radical to recover. I felt it was his to lose. He didn't need to get thrown out, but he was tone-deaf. He could have focused on the board, put in real governance, limited his flexibility, brought back—whether it was Scott, Havens, Vikram—but he would never admit he was wrong." On further deliberation, the banker says, "Compromise isn't always so good. It was better for him to leave."

Nearly two months after the Group of Eight sent their first letter to the board, three directors finally agreed to meet with three of the dissidents. Parker Gilbert recalls that "the condition under which they would meet with us was that the one subject we would not even talk about was the termination of Purcell." The group decided, as Bob Scott says, "If we got that audience we should offer them a way to suffer defeat gracefully." Accordingly, they prepared a plan for the firm to be split into two separate entities. Morgan Stanley would consist of Institutional Securities, Institutional Investment Management, and Private Wealth Management. Dean Witter Discover would include the Individual Investor Group, Retail Investment Management, and Discover. If the plan were adopted it would be an admission that the merger had failed, and that the two firms would never find a way to coexist, certainly not with Purcell at the helm. In a twenty-one-page proposal, the Eight showed how the split could create a sum-of-the-parts valuation of $62 a share.

The plan offered Purcell and the board a way to save face by giving the Dean Witter Discover businesses back to Purcell. Bob Scott says, "We'd figured out that the board was bound and determined to protect

Phil, and we thought it was important that we offer a suggestion that gave him some air cover."

On April 22, Michael Miles, Robert Kidder, and John Madigan met with Parker Gilbert, Lewis Bernard, and Bob Scott in a conference room in Marty Lipton's office, although Lipton wasn't there. Kidder ran the meeting in a pleasant, noncommittal way. Madigan didn't say much, but Miles, who had been on the Sears board and had been through the wars with Brennan, Lipton, and Purcell, was seething. From time to time, his face would get red and he would erupt, and then apologize. He was doodling on a yellow pad; Scott looked over and saw that he was drawing a gallows.

Gilbert, Scott, and Bernard gave the directors copies of their proposal for the spin-off. They had filled in most of the names on the Morgan Stanley organization chart. Scott would be Interim CEO; Steve Newhouse and Joe Perella would be vice chairmen; and Cruz and Pandit would be copresidents. Havens would be Head of Equities, with a senior position for Jerker Johansson; Neal Shear would be Head of Fixed Income; Terry Meguid would be chairman of Investment Banking with Cordell Spencer and Mike Uva as coheads. The Head of Asset Management was "to be determined."

Parker Gilbert says, "It was not a good meeting. I said, 'I beg you to look at what the firm needs and to help the firm by getting rid of Phil Purcell. I beg you to do this.'" At the end, Bob Kidder asked him, "What else do you think we should do?" which Gilbert took to mean, what they should do short of asking Purcell to resign. Gilbert says, "This is it. This is what you've got to do."

Strategy aside, there were two major flaws in the Eight's plan: Cruz and Pandit were incapable of working together; and while the Eight had reason to believe they could count on Havens, Newhouse, Pandit, Perella, and Meguid, they had not agreed to return.

As per their contracts, Perella and Meguid immediately issued statements that they had not known about the plan, nor had they authorized the use of their names. The other directors had not been notified about the meeting until it was over, and when they heard that the Eight had proposed splitting up the firm, as one said, "It seemed like they had reached a point of desperation. They thought they were giving us something to do as a way to get Phil out. We thought, 'Now they're coming up with plans out of the blue, no longer based on analysis because they want to get their way.' It didn't help their cause." Once again, the board was drawing conclusions based on incomplete evidence.

Twelve

"I DON'T CARE IF THEY FIRE ME."
(AND "I QUIT.")

Joe Perella stayed at the firm for five weeks after he resigned, and while he was still working there, he invited analyst Mary Meeker and Ruth Porat, the vice chairman of Investment Banking, to dinner at an Italian restaurant, Sistina. "He was reaching out," Meeker says. "He encouraged us: 'Voice your opinions and let them be known,' he said. 'Write a letter.'"

Porat, tall and slim, with long brown hair, was in her late forties. She graduated from Stanford in 1979 and received an MBA from Wharton in 1987. She was working at Morgan Stanley when Bob Greenhill left and followed him to Smith Barney. When that blew up, John Mack and Joe Perella encouraged Porat to return to Morgan Stanley. She was the only one of the people who left with Greenhill who was asked back. At the time of the Monday Massacre, she was in Florida on spring break with her three sons. Her husband sent her the CNBC update about the devastation of the Institutional Securities business early on the morning of March 29, and then Perella called her. Porat had worked with Pandit and Havens for fifteen years, and she spoke to both of them later that day. "It was completely emotional," she says. "Devastating. I thought the world of Vikram—he is extremely smart." As for Havens, "At the core, John just loved the franchise and cared immensely about it. He would quote J. P. Morgan, and say if you don't trust a man, don't do business with him." She couldn't imagine that she wouldn't be working with them anymore.

She was in Perella's office shortly after he resigned, when Purcell walked in and to her surprise gave her a hug and said, "We're going to have fun now, aren't we?" Porat says, "I said no, and walked out."

That night in late April, Perella told Porat and Meeker over dinner, as Porat recalls, "The pressure was mounting, but it wasn't clear to the board how broad-based the issues were, how much of a problem it was. If we cared about the firm, our collective responsibility as leaders was to do the right thing."

Porat had been hearing similar comments from clients, who called to offer her and the firm moral support. "They were calling me, saying don't leave. One said, 'Leadership is loyalty in times of adversity.' He was talking about loyalty to one another, to the institution, to what we stand for. That was a very potent statement to come from a client. To stabilize the ship."

Mary Meeker left the dinner thinking, "One of the wonderful things about Dick Fisher, he would sit at the round table in his side office, and he'd ask everyone in the room, 'What's your view?' He wouldn't jump in, or cut you off, or ignore you if he disagreed with you. Then he'd ask some prodding questions, and his wonderful skill was he'd come up with a solution that was hard to argue with, usually for the greater good. Everyone always had a voice. What was lost, those voices weren't being listened to."

She said to herself, "Let's get our voices back."

At eleven o'clock that night she sat down at her computer and wrote the draft of a letter to Zoe Cruz and Steve Crawford. "The point wasn't let's get rid of Phil. I like Phil as a person; he was always good to me. But we had the wrong people in some of the important jobs, and Phil was the wrong person to run the complex Institutional Securities business. He did a brilliant job with Discover, but the Institutional Securities business, with its rapid-fire, day-to-day risk dynamics, was different.

"The point of the letter was: Listen. Board, *listen*. If you listen you will learn what is wrong, what is right, how people care, and what we need to do. You aren't even listening. Create a forum."

Meeker had overcome the precipitous slide in Internet stocks, and in 2005, the word on Wall Street was still "Hail Mary," as *New York* magazine once proclaimed. For Morgan Stanley to lose her would be a shocking blow, but she wasn't going anywhere. She was going to follow Perella's advice and let her voice be heard. She let the draft of her letter marinate for a couple of days, and then she went to see her colleague Stephen Roach, Morgan Stanley's chief economist and director of Global Economic Analysis. She told Roach, "I could send this on my own, but it would be more powerful if the two of us sent it."

Roach was an important member of the Morgan Stanley brain trust. A California boy who grew up in Beverly Hills, he received his bachelor's degree in economics from the University of Wisconsin and his Ph.D. in economics from New York University. He had been at Morgan Stanley for more than two decades. Known for his bearish stand, he had been called "The Human Contrarian" and "Mr. Permabear." He was prone to such expressions of pessimism as "economic Armageddon," and his version of an enthusiastic endorsement was "so far, so good." His skeptical approach to markets and macroeconomics was balanced by a boyish enthusiasm and a wry sense of humor. He loved the firm and his job. He says, "You work at Morgan Stanley for twenty-three years and truly, this sounds corny, every day you're excited about coming to work."

Roach was getting calls from people who worked for him all over the world. Sentiment was solidly against Purcell. He was one of the senior executives who believed that one of their most important roles during the spring of 2005 was keeping morale up, but it was difficult, especially as he assumed, as many others did, that the phones were not secure, and he was taking calls on his cell phone.

When Meeker showed Roach the letter she had drafted, he said, "I'm in. I don't care if I get fired."

Meeker agreed. "I didn't care if there were negative repercussions. I would have welcomed them. If what we said wasn't understood, heeded, and listened to, this wasn't the kind of organization I wanted to be a part of. I wanted to get clarity on it. I was at a point in my life, if I stay here, I want it to be the best place it could be. The reason I stayed as long as I did, there's something special; the J. P. Morgan 'first-class business' is a core value. We attempted, in our own small way, to reenergize and refocus that. It was important to take a stand."

They addressed the letter to Cruz and Crawford, hoping to help push a productive dialogue that would work toward restoring the ethos of the firm and lead to substantive change.

Roach and Meeker worked on the draft, using their personal e-mail accounts to be sure it remained confidential. "We had no desire for this letter to get into the public domain; we were not playing public relations games," Meeker says. They wanted the letter to come from a small group and wanted to ensure that they had a 100 percent "hit rate" of those who were asked to sign, and they offered the letter to a few senior people in Investment Banking. But the bankers said they wanted to take a different approach. There was an ongoing debate inside the Investment Banking Division about writing their own letter, but it didn't look as though enough people would take the risk of losing their jobs to participate. The bankers decided that if they sent a letter that was not signed by the majority of the team, the board would think that the division was split. That would add to the confusion. They said they were going to try to work one-on-one with directors. Ruth Porat says, "Our view was that we would do anything on the spectrum from continuing to work with directors and providing them with things they needed to think about, to keeping an open channel of communications." On their list was appointing a lead director and getting rid of directors who weren't acting independently of Purcell. The bankers had in-depth experience working with boards, and they decided to operate more informally, so the directors didn't have to worry about a conspiracy.

Meeker and Roach next approached Byron Wien, who had the same "what-the-hell" reaction about the effect on his job security. Wien, who was famous for his annual "Ten Surprises" predictions for the coming year, was not afraid to take a position. As he wrote each year in the preface to the "Surprises," the ground rules were "that the consensus would assign only a one-in-three probability to each of them, but my view is that each has a 50 percent chance or better of taking place. Usually more than half of the component elements take place during the year."

As for signing the letter, Wien says, "I have nothing to lose. I am way beyond retirement age. [He was seventy-two at the time.] I have plenty of money. I view myself as the culture czar." Wien also had significant stature on Wall Street. In 2006, he would be the only Morgan Stanley executive included on a list of the sixteen most influential financial people in New York. (Stanley O'Neal of Merrill Lynch and Henry Paulson at Goldman Sachs were among the others.) Wien is a good editor and writer; Meeker and Roach asked him to read the letter, but not to change it or copy it. Wien signed.

He suggested that they add thirty-six-year-old Henry McVey, Chief U.S. Investment Strategist, whom Wien had picked to step into his shoes. McVey was a member of the younger generation for whom Morgan Stanley had not been the same kind of wealth-creation machine it was for others who had amassed more stock over time. He had invested ten years in the firm, and the stock was flat. Looking back, McVey says, "I blame the board, who didn't understand what was going on, and didn't understand the fabric of the firm; and I fault myself and others. When you have a service-based organization and you do not have leadership that's reflective of the firm, you have to stand up and say that's not acceptable. People at Morgan Stanley weren't doing that, and it went against the culture of the firm." It wasn't until Pandit and Havens left and the exodus began that people "woke up," he says. Meeker recalls that McVey told her, "This is a bigger deal for me than it is for you. I'm part of the next generation. I really care about this. And I don't care if I get fired." He also agreed to sign.

Meeker was traveling and was hampered by basic print and delivery challenges, so she e-mailed the letter to a friend at a law firm that didn't do business with Morgan Stanley, so it could be printed in utter secrecy. She and Roach and Wien were out of the office, and the letter had to be hand-delivered. Meeker remembers asking Henry McVey if he minded taking it to Steve and Zoe. McVey's response was something like, "Oh, that's a lot of fun." Cruz and Crawford might interpret the letter as a gesture of solidarity from people who were loyal to the firm, but given the atmosphere of suspicion and mistrust, they might also see it as an attack from some of the firm's best-known and most influential people.

On April 22, McVey delivered a copy of the letter to each of the co-presidents. To read it is to understand some of the qualities that made Morgan Stanley worth fighting for. They wrote that traditionally, at Morgan Stanley, "through a process of dialog and debate we have developed a trust that the right things ultimately happen at our firm. We are now questioning this."

They reminded Cruz and Crawford that all of them had turned down jobs at other firms for more money and "often, more balanced lifestyles, with a simple, proud response—Morgan Stanley's institutional securities business is the best on Wall Street. It is a meritocracy," in which debate and argument lead to "the right place far more often than not." "The hallmark of our culture," they wrote, "is our core value system based on integrity, trust, and respect for one another and a passion for the franchise."

Now, they wrote, "*current outside board members* do not seem to be in touch with employees . . . Most of our *advisory directors* now seem to be unsupportive of the firm . . . They have proven . . . through their mentorship and relationships, to be significant assets to the organization. That is now at risk . . . Many of our *senior partners* have left the firm over the past month." Describing them as "talented and experienced leaders . . . with hundreds of years of Wall Street experience . . . A clear indication of their value to the firm is that they were paid tens of millions of dollars in F2004.

"For the first time in our careers at the firm, the majority of people we know are not politely hanging up on inbound recruiting queries."

While welcoming productive change they warned that "the process by which change is brought about must be above reproach. In our view, the recent process by which the firm has introduced change falls well short of this standard."

Asking for Cruz's and Crawford's help "in endeavoring to end the animosity that has developed within the firm," they urged them "to invite a small group of senior leaders (current and former) to convey to you specific steps that may be needed to stabilize the organization and reignite the passion and energy that drive our businesses." Calling such a meeting "at a minimum . . . basic due diligence and a reasonable act of fiduciary responsibility," they wrote that the co-presidents "should listen and we believe you should do this very soon.

"Forget the public letter salvos," they wrote. "Get in a room and hash it out—it has been the Morgan Stanley way. And, time and again, it has proven that it works."

Finally, they encouraged Cruz and Crawford to share the letter with other members of the board.

When Crawford received the letter he asked Meeker to come to see him. Her recollection is that he said, "Great letter. I hear you, it's thoughtful, but it's also general. What are the action items?"

That seemed clear from the text, but Meeker elaborated that the firm should set up focused meetings to discuss the most problematic areas and develop some approaches—"hashing it out"—and make tough decisions.

Cruz and Crawford held two meetings with the four signers, the first in a conference room on the thirty-ninth floor, and the second in Cruz's office. She started the meeting by saying that she supported Purcell and was loyal to the firm. Overall, Meeker's impression was that she was in tune with the spirit of the letter and understood the crucial need to restore the Morgan Stanley values, standards, and spirit. Meeker says, "I know that's the kind of culture Zoe wants to have at Morgan Stanley."

But on Saturday, April 30, when the board held a special meeting in Chicago, Cruz and Crawford did not share the Meeker/Roach/Wien/ McVey letter with the directors. Cruz later said she felt it was not the appropriate time and way to raise this letter with the board.

The board reached a crossroads at that meeting. Purcell and Marty Lipton began by announcing that they had decided to hire David Heleniak, senior partner of the prestigious law firm Shearman & Sterling, as vice chairman of Morgan Stanley. He would also become a member of the denuded management committee, a managing director, and an advisor to Purcell. They indicated that with Heleniak on the team and some proposed governance changes they could stabilize the firm.

One director says that Purcell and Lipton presented Heleniak's appointment as "This is what we're going to do, and it's going to be fine."

Heleniak was not a controversial figure; he had a thirty-one-year career at Shearman & Sterling, where he was the head of their Mergers and Acquisitions Group, and Morgan Stanley had been a client for twenty years. But this was the first time most of the directors had heard about what would be a major appointment.

Purcell and Lipton were taken aback when the nonexecutive directors told them they were not willing to ratify the decision until they had a meeting—without either of them present.

When Purcell and Lipton left, the nonexecutive directors shared what they had heard from influential investors. Mike Miles had gone to Baltimore with Purcell to meet with T. Rowe Price, whose executives said they would see Purcell, but only if he were to be accompanied by a director. A. T. Rowe Price executive had made one of the few public statements from a major institutional investor in support of the Group of Eight, and the firm's suspension of trading with Morgan Stanley began the day John Havens left, and continued long enough to make their disapproval clear. Chuck Knight reported that he too was hearing from investors that "you can't stick with Phil," one director says. Three weeks earlier, it seemed that Purcell could hold on if he could tough it out. Some of the directors now sensed that he might last for another year, but probably less. There was no single dramatic moment, but as the directors went around the room, it was evident that even Purcell's closest associates were shaken. Ed Brennan, who would always be painted as supporting Purcell regardless of the evidence, was surprisingly balanced. Even people who felt that the problem was among the people who had left the firm, not with Purcell, could not comfortably maintain that view, although perhaps half the board was still opposed to asking him to leave.

At least one director went into the April 30 meeting prepared to resign if serious action wasn't taken. But after that meeting, even the directors who were most dubious about Purcell's leadership stayed to see the situation out.

The board voted to institute a simple majority to fire the CEO, in place of the bylaw that required a 75 percent majority. They changed the way his successor would be chosen; instead of involving the entire board, including Purcell, the responsibility was transferred to the compensation committee. It was, however, headed by Chuck Knight, still one of Purcell's intransigent supporters. The board also agreed to appoint a lead director, and chose Miles Marsh, who was one of the moderates. They also voted to seek two new independent directors, which would bring the count up from thirteen to fifteen.

The board approved David Heleniak's appointment, and the firm made the announcement the next week. Heleniak would start halfway through the year, and would be paid $20 million for the six months that remained in 2005.

Perhaps the board thought they had done enough to indicate that they were on top of the situation, and possibly even to quell the mutiny, and they issued another statement supporting Purcell. "We have said consistently that management enjoys the confidence of the board and we reiterate that commitment today. We have thoroughly examined all the issues surrounding leadership, structure and strategy and conclude that it is in the best interest of shareholders that we support management and not split up the company."

Bob Scott responded on behalf of the Group of Eight: "The changes fail to address the fundamental cause of the crisis at Morgan Stanley, which is the failure in Philip Purcell's leadership."

Richard Bove commented, "It is Philip Purcell's board. They are trying to protect themselves and are trying to protect him, but keep losing battle after battle."

Bob Greenhill told the Eight, "The board will back Phil until they don't." He advised them to stay the course and not get discouraged.

The market response to the board's support of Purcell was negative. Morgan Stanley stock traded down 4 percent, at $50.

Thirteen

FALLOUT

V ery few deals thoroughly embarrassed the House of Morgan or seriously affected the fate of the firm; two of the most notorious were mounted during times of "irrational exuberance," and the most recent was playing out in the spring of 2005. The first truly humiliating debacle was the connection with the Alleghany Corporation, which began in the Roaring Twenties at J. P. Morgan & Co. and ended in 1935. The other was the Coleman/Sunbeam affair, set in motion when Morgan Stanley did its first deal with Ronald Perelman in 1986, and which reached a crisis point in May 2005.

The Alleghany story and the Perelman fiasco had certain common elements. The principals were not the sort of clients the bank had traditionally looked for as business partners; both deals involved high-profile leveraged buyout engineers; and they both dealt crushing blows to the firm's reputation and balance sheet.

The central characters in the Alleghany saga were Oris P. and Mantis J. Van Sweringen, small, monosyllabic, antisocial bachelor twins who lived in a faux Alpine chalet on a farm outside of Cleveland, Ohio, and were so inseparable they slept in the same room. The Van Sweringens careened onto the scene in the ebullient 1920s; they began their rise to the financial stratosphere by developing Shaker Heights, then moving into railroads. They leveraged one deal on top of the next until Alleghany controlled the fifth-largest railroad system in the United States. Everything the Van Sweringens owned was pledged as collateral for something else. Ron Chernow calls their enterprise "a pyramid of debt . . . built of nothing but faith." In 1929, the twins went to J. P. Morgan and Guaranty Trust to finance their Alleghany Corporation with a $200 million offering. A year later, their empire fell apart, the stock dropped from $56 to $10, and they were $40 million in debt.

J. P. Morgan and Guaranty Trust put together a syndicate to cover the Van Sweringens and offer some protection to investors, but it was far too late. In 1935, Alleghany auctioned off its holdings for $3 million; J. P. Morgan and Guaranty Trust each lost $9 million. As Chernow observed, for Morgan to get involved with the overleveraged little twins "showed how the recklessness of the 1920s had at last infected the citadel of respectability."

The downfall of Alleghany coincided with the Pecora investigation. Pecora was able to show that Morgan had offered Alleghany stock to a "preferred list" of clients and friends at a price well under the market. Alleghany provided the kind of evidence that led to Glass-Steagall, the truncation of J. P. Morgan's business, and the founding of Morgan Stanley.

Ronald Perelman was smoother and more sophisticated than the Van Sweringens, but like them he was a corporate raider and a specialist in the highly leveraged deal. Bald as a stone, short, stocky, and fit, Perelman galloped through a series of glamorous wives and highly public divorces, and was known to be ruthless in his personal and business lives. He was such a master of the leveraged buyout that he even leveraged his leverage. In 1985 Drexel Burnham underwrote a $761 million junk bond for him that was purely to be used for acquisitions; the only asset the buyers got was their belief that Perelman would continue to find, and turn around, underpriced and undermanaged companies. In 1986, Morgan Stanley managed Perelman's $2.5 billion hostile takeover of Revlon, and over the next twenty years, the firm did twenty-seven deals with him.

In 1998, Morgan Stanley loaned Sunbeam Corp., an appliance manufacturer, $680 million, and underwrote Sunbeam's $750 million debt offering. The chairman of Sunbeam, Albert Dunlap, was known as "Chainsaw Al," a reference to his tactic of using deep and painful cuts to increase earnings. Dunlap was as tough as Ron Perelman, but not nearly as good a businessman. In 1998, Perelman was interested in buying Sunbeam for the stable of companies in which he owned the majority shares. They included the Coleman Company, the camping gear manufacturer, known for its Coleman Lanterns. Perelman would make a stock swap—Coleman for Sunbeam—giving him 14 million shares (about $600 million) of Sunbeam stock, and $160 million in cash. Coleman would also lay off $500 million of debt on Sunbeam.

The deal was a couple of weeks from closing when Sunbeam announced that first-quarter sales would fall short of expectations. Perelman asked Morgan Stanley if everything was still okay; the firm assured him that it was, and the deal closed on March 30, 1998. Perelman's lawyer was Martin Lipton's firm, Wachtell, Lipton, Rosen & Katz.

Over the next three months, a series of bad to terrible news flowed out of Sunbeam. A second announcement about quarterly results further downgraded expectations. Board investigations turned up sufficient corporate irregularities that "Chainsaw Al" was fired. Sunbeam filed for bankruptcy in 2001, and that was the end of Perelman's $600 million.

Perelman believed he had been duped and began his efforts to recoup by suing Sunbeam's auditor, Arthur Andersen, which settled for $75 million. It took him a couple more years to decide to take on the investment bank he believed had knowingly misled him.

By 2003, Donald Kempf had been Morgan Stanley's general counsel since the end of 1999. When Jonathan Clark was general counsel, he had always cooperated with the regulators and tried to anticipate trouble, but Kempf was more aggressive and adversarial. Investigations, lawsuits, fines, and expensive settlements piled up, and it appeared that the firm's standards of behavior weren't being monitored closely enough, and were dropping. Morgan Stanley was involved in litigation with the states of Massachusetts, New York, West Virginia, New Hampshire, and California. Class action suits proliferated. The SEC and NASD investigated the firm, among others, for such matters as IPO allocations, pricing and commissions; mutual fund sales practices, including sales contests to reward brokers for selling in-house funds; late trading and market timing of mutual funds, research conflict of interest; failure to produce documents; and retention of e-mails. Governance of its mutual funds was another issue. Morgan Stanley's funds had seven independent directors, two of whom had been executives at Sears and Allstate respectively.

Despite Kempf's aggressive stance, or perhaps because of it, Morgan Stanley continued to be the target of investigations and to be slapped with fines and adverse judgments. As one executive said, "Don fought for unconditional surrender and he usually got unconditional defeat."

When Perelman decided to sue Morgan Stanley, he hired another top Chicago attorney; he and Kempf knew each other, and they held a meeting. Perelman's lawyer showed Kempf a slide presentation that indicated that Morgan Stanley had been aware that Sunbeam was not as healthy as the bank had asserted. Perelman thought Morgan Stanley owed him $500 million.

It did not take long for the number to be whittled down. In the spring of 2003, over dinner in New York, Perelman's lawyer told Kempf that Perelman wanted $10 to $20 million to go away.

As the deal came out of Investment Banking, part of Kempf's due diligence was to find out whether Terry Meguid, as head of the division, thought the firm should pay Perelman the $20 million. But instead of going to see Meguid, or calling him, he sent one of the firm's lawyers to ask his opinion. Meguid's reaction was that if Perelman had started asking for $500 million and, without noticeably negotiating, had dropped the price to $20 million, it didn't sound as though he thought he had a case. If the money were to come out of the Investment Banking Division's profits, it would make a dent. Meguid said he didn't see why the firm should pay, but as he wasn't a lawyer it wasn't up to him to decide if Perelman had a case or not. It certainly did not sound as though Kempf was taking it very seriously if he didn't discuss it with Meguid himself.

Kempf later said he hadn't spent much time on the issue because "it was viewed as a nuisance case," in comparison to the regulatory matters he was handling. Given Perelman's reputation for tenacity, it would have seemed more reasonable to treat him like a crocodile in the swimming pool than a fruit fly floating over the bananas.

The Morgan Stanley legal department prepared a PowerPoint presentation intended to scare Perelman off and invited him to watch it.

Perelman told a *New York Times* reporter that the gist of it was that, if he didn't back off, "they were going to attack me personally . . . It was a very clear threat." It was also a very bad tactic.

Perelman filed suit against Morgan Stanley in May 2003 in West Palm Beach, Florida. Perelman had a house in Palm Beach, and Sunbeam had been headquartered there, which may have accounted for the firm's name. Florida was not a good venue for the defense: in New York, a sophisticated investor was assumed to be able to do enough due diligence to protect himself; Florida law was more sympathetic to the plaintiff.

Kempf turned the case over to his old law firm, Kirkland & Ellis, with a three-person team from Morgan Stanley as backup. The Honorable Elizabeth T. Maass was on the bench.

Judge Maass was a 1978 Princeton University graduate who majored in economics, and graduated from Columbia University School of Law in 1981. When she started in private practice, her specialty was in commercial, corporate, and appellate law. She was a county court judge from 1990 to 2001, and then she was appointed to the Fifteenth Judicial Circuit of Florida, where the Perelman case was tried. Judge Maass looked like a Junior Leaguer, with blond hair that she often tucked behind her ears, a perky nose, and big blue eyes, but that was misleading. She appeared to be in her thirties, but she was forty-nine, experienced, thorough, and tough. In the Palm Beach Judicial Evaluation, she received an "E" for "Excellent" rating of 88 percent for "Knowledge & Application of Law" and "Diligence and Preparedness"; and 86 percent for "Impartiality (Freedom from Bias & Prejudice)." Overall, her ratings averaged 86.4 percent.

One of the many bloggers who followed the case, "Wall Street Free Thinker," wrote, "Mr. Perelman's company, Coleman, unpacked its tent and sleeping bags for Sunbeam, Sunbeam went to take a leak and they found Morgan's client the next day, broke and dead in the old appliance graveyard." That was just about what happened.

The question was who knew what at Morgan Stanley, and when they knew it, evidence that might have been ferreted out from the firm's e-mails, which it was required to retain. First, Morgan Stanley said the firm didn't have its e-mails for the relevant period; then that they might have them, but that they were stored on thousands of tapes that would be nearly impossible to unravel; then reported that the tapes had been converted to electronic files, but the files didn't go back to the relevant period; then found 1,423 missing tapes in a closet in Brooklyn and admitted that the firm was on the verge of converting the tapes but hadn't done it yet. All along, there were substantial time lags between the "discoveries" of the tapes and the status of the conversion process, and reporting the findings to the court.

By January 2005, the situation was already bleak for Morgan Stanley when a new embarrassment emerged: at the time of the Sunbeam deal, Morgan Stanley's lead banker, Chicago-based William Strong, vice chairman of investment banking, had been accused of having participated in a corruption scandal and was facing criminal charges in Italy. Judge Maass had asked Morgan Stanley to "produce all documents relating to Strong's 'truthfulness, veracity, or moral turpitude.'" The criminal charges had been dropped, but the bank neglected to mention that, at the time of the deal, the lead banker was under indictment.

As journalist Susan Beck commented in her thorough review of the case in *American Lawyer,* "The Morgan Stanley team didn't seem to have a strong leader." Finally in February, a senior Kirkland & Ellis partner with an effective record in trial law was sent to Florida on a rescue mission.

Don Kempf was otherwise engaged. He was coping with a series of private plaintiffs' IPO suits, in which Morgan Stanley was one of the defendants in cases that could add up to $1 billion in claims to be shared among a group of securities firms. When he heard that the Perelman case was going badly, he blamed Kirkland but continued to leave it up to his old law firm to cope.

A year and a half into the discovery phase, Judge Maass ran out of patience. On March 1, 2005, she declared that Morgan Stanley's counsel had showed "lack of candor" and accused the lawyers of "willful and gross abuse of discovery obligations." Coincidentally, that was two days before the Group of Eight sent their first letter. Perelman's legal team asked for a default judgment. Instead, Judge Maass told Morgan Stanley that the burden of proof was on the firm "to prove that it didn't know about the fraud at Sunbeam."

In mid-March, one of Perelman's counsels told the court, "We are dealing with a corporate defendant that has no conscience, that is morally bankrupt." The Kirkland & Ellis lawyer who had been called in on the rescue mission apologized to the court, saying that in thirty years of practice, this was the most "painful" case he had ever been involved in. "No excuses," he said.

That was the way things stood when Kempf showed up in Florida—during the week of the Monday Massacre in New York. He had prepared his own bloodbath: he shocked the lawyers from his old firm by announcing to the bench that Morgan Stanley was firing Kirkland & Ellis and might sue the law firm for malpractice, and asked the court for a six-month delay.

A Morgan Stanley executive who was close to the case asked him, "What genius had that idea?"

Judge Maass denied the request for a recess and gave Morgan Stanley one week to get its affairs in order. She wrote that Morgan Stanley "has contumaciously violated numerous discovery orders . . . *The judicial system cannot function this way.*"

On April 4, the same day Purcell announced the intention to spin off Discover, and the Group of Eight announced its plan to replace Purcell with Bob Scott, Morgan Stanley reported that it had added $100 million to its reserves for the Ron Perelman case, up to $360 million—eighteen times the amount Perelman would have settled for two years earlier.

When the trial opened, on April 8, Judge Maass instructed the jury to assume that Morgan Stanley had conspired with Sunbeam to defraud Perelman. The question was now no longer whether Morgan Stanley was guilty; it was how much the jury should award Perelman in compensatory and punitive damages.

That morning an investment banker who received the early edition of the *Wall Street Journal* at home, and a later edition in the office, read Suzanne Craig's story "Morgan Stanley May Get Sunbeam Burn" over breakfast. When the $20 million offer was mentioned, the story read, "The only other settlement overture came well before this, when Mr. Perelman's side offered $20 million to settle—which Morgan Stanley rejected." The banker was, therefore, somewhat startled to see the firm's spin in a later edition of the *Journal*. The story now read, "Morgan Stanley rejected this offer despite a recommendation by the firm's legal division, led by the chief legal officer Donald Kempf, to accept it, according to a person familiar with the matter." However, executives familiar with the case say that the legal division merely communicated the settlement offer to the Head of Investment Banking and never recommended that it be accepted.

Jurors were permitted to ask questions. Kempf watched them, and as he confided to a journalist who was covering the case, he thought he had identified three who were definitely sympathetic to Morgan Stanley.

In May, everyone was flailing in the water. No one was drowning yet, but Purcell, the Eight, and the board were all a long way from shore, and the firm was suffering.

Purcell looked gray, exhausted, and years older than he had looked a few months earlier. A managing director who saw him standing alone at a firm event went over to say hello and asked him how he was doing. "I'm surprised you asked," he said. "Nobody wants to talk to me." Just about the only thing that seemed to be going in his favor was that the Dublin-based online betting system, intrade.com, gave him a 71 percent chance of keeping his job—for now. There were only 1,500 intrade contracts out, amounting to a puny $16,000, but a spokesman said that was enough to indicate a trend. In 2004, when intrade took bets on the U.S. Senate races, they only missed one out of thirty-four, the Alaska race.

A reporter wrote that he had heard that headhunters were preparing "face books" for their clients, featuring prime Morgan Stanley executives who might be induced to leave. The preceding September Merrill Lynch had hired Morgan's head of Global Equity Trading and six members of his team, and had recently hired a Morgan Stanley investment banker and three high-net-worth brokers from the Boston office. Purcell instructed the firm to curtail trading with Merrill to punish the firm for poaching.

Between mid-April and early June, there would be some fifty top-level defections, and every time one person left, tens of others rethought their commitment to stay. They weren't all stars, but the departing executives included the High-Yield Bond Head William Kourakos. David J. Topper, a twenty-two-year veteran of Morgan

Stanley, chairman of the Equity Capital Committee and a member of Perella's team, went to J. P. Morgan Chase as cohead of the U.S. Equity Capital Markets Division. Mayree C. Clark resigned as head of the International Individual Investor Group. Citigroup hired Marianne Hay, head of Private Wealth Management in Europe and the Middle East, as chief of Citi's European wealth-management division, with "the mandate to acquire an international or regional private bank." Raymond J. McGuire, the elegant cohead of the M & A division, left to join Citigroup Inc., where he became global cohead of Investment Banking. McGuire, forty-eight, a Harvard College, Harvard Business School, and Harvard Law School graduate and a Perella protégé, was one of the top-ranking African-Americans on Wall Street. He was well connected, an art collector, and a trustee of the Whitney Museum of American Art. The most dramatic departures were when entire teams left. The eight institutional traders who went to Deutsche Bank left a big hole, and on June 10, nine equity derivatives traders, including three managing directors, left en masse to join Wachovia Corp.

Purcell refilled the management committee and expanded it to a total of sixteen members. Jerker Johansson, now Global Head of Equity, and Michael Uva, cohead of Global Investment Banking, both based in London, were added to the committee in April; along with New York–based Neal Shear, Global Head of Fixed Income, and Cordell Spencer, cohead of Global Investment Banking. Jonathan Chenevix-Trench, chairman of Morgan Stanley's European Operating Committee, and Alasdair Morrison, chairman and CEO of Morgan Stanley Asia, were added in late May. The high quality of the new members was a testament to the claim that the firm had a plethora of talent, and that some significant younger managing directors were staying on board.

The departures fed the media; the story had gone on far longer than anyone expected, and the fallout was more severe. There was a sense of impending drama: either one of the new developments would finish off Purcell, or he would show that he had superhuman staying power and the Eight would take themselves out of the fight.

By late April, it was apparent that Purcell might hold out, but the Eight not only weren't quitting, the group was expanding to become the Gridiron Eleven. Three former Morgan Stanley executives were now openly part of the team. The first to volunteer his support had been Robert C. McCormack, a Morgan Stanley alumnus and prominent Chicago investor whom Bob Baldwin had recruited in 1981, when McCormack was working for a rival firm in Chicago. Baldwin invited him to dinner at the Chicago Club and told him that he was one of the few people who took business away from Morgan Stanley, and suggested that he join the firm. McCormack said, "This can be the long version or the short version: I'm in." Baldwin proceeded to sell him on the firm anyway, and McCormack said, "Bob, you're not listening: I'm in." Later, Baldwin called Parker Gilbert, who asked, "How much did you tell him we're going to pay him?" Baldwin said, "We didn't talk about that."

McCormack helped build the firm's technology investment banking group, left in 1987 to become special assistant to Caspar Weinberger at the Department of Defense, then started his own highly successful venture capital firm, Trident, which specialized in information technology, investing in such companies as MapQuest. McCormack was part of the business, social, and philanthropic leadership in Chicago, and he knew most of the Morgan Stanley directors from the Midwest. He was also a large Morgan Stanley shareholder.

When he read the Group of Eight's first letter in the *Wall Street Journal*, he called Fred Whittemore, who was his neighbor in the summer in Watch Hill, and Bob Greenhill, and said, "You guys are doing the heavy lifting for the rest of us. I want to send you a check." McCormack wrote his first check, this one for $50,000, and joined the Group of Eight meetings via conference call a couple of times a week. He says, "I was their link to the Chicago directors. Brennan, and Miles, and Madigan are good friends of mine." They were all members of Old Elm, where they played golf, and they saw one another at events in Chicago and in the suburbs where most of them lived. But when McCormack talked to his friends, and told them that Purcell was "destroying the franchise," he says, "the conversations went nowhere. They thought everything was fine, that I was just a disgruntled former partner."

For most of the spring, McCormack reports, "the Chicago business community was pro-Purcell." The Midwest-versus-Eastern Establishment rivalry influenced that attitude. McCormack says, "Mike Miles kept referring to me as a 'Yalie,' even though he knew perfectly well that I went to the University of North Carolina and Chicago Business School."

The *Chicago Tribune*, where Morgan Stanley director John Madigan had just retired as chairman of the Tribune Company, was mute on the fight, even when it was being covered extensively in the *New York Times* and the *Wall Street Journal*. Eventually, McCormack called the publisher—also a friend—and said, "How come your business section doesn't cover the biggest Wall Street story in years? Is it anything to do with Madigan?" The publisher assured him that wasn't the case, and McCormack said, "You're going to look awfully stupid when this thing is over."

Because of the respect he commanded in Chicago, as well as his easy manner, McCormack was able to organize one of the very few face-to-face encounters between members of the Group of Eight and any of the directors. In April, Fred Whittemore called McCormack and said, "Everyone is away, Mac. All that's left is you and me. Let's plan something." McCormack told him that Miles, Brennan, and Madigan wouldn't talk to him, but, even though he didn't know Miles Marsh, they were neighbors and he would call him at home and introduce himself. They had a cordial conversation, and McCormack invited Marsh to have lunch with him and Parker Gilbert at the Links Club in New York the following week.

The next Tuesday, Gilbert, McCormack, and Marsh sat upstairs in the green-walled back dining room at the Links, and Gilbert laid out their case.

McCormack added, "Let me sum this up in one sentence: anyone who can lose a lawsuit over ethics to Ron Perelman has a serious problem."

Then McCormack recalls, Miles told them, "I know you guys are here as advocates for John Mack, but forget it."

"We looked at him and said, We're not here pushing Mack. *You* have to figure out who can run this company."

McCormack speculates that by disabusing Marsh, and consequently other members of the board, of the belief that the Eight had mounted the fight to bring Mack back, they greatly increased his chances of getting the job.

Two others joined the Eight in late April. Donald Brennan was one of the rare Morgan Stanley alumni who came to Morgan Stanley in midcareer. He joined the firm in 1982 from International Paper Company, and ran Morgan Stanley's merchant banking, private equity, and venture capital businesses, under the sponsorship and support of Parker Gilbert. Brennan's first career in industry gave him an insight into the way CEOs of manufacturing companies thought about investment bankers, and as he watched the Morgan Stanley board stonewalling the Eight, he understood that they were engaged in another kind of culture war. Brennan says, "When a group of CEOs gets together, one of the things they can all agree on is that they hate investment bankers. They say bankers don't really know how to run a business, they haven't been in the trenches, they're here to sell us on ideas so they can make big incomes. With some notable exceptions, the board of Morgan Stanley made disparaging remarks about the firm that you would never have heard from the board at Merrill Lynch or Goldman Sachs."

The board's lack of experience in Institutional Securities created a potentially dangerous problem. Brennan says, "If you lose a notch or two on your credit rating as a highly leveraged investment bank, it can cost you hundreds of millions a year in the increased cost of financing. That's not true in manufacturing. That board should have been asking, 'What's our cost of capital?' If they didn't, it would be like going to your doctor for a physical and only allowing him to take your pulse."

Brennan says, "I have created and chaired many boards of public and private companies. The biggest mistake [the Morgan Stanley board made] was that they went along with a dictatorial, monolithic approach to organization and management. A large and complex organization requires the talents and skills of a host of executives. To have the ego and the arrogance to think that one person was infallible, and everybody else was there to execute—the board had allowed an atmosphere where there was only one voice, and that voice didn't tolerate dissent or consensus building. Even the pope has a College of Cardinals."

It was the behavior of the board, above all, that persuaded Brennan to join the Eight—that, and his admiration and respect for Parker Gilbert. As he and Gilbert talked about the battle, they discussed how to keep the fire from getting out of control. Brennan says, "We had to be careful. If we created too much hell, we could take an A-plus credit rating and turn it into a B-minus" and sink the company.

The third alumnus to join the Eight, William J. Kneisel, joined Morgan Stanley in 1974, out of Harvard Business School. He worked closely with Lewis Bernard, and later with Vikram Pandit in capital markets—he says Vikram was "a genius"—then went into the mergers and acquisitions business when it was booming under Bob Greenhill and Joe Fogg. In 1986, he was sent to London to take responsibility for the European investment business, which he ran until 1992. When he returned, Bob Scott was running capital markets, and Kneisel was responsible for the equity capital markets business. At that time Morgan Stanley's Chicago office pitched the business to Sears, and Kneisel was the senior banker on the Dean Witter IPO. By the time he left in the late 1990s, he had worked closely with most of the future Group of Eight, and he and Fred Whittemore, who were both Dartmouth graduates, had been active at the college. At the end of March 2005, Kneisel was in South Carolina with some bankers from Goldman Sachs, and the Morgan Stanley fight had just become public. He was disturbed that "it was all the talk," he said.

In late April, he got a call from Anson Beard, who said, "We're thinking about increasing the size of the group; you're a large shareholder. I think Parker would like to talk to you." Kneisel says, "These are two guys I absolutely adore. It was a fairly easy decision. I thought, If this seemed important to them, then, okay."

The Kneisels' youngest son had recently graduated from college and was working in private wealth management at Morgan Stanley. Kneisel said, "The last thing I wanted to do was get into an entanglement" that would hurt him. But, "I have such deep affection for and respect for the core values of what Morgan Stanley was, and having spent twenty-five years of my professional life there, if there was an opportunity to reassert those values in a meaningful way, I wanted to help."

He added, "A business that gets started on the idea of a first class business in a first class way, that's the kind of world that Parker and Greenie and the rest of them exemplify."

Joining the Eight meant not only participating in developing strategy and using their influence with other major investors, but also putting up serious money for the next phase, which could turn into a proxy fight. When word reached Purcell and some of the directors that the Group of Eight was not packing their bags for summer vacation, but were expanding their ranks and their bank account, it added weight to the fight, just as the investment community was beginning to turn around.

Major institutional investors were calling members of the board and telling them to buck up and get rid of Purcell before the fight did any more damage. Aggressive hedge fund managers, entrepreneurs who didn't have to answer to the rules of big companies, were outspoken and insistent. People who hadn't had much of an opinion one way or the other about Purcell's leadership before were not impressed by the way he handled the challenge. As he continued to turn down interviews and to issue "no comment" responses, he was not making a case for himself. Melissa Lee at CNBC was still posted outside the Morgan Stanley building and implored him—on air—to come downstairs and tell his side of the story, providing a little sideshow in the Times Square area. The daily newspapers had been covering the story all along, and in May the monthly magazines, which had longer lead times and had assigned pieces early in the fight, broke the next stories.

Institutional Investor published "Morgan Stanley's White-Shoe Blues," which predicted that the efforts by the Group of Eight "ironically, could lead to . . . a deal in which a weakened Morgan Stanley gets even bigger by merging with or being acquired by a rival seizing a once-in-a-lifetime opportunity."

Fortune reporters Bethany McLean—coauthor of *Enron: The Smartest Guys in the Room*—Andrew Serwer, and Nicholas Varchaver wrote a six-page story, "Brahmins at the Gate," which featured head shots of all members of the Group of Eight and was subtitled, "When Morgan Stanley choked on its own merger, the ugliest civil war in recent Wall Street history broke out. Now the old guard is on the march . . ."

The authors described the fight as "open warfare" and "clearly personal," and quoted Bob Scott, who described the situation at the firm as "congealed mediocrity." It was an unintentional echo of Fred

Whittemore's warning to managing directors a few years earlier to beware of the sin of "congealed arrogance." The most damaging part of the story was the accompanying chart of directors' interlocking connections. The reporters gave Purcell the opportunity to put forward a defense, but he declined.

Newsweek reporter Charles Gasparino, author of *Blood on the Street: The Sensational Inside Story of How Wall Street Analysts Duped a Generation of Investors,* wrote "A War Without Winners." The story was illustrated by a photograph of Purcell, who looked as though he was trying to smile for the camera but felt too ill. Gasparino wrote that the board wasn't as solidly behind Purcell as reports indicated, and the directors were considering "splitting his job of chairman and CEO in two." He also indicated that Purcell might be weighing a counterattack, "suing the Group of Eight for 'torturous interference.'" (Both subjects had been briefly discussed.) Gasparino observed that Morgan Stanley could be the big loser in the fight, given the brain drain, the low morale, and the stock price.

The *New York Times Magazine* published a two-page comic strip, "Morgan v. Stanley v. Morgan Stanley," which sent up both Purcell and the Group of Eight. It depicted the dissidents in a centipedelike drawing of heads emerging from a single long white shirt. They mislabeled a couple of members of the group, switching the bearded Bob Scott with the clean-shaven Fred Whittemore, but told an ultraconcise version of the story, ending with the Eight trying to saw off the top of 1585 Broadway, while an enormous Purcell hangs on and shouts "No!" A tiny figure watches with binoculars from the roof of a smaller building. The bubble over his head reads "What's wrong with living in Chicago?"

The publicity was so bad that Morgan Stanley's media-buying agency, Publicis Group SA, changed the firm's existing contracts, requiring advance notification of negative stories, with the right to pull its ads. The clause read, "In the event that objectionable editorial coverage is planned, agency must be notified as a last-minute change may be necessary. If an issue arises after-hours or a call cannot be made, immediately cancel all Morgan Stanley ads for a minimum of 48 hours." The *New York Times,* the *Wall Street Journal,* and *USA Today* were among the publications that were notified of the change in their contracts with Morgan Stanley. That sort of insurance was usually reserved for major crises; airlines sometimes had similar clauses in the contracts so ads could be pulled in the immediate wake of a plane crash. Robert Dilenschneider, a dean of the financial and corporate strategic communications world, said the move was the sort of thing a company does, "when you have totally lost control and you have lost your wits and you don't have a good story to tell—that's what it signals."

Someone must have seen a draft of the letter from Mary Meeker, Steve Roach, Byron Wien, and Henry McVey, and it was leaked to the *Wall Street Journal*. They had done everything they could to keep their letter confidential, but as Roach says, "It was a time when people were dying for anything [about Morgan Stanley] to put on the front page."

On Saturday, May 8, Roach, who was just back from China, where he had been more than fifty times in the past few years, was watching his fourteen-year-old daughter play field hockey when he got a call on his cell phone from Randy Smith at the *Journal*. "I was in the stands with all these parents," Roach says. "My daughter looks up and says, 'There's Dad on the phone again.'"

Smith didn't have the letter, but he said he had spoken to at least three people who confirmed what it said. Roach and Meeker went on damage control and called Morgan Stanley's Head of Public Relations, Ray O'Rourke, and Zoe Cruz to warn them that a story was brewing. Meeker says, "We took this very seriously. I was horrified when it leaked to the media."

As Smith wrote, "The signers were the first employees known to have expressed themselves on the record, albeit privately, to management during the conflict that has wracked the firm." He added, "Because of their stature on Wall Street, they would have less to fear than others about any adverse consequences from the letter." The letter itself remained closely held and the text appeared in the media.

On Monday, May 10, Roach issued a brief statement "at the behest of company management" saying that the letter was written "in a positive and constructive spirit."

When the authors of the letter got to the office the morning the story broke, they found themselves getting "high fives" and greetings, many of them from people they didn't know. Meeker says, "We were taken aback by the reaction; it was as though news of the letter and its content helped give some folks more courage."

Directors who read about the letter for the first time in the *Journal* wondered what else the management team was keeping from them.

A day after the *Journal* story appeared, Purcell made his first official public appearance since the Monday Massacre. On May 10, UBS held its Global Financial Services Conference, and Purcell, Cruz, and Crawford spoke to a standing-room-only crowd, principally of institutional investors. Purcell admitted to "middle of the pack" performance in some areas, and said he had "taken to heart" criticism of the firm's lag in its price-to-earnings ratio and its stock price. "Being in the paper every day doesn't help morale in investment banking," Purcell said, while the publicity had aroused fears in the retail brokerage division, where brokers were afraid that their business was going to be spun off.

The presentations were long and detailed, but reactions were lukewarm. Sanford Bernstein's Brad Hintz said it sounded like "more of the same." Reporters privately remarked that Purcell, Cruz, and Crawford didn't look comfortable as a team. Richard Bove remarked, "Everybody walked away with negativity in their souls." It wasn't that the ideas were bad, it was that Purcell hadn't been able to execute them effectively before, and investors had less and less faith that he could do it now, just because he said he would.

Purcell had been criticized because he didn't spend enough time meeting with employees, but that winter and spring, he had been touring the territories. He had started with the regional managers' meeting in Scottsdale in January, made a rare stop for an all-hands meeting in London immediately after the G-8's first ad came out, and in mid-May he was in Asia with about a dozen Morgan Stanley executives. They were led by Alasdair Morrison, Head of Asia, who was about to be appointed to the management committee. Morrison was an impressive and attractive Englishman who had been the head of Jardine Mathiesson before he joined Morgan Stanley.

By the time Purcell got to Asia, he was tired and disheartened. His face was bloated, his color was bad, his eyes were surrounded in big puffs, he needed a haircut, and he looked soft around the middle. Traveling with him while he was fighting for his life was awkward. Once, when he and Steve Roach were going somewhere in a car, Purcell asked Roach why he and the others had written the letter to Cruz and Crawford.

"I care a lot about Morgan Stanley," Roach said.

Purcell countered, "It's caused a lot of problems."

"There *are* a lot of problems," Roach answered.

On their last day in China, the team was waiting to see the chairman of one of the big China banks, and Roach suggested they "play the Chinese card game" to pass the time. When Morgan Stanley executives went to Asia they were given business cards with their names translated into Chinese characters on the back, and they asked the translator to tell them what each of their names meant in Chinese. When the translator got to Purcell, he gave an unctuous response. "He said it meant something like 'shining light,'" Roach recalls.

Roach asked the translator to give him the card and pretended to read it. Then he looked at Purcell and joked, "I read Mandarin; what it really says is 'Bob Scott.'"

There was a "Is-this-guy-nuts?" silence among the rest of the group, and then Purcell said, "Roach, you really are a shithead." The tension had broken, but not for long.

While Purcell was in Asia, the Florida jury in the Coleman case set the fines and damages against Morgan Stanley. They awarded Perelman $604.3 million in damages on May 16, and two days later added another $850 million in punitive damages. If the verdict was upheld the total cost to Morgan Stanley would be $1.45 billion, not including the millions of dollars the firm spent on legal defense. Purcell was up most of the night, talking to lawyers in New York and Florida.

The team went on to Japan, and on May 20 Purcell held a meeting at the Tokyo office, which was video-conferenced throughout Asia and the Pacific.

Purcell declared, "We have weathered the storm with the Group of Eight who are criticizing us." He repeated his statistics about the firm's performance—number one in Equities for the first time since 1982, number one in announced M & A, and so on—but the Perelman story was preoccupying everyone. When an executive calling in from Singapore politely remarked that "the spate of bad news is impacting business somewhat," Purcell said Coleman was "an unprecedented case. The judge had a bias and a prejudice of our firm. She didn't like our production of e-mails . . . She changed the rules of the game of jurisprudence, put the burden of proof on us." He claimed that "three of the jurors were tampered with by the other side," called Elizabeth Maass "a rogue judge and a total aberration for the way the legal system is supposed to work," and said the case was "unprecedented."

"The top priority for us in the U.S.," he said, "is to get out of the newspapers. We have the best momentum we've ever had. Most of the publicity generated by the G-8 . . . I believe they have lost credibility with investors and internally. I would hope that they stop going to the press, trying to bring negative publicity every day. To say negative things about the firm that made all of them rich . . . all the money they've made in the firm they've made since they retired. *You've* made them rich," he told the current executives, "and for them to hurt the firm and hurt the share price . . ." He shook his head. Almost as though he were talking to himself, he said, "I just can't understand what kind of a mind would do that."

Fourteen

"ANYONE BUT JOHN MACK"

Purcell was on the high seas in the midst of a "perfect storm," but he was still on board, and the Eight were tapping their feet in frustration. They hired a proxy advisor and agreed that they would let it be known that they were considering challenging Purcell and the entire board in a proxy fight, if he didn't step down. That could cost them $15 to $20 million of their own money. On June 7, Bob Scott, Joe Fogg, and Anson Beard held a conference call with about forty members of the Council of Institutional Investors. When someone on the call asked about a proxy, Fogg, as the M & A expert in the group, took the question. He confirmed that they were exploring the option with a proxy firm. Within hours the directors had heard the news.

Unbeknownst to the Eight, the board was already making final preparations to give them what they wanted. Clients and institutional investors were irate. The Perelman fiasco could cost the firm one quarter's profits, and second-quarter earnings per share, which would shortly be announced, were down 24 percent from the same period in 2004. The loss of talent and the threat that more people were considering leaving was leaching energy out of the firm. The directors were under scrutiny by the nonprofit governance watchdog, the Corporate Library, which gave the Morgan Stanley board a grade of D. That could lead to unwelcome attention by regulators whom Purcell and Don Kempf had already antagonized, and to stockholder lawsuits.

No one wanted to be remembered as a loser in a fight that made Wall Street history. Whatever the directors did now, the fight for the soul of Morgan Stanley would be a line in many of their obituaries. It

was time to act before regulators decided to investigate whether the
board had failed in its fiduciary responsibility.

On a nonexecutive directors conference call in late May, Chuck
Knight reported that investors were telling him that he could not
stick with Purcell any longer. He had decided Purcell had to go. As
someone who was there said, "After that, they didn't waste any time."
Another said, "It was just a matter of what the process should be: if
Phil should step down after a certain number of months, if he should
step down as CEO and become chairman; and if we were going to go
down that road, what it was going to look like."

Over Memorial Day weekend, Bob Scott heard that a couple of directors had started discussions with Purcell to begin the disengagement
process and discuss what they would have to give Purcell for him to
leave. The final negotiations for the divorce continued in the utmost
secrecy in Chicago, New York, Utah, and on conference calls. Purcell
had demonstrated what an implacable negotiator he was during the
Morgan Stanley Dean Witter merger; defeat made him even tougher.
The board was eager to finish the process so Morgan Stanley could get
back on track, and they could get on with their lives. They made significant concessions and dispensed a large chunk of stockholders' money
to complete the process. They agreed to call Purcell's departure "retirement." If he had been fired, which was being proposed by a number of
critics outside the firm, the value of his "platinum parachute" would
have been reduced significantly.

Purcell's total package amounted to $113.7 million, including the
$34.7 million in restricted stock, approximately $20.1 million in stock
options, and a $42.7 million "departure bonus." The exact amount of
the bonus was based on 2005 profits; it would be higher if profits were
up, and he would get less if they were down. Ironically, if his successor
turned the firm around, Purcell would make even more money. That
added up to $97.5 million so far, and he would receive another $11 million in retirement benefits: $250,000 outright per year; a secretary at
$115,000 a year, office and administrative expenses, medical benefits,
and $250,000 a year in charitable donations, which Morgan Stanley
would give in his name to institutions of his choice.

Purcell took care of his loyalists. Steve Crawford, who had been copresident for three months, was promised $16 million a year for two years, or $32 million if he chose to leave before August 3. Someone who was there said the board felt badly because by agreeing that Crawford and Cruz should be copresidents under a CEO who was fighting for his life, they might have ruined their careers. It was not likely that Purcell's successor would want either of them around; as someone said, Crawford's package was "guilt money."

Zoe Cruz refused a Crawford-type deal. She continued without a contract while she waited to find out whom she would be working for, and whether she would still have a job under the new CEO. She and Crawford remained on the board during the search.

Other Purcell lieutenants with special pay packages were John Schaefer, head of Retail Brokerage, and Mitchell Merin, Head of Asset Management, the two areas of the firm that had repeatedly been singled out for their poor performance.

CFO David Sidwell was guaranteed a minimum of $10.5 million if he stayed until mid-October. He would get $21 million if he resigned or was fired without cause. (Sidwell remained with the firm until 2007, and in November 2005, he agreed to revise his contract. The $21 million clause was canceled and he received a onetime special award of $8 million in restricted stock. He left Morgan Stanley in 2007.)

The agreements, which were made before the new chairman and CEO was hired, would be part of Purcell's legacy.

Marty Lipton, who had advised the board to stonewall the Group of Eight and back Purcell, and was still advising the board when they determined the severance pay for Purcell and the others, charged Morgan Stanley a fee said to be in the $25 million range.

Purcell held out for revenge, or perhaps he thought of it as justification. He was adamant that the board should not replace him with any member of the Group of Eight; anyone who left during the fight, including Pandit, Havens, Newhouse, Perella, and Meguid; or John Mack. He could not get successor exclusions in writing, but Chuck Knight, Head of the Compensation, Management Development, and Succession Committee, wanted to announce the names of people who would not be considered. Other directors told Knight that making that kind of public announcement would be counterproductive, narrow the pool, and prolong the fight, and exhorted him not to do it. The Morgan Stanley board needed to look dignified and in control, not petty and vengeful.

By that time, they were openly divided. The early-warning group was represented by Laura Tyson, who had proposed that they perform some serious due diligence six months earlier, and had been outspoken all along, despite being shouted down when the discussions got heated. Sir Howard Davies was another warning voice. Some of the former CEOs of industrial and manufacturing companies, who came out of more autocratic systems, in particular Chuck Knight and Mike Miles, were angry that they had been cornered. Bob Kidder and Miles Marsh had moved toward the center.

Purcell continued to try to influence the decision about his successor. Jeffrey Sonnenfeld, associate dean at Yale School of Management, said, "A board should never accommodate a dethroned leader because they become a wounded animal and can act vindictively."

As all of this was still happening behind the scenes, the Group of Eight believed that the fight was still on. Then, toward the end of the second week in June, Bob Scott was getting urgent "calls and whispers" that the date of execution was close. He heard that, on Thursday or Friday, June 9 or 10, Zoe Cruz and Steve Crawford were told to drop whatever they were doing and were flown to an urgent unscheduled meeting in Chicago on one of the Morgan Stanley planes. That weekend, Scott, who was at his house in Vermont, heard that the board was "preparing to shoot Phil," and made calls to other members of the group to alert them.

On Sunday, June 12, the Morgan Stanley directors met in New York and agreed to accept Purcell's decision to retire, on his terms.

At six-thirty in the morning, on Monday, June 13, CNBC's Maria Bartiromo scooped the financial media and reported that Philip Purcell would announce his plan to retire later that day.

Anson Beard was the first of the Eight to hear the news. His assistant, Farah Santoro, who had maintained her sanity and good nature through a board fight and plans for Beard's imminent wedding, heard Bartiromo's scoop and called him at home. Beard says, "I'd heard that he was working on the second quarter earnings release and that Zoe and Crawford had been flown out to Chicago on short notice. We didn't

know what it was about, and you never know when the board was going to break, but we were relentless."

Parker and Gail Gilbert were in Bilbao, Spain, where they had gone
to see the Frank Gehry–designed Guggenheim Museum of Art. They
were in a restaurant having lunch with another couple when Gilbert
got a call on his friend's cell phone. Bob Greenhill's assistant had
tracked him down. "Congratulations!" she said. "You've done it!"

Gilbert says, "I was surprised. I was absolutely thrilled. It was a de-
fining moment. You had to feel good about the way it was working out."

Bob Scott was driving back to New York when he heard on his car
radio that the deed was done. "After the calls over the weekend, I
wasn't surprised," he says, "but I was gratified, and obviously I was
happy that, through applying this pressure, the board had finally done
the right thing. I had the feeling, Phil is gone, but that doesn't necessarily solve the problem, it depends on what the board does in choosing
a new CEO."

At 1585 Broadway, Steve Roach was preparing to hold his regular
early-morning Monday Strategy Forum when he was alerted that
there would be a change in the format. About one hundred managing
directors were settling on the chairs in the sixth-floor auditorium when
Roach came in and sat at one end of the long dark-wood table on the
dais that stretched along the front of the room. Two large electronic
screens with charts were mounted behind him on a "Morgan Stanley
blue" wall, patterned with the firm's logo and the little triangle. Purcell, Cruz, and Crawford filed in, seated themselves, and looked out
over row after row of white shirts. The conversations subsided when
they sat down; everyone had heard Maria Bartiromo's scoop.

Cruz busied herself setting out her coffee cup and her papers; Crawford was looking down, grave and inward; Purcell, in a gray suit and
dark red tie, sat between them, smiling quietly, waiting for Roach to
begin. Roach cleared his throat and announced in a matter-of-fact
voice, "All right . . . in lieu of our regularly scheduled program, we
have a news special today that"——he cleared his throat again——"will
be brought to you by our three top brass." His face was expressionless.
He leaned over toward the center of the table and said, "Phil . . ."

Purcell searched for the controls of the microphone, and Roach said, "Hit the button."

Purcell stood to read his remarks, looking healthier than he had for weeks. As he spoke, he continued to smile; he seemed relieved, and even when his anger broke through, he talked in a steady, even tone.

He began, "The strategy forums that Steve hosts usually address the best investment ideas we have for our clients . . . Today I want to talk about our firm and specifically what's in the best interests of all of Morgan Stanley.

"Like most of you I look forward to getting to the office early, opening mail, answering client calls, and taking a brief look at the morning papers. But that hasn't been true over the last several months.

"There's been an unrelenting stream of criticism directed at me. And it has negatively affected how Morgan Stanley is seen, and it's clear that this is likely to continue, and it's clear what I should do.

"This morning, I am announcing my intention to retire by the time of our next annual shareholder meeting in March of 2006. I believe this is the best thing I can do for you, our clients, and our shareholders. You have all done an extraordinary job . . . despite these daily distractions. I feel strongly the attacks are unjustified, but unfortunately they show no signs of abating . . . people are spending more time reading about the acrimony," he said, than about the "outstanding work" done at the firm. "The whole is greater than the sum of its parts, and of any one part," he said, and he would "retire when my successor is appointed."

He added that he was sad that, as "the firm's integrated strategy is coming together," he would not be there to see it. Defending his leadership, he said, "We have gained share in almost every market category . . . Since the merger our stock price has outperformed the S&P by threefold," eliding over the fact that Morgan Stanley did not compare itself with 500 firms, but with a handful of its peers, and in that universe, the stock had underperformed since 2001. As for market share, he had just gotten rid of the leaders of the divisions that had gained the most.

"There is no finer firm on Wall Street," he continued. "The test of a leader is the performance of the institution he leaves behind. Morgan

Stanley has great depth of talent ... [and] a strong independent board ... [that has] recently appointed Miles Marsh lead director."

He paused briefly, then composed himself, and concluded, "It will not be easy for me to leave ... I have enormous faith that the best years of Morgan Stanley will be lived in the days and years ahead." He wrapped up with, "I have one last thing to say ... let's get back to work. We'd be happy to answer questions."

There was no applause; the audience was quiet, as though they were waiting for him to finish, so they could go back to their desks and try to pick up the pieces.

Purcell broke the tense silence with a little joke. "We need Byron Wien," he said; Wien could usually be counted on to ask a question. "Where's Byron?"

Roach covered the microphone and made a quick remark, and Purcell laughed. "Steve says he's, uh, talking to the search committee. He's the perfect age for Zoe and Steve." He was referring to the fact that Wien was over seventy, beyond the age for consideration. "Chuck Knight is here," Purcell said, looking out over the audience for a friendly face. "I think we should consider Byron."

With that, he sat down and crossed his arms over his chest.

Crawford, sitting on his right, was holding the side of his head in the palm of his hand. Cruz bridged the awkward moment. "Before we open it to questions and answers and before we get back to work, Phil," she began, "I want to personally thank Phil."

After the meeting, the traders went downstairs to an atmosphere of barely controlled hysteria and relief. One reported joining a spontaneous sing-along of "Ding Dong! The Wicked Witch Is Dead" while other traders danced a reel.

Purcell e-mailed his message firmwide in a "Letter to My Colleagues," which was released to the media, and Miles Marsh issued a statement on behalf of the board. He said, "Phil and the board have independently been considering the right course of action. In the last week, Phil came to us with the conclusion that he should remove himself for things to settle down." In what sounded like a near-admission that Purcell had been asked to leave, Marsh told the *Wall*

Street Journal's Ann Davis, "The board finally said, 'Look, from the point of view of the firm, we just can't engage in an endless situation like this, as much as we feel that some of it was unfair.'"

The media had earned its name; it was the mediator in the fight, and journalists who had been covering the story offered their observations. The postmortem pile-on was so one-sided that one reporter told a friend that he was beginning to feel some sympathy for Purcell. "I kind of like him better now that he's out," he said.

An unsigned editorial on the *New York Times* Web site titled "In Business, Tough Guys Finish Last" summed up the criticisms. The *Times* called Purcell "ruthless, autocratic and remote. He had no tolerance for dissent or even argument. He pushed away strong executives and surrounded himself with yes men and women. He demanded loyalty to himself over the organization. He played power games. He had little contact with rank and file . . . Is it a surprise that he was loathed by many executives, especially those on the Morgan Stanley side of the divide? Or that they finally took their revenge?" The story ended by noting that Purcell had no "reservoir of good will . . . [to] draw upon . . . That's what killed him."

Forbes's David Andelman wrote, "The saddest part . . . is that even in defeat, Purcell himself was unable or unwilling to admit his own very personal role in his slow rise and precipitous fall. He laid his 'decision' to step down directly at the feet of 'the continuing personal attacks on me . . .' To translate: Purcell's demise should in no sense be attributed to his extraordinary hubris, nor to his efforts to place his personal stamp on an institution where the individual had always been subordinate to the greater good and where performance or brilliance invariably trumped personal loyalty."

Purcell told the *Financial Times* that the Group of Eight was at the root of his troubles. "If it's good they make it look bad and if it's bad they make it look worse," he said. As the *FT* noted, Purcell's letter "oozes wounded pride."

Ann Davis's summary in the *Wall Street Journal* was titled "Closing Bell." Purcell told her "you had a jihad and it wasn't going to stop," and that "he was going to retire anyway before long."

Chuck Knight prevailed over the directors who did not want him to make a public statement ruling out certain possible successors. Knight announced, "Members of the Group of Eight, the five recently departed management committee members, and John Mack are not being considered as candidates for Phil's replacement."

Purcell and CFO David Sidwell held a conference call at ten-thirty that morning, attended by analysts from UBS, J. P. Morgan, Merrill Lynch, Lehman Brothers, and CIBC World Markets. No member of the board joined the call. Purcell repeated that the crisis had been precipitated because "way too much attention is being paid to acrimony and criticisms, most of it directed at me. It is not good for Morgan Stanley, so the best thing for me to do is . . . to retire, and it is best for all our people." When one of the analysts asked whether the firm would be "more vulnerable to further defections" because his plan to leave had been announced before a successor was named, Purcell argued that attrition was not any higher than usual. "The big difference is that this year every person that leaves is in the newspaper," he said bitterly.

Merrill Lynch's Guy Moszkowski asked Purcell to comment on Knight's announcement about the people who wouldn't be considered for his job.

Purcell replied, "I would speculate that the board just made a decision three months ago to have Zoe and Steve be copresidents . . . And if they pick them over the five that recently departed, it would be very unusual that they would consider any of those five ahead of Zoe or Steve. On the other ones [John Mack and the members of the Group of Eight] I just think it is the board is very familiar with them, worked with them for many years, knows their qualifications, knows the qualifications that they are looking for in leadership for this phenomenal firm, a great franchise. And obviously, from what Chuck said, they have decided they don't make the cut."

By coincidence, the National Press Club in Washington, D.C., was holding a panel discussion that day, titled "The End of the Imperial CEO."

Marty Lipton was batting zero-for-two in the highest-profile non-criminal CEO stories of the year, the Richard Grasso pay debacle at the New York Stock Exchange and the Purcell defense. The day Purcell resigned, Lipton paid a visit to Goldman Sachs CEO Henry Paulson, one of the NYSE directors who had been most incensed by the Grasso pay package. A person to whom Paulson mentioned the visit later that day said he had the impression that Lipton wanted to explain how the "Eight Grumpy Old Men" got the better of him.

The Eight issued a brief statement: "As shareholders of Morgan Stanley, we are pleased that the board has taken this important and necessary first step. We hope that this and future actions will stem the recent tide of departures from the firm and restore a culture and business environment capable of attracting and retaining the best professional talent to Morgan Stanley."

The Eight were jubilant, but wary. They hoped they would be consulted about the choice of the new chairman and CEO, but they did not expect that the board they had opposed, and which had stonewalled them for three months, would be eager to talk with them. They agreed to stay out of the press, but they let it be known that the threat of a proxy fight wasn't dead. If the directors didn't bring in a first-class chairman and CEO, and if some of the more obdurate Purcell supporters didn't resign, they would be back.

As Parker Gilbert says ruefully, "It was over. There wasn't anything else for us to do." It was a triumph and a letdown.

A story that started with one wedding ended with another. Eight years earlier, Dick Fisher and Jeanne Donovan were married on a day that coincided with a crossroads in Morgan Stanley history. On June 17, 2005, Anson Beard and Debra de Pasquale's marriage ceremony was held in the tiny private chapel that Beard's Yale roommate Frolic Weymouth built in the woods on his property in Chadds Ford, Pennsylvania. Weymouth, the eccentric and brilliant artist who started the Brandywine Valley Trust, one of the first land trusts in the country, and the Brandywine River Museum, was a famous coaching driver and collector of antique coaches, and the couple arrived for the ceremony in one of the open, horse-drawn carriages that outgoing president James Buchanan had loaned to Abraham Lincoln for his inauguration. The informal ceremony was witnessed by a few dozen friends and family members.

The next day, the Beards flew up to Greenwich, Connecticut, where they held a dinner dance for 350 guests in black-and-white-striped tents.

Before dinner, in the soft light of a warm June evening, little groups stood on the lawn, "women in their light summer dresses," men in summer suits and blazers. People who hadn't been part of the fight gathered around members of the Group of Eight to discuss how they had pulled off the coup, what turned the board around, and whether they thought John Mack would get the job, despite Chuck Knight's pronouncement. No one had yet heard about the scale of Purcell's departure package.

Beard welcomed their friends and announced there would only be one toast, and he would give it. He raised his glass and said that he and Debbie had asked for everyone's presence, but no presents, but that they had received one phenomenal wedding present, that Monday when they heard that a certain CEO was relieved of his responsibilities by a board whose decision was overdue. It was their only and best wedding gift. As Beard says, "The place went crazy."

In the midst of dinner, as the orchestra broke into loud Brazilian music, a band of Brazilian dancers and drummers in enormous headdresses and glittery Copacabana costumes shimmied into the tent, banging drums and shaking tambourines, singing and chanting. Immediately, everyone was on their feet, clapping and cheering as a dancer on stilts led them in a conga line around the dance floor. They snaked through the tables, holding on to one another's waists, bobbing and laughing, and the "Grumpy Old Men" kicked to the left and right, and danced on.

That weekend the Cypress Point golf club overlooking the Pacific Ocean on California's Monterey Peninsula held its annual "Hook and Eye" tournament. Cypress Point, designed by Alister MacKenzie, who also designed Augusta National, was among the world's most spectacular courses, and the Hook and Eye attracted many of the nation's most successful business leaders. Purcell was still chairman and

CEO of Morgan Stanley until his replacement was chosen, and he and Chuck Knight flew to California to play in the tournament. It was hard to know what Purcell was thinking, but it appeared that he believed that no shame attached to him, and that he had agreed to leave to protect the firm from further depredations, rather than because he had failed.

The board hired the executive search firm Spencer Stuart, and its U.S. chairman Thomas J. Neff, and proceeded to gather the names of candidates to succeed Purcell. *Fortune* magazine's Patricia Sellers wrote, "The prescription for new leadership at Morgan Stanley: a strong manager with instant credibility and high E.Q.—emotional intelligence. The assignment: re-establish trust and cooperation at a company traumatized by infighting and poor judgment at the top." Most of the logical candidates were well known in the financial community. Robert Rubin, who had served as Treasury secretary under President Bill Clinton, was now at Citigroup and he was an interesting possibility. Richard Fuld, chairman and CEO of Lehman Brothers, was so attractive that there was even talk that Morgan Stanley might think of acquiring Lehman to get Fuld.

The Group of Eight was still hoping that Vikram Pandit, John Havens, Joe Perella, and Terry Meguid could return; Pandit was their first choice as chairman. Miles Marsh and Tom Neff met briefly with representatives of the Eight, but they felt the meeting was purely pro forma. Anyone they suggested would be tainted.

At that point, a number of people who were witnesses to the board discussions described the situation as "chaos," and most of the directors as "clueless." Inside the firm, Purcell's credit, which had declined to the single digits, went down to zero, as someone said, when it appeared that he was blocking Mack's return.

A small pro-Zoe group suggested that she should be appointed CEO, and that Steve Newhouse be asked to return as nonexecutive chairman.

Chuck Knight spoke with Morgan Stanley alumnus Robert E. Diamond Jr., the president of Barclays Capital, who quashed talk of returning to the firm but pointedly commented on the importance of "talent and culture" in the selection process.

The person who came closest to getting the job was the lanky, well-respected Laurence D. Fink, fifty-three, chairman and CEO of BlackRock, the investment management firm he founded in 1988, and took public in 1999 under a plan that involved broad employee ownership. BlackRock now had a $391 billion asset pool and the strength in asset management that Morgan Stanley was seeking.

One of the most controversial elements in the internal warfare at Morgan Stanley had been over risk management. Purcell's aversion to risk had cost the firm significant opportunities, and one of Fink's skills was his understanding of risk. He was a pioneer of asset-backed securities, he was in his early thirties in 1986 when he made a pile of money as a bond trader, then got clobbered the same year with a $100 million loss in the mortgage market. He never forgot that lesson. BlackRock had been so successful in managing risk for its own products that the firm had been marketing its risk management strategies to its clients.

Fink was one of the gregarious members of the tribe that included John Mack and Joe Perella. All of them lunched at San Pietro—like Perella, Fink had his own table. He was a connoisseur and collector of fine wines, and invited small groups of young managing directors to dinners where he shared rare vintages and leaned back with his hands behind his head, to give them blunt appraisals of the business and the competition and answer questions. He was accessible, he was personable, and he had built enormous stockholder value.

Like many heads of almost all the major securities firms, Fink came out of the bond side of the business. Dick Fuld at Lehman Brothers; Lloyd Blankfein, who would take over at Goldman Sachs in 2006; and John Mack had all been bond traders or salesmen. As Fink explains, "Bonds is all about teamwork. All for one and one for all. To be good in bonds you have to build culture, teams, organization." Morgan Stanley needed to rebuild its teams. Fink had successfully emphasized an approach known as "One BlackRock" that was similar to John Mack's "one-firm firm," based on meeting individual client and global needs while promoting teamwork, global consistency, and a single message that all employees understood and conveyed.

Fink says the situation at Morgan Stanley "was a tragic story, a misjudgment of needs, interests and personalities. It was a wonderful platform; the notion of the merger could have worked," although he says the two firms were an odd match: "In '97 Morgan Stanley was rocking, and Dean Witter was . . . Dean Witter."

Tom Neff interviewed Fink and ascertained that he was interested, however, with conditions. Fink next met with Neff and Knight, and after that, at a series of meetings that more and more directors attended. He told them that he wasn't against the integrated strategy, and advised them not to spin off Discover, which "makes 15 percent on equity, until the firm was stabilized. Why would you sell an asset so many people would covet, until you know if Morgan Stanley is going to be independent or sold?"

Remarking that Morgan Stanley was "terrible" in Asset Management and had an incomplete bond business, Fink proposed some kind of merger with BlackRock. He discussed the missed opportunities in asset-backed securities and explained that while "Morgan Stanley was doing better in the credit markets, its position was deteriorating" by comparison to the competition. As for the Dean Witter side, he said, "it needed to be reenergized."

Fink told the board, "It was very important for Morgan Stanley to build its intellectual capability in those areas." He was in favor of bringing back Vikram Pandit and John Havens but recognized that they wouldn't return while Cruz was there.

Finally, he told the board, "Phil was never as good as people said he was when he was a star, and never as bad as people said he was. But if Phil *is* this bad and you supported him, you should all quit." Chuck Knight's response was, "You're right."

That was Fink's last interview.

The biggest challenge, Fink says, "was to bring back community fast." He told the board that no one could do that better than John Mack.

The board was getting a blitz of calls and letters from clients and investors urging them to consider Mack. Allianz Global Investors wrote the directors a starchy letter, criticizing them for eliminating Mack and other former Morgan Stanley executives. Eric Gleacher, the investment banker who worked with Mack at Morgan Stanley (and who brought Ronald Perelman to the firm as a client) and now headed his own firm, Gleacher Partners, told the *Times*, "John Mack has the culture of Morgan Stanley embedded in his body. This place can be resurrected, and I think he can do it." The wording "this place" was an indication of the way many Morgan Stanley alumni felt about the firm. They might not work there anymore, but it never quite became "*that* place." Miles Marsh told his fellow directors that even the competition was advising them to hire Mack.

Byron Wien was among the firm leaders who were unabashedly lobbying for Mack to return, even though that would create an awkward situation for Wien, who had agreed to follow Mack to Pequot Capital. If Mack went back to Morgan Stanley and Wien stayed, they would both disappoint Pequot's founder and CEO Art Samberg. (Wien did go to Pequot but continued to consult for Morgan Stanley.)

"Bring back Mack" had begun to sound like a chant at a football game.

Finally, Tom Neff called Mack, and they arranged to have dinner at the apartment of a friend at the Carlyle Hotel with Chuck Knight and Miles Marsh. Knight told Mack that he had never been against his candidacy. Mack says his explanation was, "The reason I said 'not John Mack' was because when Disney didn't eliminate Iger they couldn't get good candidates." Knight was referring to the Disney search for a successor to embattled chairman and CEO Michael Eisner. Robert A. Iger, who was already president and CEO, was such a logical choice that other qualified candidates were discouraged. Knight said that if he hadn't specifically ruled out Mack, other people might have been reluctant to be considered.

At the end of dinner, Knight said to Mack, "I'm disappointed that you don't seem very excited about coming back."

Mack answered, "It's not about excitement. There are two points: first I like what I'm doing now. And second, when I walked out of the firm not one of you asked me to stay and it's the same board today."

When he got home, he told his wife, Christy, "I don't think I'm going to take it."

The next morning, people close to Mack say he told them, "I woke up and I said, maybe I am going to take it."

They were already interviewing Mack when Chuck Knight reiterated his announcement about the exclusion of certain candidates, and was quoted in the *New York Times* as saying the "ground rules are still in place."

The Macks were planning to go to Europe on vacation, and to see their daughter, Jenna, who lived in London. The trip coincided with the Morgan Stanley courtship, but Mack decided to go. While he was away, he considered the terms under which he would return. He says, "I want Perella back. I want Vikram back. I called Vikram, told him I wanted him to run planning. He says no, I want to be president." Mack declined to make that decision, and Vikram said, "You've got to talk to Parker." The Macks were in London, staying at the Dorchester, and Gilbert reached him there, but Mack didn't change his mind.

When the market understood that Mack was likely to be returning, Morgan Stanley stock traded 5 percent higher over two days, although it was still only at $53.12.

B y the end of June, Purcell's office was filled with packed boxes. Mack returned from London on Sunday, June 26. A June 27 offsite meeting for about eighty managing directors, to be led by Cruz and Crawford to discuss new efforts to integrate the businesses, was indefinitely postponed, awaiting developments.

On Monday, June 27, Chuck Knight publicly acknowledged that the board was eager to bring Mack back. Miles Marsh told *Newsweek*'s Charles Gasparino that as a search tactic, Mack "was initially ruled out . . . to make sure he wanted the job."

The negotiations had uncomfortable undertones: eight of the outside directors had been on the board in 2001 when they accepted Mack's resignation. Ed Brennan would turn seventy-two in January 2006 and would have to retire, but Knight, Madigan, and Miles had been strong Purcell supporters.

S eventeen days after Phil Purcell announced that he would resign, late in the morning of June 30, 2005, the Morgan Stanley directors met at 1585 Broadway and unanimously elected John J. Mack chairman and CEO, effective immediately.

The sixth-floor auditorium was alive with excitement later that day as the managing directors waited to welcome Mack. He walked in quietly and stood behind the long table on the dais. Immediately, the managing directors were on their feet, erupting in a great burst of applause and shouts. He smiled, and as the ovation went on and on, he raised a bottle of water and took a swig, then looked down almost shyly, seemingly overwhelmed. After a while, he held his hands up and pushed against the air to quiet the crowd, but no one sat down.

Miles Marsh had come in behind him, and now he took the microphone and smiled. "I guess we made the right decision," he said, and the applause started again. "We've had a momentous five weeks," Marsh said, but that was now over, and he was about to announce "the world's worst-kept secret: John Mack is the new chairman and CEO of Morgan Stanley."

Christy Mack sat next to Zoe Cruz in the front row; Steve Crawford sat on Cruz's other side. Cruz, at least, had a reprieve: Mack had trained her, promoted her, and tried to hire her at CSFB. That might balance the fact that she had supported Purcell. Across the aisle, Mary Meeker, Byron Wien, and Steve Roach stood together, proud that they had taken a stand and stuck it out.

Purcell had vacated his office and was not there to welcome his successor, but Miles Marsh began by thanking him, briefly citing Purcell's legacy, "most significantly the merged companies and Discover Card." He added, "I'm sure you will all join the board and me," in wishing Phil and his family the very best. That was a cue for applause, but no one took it.

Marsh led into his introduction of Mack by talking about his contributions to the firm, in particular its "very strong position in the Chinese market," which, he said, "owes a lot" to Mack's efforts. He remarked that "when John felt he needed to run his own shop . . . something that comes to people who are natural leaders," and left Morgan Stanley in 2001, "he never criticized the team on the field . . . no sniping." That sounded like a reference to the Group of Eight, none of whom were invited to the meeting.

Explaining the board's earlier "not John Mack" position, he said, "John was always on our minds as a candidate," but the directors wanted to be sure that "John was interested in coming back to us. We were concerned that a groundswell of support for John could overwhelm the search process . . . but frankly, once we were certain that John was interested in coming back, that made the choice academic." The board "received a lot of help" from employees, alumni, investors, and competitors, who advocated Mack's return. He smiled and added, "Even the news media might have mentioned John Mack once or twice."

Marsh's equable manner made him well suited to try to explain the board's intransigence. He had a nice face, with blond hair going white, and a pleasant South African accent. He spoke of "our" firm and told the employees that their guidance about leadership and corporate governance had been more helpful than they could know. Finally, he said, "I give you your new chairman and CEO, John Mack." The managing directors stood and cheered again, until Mack held up his hands for silence.

"I had no idea I'd be comin' back home," he said, and began an anecdote that made it seem as though he had never left. "About thirteen months ago," he said, "I was getting a haircut downstairs"—he paused as the managing directors laughed fondly, as though to acknowledge that he hadn't really been completely gone—"and I saw this grumpy-looking old fellow with old clothes. It was Byron Wien. I said, 'Byron, how many years have you owned that suit?' It was threadbare." He looked out into the audience and asked, "Byron, are you wearing that suit I got you?" (Mack had told Wien he couldn't wear the old suit anymore and sent him a replacement from Brooks Brothers.) There was a ripple of fond laughter, and Mack continued, speaking extemporaneously in a manner that felt more like a conversation with a small group than a speech to a packed crowd. He began by calling his appointment an honor and an opportunity, then said, "You've been in the press so much, it kind of beats you down. From now on, when we're in the press it's going to be positive."

He spoke of the "one firm" idea, the momentum, the franchise, and the people. As for "people who have left us," he said, "we want them back . . . but as team players. No individual agendas."

He reminded them of his open-door policy and invited them to "call me on my mistakes. A successful firm that is this large needs everyone to be together and pull together." He did not commit to a decision as to whether the firm would stay together, spin off divisions, or merge with a bigger bank, but said, "We'll take some time and analyze the strategy." The other subject that had burned the firm and injured its pride was the recent spate of legal actions and fines. He promised that Morgan Stanley would take the lead in a productive interface with regulators to restore the good name of the firm and the industry.

He looked out at the colleagues he had worked with for most of his life, and the new, younger people he didn't know yet. Most of them hoped he would be the kind of leader they could follow. "*This* is the gold standard," he said, and his voice broke and his eyes filled with tears, "and I need all of you to *deliver.*"

The audience stood and cheered again, and he left the room shaking hands and smiling.

E arlier that spring, when Mack's whimsical side took over, he was reported to have remarked in the low-key, laconic southern accent, which was stronger when he was teasing, that, while he was still refraining from commenting on the fight, if he did come back it would "make a great ending to the book."

Fifteen

MACK IS BACK

In the summer of 2005, everything at Morgan Stanley was an urgent priority. Get out of the press and stay out. Replace the heads of important divisions in Institutional Securities and the heads of Retail and Asset Management. Talk to the five senior executives who left after the Easter Monday Massacre. Replace most of the board, which was battered, reeling, and publicly embarrassed. Hire a new general counsel. Sell the aircraft-leasing business, and swallow the write-down. Keep Discover, or sell Discover—but do something. Move the share price up. Move up the return on equity. Move the chairman and presidents' offices back to the fortieth floor. Restore morale, and keep it high. Correct the firm's official Web site so it accurately dates Morgan Stanley's founding to 1935, rather than 1997, the year Purcell took over. Change the firm's New York Stock Exchange symbol, from MWD to MS. And get rid of the triangle logo—not exactly at the top of the list, but symbolic of the previous administration's failure to understand that the only logo Morgan Stanley needed was its name.

Of all the hangovers from the last regime, the ones with the longest half-life were the exit packages the board granted Phil Purcell and Steve Crawford. When the amounts were reported in early July, people both in and out of the firm expressed the view that it was disgraceful for the board to have agreed that the shareholders should pay such a steep price for Purcell's departure. The decision was seen as another example of questionable advice from counsel Marty Lipton. The editors of the *New York Times*, who rarely interested themselves in

Wall Street's wars unless they involved criminal behavior, ran an editorial titled "The Wages of Failure on Wall Street," writing, "Stockholders and employees are properly seething at the deal cut for Mr. Crawford . . . by a board that was oblivious to protecting the bank's reputation as it over-rewarded his fealty to Philip Purcell." Calling Purcell's departure package "ludicrous," and "failure's rewards," the *Times* wrote, "Few of life's losers land so affluently." Addressing the other exit packages, the editors added, "Now others from his team of loyalists— sycophants is the term outraged critics prefer—are lining up to walk the platinum plank behind Mr. Crawford, who never ran a business division at the bank yet rose to the top as Mr. Purcell's attentive protégé."

Steve Crawford resigned on July 11. He took the $32 million, roughly triple what he had made in 2004, and was allowed to vest his stock.

The *New York Times* editorial changed the dynamics of public opinion in Chicago. Bob McCormack recalls that people who read it said, "'This is really awful.' They were shocked. We couldn't have written an editorial making a better case that the directors should immediately resign."

Nicholas D. Kristof announced an "Award for Greed" in another *Times* column, and proclaimed three winners. First place went to Andrew Wiederhorn, chairman and CEO of Fog Cutter Capital Group; Wiederhorn was serving eighteen months in federal prison for pleading guilty to two of the more minor deeds of which he was accused. Fog Cutter's annual report described him as being "on leave of absence" and continued to pay his full salary, plus an extra $2 million to help cover the restitution portion of his sentence. There were two runners-up: John Rigas, former CEO of Adelphia Communications, who was serving a fifteen-year prison sentence for stealing $100 million from the company; the other was the Morgan Stanley board, "which threw $113 million at . . . Philip Purcell, when he was finally booted for driving away talent."

Purcell's financial arrangements tainted the reception of Mack's initial contract, which stipulated that in the first eighteen months, his compensation would be based on the average of his peers at Bear Stearns,

Merrill Lynch, Lehman Brothers, and Goldman Sachs, with an annual cap of $25 million. He would also receive a onetime grant of 500,000 shares of Morgan Stanley stock, valued at $26.9 million. As the news was released, Mack recognized that an outcry was in the offing and briskly corrected course. Within hours, he sent Morgan Stanley employees a memo reporting that he had changed the terms. "I don't want anyone to think that I am entitled to something that others are not," he wrote. "I will amend my employment agreement. No guarantee. No industry benchmark. The Board will set my pay after our results are in based strictly on our performance as a Firm." He added, "This business is based on trust." The Morgan Stanley tradition, which had never been abrogated until the merger, was that no employee was given a contract or a guarantee. Too much had changed for the "no contract" culture to continue, but Mack's decision restored the understanding that compensation had to be earned.

B ack in Utah, Purcell was simmering over the circumstances of his departure and enjoying the fruits of his most recent successful negotiation. In August, when another of the Purcells' seven sons was married, he looked tired and older, but the Purcells' 2005 Christmas card, taken at the wedding, is the portrait of a wholesome, attractive American family. The children stand in front, four little girls in sleeveless white dresses, with white barrettes in their hair, holding nosegays of white flowers; and the boys in dark suits with white boutonnieres. Anne, in black lace, beams.

On August 21, the *New York Times* wrapped up Purcell's career at Morgan Stanley on the first page of the SundayBusiness section. The piece, titled "Exile from Wall Street," is accompanied by a full-color photograph that occupies most of the top half of the page. Purcell is posed, Clint Eastwood–style, leaning on a rail fence with one foot up, a hand on one hip and another resting on the top of the gate. His jeans are worn low with a tooled leather belt, and his long-sleeved navy blue cotton shirt is open at the neck. Behind him, two horses are lying in a field, and white farm buildings are clustered in the lee of green mountains.

Purcell drove through the landscape in his Mercedes jeep, playing country music, exhilarated to be home. He did not admit, or believe, that he might have failed the firm, and reporter Landon Thomas wrote that he was "like a wounded gunslinger, beaten to the draw by a slicker, more audacious foe ... Underneath the taciturn reserve lies a man who has not made his peace with the injustice of it all." Purcell still insisted that the Group of Eight's position "wasn't fair or accurate," but recalled his father's warning not to expect life to be fair. A senior Morgan Stanley executive who read that line would later exclaim in disgust: "Not fair? What was the most he made before he came to Morgan Stanley? *Millions of dollars a year?* And then what? *Tens of millions!* Very few cultures on Wall Street would have tolerated such poor performance for as long as we did. At other firms there would have been a riot from within," but the executive added, "this is a somewhat gentlemanly culture."

"This is my new life," Purcell said. "If it were not for the articles and possible books, this would be a wonderful way to live the rest of your life."

The media phase of the old life wasn't finished yet: at the end of the year, Purcell was featured in a grand finale of unfriendly attention. Gretchen Morgenson assembled her annual financial rogues gallery for the *New York Times* and called it "The Big Winner, Again, Is 'Scandalot.'" A half-page full-color cartoon showed some of the year's corporate wrongdoers on a theater stage littered with cash. Tyco's former CEO L. Dennis Kozlowski and Bernard J. Ebbers, former chairman and CEO of WorldCom, dressed in orange jumpsuits with their hands cuffed behind their backs, are being marched offstage by a guard wearing dark glasses. Eliot Spitzer is chasing A.I.G.'s chairman and CEO Maurice R. "Hank" Greenberg, who is running off into the wings, and an unidentified character is lugging bags of money slips out through the curtains. Front and center, Phil Purcell, with an enormous swelled head and a big grin, stands at the microphone with a briefcase labeled MORGAN STANLEY. From behind the side curtains, a hand emerges holding a long cane, and hooks it around Purcell's neck to drag him offstage, vaudeville style. Morgenson gives Purcell the "Tough Guys Finish Last Award," remarking, "Hardball can sometimes backfire, even on veteran players."

Inevitably, a lawsuit was brought against the board, with the focus on Purcell's platinum helicopter and Crawford's golden parachute. The plaintiff was the Central Laborers' Pension Fund, which sued Purcell and the other directors for "Negligent Breach of Fiduciary Duties, Waste, Unjust Enrichment, Abuse of Control and Gross Mismanagement." The pertinent complaint was:

> After Purcell's hand-picked Board passively tolerated years of poor business and stock performance and a massive exodus of Morgan Stanley's top managers, which resulted in a shareholder revolt, Purcell's Board rewarded Purcell and Stephen S. Crawford, his top lieutenant, for their failures with departure payoffs of over $100 million to secure their silence and cooperation, while attempting to release them from valuable and viable corporate causes of action against them.

As of May 2007, the suit had not been resolved.

During the fight, Purcell declared that he would not enter into a dialogue with the dissidents, and let them shadowbox until they got tired of the exercise, yet in the end he did fight. One evening during the siege, as the story went—and by then there were so many stories—he rode down in the elevator with another senior employee, who said sympathetically, "I'm sorry you're going through all this difficulty." Purcell's reported response was something to the effect that it wasn't all that hard on him; he liked a good fight. When he did put on the gloves, the crowd saw how he conducted himself in the ring, then watched him lose the fight, and walk off with the money.

In August 2006, Phil Purcell opened a firm to invest his own money in small financial services and growth firms. It was located in Chicago, and he shared office space with a hedge fund started by two of his sons.

The only senior executive still in place who had been part of Purcell's March 28 restructuring was Zoe Cruz, who became acting president after Crawford resigned. Her future at the firm would be the subject of intense speculation for many months, as Mack neither upgraded her from "acting" nor downgraded her to "departing." The Group of Eight couldn't understand why she survived after having backed Purcell, even if, as she said, she had supported him in order to help stabilize the firm. But the fact that she had declined any financial exit package was positive, her history with Mack was in her favor, and she had been an advocate with the board for his return.

The Eight believed that it would be in the firm's best interests to ask Steve Newhouse, Vikram Pandit, Joe Perella, John Havens, and Terry Meguid to come back. Newhouse had invaluable international client relationships and experience; Perella had a reputation, a Rolodex (or Palm Pilot), a track record, and a personality no one could match; Pandit's gravitas, stature, brilliance, and mannerly demeanor had earned him respect and affection; and Havens and Meguid, both natural leaders, were close on their heels. The chief obstacle to any of them wanting to return was Cruz, who continued to say that one of the reasons she had supported Purcell was to prevent Pandit from getting the job. The former dissidents remarked that they didn't understand why Mack would pick one person—Cruz—if that prevented him from getting five talented, experienced senior executives back. "It doesn't make sense," they would say. "To give up five for one? Just do the math."

Mack had separate lunches with Perella and Meguid, one breakfast with Pandit, and another with Havens, although members of the Group of Eight said that he maintained that he didn't want "a gun to his head" about whom he should hire, and was determined to make his own decisions as to who might return and under what circumstances. None of the five went back. After their meetings with Mack, Perella and Meguid began preparing to start their own firm; Pandit and Havens rented temporary offices for a new hedge fund and a private equity fund. Newhouse was moving back to the United States from London and would serve on corporate boards.

In October 2005, Pandit, Havens, Guru Ramakrishnan, and Brian Leach, Morgan Stanley's former risk management executive, announced that they had formed Old Lane Management. Old Lane opened the following April, with a $3.5 billion multistrategy hedge fund, a $500 million India-focused private equity fund with two offices in India, the head office and one other in the United States, an office in London, and about one hundred employees.

The settlement for Newhouse, Pandit, and Havens fell between the cracks until November, when a longtime Mack colleague, Thomas R. Nides, returned to the firm as chief administrative officer and completed the process. Newhouse would be paid $17.4 million, approximately what he earned in 2004; Pandit would get $9 million, and Havens $7.9 million. The agreements stipulated that they could not talk about the firm for thirty-six months.

Perella and Meguid geared up to start a corporate advisory and investment firm that Perella jokingly called "Noco," as in "no company," a reference to "Newco," the term used for a new business that hadn't yet picked a name. When Peter Weinberg, former CEO of Goldman Sachs International, joined them, the firm was titled Perella Weinberg. The new partner was highly respected and well liked, with a stellar Wall Street pedigree. A tall man in his late forties, with spectacles and a friendly demeanor, Weinberg had spent the first seven years of his career at Morgan Stanley, then moved over to Goldman Sachs, where he was the third generation of the family that had led the firm between 1930 and 1990. His grandfather was the legendary senior partner, Sidney Weinberg, and his uncle John L. Weinberg was co-senior partner and then the sole senior partner from 1974 until 1990. Perella Weinberg opened on June 15, 2006, with $1 billion in seed capital and offices in the General Motors Building across from the Plaza Hotel on Fifth Avenue; and on Grafton Street in London.

By the time Old Lane and Perella Weinberg were in business, John Mack had appointed Zoe Cruz copresident with Robert Scully, a fifty-six-year-old veteran investment banker who had been chairman of Global Markets and vice-chairman of Investment Banking, and a steadying influence during the spring and summer of 2005. Mack said that Cruz provides "outstanding leadership ability, deep insight into our business and culture, and a strong commitment to the Firm and our clients." He also cited her twenty-four years at the firm, during which she "consistently built successful businesses and delivered bottom-line results." Under her leadership, the Fixed Income business had more than doubled its revenues from 2000 to 2004. The appointment ended any residual speculation about her role. In August 2006, *Forbes* named Cruz number ten on its list of the 100 Most Powerful Women worldwide. The top three spots were taken by German chancellor Angela Merkel, U.S. secretary of state Condoleeza Rice, and Wu Yi, the vice premier of China. Cruz ranked ahead of Oprah Winfrey (number fourteen), Hillary Clinton (number eighteen), and Melinda Gates (number twelve).

Steve Crawford became one of three founders of Centerview Partners, a boutique investment firm that engaged in advisory and investment businesses. James M. Kilts, who joined Centerview as head of its private equity fund, was another executive whose payout had stimulated shareholder outrage; he received $175 million in 2005 when he was chairman and CEO of Gillette, after Gillette was sold to Procter and Gamble. One of Centerview's first assignments was a defense against a proxy fight mounted by a large shareholder, Nelson Peltz.

Mack and his new team initiated some changes in Institutional Securities. Vikram Pandit's title was retired, and Mack gave Zoe Cruz responsibility for overseeing the division. Jerker Johansson, who had succeeded John Havens as Head of Equities, and Neal Shear, who replaced Cruz as Head of Fixed Income were appointed co-Heads of Sales and Trading in a move to integrate the divisions. A year and a half later, after achieving record results in the division, Cruz took a bold step: she replaced the traditional equities and fixed income divisions with a Trading Group under Shear, and a Clients and Services Group under Johansson. The new structure, which reflected the blurring of product distinctions in the industry, was designed to provide better service to clients, offer a broader view of investment opportunities, and improve risk management across asset classes.

Investment banking had lost Terry Meguid and Joe Perella, and the firm's legacy business needed a leader with a strong client-oriented personality. It was a role that fit the Lebanese-born Walid Chammah, Head of Global Capital Markets, whom Mack had tried to persuade to join him as CSFB. Chammah had worked in Fixed Income with Cruz and he would report to her. Cordell Spencer, known as "Corey," became Deputy Head of Investment Banking.

The Institutional Securities business started putting more of the firm's capital to work, enhancing Morgan Stanley's risk-taking and stepping up its principal investing activities. The firm extended its leadership position in such key businesses as investment banking and prime brokerage, invested in growth areas like leveraged finance and equity derivatives, and made bolt-on acquisitions to help strengthen its commodities and residential mortgage business. Mack also moved quickly to strengthen Morgan Stanley's presence in key emerging markets including Russia, China, and India. The firm had been the first of its peers to build a local presence in the Middle East and it built on those early moves by opening new offices in Dubai and Qatar, attracting experienced talent to the region and forming a joint venture with The Capital Group, a well-respected bank in Saudi Arabia.

Purcell appointees were still heading the Retail, Asset Management, and Discover divisions. Retail and Asset Management were the worst performers, in part because Purcell had been unwilling to invest in people, products, or technology. In 2004, the Individual Investor Group's (Retail) profit margin was 8 percent, compared with 19 percent at Merrill Lynch, and 22 percent at Citigroup. The Private Wealth Management Division, which served clients who could invest $10 million or more, had fewer advisors in 2005 than in 1997, and Private Wealth advisors had been shoved onto an outdated platform, hampering their ability to handle more complex investments. Earlier in 2005, John Schaefer told Purcell he wanted to retire as Head of Retail, but the plan was held in abeyance while the firm was in turmoil. On July 15, Schaefer left with an exit package estimated at $7 million, his full pay for the year. Mack didn't wait to commence surgery. Zoe Cruz, who was overseeing the division, announced that the firm would cut about one thousand financial advisors, some 10 percent of the total, and would recruit less than half as many new brokers as in recent years. Mack commented, "There may be further reductions. That was clearly a first step, and a step I would argue should have been taken in the past."

Purcell had talked to James P. Gorman about coming over from Merrill Lynch to head the Individual Investor Group. At the time, the forty-seven-year-old Gorman was president of Merrill's Global Private Client Group, overseeing 14,000 retail brokers. Gorman turned Purcell down, and Merrill had just promoted him to executive vice president and head of Corporate Acquisitions, Strategy and Research, when Mack and Cruz approached him, and he agreed to become president and COO of the Individual Investor Group. Gorman's contract with Merrill didn't permit him to start his new job until February 2006.

Gorman revamped the entire senior management team, streamlined the organizational structure, stabilized and reinvigorated the sales force, and improved recruiting and training. The division introduced a new compensation plan for financial advisors, and continued to address platform, infrastructure, and legal and compliance issues. They broadened product offerings and expanded and enhanced the bank deposit program, deposits grew from $1.7 billion in 2005 to more than $16 billion in the first quarter of 2007. Retail delivered its highest quarterly revenues since 2000 in that first quarter. Margins improved from 2 percent in mid-2005 to 15 percent in the first quarter of 2007, and financial advisor productivity and net new client assets reached all-time highs.

Under Gorman, the Retail business also started building a much closer relationship with Institutional Securities, leveraging the firm's strengths and expertise to market products to retail clients. On March 31, 2007, the firm officially merged its two broker dealers to create a single legal entity. Morgan Stanley was finally beginning to realize the potential of the merger, almost ten years after it took place.

Because of Morgan Stanley's experience doing business in China, it was able to launch the first fund to invest in China's mainland "A-Share companies"; the fund sold out in forty-five minutes. In April 2007, Chief Economist Stephen Roach, one of the authors of the 2005 "values" letter to Cruz and Crawford, was promoted to become Chairman of Morgan Stanley Asia, with plans to move to Hong Kong in September. A superb relationship banker, in part because he is so outspoken that he is widely trusted to "call 'em as he sees 'em," he will try to obtain a brokerage license in China for the firm, among his other tasks. While Roach is famously cautious (a.k.a. pessimistic) in his market outlooks, his view of the potential of the Chinese economy is uncharacteristically enthusiastic.

In Asset Management, Mitchell Merin, whom Purcell had brought in from Dean Witter, left with an exit package of an estimated $11.5 million. Mack appointed a soft-spoken southerner, Owen Thomas, who had a first-class record running the Institutional Securities real estate business, to lead the turnaround of the division, now renamed Investment Management. The biggest growth opportunity Morgan Stanley missed was in alternatives, and to build that business, the firm purchased FrontPoint Partners, a hedge fund with $5.5 billion under management; made significant minority investments in three other hedge funds; and purchased two additional smaller hedge funds outright. Owen Thomas moved quickly to correct years of underinvestment, to

fill gaps in product offerings, and to build new high-net-worth investment teams. In 2006, the firm launched fifty-eight new products, thirty-
four of them in alternative investments—up from only three new
products in 2005. By the first quarter of 2007, Morgan Stanley Investment Management had recorded two quarters of fund inflows, had re-
entered the private equity business, and launched a promising new
infrastructure initiative. Although the long-term plan for growth in
Asset Management was expected to take three to five years, there were
clear signs of progress throughout the business.

To address the issues that had plagued the legal department during
the tenures of Christine Edwards and Donald Kempf, Mack hired
the youthful, white-haired Gary G. Lynch as general counsel. Lynch
was executive vice chairman of CSFB, a former director of the enforcement division of the SEC, and a former partner of Davis Polk. Stuart
Breslow, CSFB's chief compliance officer, joined Morgan Stanley as
Head of Compliance to shore up the firm's practice and reputation with
regulators. Lynch and his team immediately began to prepare the appeal to the Perelman/Coleman verdict. Their preparation and Lynch's
new approach paid off—coincidentally on the same day that Morgan
Stanley announced record first-quarter results—when the District
Court of Appeal of the State of Florida overturned the entire judgment
against the firm and denied Perelman a retrial of the case. It was a
stunning win. Perelman vowed to appeal, and did, but legal analysts
said it would face an uphill battle. The *New York Times* called it a
"major victory in the legal arena" that together with robust financial
results sent "a message to the marketplace that Morgan Stanley under
[Mack's] watch is a starkly different firm."

Discover's future as part of Morgan Stanley had always been uncer-
tain. In the summer of 2005, Mack announced that the firm would not
spin off the division to shareholders, reversing Purcell's earlier decision.
Mack called Discover "a unique, successful franchise with growth opportunities that gives Morgan Stanley a consistent stream of stable,
high-quality earnings and substantial cash flow." Then, late in 2006, following dramatically improved performance, both at Discover and in the
firm's core securities business, Mack announced that it was now time to
part ways, and that the firm would spin off Discover to Morgan Stanley

shareholders. On the fourth-quarter-earnings call, he explained, "When I came in here, the firm was really in turmoil. And Discover was one of our best businesses at the time. We had weaknesses in our others, and we had, I think, real growth issues. So with the performance that we've seen in our other businesses, and having the momentum and strength we have right now, I think both Morgan Stanley and Discover can go their own paths and really create a lot more value for shareholders." Discover was spun off in the summer of 2007, and that meant that Phil Purcell's most substantial achievement would become past history at Morgan Stanley.

Mack could not fire the Purcell-era board; they had to quit, and most of them did. By the end of 2005, all but four directors had resigned. Chuck Knight, Mike Miles, and John Jacobs resigned in September around the time that Knight's book, *Performance Without Compromise*, was published by Harvard Business School Press. Miles Marsh, Ed Brennan, and John Madigan announced that they would resign in December. That left Laura Tyson, Sir Howard Davies, Robert Kidder, and Klaus Zumwinkel.

The board looked very different by the end of 2006. It was diverse, distinguished, and included directors with a great deal more financial services experience. Erskine B. Bowles, who like Mack was a native of North Carolina, joined shortly before he took office as president of the University of North Carolina's sixteen-campus system. Bowles had worked at Morgan Stanley from 1969 until 1972, then returned to North Carolina and founded and served as chairman and CEO of an investment banking firm, a venture capital company, and a private equity company. He then moved into the public sector as Director of the Small Business Administration, a member of the National Economic Council and the National Security Council, and served as President Bill Clinton's chief of staff.

Two other new board members were Morgan Stanley alumni. O. Griffith Sexton, adjunct professor of finance at Columbia Business School and a visiting lecturer at Princeton, had been a managing director and investment banker at the firm from 1973 to 1995. Sexton, who was a former U.S. Navy aviator and Vietnam veteran, had military service in common with another Morgan Stanley alumnus, Charles E. Phillips Jr., who would join the board in June 2006. A former Marine Corps captain, Phillips was a graduate of the United States Air Force Academy, where he received his BS in computer science. Phillips, an African-American, held an MBA from historically black Hampton University in southern Virginia and a JD from New York Law School. He had been a managing director at Morgan Stanley in Equity Research until 2003, when he joined Oracle Corporation, where he was now president and a director.

Roy J. Bostock was a Duke graduate and a trustee emeritus of Duke, where he and Mack had served together on the board. A Harvard MBA, Bostock was the former chairman of BCom3 Group, a conglomerate of major advertising and marketing agencies, and was now using his communications skills as chairman of the Partnership for a Drug-Free America.

The board now had two women members. Laura Tyson, the only remaining director from pre-merger Morgan Stanley, was joined by the lively, bright Hutham S. Olayan, president and CEO of Olayan America, an arm of a multinational company with business and investment interests, and roots in Saudi Arabia. Olayan been recruited as a trustee of the American University in Beirut by Dick Debs when he was the chairman of the university. A founding member of the Arab Bankers Association of North America, and active in the Council on Foreign Relations, she contributed a sophisticated understanding of international finance and interests.

Regulatory experience and accounting skills came with Donald T. Nicolaisen, who was chief accountant for the SEC until November 2005 and formerly a senior partner at PricewaterhouseCoopers, and Charles H. Noski, former vice president and CFO of Northrop Grumman Corporation. He had been senior executive vice president and chief financial officer of AT&T, vice chairman of the AT&T board, and senior advisor to the Blackstone Group.

This new board would be actively involved with the firm's senior executives. Mack invited the members of the management committee to every board meeting and dinner, and as one member says, the directors "ask good questions and spend plenty of time. I've had meals, one-on-one, with a large number of directors, who want to know what's going on." As an investment banker who has made presentations to dozens of boards says of the Purcell-era directors, "I can't imagine another board that would not have spent time with senior people." He added, referring to the occasion when Dick Fisher wanted to address the board about Mack's resignation, "There's not a single person on one of those boards who would have refused to see the former chairman."

Morale, the most complex and subtle problem, was difficult to measure, but low morale was the most pervasive residue of the Purcell era. With Mack's return, a sense of relief resonated throughout the firm as he reasserted clear and present leadership. He had willing and eager support. Although the firm lost a lot of talent, a senior investment banker says, "It was a tribute to our culture that we were able to keep many of our best people here. I had an obligation to the people, younger managing directors in particular, and when they would ask me if I was leaving, or if they were thinking of leaving themselves, I would say, This too shall pass. It's a difficult period, but it will play out. Phil will inevitably go. If he decides he wants to leave, it will be easier on all of us. The more senior you were, the more you knew that the only way to resolve the situation was for Phil to leave. The G-8 made that clear. If he had left a year earlier, everyone would have celebrated him, wished him good luck, been very nice about it, and said to ourselves, Thank goodness we're moving on. The way he left was his choice. I told people, This is transitory; just do great work for our clients. Stay focused."

"By and large," he says, "that's what people did. I sat on the trading floor, and I would see people come in who had just read about us in the *New York Post*, but they would get over it, and go back to focusing on clients."

Mack's morale-boosting featured events that emphasized the "open door policy." They included quarterly Open Forums that employees patched into globally to talk about the business; regular meetings between management committee members and managing directors; and Mack's most popular innovation, Open Door breakfasts. In May 2006, an e-mail invitation for a first-come-first-served breakfast was sent to all employees in New York. In the first forty-five seconds, 250 responses shot in; there were more than one thousand responses within six minutes. Mack held dozens of those breakfasts, and copresidents Zoe Cruz and Bob Scully chaired dozens more. The people who attended carried their impressions of Mack, Cruz, Scully, and the reenergized firm back to hundreds of others.

Stories circulated that conveyed the message that Morgan Stanley was once more "the Culture of YES." In August 2005, shortly after Mack returned, a trader came to see him and explained that he wanted to start a new fund, but there had been delays in getting it approved. Mack picked up the phone and called the trader's manager and asked him, "Do you think he can do this?" The manager said, "Yes, have him call me." Instead, Mack accompanied the trader down to the manager's office on the fourth floor and said, "Let's get things rolling today."

The same month, a week after announcing major decisions on Discover, the aircraft-leasing business, and Retail, Mack was on a short vacation when he got a call from some of the firm's bankers in China, who told him that it was important to their clients that they meet with him as soon as possible, to demonstrate his commitment to the region. Mack flew to China, arriving in the evening for a client dinner, and participating in six client meetings the next day.

As the firm stabilized and the businesses began to move toward record results, there was time for a little fun. In the fall of 2006, Mack hosted a family-style pig roast at the Westchester campus for management committee members and their families and younger members of the firm. They played basketball, volleyball, soccer, and horseshoes, and Mack arranged to have Bill Ellis Barbecue drive its famous pork barbecue from North Carolina for an authentic southern picnic. In late October, the firm held a "State Fair" for thousands of employees who came to the Westchester campus with their families to ride the Ferris wheel and the carousel, paint pumpkins and faces, check out the petting zoo, and enjoy the fairground food. The featured attraction was the CEO-dunking booth, where a swarm of people converged to see John Mack get submerged in a tank of water for a good cause.

Before the fair, the firm had conducted an online auction for a chance to dunk Mack, proceeds to benefit Morgan Stanley Children's Hospital. The high bidders—who included Zoe Cruz; Bob Scully; Eileen Murray, the new Head of Global Operations and Technology; and a couple of teams from Prime Brokerage and Global Capital Markets—would each have three chances to throw a softball that triggered the "dunk." Mack, wearing track pants and a sweatshirt, sat on the dunking chair and egged on anyone who stepped up to the plate. No one hit the target during the morning session, but Tom Nides persuaded his seven-year-old daughter to rush the tank, and Mack was plunged into the water. In the afternoon session, two pitchers hit the mark. After the fair, John and Christy Mack invited the auction winners, their spouses, and families—about forty people—back to their house in Rye for dinner. The auction raised more than $120,000 for Morgan Stanley Children's Hospital.

When Mack talked to employees, his message was consistent. At the end of 2005, only months after the turmoil had ended, he told them, "You are the leaders of this firm now. You have to help set the tone and shape the culture of this organization. You have a responsibility to manage the people you work with and mentor your younger colleagues, to be honest and direct with them and listen to what they have to say. This firm has traditionally had a partnership culture, and while it's hard to go back to a true partnership with 53,000 people, we can have the spirit of a partnership. We can trust each other and be honest with each other. We can make sure we're all working toward the same goals. And we can act like owners. That's how we are going to really succeed." The concept of employee-owners was a regular refrain in Mack's talks and firmwide messages.

It didn't take long for word to get out that Morgan Stanley was a good place to work again. Mack created a new position, Chief Talent Officer, and appointed Linda Riefler to the job. Riefler, who briefly left the firm in mid-2005 during the crisis, joined the management committee. The new department was a signal that the firm was making meritocracy a priority again. Mack let his management team know that he would personally make recruiting calls for them, which Purcell had consistently declined to do, and he played a pivotal role in recruiting key talent and high-net-worth brokers.

In 2006, Morgan Stanley had the best revenues and earnings in its history. Net revenue, at $33.9 billion, was up 26 percent from 2005. Income from continuing operations was $7.5 billion, up 44 percent. Diluted earnings per share from continuing operations were $7.09, up 47 percent, and return on equity was more than 20 percent for five straight quarters. Institutional Securities had its best full-year results ever, with record revenues of $21.6 billion and record profit before taxes of $8.2 billion, up 72 percent. In Global Wealth Management, revenues had grown a more modest 10 percent, but at $5.58 billion they were the highest in six years. Financial advisor productivity and assets per global representative reached record highs, and Discover's fiscal year 2006 net revenues of $4.3 billion were up 24 percent and showed record profit before taxes of $1.6 billion, up 72 percent.

Based on the firm's performance, John Mack, who had turned down the guarantee of a maximum of $25 million a year when he made his point about merit-based compensation, earned $40 million in 2006. The firm's progress continued in the first quarter of 2007, when it announced another round of record results, with earnings up 70 percent from the same period in the prior year. A key driver of the improved financial performance was increased risk-taking, led by Zoe Cruz and the team in Institutional Securities. On March 31, 2007, CNBC Wall Street reporter Charles Gasparino said, "You have to give credit to Zoe Cruz for that, because essentially she's the one leading the charge here." Financial analysts Meredith Whitney and Gary Lee of CIBC World Markets observed in a note to investors that, by the first quarter of 2007, Morgan Stanley achieved "the best performance among its peers by a comfortable margin."

The most dramatic change, though, was in Morgan Stanley's share price. On June 22, 2005, the day before it was first reported that Mack might return, Morgan Stanley's stock was trading at $50.52. At the end of the fiscal year in November 2006, it closed at $81.42, up 61.2 percent.

Phil Purcell had compiled his own numbers in the summer of 2005, when the *New York Times* interviewed him in Salt Lake City. He had prepared a chart indicating that between the time Dean Witter went public in 1993 and the time he left the firm, Morgan Stanley stock showed a 690 percent increase. But for the Group of Eight the relevant numbers started on June 1, 1997, the first day of trading after the merger became official. During the eight years of Purcell's tenure with the combined firm, the stock nearly tripled—but for the period from 2001 through 2004, it trailed behind its major competitors—and rose 15.5 percent per year on average.

After the fourth-quarter 2006 earnings were announced, Mack held a firmwide town hall meeting. "You know," he said, "when you do this long enough, you think you get immune to it, you get calloused by it, that it's business as usual. I've been doing this a long time, but to me every day, it's not business as usual. What I like about this business is the enthusiasm and the intellect and the challenges here—and that's you.

"We've had a great year, a record year by any measure. We have an opportunity to return this firm to where it belongs. We can celebrate, but we cannot be satisfied. Our goal is to be the best firm in financial services. Why did this firm come back so quickly? Because its DNA is the DNA of excellence. If we are excellent in our job, if we are excellent in the way we deal with our clients, and if we treat ourselves and our friends here as partners, this firm, over time, will be the best firm by any measure."

He met his goal in mid-2007, when the firm announced its second-quarter results. Morgan Stanley outperformed every firm in its class, with better net income, profitability, and growth. By comparison to Goldman Sachs, Morgan Stanley had revenues of $22.5 billion, with a 21 percent growth rate; Goldman's $22.9 billion revenues showed an 11 percent growth rate; and while Goldman's profitability grew by 15 percent, Morgan Stanley's grew 50 percent. The firm's growth on non-Discover business was 67 percent. The day the results were announced, the stock hit $90.

Mack's rapid success in turning the firm around was also partly due to his attention to clients. While Purcell never lived up to his predecessors in terms of the number of client meetings he held, by June 2007, Mack could say that in the last seven months alone, he had held meetings or been on calls with 250 clients.

The top people Purcell had pushed out were also flourishing. Within eighteen months after Vikram Pandit and John Havens started their hedge fund, Old Lane, it was managing $4.5 billion in assets. Pandit and Havens were considered so valuable in themselves that Citigroup chairman Charles O. Prince III spent most of Old Lane's first year courting them. In the spring of 2007, Citi, the biggest bank in the world, succeeded in acquiring Old Lane for an estimated $800 million. Pandit became head of Citi's Alternative Investments Group, managing some $54.5 billion; the deal put him on center stage as a favored candidate to become Citi's CEO. Old Lane's top team, in particular John Havens and Guru Ramakrishnan, were also mentioned as among the "assets" Citi was acquiring. In the *Wall Street Journal* story that began "Is Vikram Pandit worth it?" the most ardent praise came from his former boss. Philip Purcell was quoted as saying "Vikram is a brilliant guy and he's got a real sense for markets and risk and an ability to lead people to the right place. He'd be a net plus for Citi." It was a gracious comment, but as one still-outraged former senior member of the management committee remarked, "Phil shoots Vikram because he's not good enough to be CEO of Morgan Stanley, but Vikram's clever enough to start a company and just over a year later, sell it to Citi. I guess Vikram and Havens should thank Phil, 'cause look where they are now."

On another front, Joe Perella, Terry Meguid, and Peter Weinberg at Perella Weinberg Partners merited a significant editorial in the *New York Times* by Thomas L. Friedman, who described the firm's leadership in a new area of mergers and acquisitions: the Green Deal. Perella Weinberg had been hired by the Environmental Defense Fund to negotiate between the Texas power company TXU and Kohlberg Kravis Roberts and Texas Pacific Group, which was offering $45 billion, described as "the biggest leveraged buyout ever," but the terms of the offer were unusual. TXU was under pressure from the Environmental Defense Fund and the Natural Resources Defense Council because of its plans to build eleven environmentally unfriendly coal-fired plants. With Perella Weinberg on the side of the angels, the deal was made, based on TXU's agreement to cut the new coal plants from eleven to three, spend nearly half a billion on energy-efficiency programs, and to purchase twice as much wind power as previously planned. The pressure was on by the time Perella Weinberg was brought into the deal, but it was their expertise that made it work. Friedman quoted Fred Krupp, president of Environmental Defense, as remarking, "what is the message when the largest buyout in history is made contingent [by the buyers] on winning praise for its greenhouse gas plan? The markets are ahead of the politicians. The world has changed, and these guys see it."

One spring afternoon, long after Phil Purcell had gone back to Chicago, and Mack's leadership was showing results, the Group of Eight met again at Parker Gilbert's apartment. Sitting around the mahogany table in the library, they talked about whether the fight had been worth the effort, the exposure, and the cost.

Bob Scott: It was absolutely worth it. The firm is immeasurably better today than it was a year ago. I do regret that the employees had to endure the public nature of the management fight. Reading about the irrational behavior of senior management and the board was disheartening.

What could have kept this from becoming a public fight?

Gilbert: If the board had been advised differently about seeing us, it would have been another story. Marty Lipton knew us. He knew me. He knows Joe [Fogg]. He knows we're not people who say something and disappear. One of the strange features of Phil's defense, when he talked about the way Morgan Stanley settles things in private, that's what we wanted to do. I remain dumbfounded to this day, why they refused to talk with us.

Anson
Beard: The fight will always be a sad phase of Morgan Stanley history. It certainly did intermediate damage to the firm, measured in lost talent. This should never have entered the public domain; it should have been resolved privately. The board of directors used incredibly poor judgment, and received consistently poor outside advice. For them to ignore us was outrageous and showed no common sense whatsoever, given our collective credentials in the business and record with the firm. They should have given us the courtesy of hearing us out.

Joe Fogg: You know, when we started this thing, none of us were thinking of replacing Phil with John Mack, but by the time Phil finally left, John was probably the only guy that could have turned things around. It looks like he is doing just that.

What about the media exposure?

Lewis Bernard wasn't there that day, but he had remarked to the others, "The most dramatic conclusion was the power of the media, particularly the cable channels. They have an enormous hole to fill and they'll fill it with just about anything. They were fascinated by our strange affair, they fanned the flames and got Phil and the Board's 'goat.' On the other hand, we succeeded because we were trusted by our former colleagues at Morgan Stanley and institutional investors who knew us well."

Fred

Whittemore: I get stopped in the elevator and the lobby, and people I don't know thank me. I was on the street during the fight, and a woman stopped me and kissed me and said, "You guys are doing a great thing for the firm. Keep it up. Don't stop."

How would you describe the story of the mutiny of 2005?

A voice: How about "The Wrist Slaps Back"? [*Some took this as a reference to Senator Orrin Hatch's remark about "limp-wristed Ivy Leaguers."*]

And the "wrist" is?

Voices: Shareholder rights.

Gilbert: This was the first time ever that institutional shareholders—hedge funds and large institutional hold-ers and pension funds—combined with a group like us and were heard in public. We unleashed a groundswell. This was a wake-up call for shareholders, demonstrating that they could be heard and effect change under ex-treme circumstances, outside a proxy contest.

Debs: Our struggle showed the fault lines in the U.S. system of corporate governance. Here we had one man who was the boss, the CEO and chairman, who was able to stack his board with friends and allies, keeping them happy with rich compensation and extensive perks, isolated from the people who worked in the firm—and all of this without any effective voice by the owners of the firm or those who worked for the firm. The system of voting for directors gave shareholders virtually no opportunity to appoint or replace directors, and this CEO and Board took full advantage of that.

Gilbert: The conventional wisdom was that institutional investors would only step forward if they had the chance to cast a vote. What was unique was that we demonstrated that pressure could be brought to bear, and change made without a proxy fight. I feel strongly that this was a new awakening for corporate democracy. I think we can take some credit for that.

Debs: Even after the Group of Eight—which you have to admit is a pretty distinguished group, responsible for the firm's growth and reputation—had raised important issues, the Board refused to communicate with us. They listened only to what was told them by the CEO and his hired counsel, even while he forced out the five most senior and competent executives, and while the firm continued to deteriorate with the loss of talent and the loss of business. The directors would have succeeded had it not been for the obstinacy of the Eight, who were finally able to turn the tide of public opinion and demonstrate the weakness and incompetence of the Board's leadership, who believed they were immune to outside criticism. The deck was loaded against us, and by a minor miracle—and perseverance—we were able to win the game.

When you talk about the soul of a firm at which the product is making money, what does "soul" mean?

Gilbert: People. Morgan Stanley worked because we hired the best people we could. That's still the most important criterion of success, more than capital or how we got into markets: keeping a flow of good people, giving them jobs to do, giving them excitement. Our people came from everywhere. It was a true meritocracy. They were committed to excellence and service, and they had a lot of the old Morgan Stanley character in them, which was first class business in a first class way.

Whittemore: It's still a meritocracy. Restored. We always had the notion that the clients came first, that it was not a business where you went into it just to make money. If it was done well, that would follow, but it was not the top priority. I think most people knew and understood that. It was a band of people who came together to try and make this kind of firm a reality.

The success of the campaign contributed to a sharper public focus on shareholder rights, which may have influenced Marty Lipton's increasingly public efforts to "protect" directors of public companies from the shareholders. In December 2006, Lipton circulated "an updated list of key issues for directors" to clients and would-be clients about "anticipating attacks" and developing "strategies to avoid or counter them." He raised the criticism of executive compensation by "the media and political gadflies" and proposed that boards "recognize the explosive nature" of the pay packages and develop "specially tailored executive compensation packages" to minimize criticism. He wrote, "Limits on executive compensation, splitting the role of chairman and CEO, and efforts to impose shareholder referenda on matters that have been the province of the board are examples of proposals that should be resisted."

In February 2007, Lipton gave the keynote address at the Institute on Federal Securities' annual meeting in Miami. He claimed that "shareholder activism is ripping through the boardrooms of public corporations and threatening the future of American business." Lipton's speech provoked one of the effective "media gadflies," Gretchen Morgenson, to write a February 11, 2007, *New York Times* article titled

"Memo to Shareholders: Shut Up." Morgenson polished off her commentary by noting, "If the public corporation is an endangered species, as Mr. Lipton argued, it is not because of shareholders. Those who owned stock in Enron, WorldCom, Adelphia, and Tyco did not create the scandals that rocked those companies and sowed mistrust among others. Selfish managers and passive directors did that work handily."

Morgenson's speculation that Lipton's "rant" was a sign of his "sheer desperation" provided a modicum of satisfaction to at least some of the Eight. They had believed from the beginning that Lipton's advice to the board, that they should neither talk to the dissidents nor respond to them in any way, had emboldened Purcell to execute the Monday Massacre that led to the loss of valuable talent, and to the public exposure they had tried to avoid.

For a few months in the spring of 2005, the Group of Eight ground their teeth and restrained themselves when Purcell accused them again and again of trying to "take down the firm" and called them ungrateful to the employees who had "made them rich"—dismissing the thirty years most of them had spent building the firm, beginning long before Phil Purcell came to Wall Street. By breaking the long-held tradition of silence and taking their challenge public, they displayed a side of the financial services industry, the collaborative striving for excellence, that is usually overshadowed in the news by the avaricious, cheats, and criminals—and made Wall Street history.

They had accomplished what they asked for in their first letter: Purcell was gone, so were the crony elements of his board, and the old principles and the spirit of the firm were healthy again. When a client sent the Group of Eight, care of Anson Beard, a small sculpture of a pair of heavy solid brass bull's balls, even the least rowdy among them could acknowledge that it was a satisfying symbol that power and reputation, once earned, are not necessarily dissipated with age, or the loss of a title.

After the fight was over, and the battle won, the Eight went back to what they had been doing all along. Parker Gilbert presided over the opening of the dramatic J. Pierpont Morgan Library addition, for which he had raised much of the $100 million. Fred Whittemore coproduced the film *Evening*, based on the book by Susan Minot, starring Meryl

Streep, Vanessa Redgrave, and Claire Danes. Dick Debs played an important role in the opening of Morgan Stanley's Dubai office, and worked with John Mack on international business. Joe Fogg's venture capital business continued to thrive. Bob Scott opened Craft in Las Vegas and the first haute sandwich kiosks, known as 'wichcraft. Lewis Bernard, Anson Beard, and John Wilson served on and headed corporate and charitable boards.

The financial rewards were an awkward subject. The Eight didn't set out to boost the value of their stock; on the contrary, they had spent millions of dollars, possibly to no avail. Yet, if they still owned the 11 million shares they had held when they began the fight (some of them had sold shares over the intervening eighteen months), their wealth would have increased by $330 million. To say that hundreds of millions of dollars was insignificant would be condescending, if not surreal, but all of the Eight insisted that the money was never the point. Even Purcell admitted that their campaign was "waged with real passion." Whatever the Eight gained, other shareholders gained as well. For those who did not enjoy great wealth, the increase in value could make a real difference.

It would be accurate to say that the doubled share price was not a goal, but a predictable side effect of a successful campaign. As Bob Scott explained, "We grew up in a culture that taught us that if we focused on our mission and did it well, the results would follow." Gilbert adds, "The fact that the stock had underperformed materially was part of the charge against Phil. By restoring the culture, if we got that right, other things would follow." In the world of finance, increasing value is an intrinsic element of doing a first class business in a first class way.

AFTERWORD

Soon after John Mack took over, an unsigned ad appeared in the business section of the *New York Times*. It read:

> ## CERTAIN CLIENTS AND SHAREHOLDERS OF MORGAN STANLEY WOULD LIKE TO:
>
> Thank Phil Purcell and his management team
> for their service to the Company;
>
> Thank the G-8 and their advisors for their courage,
> perseverance and confidence in the Firm;
>
> Thank existing employees for their loyalty,
> patience and confidence in each other;
>
> Thank shareholders for speaking
> and the Board of Directors for listening;
>
> Welcome back John Mack and others who we hope
> Will return to Morgan Stanley.
>
> WE ARE GRATEFUL FOR THIS UNIQUE FRANCHISE.

EPILOGUE

Three Years Later . . .

John Mack had eighteen months to rebuild flagging businesses and restore morale at Morgan Stanley, before the markets were roiled by the worst credit crisis since the Great Depression. Beginning in the late summer of 2007 and escalating quickly, one financial services firm after another announced write-downs in the billions of dollars, leading to the forced resignations of some of Wall Street's most senior executives. They included Merrill Lynch chairman and CEO Stanley O'Neal, Citigroup's beleaguered chairman and chief executive Charles Prince, and Peter Wuffli, CEO of UBS. Bear Stearns CEO James Cayne gave up his job amid cries of outrage when the media revealed that he had been pursuing a busy golf-and-bridge schedule while Bear was sinking. Bear Stearns only avoided bankruptcy because J. P. Morgan Chase, led by chairman and CEO Jamie Dimon, stepped in to buy the firm in mid-March 2008. The purchase was backed by the Federal Reserve, which agreed to take over $29 billion of Bear's "most toxic assets" in a highly unusual and possibly unprecedented move: Fed chairman Ben Bernanke said the Fed was intervening not solely to prop up a single failing firm but "to preserve the integrity and viability of the American financial system."

On the Sunday night before the announcement Bernanke held a last-minute all-hands conference call with the heads of the major Wall Street firms and international banks. Mack went to his office to take the call. Bernanke wanted to be sure the participants were solidly behind him; a global run on Bear could lead to an inter-national financial meltdown. The similarity between that call and the night a century earlier, when J. P. Morgan assembled top bankers at his library to press for an agreement to stabilize the markets, was uncanny. In 1907, the issue had been that troubled trust companies had backed loans with failing securities, placing an entire economic system in peril. Substitute "failing securities" with "mortgage-backed securities" and the problems were disturbingly alike.

Bear Stearns's toxic assets were, for the most part, subprime mortgage packages, which were backed by questionable collateral. The losses, which affected markets in Europe as well as the United States, were so severe that humor was one of the few ways to get even momentary relief. That accounted for the extraordinary popularity of a pair of middle-aged British comedians, John Fortune and John Bird, known as "The Long Johns," who performed a routine on subprime mortgages that attracted more than two million hits on YouTube.

Starting around 2002, Wall Street firms, with the notable exception of Morgan Stanley, had been making tremendous profits packaging and selling pools of mortgages, contributing to stunning pay packages for financial executives. In one much-noted instance, the Goldman Sachs bonus pool for 2006 was $16.9 billion. Journalist Arnaud de Borchgrave recalled that he wrote a column for United Press International about Goldman's bonus pool that year. The column featured a story about a disgruntled Goldman trader who received $70 million, claimed he was worth at least $100 million, and quit in a fit of pique. The atmosphere and the expectations were, to say the least, surreal.

When John Mack returned to Morgan Stanley in late June 2005, Wall Street was operating in a state of mortgage-backed euphoria, but the firm wasn't benefiting from the surge. Phil Purcell had avoided investing in the residential mortgage business, and Mack and Zoe Cruz were now chafing at the lost opportunities. They agreed to expand the firm's mortgage business and take a more aggressive stance in proprietary trading.

As co-president, Cruz oversaw the firm's trading and risk operations, and with her encouragement, traders increased their exposure to the subprime market, mounting a series of short bets, hedged by longs.

But by mid-2007, they were learning that their substantial short position was not going to remain short if the subprime market continued to deteriorate beyond what they—and most others—had expected. To cover their positions, they bought swaps and derivatives rather than investing in more liquid instruments. When it was time to sell, the only way to unwind those contracts was to offer them to the counterparties, at whatever price they could get.

Trouble was looming in the early summer of 2007, but Cruz consistently maintained that the firm was appropriately short subprime and would profit as the market dropped. In September, Morgan Stanley announced a $1.8 billion write-down. Most of that was related to leveraged loans, and comparatively little reflected subprime problems. Then, on November 7, the firm revealed, in the first of several such announcements, that it had suffered an additional $3.7 billion loss from a debacle in its subprime trading position. Particularly galling was the fact that Goldman Sachs was the counterparty that profited from some of Morgan Stanley's now devalued contracts.

As the positions were unraveling, senior Morgan Stanley executives continued to believe that Cruz's job was not in jeopardy. In mid-November John and Christy Mack had dinner with Zoe and Ernesto Cruz at the restaurant San Pietro. No one saw this as a farewell dinner. But by the end of the month, Mack faced the unwelcome evidence: Cruz's lapse in judgment or oversight, and her failure to reveal the severity of pending losses soon enough, combined with a combative management style that other senior executives admitted made them loath to cross her, had undermined her ability to lead the firm effectively. On November 29, Mack called Cruz into his office and told her that her twenty-five-year career at Morgan Stanley, where it was estimated that she had earned some $100 million, was over. She left that day.

On December 19, the firm announced a total of $9.4 billion in mostly mortgage-related write-downs as of the fourth quarter.

When news of the losses broke, critics asked why Mack had failed to recognize what was happening in time to stem the hemorrhage. Some blamed the management structure: the risk management team reported to Cruz rather than to Mack. Sanford Bernstein's Brad Hintz disagreed. He attributed the losses to "a failure of execution of a trading strategy rather than a failure of risk management."

The losses and negative publicity—as well as the dramatic drop in the stock's trading price that accompanied them—eroded morale. Mack responded by making a series of management and organizational changes. He also told the management committee that he intended to forgo his 2007 bonus. (Based on his 2006 pay, that could have amounted to more than $40 million.) The decision epitomized his policy of "pay for performance." He said he was responsible for the firm's overall health, and when something went wrong, the buck stopped with him. He evidently also conveyed the message that "we're all in this together." After the meeting, a member of the committee privately told Mack, "That's the right thing to do. I don't want a bonus either." Mack thanked him but assured him that he'd done a great job and would get his bonus. The offer was a heartening reminder of the partnership attitude that underlay the Morgan Stanley culture.

Zoe Cruz had been a controversial choice when Purcell picked her as co-president, and that was still there when Mack confirmed the appointment. Those who criticized his decision replayed the events of the summer of 2005, when her continued presence at the firm became an implacable obstacle to the return of Vikram Pandit, John Havens, Stephen Newhouse, Joseph Perella, and Tarek Abdel-Meguid (most commonly referred to as Terry Meguid). All of them were thriving, most notably Pandit, whom Purcell had fired because he suspected him of disloyalty, and whom Cruz had insisted would be a worse CEO than Purcell. Citigroup promoted Pandit to CEO in early December 2007, and Pandit named Havens to head Citi's Investment Banking business. (In early 2008, Jerker Johansson, whom Purcell had promoted to take over from Havens, was hired away to head the UBS Investment Bank.) Over at the GM Building on Fifth Avenue, Joe Perella and Terry Meguid, with partner Peter Weinberg, steadily continued to build Perella Weinberg, which ended 2007 with 135 professionals, $2.5 billion in assets under management in five asset management businesses, and $80 billion in M & A deals. Cruz's downfall confirmed that Mack had backed the wrong horse.

There are many theories about why John Mack chose Cruz, thus inevitably losing the others. Mack said at the time that he didn't want a gun to his head about whom he should hire or fire, or what jobs they should have. But he also may have been focused on putting a fresh team in place rather than reassembling a group of superstar warriors. Nevertheless, Mack must have had some doubts about Cruz, which were exacerbated by reports that, as he was trying to restore the culture of debate and discussion, she had a reputation for suppressing and sometimes punishing dissent.

When, after eight months, Mack finally appointed Cruz co-president, she was acknowledged to be among the two or three most powerful women on Wall Street. In October 2007, only a month before she left the firm, *Fortune* magazine named her sixteenth on its list of the fifty most powerful women in business. Even as late as November 9, two days after the firm announced the additional $3.7 billion in write-downs, the *New York Times* suggested that she might be the leading candidate to succeed Mack. After the story appeared, Morgan Stanley insiders insisted that the firm had not given any indication that she had been anointed as Mack's sole successor, but Cruz was on the "what if the CEO is hit by a bus" list he had submitted to the board of directors. Succession was a sensitive subject, given Purcell's lack of satisfactory backup and his board's limited contact with the heads of the firm's businesses. Under Mack, the board had plenty of opportunity to appraise potential successors: he had revived the pre-Purcell policy of inviting management committee members to all board meetings, and he encouraged the directors to contact members of the management committee if they had questions.

The subprime losses and Cruz's abrupt departure overshadowed the successes of Mack's new team. By the end of 2007, the executive ranks were headed by people from within the firm, whom Mack had repositioned or promoted, and stars he had enticed to come to Morgan Stanley from competitors. They included Walid Chammah, whom Mack elevated to Head of Investment Banking in 2005, and James Gorman, formerly of Merrill Lynch, whom Mack hired to overhaul Morgan Stanley Global Wealth Management (Dean Witter's former Retail business). *MarketWatch*'s David Weidner wrote that acquiring Gorman, who had been considered a CEO contender at Merrill Lynch, was "one of the best Wall Street poach jobs in the past five years." In 2007, under Gorman, Global Wealth Management's pre-tax income rose 127 percent to \$1.2 billion while net revenues grew 20 percent to \$6.6 billion. Despite the Street-wide downturn in the fourth quarter of 2007, GWM delivered a 21 percent pre-tax margin, the highest since 2000, and up from just 2 percent in the first quarter of 2006, when Gorman joined the firm. Later, when minus signs were bring posted all over Wall Street at the end of the second quarter of 2008, GWM revenues rose 4 percent and the business generated its second-highest net new assets of \$13.3 billion.

After Cruz left, Mack moved her co-president, Robert Scully, into the Office of the Chairman, and promoted Gorman and Walid Chammah as co-presidents. Chammah was a strong client-relationship banker who oversaw record investment banking revenues in 2007. He had spent 2007 based in London, where he focused on building the firm's robust international business. In his new role as co-president, he was assigned to take charge of the Institutional franchise.

In addition to Global Wealth Management, the other underperforming business with roots in Dean Witter was Asset Management. Mack had assigned Owen Thomas to head that business in 2005, and in two years Thomas grew assets under management 29 percent. In 2007, he helped deliver record results, with revenues up 59 percent and profit before taxes (PBT) up 72 percent. By early 2008, Asset Management had delivered six consecutive quarters of positive client inflows. Even so, Mack acknowledged there was still a lot more work to do, as the second quarter of 2008 would prove, when the division lost \$227 million, as compared to a gain of \$161 million in the previous quarter.

Mack promoted Thomas again in 2008, making him CEO of Morgan Stanley Asia, where Steve Roach served as Chairman and expansion was a priority. The firm had secured a Chinese banking license; applied for security, trust, and asset management licenses; and tripled its revenues in China since 2006. At the end of 2007, Morgan Stanley was ranked number one in China-related international IPOs by Thompson Financial. That December, when financial service firms and banks were looking to sovereign funds to replenish their capital in the wake of their subprime losses, the China Investment Corporation made a \$5 billion investment in Morgan Stanley, giving the state-owned bank a 9.9 percent stake in the firm.

As Morgan Stanley expanded its global franchise, Mack traveled tirelessly, holding meetings throughout Europe, Asia, and South America. He visited the Middle East seven times in 2006 and 2007, helping Morgan Stanley open new offices in the region and forming a joint venture with the Saudi Arabian firm Capital Group. In less than three years, revenues from the firm's Middle East business grew some 90 percent.

To avoid becoming entangled in future destabilizing risks, Mack transferred risk management into the Office of the Chairman and hired Kenneth M. deRegt as Chief Risk Officer, reporting directly to him. DeRegt had been head of Fixed Income at Morgan Stanley, and had extensive experience in capital markets and trading, but he had left during the Purcell era.

Others moved in and up, creating a roster of "names to watch." Cordell Spencer was promoted from co-head of Investment Banking to Deputy Head of Institutional Securities, working with Chammah. Paul Taubman was promoted from Head of Mergers and Acquisitions to Head of Investment Banking. Under Taubman's leadership, Morgan Stanley ranked number two in global M & A at the end of 2007, and the firm continued to advise on some of the biggest deals in the marketplace, among them Microsoft's high-profile bid for Yahoo in 2008. M & A also advised on the largest airline merger (Northwest/Delta) and the largest media deal, the spin-off of Time Warner Cable. Merrill Lynch analyst Guy Moszkowski attributed much of the firm's success in navigating the difficult markets to "a rapid shift back to a culture of debate, inter-unit questioning of trading strategy, and sharp discipline."

Good news in the legal arena spread some cheer to alleviate the subprime gloom. One of Mack's first hires, chief legal officer Gary Lynch, brought in a triumphant reversal of the $1.58 billion judgment against the firm in the Coleman case. The judgment had been overturned once in an appeal, but Ronald Perelman took it to the Florida Supreme court, which rejected his second appeal by a 5–0 vote on December 12, 2007. Lynch also reached settlements on legacy issues in Wealth Management, including the long-standing SEC case related to the firm's handling of email after 9/11, and class-action suits brought by female, African-American, and Latino financial advisors. Among Lynch's mandates was to repair damaged relationships with regulators, which would be particularly important as the markets became increasingly scrambled and the financial services community had to work closely with government officials to deal with the monumental industry-wide problems.

As the industry continued battling an increasingly challenging market environment, Mack and his team reviewed the firm's strategy and priorities. A colleague commented to Mack that the still buried subprime losses and vulnerabilities reminded him of scenes in World War II movies, where soldiers crawled across mine fields, poking through the sand with bayonets to find out where the mines were hidden. There were still more mines to be exploded. In a story headlined "Nearly Half of Wall Street Bank Profits Are Gone," *New York Times* reporter Louise Story wrote that, while seven of the major U.S. financial institutions had earned a combined $254 billion in profits between 2004 and mid-2007, the same institutions (Bank of America, J. P. Morgan Chase, Citigroup, Lehman Brothers, Merrill Lynch, Goldman Sachs, and Morgan Stanley) had now written down $107.2 billion, mostly related to the subprime fiasco but also exacerbated by the dramatic rise in oil prices. Despite the need for caution, Mack believed that the firm's basic strategy was sound and encouraged his people to capitalize on the opportunities that difficult markets can present. The firm would proceed with plans for growth, particularly in the international sphere, but would dial back market risk, place tighter controls on expenses, and resize some businesses to reflect market conditions. Other firms were also reacting to tough market conditions; by the summer, 83,000 financial service employees worldwide had lost their jobs.

Chaos and uncertainty even damaged Morgan Stanley's famously strong Institutional Securities business, where profits were down 77 percent from 2007 by the second quarter, with Fixed Income sales and trading down 85 percent. The unit was hurt by nearly $800 million in trading and leveraged loan losses, a figure that included a $121 million charge due to the activities of a young London-based trader who had improperly overvalued trades.

Streetwide, the second quarter of fiscal 2008 was purgatory for Investment Banking. One of the best-known private equity firms, Kohlberg Kravis Roberts, had filed its own IPO in 2007; nearly a year later, the IPO was still sitting on the shelf. According to one account, KKR's "deal-making has all but stopped."

Mack took steps to maintain the firm's strong capital base and to increase liquidity, instructing that the balance sheet be more flexible. By the end of the first quarter of 2008, the firm had some $200 billion in total capital. He took steps to maintain the firm's strong capital base and to increase liquidity, giving instructions that the balance sheet be more flexible. By the end of the first quarter of 2008, the firm had some $200 billion in total capital. He continued to enhance the risk management function and held more frequent risk meetings and dialogues across the firm. The plan was to be conservative, but to remain nimble and move ahead when the time was right.

The firm didn't have to wait long. In a single week in February 2008, Morgan Stanley embarked on a series of transactions that helped reopen some of the most problematic credit markets. When, as the *Wall Street Journal's* Heidi Moore reported, "getting a financing done . . . seems like it requires a Profile in Courage," Morgan Stanley arranged the first client-driven collateralized loan obligation (CLO) deal of the year, the year's first commercial mortgage-backed securities (CMBS) markets deal, and the year's first refinancing deal in the failed auction-rate securities market. The *Journal's* Moore explained that the firm's approach was "take a haircut, accept fewer buyers, and keep the terms of the deal as far as possible from being influenced by any market movements."

In March 2008, as the financial community prepared to release first quarter results, Bear Stearns abruptly collapsed under the weight of its failed funds, with hedge fund investors pulling out at a fatal rate amid market concerns about the firm's liquidity. It was then that Federal Reserve Chairman Ben Bernanke took the drastic step of bailing Bear out. The Federal Reserve's decision to use taxpayer money to shore up a failing firm was controversial, but *New Yorker* finance columnist James Surowiecki took a practical approach, writing, "The threat of moral hazard in this case was simply less dire than the threat of financial contagion." The Fed continued to reduce interest rates and, for the first time in its history, opened its discount borrowing window to broker-dealers, not just to commercial banks.

That helped, but the contagion *was* spreading. When Lehman Brothers announced its second quarter results, chairman Richard Fuld reported that Lehman had experienced its first quarterly loss ever: $2.8 billion. (In 2005, Fuld was considered such a formidable leader that there was talk that Morgan Stanley might buy Lehman, just to get him to head up the combined firm.) In response to the write-down, Fuld made some top management changes and announced he would forgo his 2008 bonus, but with the stock trading at $19, down from a 52-week high of $82, there were rumors and news items indicating that Lehman was a takeover target, possibly at a steep discount.

In a climate of worldwide anxiety, exacerbated by Bear Stearns's near death experience, some pundits and investors estimated that the crisis would rampage on until the write-downs reached $500 billion, then increased the estimate to $1 trillion and upward. Yet in the first quarter, many firms showed results that indicated that the worst might be over. Morgan Stanley led its core competitors in return on equity, with a 20 percent ROE, while Goldman delivered 15 percent and Lehman 9 percent. Morgan's net income of $1.6 billion for the quarter just topped Goldman's $1.5 billion, with smaller Lehman coming in at $489 million. Mack noted that he was "satisfied with how Morgan Stanley navigated the ongoing market turbulence."

After the first quarter 2008 results were announced, Merrill Lynch's Guy Moszkowski commented, "Morgan Stanley profitably far outperformed major competitors. . . . We are impressed with the firm's ability to generate such returns in the face of substantial asset write-downs." UBS analyst Glenn Schorr remarked on "a strong showing for MS," suggested that the results "highlight the strength of the core client franchise," and praised Mack and his management team for doing a "good job" in reducing the firm's mortgage exposures. Goldman analyst William F. Tanona reported, "Morgan Stanley is one of the better-positioned firms . . . as it has an enviable business mix with a strong international presence. . . . The firm is also likely to benefit from recent market dislocations, particularly in prime brokerage." At the April 2008 Annual Meeting, Mack was able to announce that, despite the firm's subprime losses, Morgan Stanley had "delivered its second highest revenues ever in 2007, including achieving record or near-record performance in all of its other businesses."

Mack attributed the improvement in part to "a new sense of openness and communication," but warned employees, "This is just the beginning. We've got to stay focused. We've got to make sure people continue to trust and rely on Morgan Stanley. And we've got to continue moving the share price up." By the end of the second quarter, however, it was clear that no one's share price was on the rise. *USA Today* ran a first-page story headlined: "Stocks off $2.1 trillion this year. June was the worst since Depression." Citigroup was trading at $16, down 67 percent, after seeing a 52-week high of $89; Lehman was down 69 percent; and Morgan Stanley, at $40, was down nearly 51 percent from its 52-week high. Goldman was the winner again, with a drop of only 20 percent; however, as Bank of America securities analyst Michael Hecht noted, "Everyone else is kind of opening up the kimono and giving us a lot more exposure than Goldman," implying that Goldman might have some less rosy news still uncovered.

One of Philip Purcell's most obvious difficulties had been Morgan Stanley's stagnant stock price, and now, mid-2008, the shares were again trading at 2005 levels (not including the value to shareholders of the Discover spin-off). The difference between Purcell's Morgan Stanley and Mack's would show up—if there was one—during the recovery, whenever that came. During the Purcell era, the firm's share price declined 51.3 percent in a four-year period, leaving it well behind its five core competitors; while, from Mack's return in mid-2005 to March 20, 2008, before the markets spiraled out of control, only Goldman exceeded Morgan Stanley's stock price growth among core competitors.

When Morgan Stanley announced its second-quarter results—which provoked the *Wall Street Journal* to headline its story "Still 'Brutal' at Morgan Stanley," while the *New York Times* led with the straightforward "Morgan Stanley Reports 58% Decrease in Profit"—the *Journal* quoted Morgan Stanley's CFO, Colm Kelleher, as describing the situation as "pretty frigging brutal." The firm's write-downs had mounted to $12.6 billion, but Kelleher explained that they were largely "tied to past exposure to subprime investments," implying—and no doubt hoping—that the worst really was over.

From time to time, someone asks what would have happened if Philip Purcell had still been chairman and CEO of Morgan Stanley when the subprime crisis hit. It is a fair question; if Purcell had stayed, Morgan Stanley would probably not have been holding substantial subprime positions. However, few experienced Wall Street observers challenge the assumption the Group of Eight made in its March 3, 2005, letter to the board that the firm was drifting toward mediocrity. It is widely believed that if Purcell had continued to head the firm, Morgan Stanley would have experienced increased talent attrition, a flattened meritocracy, continued underperformance in Global Wealth Management and Asset Management, and unsatisfactory return on equity. As the Eight noted in 2005, the firm's "total return had trailed the S&P Diversified Financial Index by nearly 40 percent" for the preceding five years.

The figures are part of the story, but the "soft" issue of leadership is another ingredient in anticipating the firm's future. Author Tom Wolfe, interviewed about Wall Street's current crisis, remarked: "It has always interested me that the word 'credit' comes from the [Latin] word 'credere,' which means 'to believe.' . . . It only works if people believe in it." By "it" Wolfe could be referring to a business, or to a leader. One of John Mack's talents is his ability to inspire belief in his leadership and in the firm's ability to work its way out of a bleak environment. It's a quality that comes naturally, like perfect pitch. Sadly for Philip Purcell, the ability to inspire belief, to amass "credit" at Morgan Stanley, wasn't part of his makeup.

From the perspective of the business and its culture, what if Purcell had stayed? A senior Morgan Stanley executive answers the question tersely: "If Phil were still here? We'd be Bank of America."

If it had played out that way, as the leaders in Institutional Securities believed was an imminent possibility, and a bank had swallowed Morgan Stanley, the culture that ran in the veins of the firm, and that each generation of leaders continued to renew, would almost certainly have become a half-remembered part of Wall Street history. The Morgan Stanley story would still have been told in business school classes, but the firm would no longer be a living organism, built on the promise to do "only a first class business, and that in a first class way."

APPENDIX

The trajectory of the challenge to Philip Purcell's leadership can be followed through six letters, published here chronologically. The first is from Scott Sipprelle; there are four from the Group of Eight; and one from Mary Meeker, Henry McVey, Stephen Roach, and Byron Wien. Of the six letters, three were intended to be private: Sipprelle's letter; the first letter from the Eight; and the letter from Meeker et al. The five that were released were done so only after the board refused to acknowledge or respond to the authors' concerns. The internal letter was never released to the media or to colleagues inside the firm. It is published here for the first time.

DECEMBER 9, 2004. *Scott Sipprelle, chairman Copper Arch Capital and a former Morgan Stanley managing director, wrote Philip Purcell and the Morgan Stanley board to tell them that his fund had bought a large block of Morgan Stanley stock, and to propose that the firm split off its Institutional Securities Division from the Retail and Discover divisions. Sipprelle did not receive an answer.*

Dear Phil and Directors of Morgan Stanley:

From multiple vantage points over the last twenty years I have been witness to the performance of Morgan Stanley. Starting as an analyst in investment banking in 1985, I commenced a personally rewarding career that culminated as a Managing Director and Head of U.S. Equity Capital Markets. I was at the helm in the aftermath of the landmark Morgan Stanley merger with Dean Witter in 1997, and it was my responsibility to implement one piece of the strategy envisioned in that combination: the marriage of Morgan Stanley's equity origination capabilities with the distribution capabilities of the Dean Witter sales force. I have seen Morgan Stanley from the inside.

Commencing in 1998, I was able to gain a new appreciation and perspective on Morgan Stanley: I became a large client of the firm. My investment firm, Copper Arch Capital, currently manages in excess of $1 billion of capital. We have our exclusive prime brokerage relationship with Morgan Stanley, we have our largest trading relationship with Morgan Stanley, and we have a great respect for the integrity and skill of our counter-parties in the firm's institutional securities operations.

More recently, after thoughtful analysis, Copper Arch Capital has become a shareholder of Morgan Stanley. Our investment is not predicated on a rosy view of the current structure and performance of the firm, but rather in spite of it. While we are strongly of the view that the current market value of the company does not fairly reflect the potential value of the franchise, we are also of the view that the firm is at present precariously positioned at a crossroads of opportunity and risk. While the performance of the firm's stock price relative to peers has been consistently poor since the 1997 merger with Dean Witter, we are deeply troubled that the current stewards of the firm are blind to the root causes of this affliction. Morgan Stanley's current ills are not temporal or cyclical in nature. **The problems are structural and they need to be addressed promptly lest the franchise value begin to erode permanently.**

With the benefit of 30 quarters of operating results to review since the consummation of the merger with Dean Witter, any objective analysis would conclude that **the original rationale for the merger was flawed and that the "added value for shareholders" that was promised at the time has simply not materialized.** Specifically: *The benefits of diversification have not been evident over several market cycles.* Morgan Stanley's stock has been a consistent under-performer relative to peers during every measurement period since 1997, with the degree of underperformance becoming more pronounced over time

(Exhibit I). When benchmarked against Goldman Sachs one conclusion becomes inescapable: MWD's share price declined 64% in the bear market that followed the year 2000 and has recovered only 69% of that prior peak to date in the market recovery that has followed. GS, by comparison, declined only 45% in the bear phase and has recovered 102% of the prior peak (Exhibit II). So if the "diversified" model does not cushion returns in the down times and lags badly in the up times, what is the attraction of the model?

The benefits of marrying product origination with retail distribution have not panned out

One of the central tenets of the Morgan Stanley–Dean Witter merger was that improved productivity would flow from the captive retail sales force armed with an enhanced assortment of product to sell. This has clearly not been the case as the performance of the Individual Investor Group has been consistently sub-par and the number of advisors contracting over time. The 2% pre-tax margin achieved in the most recent quarter should be an impetus to action. The current strategy for this under-performing business seems to be to wait for operating leverage to return with a recovery in revenue growth. There can be no guarantee that the waves of product opportunity that periodically wash across the retail brokerage landscape will provide much succor for IIG. We have been surprised to see that the mortgage boom, which has fattened the coffers of better-positioned competitors, seems to have eluded Dean Witter almost entirely. We would submit that "watch and wait" is the embodiment of the absence of a strategy.

It's not about mass, it's about mastery

One cannot read the press clippings from February of 1997 without being struck by the giddiness over the scale of the business that had been created. The "global powerhouse" with a market value vastly in excess of any other pure securities firm also created with the stroke of a pen the largest collection of assets under management of any securities business of the day. As time has elapsed, it has become clear that scale can be the enemy of performance. The Investment Management operations have

suffered steady net outflows in the last several years, the result
of mediocre investment returns. While profitability in this operation has been stabilized through product consolidation and
aggressive cost cutting, this has come at the cost of decreasing
product prestige, increasing personnel turnover, and deteriorating morale.

Although the Discover operation gives heft to Morgan Stanley as a financial conglomerate, its strategic importance to the rest
of the company is not apparent. While the performance of this
operation has been sound, the competitive headwinds and rein-
vestment requirements in the credit card business are increasing
and the Discover operation remains frozen at a shrinking, sub-
scale market share in a land of giants. Status quo in this business
also does not appear to be a viable long-term strategy.

The institutional securities business is the key to the com-
pany's future

An objective analysis of Morgan Stanley's portfolio of businesses will conclude that the institutional securities business
has the strongest brand position, the largest pool of profit potential, the best growth prospects, and the greatest opportunity for overall value creation. This business is the key to Morgan
Stanley's future and it must not be encumbered by a corporate
strategy wedded to reinvesting in ailing operations with un-
certain opportunity for value enhancement. As long as those
charged with the oversight of the direction of the company do
not acknowledge and forcefully address the firm's challenged
operating entities, the company's crown jewel will be increasingly vulnerable to attrition, to distraction, and ultimately to
decay.

It is ironic that Morgan Stanley, a firm that has been such
an agent for change in the capital markets through strategic
restructuring advice to corporate clients, through direct investments in under-performing businesses, and through erudite research promoting strategies for enhancing corporate productivity has become intransigent when the issue of optimal levels of
performance relate to its own portfolio of businesses. It is indeed
time for Morgan Stanley to look in the mirror.

Our proposal for restructuring Morgan Stanley is very simple:

return the company to its roots. We recommend the following steps be undertaken as soon as practicable:

1) Sell or spin-off Discover
2) Sell or spin-off the investment management operations
3) Sell the retail brokerage business
4) Selectively shrink the balance sheet and aggressively deploy the surplus capital to buy back stock with an interim goal of returning return on equity to above 20%

These steps, if acted on successfully, would result in significant brand enhancement with clients and investors, with derivative benefits as well in terms of mission clarity and valuation premium accorded. The value creation would likely be significant (Exhibit III). As Directors of a public company, you are charged with a fiduciary responsibility to safeguard the value of the company that has been entrusted, temporarily, to your care. We are asking that you, as our representatives, give serious consideration to the proposal that we have outlined above. **Should there be no constructive steps made toward addressing our concerns, we intend to oppose strongly the re-election of each of the Directors.**

We would appreciate the opportunity to discuss our analysis and proposals with you more fully and eagerly await your response.

Scott Sipprelle
Chairman, Copper Arch Capital

EXHIBIT I
Stock Performance of MWD Relative to Peers*

1997 to Date 4 out of 5
1998 to Date 5 out of 6
1999 to Date 5 out of 6
2000 to Date 6 out of 6
2001 to Date 6 out of 6
2002 to Date 6 out of 6

*Peer group: GS (since 1998), MER, JPM, LEH, BSC

EXHIBIT II

Stock Performance of the Diversified Model Relative to Peers

<u>*Bear Market Performance* Recovery Performance*</u>[+]

MWD–64% 69%

GS–45% 102%

MER–59% 90%

**Stock price decline from end of 2000 to subsequent low.*

[+] *Current stock price as a percent of 2000 level.*

EXHIBIT III

Value Creation Opportunity

<u>Value per MWD Share</u>

Discover $10.45 *15% premium to receivables*

Investment Management $10.80 *3% of AUM*

Retail Brokerage $2.65 *15x normalized earnings*

Institutional Securities <u>$49.75</u> *2.5x Pro-forma book value*

$73.65

MARCH 3, 2005. *The Group of Eight wrote the following letter to Philip Purcell and the Morgan Stanley board, proposing that he resign or be asked to leave. They did not receive an answer.*

Dear Mr. Purcell:

As retired senior executives of Morgan Stanley and significant shareholders, we care deeply about the Firm, its employees and its reputation for integrity and excellence. The Firm's commitment to excellence is the product of generations of professionals who worked, and sacrificed, tirelessly to assure that Morgan Stanley provided its clients with products and services which represented the highest standards in the industry.

Unfortunately, Morgan Stanley's performance over the past few years and its reputation have declined to the point where we are greatly concerned about the Firm's ability to regain its position as the premier global financial services firm.

Our perception of Morgan Stanley's decline is corroborated

by the judgment of the equity markets. For example, the Morgan Stanley 2005 Proxy Materials show that, over the last five years, the Firm's total return has trailed the S&P Diversified Financial Index by nearly 40 percent, a stunning vote of no confidence for a company that has historically been a market leader. According to an article published in the *International Herald Tribune* on February 9, 2005, Morgan Stanley's stock was down 27 percent over the past four years, compared with a 4 percent gain for Goldman Sachs, an 18 percent gain for Lehman Brothers and an 11 percent decline for Merrill Lynch. Moreover, the Firm's stock price volatility has been significantly higher than that of other companies in its peer group, a fact which belies the claimed benefits of the Firm's diversified business portfolio.

We believe that the stock's poor performance and price volatility are a function of many factors, including:

the failure to continue to earn a premium return on equity;
the failure to maintain earnings growth relative to its peers; and
the weak performance of the Firm's retail and investment management businesses over the past five years.

More fundamentally, we believe that the overriding cause of the Firm's poor performance is a failure of leadership by you as the Firm's CEO.

Morgan Stanley's role as a leader in the securities industry and its reputation for excellence have always been a function of its ability to attract outstanding professionals and provide strong and supportive leadership. We are deeply concerned that there is a crisis of confidence in the Firm's leadership and governance not only in the market, but also, we fear, among employees of the Firm. We believe that you will not be able to inspire and lead the Firm back to its rightful position in the financial services industry. We also question whether you have the respect of industry peers or the Firm's regulators necessary to the task of regaining Morgan Stanley's leadership position in our industry.

We note that there is very little financial services experience among the independent directors and there is no Institutional

Securities executive on the Board despite that unit's dispropor-
tionate contribution to the Firm's profits and reputation. In addition, while the Firm is headquartered in New York, the financial
capital of the world, neither the Chairman nor any members of
the Board reside in the New York area.

We believe that the loss of morale caused by these factors puts
Morgan Stanley at great risk of losing more key professionals
which would adversely impact the Firm's ability to serve its clients
and to attract the staff necessary to carry on its businesses.

For all these reasons it is imperative that the Board act promptly
to change the leadership and governance of Morgan Stanley. It
is absolutely critical that your successor be experienced and well
respected by the senior executive group. This change should be
accomplished as soon as possible.

We would also recommend the appointment of three outside
directors with experience in financial services. At least one of
these directors should have experience in institutional securities while another should be experienced in the retail securities
business. These additions to the Board could be accomplished
with or without increasing the size of the Board.

The signers of this letter include a number of former senior
executives and board members of Morgan Stanley. We are fearful that in reaction to this letter you may reassign or remove
more of the senior executives from the Institutional Securities
Group. Such action would damage the Firm's ability to improve
its long-term business prospects, would undermine the Firm's
reputation and, perhaps irretrievably, injure its ability to attract
and retain talented professionals.

We are united in our strong support of Morgan Stanley and
our concern for its future. While we have not discussed this letter with a wider group of Advisory Directors or others who may
share our concerns, we are confident that support for our recommendations will be widespread within and outside of the Firm.

We write this letter with a grave sense of our responsibilities to fellow Morgan Stanley shareholders and employees. We
request the opportunity to discuss in private with the independent
directors the issues and recommendations contained in this letter.
We can be reached through our financial advisor, Robert F. Greenhill, at Greenhill & Co. We hope that constructive discussion

between ourselves and the Board can result in mutual commitment to a plan which can allow the Firm to regain its position as the premier financial services firm.

Respectfully,

MARCH 31, 2005. *The Group of Eight published this letter to Philip Purcell in an ad in the* Wall Street Journal, *following the Easter Monday Massacre, when Purcell fired Stephen Newhouse, president; Vikram Pandit, Head of Institutional Securities; and John Havens, Head of Equities.*

Dear Mr. Purcell:

We regret that we must resort to another letter, but given your refusal to meet with us, we have concluded that this is the only way we can communicate with you. We are shareholders concerned with the best interests of the Firm, and we are expressing our concerns to you, our Board of Directors.

The issues which are foremost in our minds as we call for a new CEO are at the heart of your responsibilities in the areas of business performance and governance. A common proxy for measuring performance is share price. Morgan Stanley's stock has dramatically underperformed the relevant market indices and its peers over the last five years. The Firm's growth in earnings per share has been negative versus positive growth for our peer companies. Morgan Stanley's premium return on equity has been eroded to where it is actually below that of our peer companies.

When you begin to look at performance by business segment, the reason for our stock's decline becomes clearer. In retail securities, we have experienced negative growth in revenues and our pre-tax margins are unacceptably low. The key to profitability in the asset management business is growth in assets under management, and our performance since 1998 has been mediocre at best.

The performance scorecard above summarizes your record since the merger. It is a failing report card.

We are also deeply concerned by the state of Morgan Stanley's relationship with regulators at both the Federal and State levels.

Our reputation has been blemished further by a series of ill-handled court cases, most recently the Perelman/Sunbeam case in Florida. This unhappy state of affairs is not consistent with strong leadership at the top.

While you point out with pride that the Board met three times to discuss our letter of March 3, we view with dismay the process by which the Board concluded that our concerns were groundless. The number of meetings obscures the question of the depth and rigor of the process: we do not believe that having brief telephone conversations with selected management members is the kind of rigorous fact finding called for under these circumstances.

And finally, we view with dismay the manner in which the Board brought this matter to a conclusion this week. The loss of several key executives who were very important contributors to the success of the highly profitable institutional securities business—because they were unwilling to swear loyalty to an ineffective CEO—is an outrage. The departed leaders are highly regarded by the majority of our institutional shareholders. We view the Board's actions, including its apparent support of this "reorganization," as a failure of corporate governance, a failure to fulfill its fiduciary duties and a failure to act in the best interests of the shareholders of Morgan Stanley.

Our worst fears, highlighted in our first letter to you, that you might remove senior executives in the Institutional Securities Group, have been realized. These departures have precipitated the worst kind of crisis for the Firm—unless immediate action is taken to reverse the loss of talent, the Firm's ability to restore its reputation and its competitive edge will be put at risk. We believe that your immediate departure would stem the tide and possibly convince those who have left to return as leaders.

Finally, please remember that we are not just a small group of dissatisfied former employees. All of us held senior positions of leadership in the Firm and together own more than 11 million shares of Morgan Stanley stock. We care deeply about the Firm and remain ready to meet with you, face to face, to discuss our concerns.

Respectfully,

APRIL 4, 2005. *The Group of Eight responded to calls from colleagues inside Morgan Stanley expressing their dismay at the disruption caused by the public nature of their challenge, by publishing this ad in the* Wall Street Journal. *The Eight encouraged employees to contact them directly through their Web site, or through Greenhill & Company. Letters poured in.*

A Message to Morgan Stanley Employees:

A Message to All the Employees of Morgan Stanley:

We understand that the events of the past seven days are disturbing to all of you; they are upsetting to us as well. To see talented, respected leaders tossed aside by the CEO for unknown reasons raises troubling questions about the leadership, governance and direction of the Firm.

While the recent turmoil is, of course, regrettable, the stakes are important. The leadership problems at the Firm must be addressed and resolved. We want to see the Firm in its entirety begin again to grow and flourish. We want all of you to benefit from an environment like the one we knew: where a commitment to excellence is a core value and where healthy debate can make us all better people.

The most important asset of Morgan Stanley is you, its people. As upsetting as the current situation is, we urge you to remain focused on your clients and your responsibilities. With your continued dedication to the Firm, we know that together we can re-create an environment where you can achieve your goals. We understand that many of you feel that there is an atmosphere of intimidation and fear at the Firm in which you may feel that you cannot express your views without fear of retaliation. We have, therefore, created a vehicle where you can express your feelings without prejudice. You can contact us through our website at **www.futureofms.com,** or through our financial advisor Greenhill & Co. We will endeavor to communicate your collective views to the Board of Directors, without attributing them to specific individuals.

Please do not lose hope. We pledge our energy and efforts to make Morgan Stanley a firm of which we can all be proud.

Committed to you all,
Anson M. Beard, Jr.
Lewis W. Bernard
Richard A. Debs
Joseph G. Fogg
S. Parker Gilbert
Robert G. Scott
Frederick B. Whittemore
John H. T. Wilson

APRIL 11, 2005. *The Group of Eight wrote the Board of Directors asking them fourteen questions. They did not receive an answer.*

Dear Board of Directors of Morgan Stanley:

Last week, in an open letter to Morgan Stanley's employees, in which he discussed recent criticisms of his performance and calls for his replacement, your CEO, Philip Purcell, wrote: "I would not have chosen this debate to be so publicly aired." We agree and demonstrated as much when we wrote to you in advance of the Company's annual meeting in March, to express our concerns and to request a private meeting with you to discuss them. You have stated that you believe there is no "fair and compelling case" to replace Mr. Purcell, yet you have not spoken to us and have so far declined our repeated requests to meet with you. You have chosen instead to react to our concerns and those of others by announcing a radical restructuring that has cost the firm some of its most talented professionals and further entrenched and insulated Mr. Purcell. Additionally, in an abrupt and poorly explained about-face in corporate strategy, you have decided to spin-off Discover.

In his carefully crafted press statements in London last week, Mr. Purcell declared victory and announced that the debate about his performance and leadership was "over." This is not a game of winning and losing. There are already too many losers among Morgan Stanley's employees, shareholders and clients. This is about corporate governance, executive leadership and creating value for shareholders. Before you pledge your continued and unconditional support of Mr. Purcell and before you expend any more corporate resources to do so, we think the Board should answer the following questions:

Given that Mr. Purcell has stated that he does not believe "it is in the custom of Morgan Stanley . . . to risk a course of action that would damage our franchise," did the Board approve the decision to relieve Messrs. Newhouse, Pandit and Havens of their responsibilities—thereby causing their departures? Does the Board believe that the departures of these senior executives, highly respected by shareholders, employees and clients, benefit the franchise and enhance shareholder value?

Did you believe that you fulfilled your obligations in approving a management restructuring, even though a key management committee member was never interviewed by directors, and most of those in institutional securities were only briefly interviewed by telephone?

How many more talented employees must leave before the Board understands that the value of the Morgan Stanley franchise is deteriorating while the Firm is facing a crisis of confidence in the Chairman and CEO?

Since the receipt of our March 3 letter, has the Board or any Board Committee approved the payment of "retention" or "stay-on" payments to key employees?

In light of the fact that the By-Laws require a 75% vote of the directors to remove the current Chairman and CEO, did you feel it was appropriate to appoint three directors to the Board, one in December of 2004 and two in April of 2005, without a shareholder vote?

In the wake of two successive shareholder votes demanding

the elimination of the staggered Board, and the Board's own recommendation to de-stagger the Board, why didn't you follow the example of other firms and immediately eliminate the staggered Board? Indeed, why did the Board appoint two of the new directors to multi-year terms, including a director appointed after shareholders approved the de-staggering of the Board?

Shouldn't you have disclosed to shareholders before the annual meeting that the Division of Enforcement of the SEC had sent the Company a "Wells notice" in January 2005 recommending that the SEC pursue an enforcement action relating to the Company's retention of e-mails and the potential violation of a previous Cease and Desist Order?

What investigation has the Board conducted in the wake of the Florida Court's finding in the Sunbeam/Perelman litigation that "contrary to federal law" the Company failed to preserve e-mails, and willfully disobeyed the Court's order?

Is it true (as has been reported in the April 8, 2005, edition of the *Wall Street Journal*) that the Sunbeam/Perelman litigation, for which $360 million has now been reserved, could have been settled for approximately $20 million in 2003, and was the Board aware of this?

Has an independent committee of the Board reviewed the quality of the Company's relationships with its primary regulators, including the SEC, NYSE, NASD and key state regulatory bodies, and do you believe that the quality of the Company's relationships with its key regulators has deteriorated over the past several years? If so, who should be held accountable for the deterioration?

What happened over the weekend of April 2–3, 2005, to cause the Board to depart from the publicly-stated strategy (reaffirmed to institutional shareholders on April 1) that Discover was an integral part of the Company's asset base?

How does the Board reconcile the inability of the CFO to answer basic questions on the April 4, 2005, analyst call about the structure of a spun-off Discover with Mr. Purcell's claim that the spin-off had been under review for months?

Did the Board meet with clients, major institutional shareholders and key employee groups, including key employees who have recently left the Company to elicit their views on the performance of the Company, the leadership of its Chairman and CEO, and the wisdom of the recently announced restructuring and spin-off of Discover?

Since Mr. Purcell declared "I would not have chosen this debate to be so publicly aired," did he recommend that the Board meet with us, and how did the Board determine that our concerns were groundless without even speaking with us?

In recent days, we have heard these and other questions from many of Morgan Stanley's constituents and believe it is critical for members of the Board to address them directly. Moreover, we believe that if the Board engages these constituents and answers these questions, it will conclude that there are "fair and compelling" reasons for Morgan Stanley to remove and replace its current Chairman and CEO. We remain willing to meet privately with the independent directors to discuss our concerns and to learn the response to our inquiries. If shareholders, clients, employees and others agree with us, are interested in learning the Board's response to our questions or have questions of their own, we urge them to contact the Board at: Morgan Stanley, Suite D, 1585 Broadway, New York, NY, 10036. Alternatively, constituents can also send questions and comments to our website, www.futureofms.com.

Respectfully,

APRIL 22, 2005. *Mary Meeker, Henry McVey, Stephen Roach, and Byron Wien write the following private letter to Zoe Cruz and Steve Crawford, expressing their concern about damage to the culture of the firm, and suggesting that Cruz and Crawford spearhead meetings to listen to employees. The general substance of the letter was later leaked to the Wall Street Journal, but the actual text was never released to the media.*

Dear Zoe and Steve,

We write you in confidence to express our deep concerns about recent events at Morgan Stanley. In general, through a process of dialog and debate we have developed a trust that the right things ultimately happen at our firm. We are now questioning this.

Over the years each of us have turned down jobs that offered higher compensation and, often, more balanced lifestyles, with a simple, proud response—Morgan Stanley's institutional securities business is the best on Wall Street. It is a meritocracy. We debate (and argue) a lot, and, in large part, because of this, we end up in the right place far more often than not. Our colleagues are creative and think out of the box. We put our clients first. We strive to be the best in the world at what we do. We lead by example. At our core is a value system based on integrity, trust, and respect for one another and a passion for the franchise. We have extraordinarily smart people in every one of our institutional business units around the world to call on for guidance. When comparing the assets and liabilities of Morgan Stanley with any other firm, Morgan Stanley comes out as the clear winner. This is the hallmark of our culture. We take pride in the fact that because of this hallmark, our clients have consistently looked to us as their trusted advisors. We have endeavored to fulfill the promise of "doing first class business in a first class way." Today, this unassailably powerful culture finds itself in a very challenged situation.

Collectively, we have served as Managing Directors for decades and have lived through various dislocations within the organization. In every situation, there were board members, advisory directors, senior partners, and peers standing ready to provide support, encouragement, and guidance. Because of these deep and close bonds, we have not only endured, we have prevailed. Now, things are different.

For the most part, *current outside board members* do not seem to be in touch with employees.

Most of our *advisory directors* now appear to be unsupportive of the firm. Over the years, this group of former leaders has served as guiding lights and mentors for many employees of the firm. They have proven time and again, through their mentorship and relationships, to be significant assets to the organization. That is now at risk.

Many of our *senior partners* have left the firm over the past month for a variety of reasons. These talented and experienced leaders were Managing Directors with hundreds of years of Wall Street experience (mostly at Morgan Stanley). A clear indication of their value to the firm is that they were paid tens of millions of dollars in F2004.

Peers are stunned by what they read and hear about the goings-on at Morgan Stanley nearly every day. For the first time in our careers at the firm, the majority of people we know are not politely hanging up on inbound recruiting queries. They are unable to explain why a business and culture that have traditionally been so well managed is so unsettled. People are embarrassed—not by what outsiders are saying but by what insiders appear to be doing.

No doubt, we find ourselves in this position in part because of change. We welcome change and recognize that it can be productive. However, in a world of transparency and objectivity and—as a public company whose assets are its people—the process by which change is brought about must be above reproach. In our view, the recent process by which the firm has introduced change falls well short of this standard.

We ask for your help in endeavoring to end the animosity that has developed within the firm. Specifically, we urge you to invite a small group of senior leaders (current and former) to convey to you specific steps that may be needed to stabilize the organization and reignite the passion and energy that drive our businesses. At a minimum, this effort is basic due diligence and a reasonable act of fiduciary responsibility. Obviously, it is your choice to evaluate what you hear, but you should listen and we believe you should do this very soon.

Unfortunately, in effect, the message that has been sent to the people of Morgan Stanley is that "your opinions are not relevant, we do not value your experience and expertise, and if you speak out, it is at your peril." This is a dysfunctional message for the thousands of Morgan Stanley decision makers who make tens—often hundreds—of judgment calls each day as they endeavor to manage complex and dynamic markets in the best interests of their clients and the profitability of our institution. The opinions, experience, and expertise of the people of Morgan Stanley are the very things that drive the business! Without these, we are nothing.

Forget the public letter salvos. Get in a room and hash it

out—it has been the Morgan Stanley way. And, time and again, it has proven that it works.

Zoe and Steve, while this letter is sent to you in confidence, we are perfectly comfortable in having you share these thoughts with your colleagues on the Board of Directors. In fact, we encourage you to do so. We care deeply about the firm and all that it stands for. As representatives of the firm's most valuable assets—its people—we ask you to stand with us in Morgan Stanley's best interests.

Sincerely,

Henry McVey   Mary Meeker   Stephen Roach   Byron Wien

MAY 12, 2005. *The Group of Eight released a "letter to the shareholders" proposing a spin-off of the Institutional Securities (Morgan Stanley legacy) business. Three members of the board of directors met with them, but established the ground rule that they would not discuss any proposals to ask Phil Purcell to leave.*

To the Shareholders of Morgan Stanley:

We are today releasing detailed materials outlining a proposal to spin off the Institutional Securities Business (available on www.futureofms.com). As has been reported, this proposal was reviewed in preliminary form with three non-executive directors of the Morgan Stanley Board on April 22, 2005. Since that meeting we have received no direct response from the Board. We have subsequently discussed a spin-off with institutional shareholders and expanded the initial proposal to reflect their input.

The proposed spin-off is motivated by a belief that the Board of Morgan Stanley faces an immediate crisis and that the Firm has been badly served by its present management and leadership. The recent improvements in corporate governance announced by the Board in reaction to pressure from shareholders are overdue, but they fail to address the leadership and structural issues that, if left alone, will continue to damage the Firm and erode shareholder value. The crisis continues and will likely deepen.

Central to any successful resolution of the current crisis is the separation of Philip Purcell from authority over Morgan Stanley's Institutional Securities Business and the installation of a new management team, which can stem the tide of departures and attract key leaders, who have recently departed, back to the Firm. If Morgan Stanley's optimum strategy is to build a fully integrated securities business—an outcome that Mr. Purcell has failed to accomplish in the eight years since the merger with Dean Witter Discover—the strategy requires the immediate replacement of the current leadership team.

Alternatively, a spin-off of the Institutional Securities Business would acknowledge the failure of the integration effort, allow the Institutional Securities Business to regain its stature and reputation and significantly improve its performance. **This could be accomplished under the leadership of the five widely respected senior executives who were forced to depart, but who we are highly confident would return to lead the Institutional Securities Business in a spin-off.**

The business strategy presented by Mr. Purcell, Ms. Cruz and Mr. Crawford at the UBS Global Financial Services Conference on Tuesday, May 10, 2005, while acknowledging the Company's underperformance, the departure of key managers from the Firm and the high likelihood of more departures in the future, offered no credible solution to the present crisis. In the eight years since the merger, Mr. Purcell has failed to successfully execute the integrated securities business model senior management promoted at the conference. Staying the course under the present leadership is not an acceptable solution. Shareholders deserve better. We strongly believe that new leadership is critical to the success of the Firm and to the creation of shareholder value. We invite you to study the spin-off proposal carefully, before the crisis worsens.

If you believe that a spin-off of the Institutional Securities Business and the return of recently departed and highly respected leaders would be beneficial to shareholders, we urge you to let us know by e-mail on our website (www.futureofms.com). We also encourage you to make your views known to the Morgan Stanley Board by contacting them directly.

Respectfully,

JUNE 30, 2005. *The Group of Eight released this statement:*

In a statement regarding John Mack's appointment as chairman and CEO of Morgan Stanley, The Group of Eight said:

"The appointment of John Mack to the position of Chairman and CEO of Morgan Stanley is another important step in the process of restoring the Firm to its position of preeminence in the financial services industry. We applaud the Board's openness in turning to John as an action clearly in the best interests of shareholders, clients and employees.

We hope that John will be able to attract back many of the talented employees who left the Firm during this stressful period, in particular the five former members of the management committee who are so important to the Firm's franchise.

We also want to thank the dedicated and loyal employees who have continued to serve Morgan Stanley's clients during this challenging period."

MAY 13, 1933. *J. P. Morgan Jr. wrote this statement in pencil on May 12, 1933, and read it into the record the next day when he testified before the Sub-Committee of the Committee on Banking and Currency of the United States Senate. For generations it has been reprinted and framed in the offices of members of the Morgan firms. The Glass-Steagall Act, passed the same year, which required banks to drop either their commercial or investment banking activities, led to J. P. Morgan closing its investment banking department, and, in 1935, to the founding of Morgan Stanley.*

I have ventured to frame a brief statement of my views on the subject of duties and uses of bankers.

The banker is a member of a profession practiced since the Middle Ages. There has grown up a code of professional ethics and customs, on the observance of which depend his reputation, his fortune, and his usefulness to the community in which he works.

Some bankers are not as observant of this code as they should be; but if, in the exercise of his profession, the banker disregards this code—which could never be expressed in legislation, but has a force far greater than any law—he will sacrifice his credit. This credit is his most valuable possession; it is the result of years of fair and honorable dealing and, while it may be quickly lost, once lost cannot be restored for a long time, if ever. The banker must at all times conduct himself so as to justify the confidence of his clients in him and thus preserve it for his successors.

If I may be permitted to speak of the firm of which I have the honor to be the senior partner, I should state that at all times the idea of doing only first class business, and that in a first class way, has been before our minds. We have never been satisfied with simply keeping within the law, but have constantly sought so to act that we might fully observe the professional code, and so maintain the credit and reputation which has been handed down to us from our predecessors in the firm. Since we have no more power of knowing the future than any other men, we have made many mistakes (who has not during the past five years?), but our mistakes have been errors of judgment and not of principle.

The banker must be ready and willing at all times to give advice to his clients to the best of his ability. If he feels unable to give this advice without reference to his own interest, he must frankly say so. The belief in the integrity of his advice is a great part of the credit of which I have spoken above, as being the best possession of any firm.

Another very important use of the banker is to serve as a channel whereby industry may be provided with capital to meet its needs for expansion and development. To this end the banker can serve well, since, as he has at stake not only his client's interests but his own reputation, he is likely to be especially careful. If he makes a public sale and puts his own name at the foot of the prospectus, he has a continuing obligation of the strongest kind to see, so far as he can, that nothing is done which will interfere with the full carrying out by the obligor of the contract with the holder of the security.

NOTES

PROLOGUE

1   Description of the January 16, 2005, meeting at Parker Gilbert's, from author interviews with Parker Gilbert and Robert Scott, and author meetings at the Gilbert apartment.

2   *an outraged John P. Havens...*: Author interviews, multiple confidential sources.

3   *"I wear Morgan Stanley blue..."*: Multiple sources.

4   *J. P. Morgan Jr. read into the record at a 1933...*: See Appendix for full text.

4   *"We weren't planning to do anything yet..."*: Author interview, Parker Gilbert.

5   *Joe Perella, who had been at the table...*: Author interviews with multiple confidential sources.

6   *to tell the New York State Comptroller...*: Author interview, confidential source.

6   *"When Vikram endorsed an underwriting..."*: Confidential source, confirmed by others.

7   *John Mack recalls a time "during a terrible market..."*: Confidential source, author interview.

8   *"The fish is rotting from the head..."*: Richard Bove in Punk, Ziegel research report, December 2004.

8   *"Morgan Stanley doesn't have to do anything..."*: See David Rynecki, "Morgan Stanley's Man on the Spot," *Fortune*, November 15, 2004, http://money.cnn.com/magazines/fortune/fortune_archive/2004/11/15/8191084/index.htm.

8   *"The firm's performance results...This is very helpful..."* and *"There was no dialogue..."*: Parker Gilbert, author interview.

9   *"STOCKS AND BLONDES: BOOZE, BABES AND A DWARF!"*: *Daily News*, July 19, 2005, 1.

10 *"And I have an awesome responsibility...":* "The Digital 50," *Time Digital*, September 27, 1999, www.time.com/time/digital/digital50/26.html.

10 *"It is time for the Skull-and-Bones Society types...":* Senator Orrin Hatch (R-Utah), *New York Times*, April 17, 2005, Business Day.

PART I: BEGINNING AND ENDINGS
1: A FIRST CLASS BUSINESS

13 *Perry E. Hall declared...:* Perry Hall, private papers, courtesy of Frederick B. Whittemore.

13 *blue chip companies of smokestack America:* Morgan Stanley issued securities worth $1.564 billion for General Motors between 1946 and 1965; $1.78 billion for Shell Oil and its subsidiaries between 1939 and 1970; twenty-five offerings that added up to $2.827 billion for the Standard Oil Companies, starting in 1926; and $1.08 billion for United States Steel between 1938 and 1968. The big utility client was Con Edison, more than $2 billion starting in 1936. GMAC was the major financial institution, at $2.65 billion. AT&T was the biggest client of all, at $4.85 billion. In 1954 the firm issued two secondary offerings, one for preferred and one for common stock for International Harvester, the conglomerate J. P. Morgan put together; and between 1938 and 1961 more than $1 billion for U.S. Steel. See *Morgan Stanley & Co, 1935–1965*, privately published for the firm, as well as other unpublished proprietary manuscripts recounting Morgan Stanley history.

14 *few bankers anywhere in the world...:* See "Mister Morgan," *Fortune*, August 1933.

14 *"industrial architecture on a Jurassic scale":* Ibid.

15 *total market cap of all American manufacturing companies:* See Ron Chernow, *The House of Morgan: An American Banking Dynasty and the Rise of Modern Finance* (New York: A Morgan Entrekin Book/Atlantic Monthly Press, 1990), 85. Chernow's Pulitzer Prize–winning history is an invaluable source, in particular for the period prior to 1960.

15 *85 percent of the U.S. farm equipment business...:* Ibid., 109.

15 *J. P. Morgan himself joined the GE board:* Jean Strouse, *Morgan, American Financier* (New York: HarperPerennial, 2000), 313.

16 *the salvation of the gold standard...:* This account and quotations are from Chernow, 71, 75, 76.

17 *"Because a man I do not trust...":* Quoted in multiple sources. Frederick Lewis Allen, *The Great Pierpoint Morgan* (1949; Harper & Row Perennial Library reprint, 1965), 8; quoted in Chernow, 154.

17 *"we had never bought anybody yet...":* Pierpont Morgan Library, ARC12161108F378, "Memorandum." This is a record written by J. P.

Morgan Jr. of his meeting with President Woodrow Wilson on July 1, 1914.

17 *3,698 on the first day...:* See Chernow, 158.

18 *saved the Allies...:* See John K. Winkler, "Profiles: Mighty Dealer in Dollars, Part II," *New Yorker,* February 9, 1929, 27.

18 *attributed to overwork:* Gilbert joined the firm in January 1931, in time to shoulder part of the partners' Depression-era debt. When Gilbert was in the hospital, shortly before his death, Jack Morgan sent him a hand-written letter, which began with a heartfelt, "We all miss you very much and . . . feel the lack of your advice and your accuracy of judgment. Incidentally, I may mention that we all enjoy having you about the place." He went on to explain, "We thought we had made ample reserves against the situation which had developed in 1930 [but] it turned out otherwise . . . The result of this miscalculation for which you were in no way to blame, is that you were loaded with a debt at the end of your first year, caused by no fault on your part which always seemed to me, and I believe to all of us, not entirely equitable."

Morgan had asked for a study to determine how much the firm should have had in reserve and told Gilbert that he was going on a short vacation and when he returned, "I shall expect to be able to tell you the amount upon which we have all agreed, which will I hope be quite satisfactory to you." Gilbert died before Morgan could act on his promise. His son, Parker Gilbert, who became chairman of Morgan Stanley nearly a half century after his father's death, does not know if Morgan followed through.

19 *"banksters"...: Time* magazine, February 1933, cited in Jackie Corr, "Ferdinand Pecora: An American Hero," http://www.counterpunch.org/corr01112003.html.

19 *"hysterically intense...":* See Ferdinand Pecora, *Wall Street Under Oath: The Story of Our Modern Money Changers* (New York: Augustus M. Kelley Publishers, 1968), 4.

19 *"possibly added to its influence...":* Vincent P. Carosso papers, Pierpont Morgan Library Archives. This comes from a notation in Carosso's handwriting, which reads, "The full citation for this item is TW Lamont Papers, File 110-2 (JPM & CO) Baker Library, Harvard Graduate School of Business Administration, Boston."

19 *"comes from the respect and esteem of the community":* Ibid, 4.

20 *"a straitwaistcoat put on you besides":* To Lord St. Just, February 2, 1939, J. Pierpont Morgan Library, J. P. Morgan Jr. papers, book 46, 196.

21 Description of Sky Farm from August 2006 visit to North Haven by the author, thanks to the courteous hospitality of Tom Lamont's grandson, the journalist and author Lansing Lamont.

22 *capital of $340 million...:* This was 1932 deposits, according to Ferdinand Pecora, *Wall Street Under Oath: The Story of Our Modern Money*

Changers (New York: Augustus M. Kelley Publishers, 1968), 15. Other sources cite $430 million, possibly accurate for 1935.

22   *Morgan and Lamont families...:* The Morgan family held about 50 percent of the stock, and Lamont held another 40 percent, according to Chernow, 388.

23   *sent by colleagues and competitors...:* Ibid.

23   *"Morgan Stanley partners raised $200 million in debt":* From "Morgan Stanley & Co Incorporated: A Brief History," 1976, by William J. Kneisel.

23   *forty truck fuls:* Chernow, 400–401.

23   *"He did though":* Ibid., 401. Chernow cites U.S. Congress, Senate Special Committee Investigating the Munitions Industry, World War Financing, p. 7485, and *Time*, January 20, 1936.

24   *the office manager still took notes...:* Frederick B. Whittemore, author interview.

24   *"Charlie, it's your mother!":* Charles Morgan, author interview.

25   *helped future chairman Dick Fisher...:* Whittemore, author interview.

25   *"the greatest twenty-two-man debating club...":* Charles Morgan, author interview.

25   *"He was a peacekeeper...":* Whittemore, author interview.

25   *kept cherry bombs in his desk...:* Whittemore, author interview.

25   *250 armed guards...:* Chernow, 301.

26   Wall Street and the Security Markets...: *See* Harold R. Medina, *Wall Street and the Security Markets: Corrected Opinion of Harold R. Medina in the United States of America, Plaintiff, v. Henry S. Morgan, Harold Stanley, et al., doing business as Morgan Stanley & Co, et al., Defendants, Filed February 4, 1954.* (Reprint Edition, Arno Press, Inc.)

27   *"cease to function in a healthy, normal fashion...":* Ibid., 15.

27   *"WHAT IS WRONG WITH US NOW?":* Perry Hall, private papers, courtesy of Fred Whittemore.

2: BUILDING THE BANK

31   *"What's wrong, young man?...":* Frederick Whittemore, author interview.

31   *"a brilliant investment banker":* Gilbert, author interview.

32   *"picking up medals...":* Whittemore, author interview.

32   *"seems to preclude even modesty...":* See Wyndham Robertson, "Future Shock at Morgan Stanley," *Fortune*, February 27, 1979, 85ff. Statistics on the firm as of 1978 are gathered from Robertson's article, a benchmark story that helps define the changes. Robertson was the first reporter given access to Morgan Stanley for a major story.

32   *"a goddamn disaster...":* Robert Baldwin, author interview.

32 *in 1970, the firm admitted six partners: Morgan Stanley 1970*, privately
    published, 9, 14.

32 *"the irreverent six"*: Baldwin, author interview.

33 *Baldwin set up three committees:* Baldwin, author interview.

33 *"They were all wrong"*: Whittemore, author interview.

33 *"We were reluctant to give up our Morgan Stanley partnership..."*: Fifti-
    eth Anniversary, Morgan Stanley & Co, Incorporated, typed manuscript
    of talk by Samuel Payne, courtesy of Fred Whittemore.

34 *"the nicest ruthless man..."*: financial journalist to a former Morgan
    Stanley executive, as reported to the author in 2006.

34 *he fell ill with paralytic polio:* In 1944, when Dick Fisher was infected
    with the polio virus, there were about twenty thousand cases of polio a
    year in the United States, only a small portion of which were of the
    paralytic variety. The severe polio epidemic took place in 1952 and
    1953, as numbers of cases more than doubled in 1952 and were up by
    one-third the next year. Many families forbade their children to swim
    in public swimming pools or go to movie theaters during those years.

35 *"...just a statistician..."*: Robert G. Scott, "Richard Fisher" (remarks at
    memorial service for Richard B. Fisher, Riverside Church, New York
    City, January 12, 2005).

37 *"I knew then I was on my own"*: John Mack member biography, The
    Horatio Alger Association of Distinguished Americans, http://www
    .horatioalger.com/members/members_info.cfm?memberid=MAC03.

37 *"a patina about Morgan Stanley...a close-knit collegial group...the firm
    was pricing...stated their view..."*: Author interview, confidential source.

38 *"Dick was very calm..."*: Author interview, confidential source.

38 *"You can't understand John Mack..."*: Chas Phillips, author interview.

38 *crossed their names off with a red pencil...:* Baldwin, author interview.
    According to Lisa Endlich in her excellent book, *Goldman Sachs: The
    Culture of Success* (New York: Alfred A. Knopf, 1999), Goldman's senior
    partner, Sidney Weinberg, also kept a tombstone ad in his office and
    crossed off the names of firms as they closed.

39 *"willing to tell you what you had to do..."*: Chas Phillips, author interview.

39 *"We're about to have a partner who is smarter..."*: Whittemore, author
    interview.

39 *Baldwin remembers Perry Hall saying...:* Baldwin, author interview.

40 *Barton Biggs as Chief Analyst:* Biggs brought in people who became fa-
    mous in their fields, including Barry Good (oil), Dennis Sherva (small
    growth companies), Ben Rosen (technology), Walter Loeb (retail), John
    Mackin (heavy industry), Byron Wien (U.S. equity markets), and Ste-
    phen Roach, who became the global economics chief.

40 *"I was coming up with ideas..."*: Byron Wien, author interview.

40 *Monday-morning meetings:* When Biggs left, Wien took over the Monday-morning meetings. Wien hired Steven Galbraith as his successor, and Galbraith was named the number one all-star strategist by *Institutional Investor.* When Galbraith moved on to a hedge fund, Wien picked his successor, Henry McVey. In time, Stephen Roach and Mary Meeker became two of Wall Street's most famous seers. Meeker was known as "Queen of the Net" for her brilliant analysis of the Internet and connectivity businesses. Roach was the bearish Chief Economist and Director of Global Economic Analysis, and took over running the Monday-morning meetings.

41 *"It was perfect for Greenie..."*: Baldwin, author interview.

41 *"electronic bugs":* "Mergers: The Billion-Dollar Game," Steve Lohr, *The Atlantic.*

41 *"What do you call your father?":* Baldwin, author interview.

42 *"We hired engineers and we did an evaluation...":* Oil company story as told to the author by Joseph G. Fogg III.

42 *"Do you think you could get Bob Greenhill...":* Baldwin, author interview.

42 *"the person that was most sympathetic...":* Gilbert, referring to William Black, author interview.

43 *"Black held the firm together...":* See Ron Chernow, *The House of Morgan: An American Banking Dynasty and the Rise of Modern Finance* (New York: A Morgan Entrekin Book/Atlantic Monthly Press, 1990), 623.

44 *Anson M. Beard Jr.:* The author was married to Anson Beard's brother, Samuel S. Beard, from 1969 to 1982.

44 *"The 'little guy,' of course...":* See Robert J. Cole, "City Retail Unit Due at Morgan Stanley," *New York Times,* September 7, 1977.

44 *"...or the small institution":* See "Morgan Stanley Hangs Out a Retail Shingle," *New York Times,* September 11, 1977.

44 *With Fred Whittemore as Head of Syndicate:* See Michael C. Jensen, "The Morgan Stanley Manner," *New York Times,* May 25, 1975.

44 *and eleven of the top twenty:* Ibid.

44 *six of the ten...:* Thomas A. Saunders III succeeded Fred Whittemore as head of Syndicate. Saunders resigned from the firm in 1989.

45 *"Saying yes to Morgan Stanley...":* Whittemore, author interview.

45 *"Oscar Mayer, had never heard of Morgan Stanley...":* This story was recounted to the author by a former Morgan Stanley investment banker, a confidential source.

45 *"I Wish I Were an Oscar Mayer Wiener...":* See Tim Metz, "Morgan Stanley Drops Its Staid Image, Battles for Securities Business," *Wall Street Journal,* July 17, 1980, 1.

45 *"It was the first time anybody had showed...":* Anson Beard, author interview.

46 "Salomon was the ten-foot giant...": Brad Hintz, author interview.

46 "We were the engine...": Joe Fogg, author interview.

47 "to stand behind a potted palm": Whittemore, author interview.

47 "Parker isn't going to be able to take the early train...": Baldwin, author interview.

47 "Leadership requires a positive nature...": Whittemore, author interview.

48 Morgan Stanley was not alone in worrying...: See Scott McMurray and Ann Monroe, "Morgan Stanley Planning to Go Public in $200 Million Stock Issue, Sources Say," Wall Street Journal, January 24, 1986.

48 "the worm can't get bigger than the apple...": Brad Hintz, author interview.

48 "a superb job of making it fair...": Anson Beard, author interview.

49 A managing director whose interest... was valued...: Author interview, confidential source.

49 "respectably rich...": Whittemore, author interview.

49 but not hugely... rich: Former chairman Perry Hall had retired and was living in Woods Hole, Massachusetts, when he realized he had outlived his savings. He sold his boat and some real estate, and when he still came up short, the firm quietly gave him an annuity of $400,000 a year for the last few years of his life.

49 "You had to be able to contemplate the billion-dollar deal...": Investment banker, confidential source; concept confirmed by multiple sources.

49 Parker Gilbert recalls commuting with a couple of colleagues...: Gilbert, author interview.

50 one of the most expensive apartments in the city... and... sold for $30 million: See Michael Gross, 740 Park: The Story of the World's Richest Apartment Building (New York: Broadway Books, 2005).

51 "Clients like our long-term commitment...": William Kneisel, quoted in Frederick Ungeheuer (in New York), Helen Hibson (in London), Barry Hillenbrand (in Tokyo), "We Don't Have to Have All of Our Cake Today," Time, February 26, 1990, Internet source.

51 Description of the "Black Monday" October 19, 1987, stock market crash from interviews with Anson Beard, who, as Head of Equities, was the most directly involved in managing the situation for the firm.

52 "one of our best managers...": Confidential source, author interview.

53 "...that they couldn't work together": Gilbert, author interview.

53 "Dick said, 'I'm not running for class president...'": Confidential source, author interview.

53 Gilbert called them into his office...: Gilbert, author interview.

53 "That wasn't a designation I particularly liked...": Gilbert, author interview.

54 "the most profitable on Wall Street...": See Kurt Eichenwald, "Morgan Stanley Chairman to Retire," New York Times, May 18, 1990.

54 *Fisher told a reporter... "Going forward, the people here expect...":*
    Ibid.

55 Vikram Pandit photograph from Columbia University Yearbook, 1976,
    courtesy of Columbia University.

56 *a friend said he'd joked...:* Author interview, confidential source.

57 Description of the skit from Byron Wien, in an interview with the au-
    thor. Text excerpts courtesy of Byron Wien.

60 *"just shows that Morgan is very much focused on shareholder returns...":*
    See Michael Siconolfi, "Morgan Stanley Puts 'Pay Cut' Back into
    Wall Street Lingo: Senior Officials Get 20% Less for Year, But at
    $6.3 Million Apiece, It's Not Too Awful," *Wall Street Journal*, April 7,
    1992, B8.

60 *"We decided we should have a planning off-site... was close to a revolu-
    tion... started breaking down silos...":* Confidential source, author inter-
    view.

61 *Fixed Income department expanded by 75 percent:* See Michael Siconolfi,
    "Morgan Stanley's Greenhill to Step Down and Mack Will Succeed
    Him as President," *Wall Street Journal*, March 3, 1993, C1.

61 *"girls' rules too...":* Morgan Stanley managing director, author inter-
    view.

61 *"I'm sure you'll make the right one":* Gilbert, author interview.

61 *"Never before had Morgan Stanley deposed its president...":* Siconolfi,
    "Morgan Stanley's Greenhill to Step Down."

62 *"hybrid vigor... fresh insight...":* From video of Perella's talk at the In-
    vestment Banking Division meeting in Barcelona, Spain, September
    29, 2004.

3: PHILIP PURCELL AND "THE GREAT AMERICAN COMPANY"

An important source for this chapter is Donald R. Katz, whom I briefly interviewed, and whose superb history of Sears, *The Big Store: Inside the Crisis
and Revolution at Sears* (New York: Penguin Books, 1987), provides facts and
insights into the corporate environment in which Purcell operated at Sears
and Dean Witter. Any inferences I have drawn from information provided
by Katz are my own.

Specific quotations are cited below, unless attributions are made within
the text.

67 *"just playing basketball and chasing Annie":* See Donald Katz, *The Big
    Store: Inside the Crisis and Revolution at Sears* (New York: Penguin
    Books, 1987), 69.

67 *"were some of the best in my life":* Philip J. Purcell, "Thoughts on Notre
    Dame Athletics," September 2006, a speech Purcell delivered at the an-

nouncement of the gift of $15 million to Notre Dame, of which the Purcells donated $12.5 million, according to the Notre Dame Web site. The Purcell Pavilion would be used for basketball.

68 *one percent of the American gross national product...:* "Sears—A Corporate Governance Case Study"; the case study was prepared as part of the Monks effort. See Robert A. G. Monks, "Corporate Governance Case Study: Sears," www.ragm.com/books/corp_gov/cases/cs_sears.html.

69 *"...powerful agent of change..."* and *"and create something new":* Katz, 67.

69 *"...hard to tell company and family apart...":* "Sears—A Corporate Governance Case Study."

70 *"a major investment in American greatness...":* Purcell, quoted in Katz, 233.

70 *"...buy a shirt and coat, and then maybe some stock":* *Wall Street Journal,* quoted in Katz, 246.

71 *"...quite separate from emotions like resentment":* Katz, 276.

71 *"treated us like some lower form of life:* Purcell, quoted in Katz, 291.

72 *...brisk and final "No":* Katz, 395.

72 *crowd "was only to be exceeded the day we went public...":* Anson Beard, author interview.

73 *"...passable 'xample of a claw hammer, too!":* Katz, 531–32.

74 *"...will visit our stores this year":* See Caroline E. Mayer, "Sears Unveils New Credit Card Intended for Use in Financial Planning," *Washington Post,* April 25, 1985.

74 *one of the ten worst executives...:* Katz, 374

76 *"somewhat aloof management style...outside the securities industry...":* Herb Greenberg and Janet Key, "Purcell New Chief at Witter," *Chicago Tribune* (pre-1997 full text), August 13, 1986, 3.

76 *"...was ridiculed for his contrarian strategies":* Spiro and Flynn, "A Star in the Gloom at Sears."

76 *"autocratic and bureaucratic":* "Last Stand at Morgan Stanley; Face Value," *Economist,* May 7, 2005.

77 *"We don't want Sears Roebuck in the banking business":* Katz, 553.

79 *"...at many times the rate of increase in pay for employees":* See Monks, "Corporate Governance Case Study: Sears."

79 *"created a patriotic argument...Pretty heady stuff":* Arthur Martinez, author interview.

80 *"...sort of geeky and lacking in stature to be running a business...":* Confidential source, author interview.

80 *"...What they knew of the company came largely from the company":* Sears executive quoted in Katz, 520.

4: THE DEAL

81 *"Dick thought the world of Phil... 'do a merger?' "*: Confidential source, author interview.

81 *"These guys are good..."*: Confidential source, author interview.

81 *"...he was extremely effective"*: William J. Kneisel, author interview.

82 *"Now we want to be independent"*: Confidential source, author interview.

82 *"to go and speak to our respective counterparties...like KGB agents... decisions were made at the top"*: Brad Hintz, author interview.

82 *"...they are not compatible"*: William J. Kneisel, author interview.

82 *"marriage of blue bloods..."*: See "Morgan Stanley, S. G. Warburg Discuss Merger: Stock Swap of $7 Billion to Bring Global Reach, $150 Billion Asset Pool," *Wall Street Journal*, December 9, 1994, 1A.

83 *"...language was German"*: Anonymous, Internet.

83 *"sound, inspirational management and success..."*: "The Fall of the House of Warburg," Jeremy Warner, *Independent* (London), February 17, 1995.

84 *"...number four worldwide in issuing debt"*: See Paula Dwyer (in London), with Leah Nathan Spiro (in New York), Robert Neff (in Tokyo), and Bill Javetski (in Paris), "Handshake in London, Hands Shaking on Wall Street," *BusinessWeek*, December 26, 1994.

84 *"...bold and opportunistic"*: Ibid.

84 *nonnegotiable... "Why did you do that?..."*: Confidential source, author interview.

85 *"behind because of lack of head count...hired right through the cycle...We became the firm to be at"*: Confidential source, author interview.

85 *"Equity Research at Morgan Stanley: What's Important"*: Mayree C. Clark, author interview; and research policy statement.

86 *"Project Edison"* and *"...a consensus-run company"*: Hintz, author interview.

86 *"...however pricing remains an issue"*: From the Project Edison Study, excerpts read to the author by Brad Hintz.

86 *"...distribution, distribution, distribution"*: See Peter Truell, "Morgan Stanley and Merrill Set to Add Money Managers," *New York Times*, June 25, 1996, D1.

86 On James Allwin: *"...in a gray universe"*: Confidential source, author interview.

87 *...subsumed by a big Wall Street bank*: See Beth Selby, "How Morgan Stanley Maps Its Moves," *Institutional Investor*, June 1, 1992, 52.

87 *"...entree into the retail business"*: See Truell, "Morgan Stanley and Merrill Set to Add Money Managers."

87 *"Individual investors control a growing percentage..."*: Barton Biggs, quoted in the *New York Times*, June 25, 1996, Internet source.

87   "...run-of-the-mill mutual-fund company...": See Patrick McGeehan, "Van Kampen Poses Marketing Dilemma," *Wall Street Journal*, November 5, 1996, C1.

88   "...mediocre retail division": Confidential source, author interview.

88   "...more of a recurring revenue stream...": Confidential source, author interview.

88   "John was the promoter and the architect...": Author interview, confidential source.

88   "Most of the calls came from Mack...": Richard Sorensen, author interview.

89   "...you have a fist": Widely quoted Krzyzewski saying.

89   "that fit together and have chemistry... Teammate of Jim Yerkovich...": See Jim Yerkovich with Patrick Kelly, SJ, *WE: A Model for Coaching and Christian Living* (Washington, D.C.: National Catholic Education Association, 2004), 9.

90   The Chinese delivery man, or pizza delivery man, story is common currency at Morgan Stanley. In fact, the delivery was breakfast, as confirmed by John Mack.

90   "Never let it happen again": CNBC, *Market Week with Maria Bartiromo*, February 5, 2002.

91   "John was the initiator... I believe him.": Author interview, confidential source.

91   *merger took on code names:* The references are to hockey legends (and former New York Rangers) Mark Messier and Wayne Gretzky.

91   *Fishers' home alarm system...:* Author interview, Jeanne Donovan Fisher.

91   *Dean Witter picked "Dr Pepper"...:* See Steven Lipin and Anita Raghavan, "The Morgan Stanley/Dean Witter Merger: The Morgan Stanley/Dean Witter Deal—Wall Street Is Surprised and Bullish," *Wall Street Journal*, February 6, 1997, C1.

91   "only 12 percent of merged corporations...": See John Gapper, "Morgan Stanley Deserves to Be Troubled," *Financial Times*, March 31, 2005.

91   *speculated that Karches and Allwin were both in line for the presidency...:* See Anita Raghavan, "Perella Pulls Back Clock to the 1980s: Morgan Stanley Is Set to Elevate Deal Maker," *Wall Street Journal*, January 16, 1997, page C1.

92   "We said, 'We'll do it at this price'...": Confidential source, author interview.

92   "biggest-ever brokerage merger": See Lipin and Raghavan, "The Morgan Stanley/Dean Witter Merger."

93   "Phil shook my hand": Confidential source, author interview.

93   ...one of Mack's closest associates... "wasn't going to do this forever": Confidential source, author interview.

93   *"John was used to doing business like that with Dick..."*: Confidential
      source, author interview.

94   *"I don't think there was ever a handshake..."*: Confidential source, au-
      thor interview.

95   *"Phil understood how important it was to control the infrastructure"*: Brad
      Hintz, author interview.

96   *"...probably listens to his own executives"*: See Anita Raghavan, "Mor-
      gan Stanley Puts More Stock Than in the Title," *Wall Street Journal*,
      February 7, 1997, C1.

97   *"They view you as an insider...Why would you want to change it now?"*:
      Parker Gilbert, author interview.

97   *"Phil...wants a 75 percent...that applies to me too"*: Author interviews,
      multiple confidential sources.

98   *"rancorous" board debate...*: See Diana B. Henriques, "Philip Morris
      Chairman Unexpectedly Resigns," *New York Times*, June 20, 1994, Fi-
      nancial Desk, D1.

99   The photograph was reprinted in the *Wall Street Journal* in 2005 under
      the headline "Mack's Back, Once Again," with a chart of Morgan Stan-
      ley's daily share price on the NYSE as part of the image. Halfway
      through 2005, it wasn't much higher than it was in 1998.

99   *"...a more gray and rainy day..."*: See Peter Truell, "$10.2 Billion Deal
      Would Create Biggest Securities Company," *New York Times*, February
      6, 1997, Business Section, Internet source.

99   *"...a lousy day for Merrill Lynch..."*: See Lipin and Raghavan, "The
      Morgan Stanley/Dean Witter Merger."

99   *"They are two fine firms and we wish them well"*: See Truell, "$10.2 Billion
      Deal."

99   *"...402 brokers and 9,725 employees"*: See Angela G. King, "Morgan
      Stanley, D Witter Pair Up," *Daily News*, February 6, 1997, Internet
      source.

100   *"...help our clients"*: See Gapper, "Morgan Stanley Deserves to Be Trou-
      bled."

100   *"...superb partnership"*: See Lipin and Raghavan, "The Morgan Stan-
      ley/Dean Witter Merger."

100   *"...an enigmatic former consultant"*: Ibid.

100   *"...often seen on Morgan Stanley's trading floors"*: See Patrick McGee-
      han and Bridget O'Brian, "The Morgan Stanley/Dean Witter Merger:
      The Morgan Stanley/Dean Witter Deal—Conflicts of Culture Could
      Occur," *Wall Street Journal*, February 6, 1997, C1.

100   *"...bloodying some noses and scraping elbows...knows where he is go-
      ing"*: See George Mannes, "Morgan Stanley, D Witter Pair Up," *Daily
      News*, February 6, 1997.

100 *"he was almost worshipful ... still CEO"*: Confidential source, author interview.

101 *"The deal stunned ... kids screaming in the background"*: See Anita Raghavan and Steven Lipin, "Brains and Brawn: Morgan Stanley Group and Dean Witter Plan an $8.8 Billion Merger—They Face Challenge Melding Elite Institutional Firm with Large Retail Broker—Biggest Securities Firm of All," *Wall Street Journal*, February 5, 1997, A1.

101 *would never have let a client ...*: Bob Greenhill, author interview.

101 *"... is the succession plan"*: Confidential source, author interview.

102 Jeane Fisher background, quotes, and details of wedding of Dick and Jeanne Donovan Fisher: Jeanne Donovan Fisher, author interview.

104 *"... have lost their job"*: Whittemore, author interview.

5: A CRISIS OF CONFIDENCE AND A CULTURE CLASH

105 *"... the guy with the white hat"*: Confidential source, author interview.

105 *"... tell you what to do"*: Confidential source, author interview.

105 *"... one of the two of us"*: Multiple sources, author interviews.

106 *"a bad symbol and not practical"*: Confidential source, author interview.

107 *"It was tacky at best ... didn't work"*: Confidential source, author interview.

107 *"Phil's lackey"*: author interviews, multiple sources.

107 *"At Dean Witter, if I told people ... why"*: Author interviews, multiple comments to the author from Advisory Directors who were present.

108 *"not a meritocracy ... talk to directors"*: From handwritten notes by Richard B. Fisher. These are undated, but he wrote "one year is enough," which dates them at around June 1998. Notes provided to the author by a confidential source.

109 *"John didn't want to embroil ..."*: Confidential source, author interview.

109 *" 'guys named Vinnie in cheap suits' "*: See Carol J. Loomis, "The Oddball Marriage Works," *Fortune*, April 26, 1999, 92ff.

109 *"Deepening turf battles were exacerbated ..."*: See Charles Gasparino and Anita Raghavan, "How Dean Witter Boss Beat Heir Apparent at Morgan Stanley for Merged Company," *Wall Street Journal*, March 22, 2001, http://online.wsj.com/PA2VJBNA4R/article.

110 *"When John and Phil ... just a chip in putting together something larger"*: Confidential source, author interview.

111 *"The re-branding of Dean Witter ... image"*: Confidential source, author interview.

112 *"... positive supportive relationship"*: Chas Phillips, author interview.

112 *... voted against her ... "apology can go a long way"*: Mayree C. Clark, author interview.

113   *"These so-called analytical ... system was opaque"*: Robert G. Scott, author interview.

113   *off-site meeting ... paid more than he was:* Confidential sources, author interviews.

114   *"... a mysterious process ... Purcell couldn't justify ..."*: Scott, author interview.

114   *"Never refer to me as your partner again"*: See Gasparino and Raghavan, "How Dean Witter Boss Beat Heir Apparent."

115   *"... That doesn't mean you want to lose $100 million ... or a billion"*: Author interview, confidential source. This attitude toward risk was voiced by many former and current Institutional Securities executives.

115   *"... never lost $400 million"*: Multiple sources, author interviews.

115   *When John Mack ran Fixed Income ... "Mack would double"*: Confidential source, author interview.

116   *"Phil had had it with Morgan Stanley's big bets"*: Author interviews, confidential sources.

117   *"Phil and I had several conversations ... 'Your figures are wrong'"*: Robert G. Scott, author interview.

117   *"creative thought" ... A regional broker ... "malfeasance at the highest levels"*: From letters sent to the Group of Eight in early April 2005, by executives in Morgan Stanley's Retail Division.

118   *"It was Phil's club ... You are the most important people ..."*: Confidential source, author interview.

119   *"You can't run ... to integrate it"*: Anson Beard, author interview.

119   *"The Dean Witter refrain was ... save more money"*: Scott, author interview.

120   *"If you wound him up ..."*: Senior banker, author interview.

120   *Purcell never called Stephen A. Schwarzman ... in eight years.* See, Ann Davis, "How Tide Turned Against Purcell in struggle at Morgan Stanley," Wall Street Journal Online, June 14, 2005.

120   *"That was a great affair you guys ... when he returned"*: Richard A. Debs, author interview.

120   *"... disconnected from his own company"*: Investment banker, author interview.

120   *he proposed a strategy to revise the client/banker structure:* See David Rynecki, "Morgan Stanley's Man on the Spot," *Fortune*, November 15, 2004, Internet source.

122   *"The person who punished Phil every day ..."*: Confidential source, author interview.

122   *"What can I do to make John happy? ..."*: Author interviews, multiple sources. This was a widely told story.

122   *"Name one thing ... Tell me. What?"*: Author interview, confidential source.

122   *"That was really puzzling ... Why fire him?"*: Confidential source, author interview.

122   *"probably is the most incompetent..."*: See Jonathan A. Knee, *The Acci-
      dental Investment Banker: Inside the Decade That Transformed Wall
      Street* (New York: Oxford University Press USA, 2006), 196.

123   *"might be the best investment bank...by inept lawyers and flacks"*: See
      Kate Kelley, "Morgan Stanley's Season in Hell," *New York Observer,*
      September 27, 1999, 29. Further citations, if not otherwise identified,
      are from this story.

124   *"We* had *a logo"*: Joe Fogg, author interview.

124   Orange County case: Author interview with a confidential source who
      was a member of the Morgan Stanley legal department at the time.

127   *"Do you think you have to buy a Ferrari..."*: Author interview, confiden-
      tial source.

128   *"a general in search of a war"*: Author interview, confidential source.
      This perception of Kempf was widely held and expressed in different
      ways by many people in the course of interviews.

128   *making life at the office "hell"...provoke the firm to fire her:* Author inter-
      view, confidential source who was a member of the management com-
      mittee at the time. Numerous other sources, including women at the
      firm, confirmed this information.

129   *"John wanted to protect us..."*: Confidential source, author interview.

129   *on the car phone...:* Senior Morgan Stanley executive, author inter-
      view.

129   *"This merger isn't working...cut it with a knife"*: Multiple sources, au-
      thor interviews.

130   *At another meeting..."How do we define success?"*: Multiple sources,
      author interviews.

130   *"fascinating"..."terrible idea"..."leadership is in denial"*: Confidential
      sources, author interviews.

130   *"welcome the bringers of change...with a real answer"*: See Ethan Raisel,
      The McKinsey Way (New York: McGraw-Hill, 1999), 27.

6: "AXE MAN"

132   Chapter title refers to the caption in Kimberly Seals, "Morgan's Machia-
      velli," *New York Post,* February 25, 2001, 54.

132   *"needed to run a consumer business"*: See Charles Gasparino and Anita
      Raghavan, "How Dean Witter Boss Beat Heir Apparent at Morgan Stan-
      ley for Merged Company," *Wall Street Journal,* March 22, 2001, Internet.

132   *"...Let's change something"*: Confidential source, author interview.

132   *"Some people left...taking risk"*: Confidential source, author interview.

132   *"Phil probably really believed...how it was made"*: Confidential source,
      author interview.

133   *"...didn't do a merger":* Confidential source, author interview.

133 *"picked up their bags and left"*: Confidential source, author interview.

133 *"John always had people thinking about him..."*: Author interview with an advisory director.

134 *...He wanted to be sure they understood...would leave with him...*: Jeanne Donovan Fisher, author interview.

135 Morgan Stanley's independent directors listed in the 2001 Annual Report were Robert P. Bauman, former CEO of SmithKline Beecham PLC; Edward A. Brennan, former chairman and CEO of Sears, Roebuck and Co.; John E. Jacob, executive vice president and chief communications officer, Anheuser-Busch Companies, Inc.; C. Robert Kidder, chairman and CEO, Borden, Inc.; Charles F. Knight, chairman, Emerson Electric Co.; John W. Madigan, chairman, president, and CEO, Tribune Corp.; Miles L. Marsh, former chairman and CEO, Fort James Corporation; Michael A. Miles, who at the time was Special Limited Partner, Forstmann Little & Co.; and Laura Tyson, dean, London Business School.

135 Scott's description of the conversation about the presidency between Purcell and Scott: Robert Scott, author interview.

135 *"There's no anger here..."*: See Patrick McGeehan, "The Markets: Market Place; Old Money Gives Way to Main Street," *New York Times*, January 25, 2001, Business/Financial Desk, C1.

136 *"The first time I ever met...he bumps me"*: Confidential source, author interview.

136 *"...that it is not compared to its peers"...among the incomparables:* See Emily Thornton (in New York) with Stanley Reed (in London), "Morgan Stanley's Midlife Crisis," *BusinessWeek Online*, June 25, 2001, http://www.businessweek.com/magazine/content/01_26/b3738095.htm.

136 *"You either allocate enough capital...or you buy a bank"*: "Morgan Stanley's Midlife Crisis," Emily Thornton and Stanley Reed, *BusinessWeek*, June 25, 2001.

137 *"Never has one small triangle...symbol of change"*: See Patrick McGeehan, "A Bank's New Look (Minus Dean Witter)," *New York Times*, April 2, 2001, Business/Financial Desk, C2.

137 *"It was unveiled...has to sell the troops"*: Author interview, former managing director.

137 *"There is a lot of room for improvement"*: See Patrick McGeehan, "Credit Suisse Shakes Up First Boston," *New York Times*, July 13, 2001, Business/Financial Desk, C1.

138 *Byron Wien produced another skit... "confusion of our clients"*: Text courtesy of Byron Wien.

139 *Kimberly Seals:* "Morgan's Machiavelli," *New York Post.*

139 *...threatened to withdraw their business:* See Philip Shenon, "Morgan Stanley Says It 'Clearly Made a Mistake' by Inviting Clinton to Speak," *New York Times*, February 11, 2002, National Desk, 34.

139 " 'personal behavior as president' ": Ibid.

140 "laying out in withering detail... time to relax and enjoy it": See Landon Thomas Jr., "Phil's Pyrrhic Win: Phil Purcell Seized the Top at Morgan Stanley—Just in Time for the Recession," *New York Observer,* April 2, 2001, 25.

140 "The Succession Procession": Text and details courtesy of Byron Wien.

142 "How about giving up Steve Crawford... shined his boots...": Confidential source, author interview.

142 "cute little Tudor": Confidential source, author interview.

143 "... There's no way in hell... could be pretty terse": Confidential source, author interview.

143 "Well, is there a landing strip there?": From "The Succession Procession," text and details courtesy of Byron Wien.

143 Unless otherwise indicated, the events during the week of September 11, 2001, were recounted to the author by Robert G. Scott.

144 *At 1585 Broadway...:* Described to the author by a management committee member.

144 "could see the flames... of the building": See Seth Schiesel and Riva D. Atlas, "By-the-Numbers Operation at Morgan Stanley Finds Its Human Side," *New York Times,* September 16, 2001, Internet source.

145 ... and it hung on the wall in his office...: See Patrick McGeehan, "After the 'Darkest Year,' a Changed Wall Street," *New York Times,* September 8, 2002, Money and Business/Financial Desk, section 3, 1.

146 "made more capital available... for clients": See Emily Thornton, "We Wanted to Maintain Confidence," *BusinessWeek Online,* September 20, 2001, http://www.businessweek.com/bwdaily/dnflash/sep2001/nf20010920_9999.htm.

146 "Communication was the most important thing...": Robert G. Scott, "Leading in a Crisis: September 11th and Its Aftermath" (remarks at Burden Auditorium, Harvard Business School, "Rising to the Challenge" Series, December 5, 2001, Harvard Business School Working Knowledge article by Catherine Walsh, http://hbswk.hbs.edu/archive/2690.html).

146 "Some good comes out of everything... one firm now": Author interviews, reported by multiple advisory directors.

147 *Purcell offered to sell the new building to Lehmann:* See Michelle Pacelle, "Morgan Stanley to Buy Tower in New York—Midtown Site Would Be Just Around the Corner from New Home Office," *Wall Street Journal,* March 28, 1994, A9.

147 "Does this make sense?... functional isolation... how did we redeploy the capital...": Confidential source, author interview.

148 "This group has never agreed on anything... say yes to Phil": Confidential source, author interview.

148   *...in 2001, it was down to $10.4 billion...*: See McGeehan, "After the 'Darkest Year,' a Changed Wall Street."

150   *"...don't owe her any of their profits...losses"*: See Per Jebsen, "Analysts Can Breathe Easier after Meeker Ruling," Reuters, August 22, 2001.

150   *"The firm reluctantly agreed to settle...conviction about"*: Author interview, confidential source.

150   *"Not one thing"*: Reported in multiple publications.

150   *"Phil took a victory...ire of the SEC to Morgan Stanley"*: Author interview, confidential source.

150   *"deeply troubled...troubling lack of conviction"*: Reported in multiple publications.

151   Citations from Morgan Stanley, *Annual Report 2002*.

151   *"It's not every day...at his ease"*: See Landon Thomas Jr. (compiled by Mark A. Stein), "Private Sector; Talking Taxes through the Roar of the Floor," *New York Times*, February 16, 2003, Money and Business/Financial Desk, section 3, 2.

152   *...net income was down 15 percent in 2002...leaning back in his chair; "grinning"*: See Patrick McGeehan and Landon Thomas Jr., "No Worry, Even Now, at Morgan Stanley," *New York Times*, Money and Business/Financial Desk, section 3, 1.

153   *"We were the first group on Wall Street...in the top five"*: Confidential source, author interview.

153   *Scott recalls...had some "interesting conversation pieces..." got off the phone*: Robert Scott, author interviews.

155   *Purcell...went to see Joe Perella..."get in the way"*: Multiple sources, author interviews.

155   *"It was one of the early events...'love you, Dick'"* and *"chilly response...a lot of us were."*: Multiple sources, author interviews.

155   *"It went on and on...touched"*: Jeanne Donovan Fisher, author interview.

156   *"The Mea Culpa Is Me Award"*: See Gretchen Morgenson, "Market Watch: A Year's Debacles, from Comic to Epic," *New York Times*, December 28, 2003, Money and Business/Financial Desk, section 3, 1.

157   *"instrumental in forging...HSBC"*: Morgan Stanley, *Annual Report 2002*.

157   *"The idea that people...didn't exist"*: Confidential source, author interview.

157   *focus on succession... "board was in tune"*: Author interview, confidential source.

158   *"definitely a managed situation"*: Mayree C. Clark, author interview.

158   *"never went to the trading floor...at night"*: Former managing director, author interview.

158   *"The essence of the situation...:"* Confidential source, author interview.

158   The expression *"the culture of NO"* was repeated in multiple author interviews.

159 *"an appalling decision...got rid of the entire team"*: Brad Hintz, author interview.

159 *"If you were a CEO with a consulting background..."*: Confidential source, author interview.

159 *"there was nobody to talk to except Wachovia...didn't say that"*: Multiple sources, author interviews.

161 *"the company did not think she should get any of the money..."*: Don Kempf, as quoted in Patrick McGeehan, "Morgan Stanley Settles Bias Suit with $54 Million," *New York Times*, July 13, 2004, Business/Financial Desk, section A, 1.

161 Descriptions and quotations from the Barcelona meeting are taken from a video made at the conference.

162 Description of the lunch conversation was provided by multiple sources.

163 *"best credit cycle..."*: Zoe Cruz, widely quoted.

163 *"The Vikram I know...old Morgan Stanley"*: Former managing director, author interview.

164 *"If you drew a green line...more red lines than green..."*: Former senior executive, author interview.

7: THE SIEGE OF PHILIP PURCELL

165 *Purcell...agreed to be interviewed:* See David Rynecki, "Morgan Stanley's Man on the Spot," *Fortune*, November 15, 2004, unless otherwise stated, Internet source.

165 *"nobody was interested in Dean Witter"*: Confidential source, author interview.

166 *"Was this with the dust bunnies..."*: See Susan Beck, "Recipe for Disaster," *American Lawyer Magazine*, April 2006, 135.

166 *his failure to articulate a clear vision for the firm... "an uncertainty discount on the stock"*: See Brad Hintz, Sanford Bernstein analyst and former Morgan Stanley managing director, quoted in Rynecki, "Morgan Stanley's Man on the Spot."

167 *the idea of reuniting the House of Morgan...:* See Ron Chernow, *The House of Morgan: An American Banking Dynasty and the Rise of Modern Finance* (New York: A Morgan Entrekin Book/Atlantic Monthly Press, 1990), 588.

167 *[Purcell] had "changed" the way Morgan Stanley investment bankers worked:* See Rynecki, "Morgan Stanley's Man on the Spot."

168 *"that would have been a disaster..."*: Former senior banker, author interview.

168 *"a bit surprised...furious with its CEO, Phil Purcell...CEO of Disney"*: Richard Bove, Punk, Ziegel, December 2004.

169   *"In my eighteen years...embarrassed to be president of Notre Dame...*
      trustees...value system of the athletic department have been totally dis-
      rupted": See Pete Thamel, "Notre Dame's President Says He Opposed
      Firing Willingham," *New York Times*, December 9, 2004, section D, 1.

169   *The Notre Dame football program contributes...*: From televised profile
      of current Notre Dame coach, October 30, 2006.

171   Letter from Scott Sipprelle: Scott Sipprelle, author interview, and quo-
      tations from his letter by permission of Scott Sipprelle.

174   *"Morgan's Machiavelli"*: See Kimberly Seals, "Morgan's Machiavelli,"
      New York Post, February 25, 2001, 54.

174   *"one of the legends...Morgan Stanley"*: Phil Purcell's memo was pub-
      lished in multiple newspapers.

175   *...begun to call "the Evil Empire"*: This phrase was repeated in a num-
      ber of author interviews with people formerly and currently working at
      Morgan Stanley.

175   "Ultimus Romanorum . . . *architect of Morgan Stanley was gone"*: E-mail
      provided and reprinted with the kind permission of Brad Hintz.

176   *Fisher told her... "Morgan Stanley way of doing this...just too sick..."*:
      Confidential source, author interview.

176   *"Each participant, no matter how long their involvement..."*: From *Mor-*
      gan Stanley 1990, privately published by Morgan Stanley, 6.

177   *"...I chose a friend...not the firm"*: Jeanne Donovan Fisher, author in-
      terview.

177   *People who were there... "this is not going away...deal with it"*: Multiple
      sources.

177   *"My phone didn't stop ringing..."*: Scott Sipprelle, author interview.

178   *"There Is No Disinfectant Like Sunlight"*: Text provided and reprinted
      by kind permission of Scott Sipprelle.

178   *Copper Arch released an eighteen-page report titled "Morgan Stanley: A*
      Time for Change": Relative Stock Performance, ROE Comparison, Earn-
      ings Growth, Benefits of Scale and Diversification ("more volatile, more
      risky"), Business Unit Analysis, Merging Origination with Distribu-
      tion: Impact on Retail Brokerage Productivity, Conglomerate Discount
      Is Indisputable, Restructuring Unlocks Value.

179   Description of meeting between Steve Crawford and Scott Sipprelle
      from author interview of Scott Sipprelle.

179   *headlines that reflected the erosion of the firm's reputation*: See Copper Arch
      Capital, "Morgan Stanley: A Time for Change," February 2005, 11.

179   *they were also geographically and socially entwined*: See Landon Thomas
      Jr., "A Path to a Seat on the Board? Try the Fairway," *New York Times*,
      March 11, 2006, section A, 1.

8: THE LAST GATHERING OF THE EAGLES

181 *on the morning of January 12 ... a record year for Morgan Stanley*: Video-tape of the meeting, by kind permission of Morgan Stanley.

182 Descriptions of Dick Fisher's memorial service are from multiple sources, a videotape and program of the service, provided by the kind permission of Jeanne Donovan Fisher, and the text of Robert Scott's talk, by his kind permission.

185 *"I've never been to a memorial service ... I told myself, 'Mary! Think about Dick!'"*: Mary Meeker, author interview.

185 *"When I saw all our former colleagues ... Don Kempf walked into the church ... no right to be here"*: Author interview, confidential source expressing a sentiment that was mentioned in interviews with others as well.

186 *"Scotty was saying ... situation"*: Author interview, confidential source.

186 *"Everybody had inhaled the fact ... Who can I call?"*: Author interview, confidential source.

187 *"last gathering of the eagles"*: Robert G. Scott, author interview.

PART II: THE BATTLE IS JOINED
9: THE LETTER

191 Description and quotes from the February 1, 2005, branch managers' meeting from video, courtesy of Morgan Stanley.

193 *"Somebody's got to do something ... come from this floor"*: Anson Beard, author interview.

194 *"Getting rid of Phil Purcell was a '10' ... in his pocket"*: Parker Gilbert, author interview.

195 *"Whoa, this is big ... a lot of money"*: Karen Scott, author interview.

195 *"All over the place ... enough people"*: Richard Debs, author interview.

195 *"I was focused on the people ... had to do something about it"*: Joe Fogg, author interview.

196 *"We wanted to save ... build"*: John Wilson, author interview.

197 *"I don't like to lose. Ever"*: Video of Anson Beard's retirement dinner.

198 *"I hope they are tapping ... leading this firm"*: Beard, author interview.

198 *"brilliant, but irascible"*: See Elliott D. Lee, "Morgan Stanley's Joseph Fogg Is Back in the Game He Pioneered: Takeovers," *Wall Street Journal*, February 3, 1988, Internet source.

198 *"Morgan Stanley's Main Merger Man"*: See John A. Byrne, "Morgan Stanley's Main Merger Man," *BusinessWeek*, June 18, 1990, Internet source.

199 *"I'm the M & A guy ... hire lawyers and a proxy firm"*: Joe Fogg, author interview.

199 *Nearly all of them were interested... to keep senior regulators apprised:* Dick Debs, author interview.

200 *"...We like credit not debt here...":* Recounted by Fred Whittemore, author interview.

201 *"...to end the Advisory Directors program":* Confidential source, author interview.

201 *"One-on-one...":* John Wilson, author interview.

202 *"We asked ourselves... to argue it out":* Anson Beard, author interview.

204 *"How about Greenhill...":* Anson Beard, author interview.

204 *"...virtual death marches...":* See Brett Cole, "Greenhill Flies Solo," *Bloomberg*, May 2005, 46.

204 *front-page article about his "comeback"... a $1 billion deal:* See Steven Lipin, "How Greenhill, with Compaq, Caps Comeback," *Wall Street Journal*, January 28, 1998.

205 *"Greenhill's IPO should be good... for you":* See Andrew Bary, "What's His Deal? Robert Greenhill's IPO Should Be Good for Him—But Not Necessarily for You," *Barrons*, May 3, 2004, 26. (In May 2006, Greenhill's stock was in the high $60s, nearly quadruple the IPO price, and the company floated a second public offering of four million shares.)

205 *stock opened at $17.50:* See Cole, "Greenhill Flies Solo."

205 *"...You want to do what?...":* As recounted to the author by people who were at the meeting.

205 *"We're the people who built the thing up... have to lead by personal example...":* Robert Greenhill, author interview.

205 *"...How do you feel about your CEO... share price?":* Scott Bok, author interview.

206 *"The most important advice... right about that...":* Parker Gilbert, speaking for the Group of Eight, author interview.

206 *"Mergers and acquisitions advice... It helps":* John Liu, author interview.

206 *"This was totally unlike... totally trust these people":* Scott Bok, author interview.

206 *"At some point... handle that?":* Bob Greenhill, author interview.

207 *"He was very up-front... think about it... The opportunity to work with... If we failed, it would have been a stupid move":* Andrew Merrill, author interview.

208 For the full text of the Group of Eight's March 3, 2005, letter, please refer to the Appendix and http://www.futureofms.com/letters_to _the_board.html.

209 *...the group was sitting in Greenhill's office... "Okay, I'll look for the letter":* As recounted by a number of people who were there.

10: REACTION

211 *A number of people heard... "This is serious":* As reported in the media, and to the author by colleagues of Perella's, to whom he spoke at the time.

212 *"it was chaotic. Deer in the headlights":* Confidential source, author interview.

212 *"It initially looked like...":* Confidential source, author interview.

213 *"Extravagant CEO Pay Is Back":* See Michael Brush, "Extravagant CEO Pay Is Back," *MSN,* March 16, 2005, http://moneycentral.msn.com/content/P110762.asp.

213 *unless return on equity was 10 percent or more:* Ibid.

213 *"brass-knuckle":* See Landon Thomas Jr., "Counselor for All Reasons," *New York Times,* July 28, 2005, C, 1.

213 *inventor of a powerful defense... Monks threatened a proxy fight:* Ibid.

216 *Gilbert was on vacation in the Caribbean... of all the remarks... those kept echoing in his head:* Parker Gilbert, author interview.

217 Information on March 15 and March 16 board meetings from a confidential source.

217 *"I was trying to be efficient"... "their representatives":* See Patrick McGeehan, "Can Meetings Restore Trust," *New York Times,* May 11, 2003, section 3, 1.

217 *"expected to attend":* See Patrick McGeehan, "This Year, More Boards Feel Pressure to Show Up," *New York Times,* March 31, 2004.

217 *"the slimmest election margin":* Associated Press, April 8, 2005.

217 *"to ascertain what they were really feeling"... "in all divisions":* Multiple author interviews.

218 *Joe Perella was hosting... and Sandy Weill:* As recounted to the author by multiple sources to whom Perella spoke at the time.

221 *"If you move these people...":* Author interview, confidential source.

221 *Crawford "was set up":* Confidential source, author interview.

222 *"we're going to do it Monday. Everybody agrees":* Author interview, confidential source.

223 *"If he had been doing... planes":* Author interview, confidential source.

223 *Byron Wien... announced... "million dollars is safe":* Byron Wien, author interview.

223 *"... I want to be with my guys":* Brad Hintz, author interview.

223 Descriptions of Monday, March 28, "massacre" from multiple sources.

225 Description of the meeting at Parker Gilbert's from people who were there.

225 *"The Gates, Central Park, New York, 1979–2005":* http:///www.christojeanneclaude.neet/tg/html.

226 *"You need to get up to Parker's apartment...I was excited...Force this out":* Andrew Merrill, interview with the author.

227 *former chauffeur told a* New Yorker *reporter... "two days running...":* See "Hackman," "Talk of the Town," *The New Yorker;* undated clipping, 1930s, J. P. Morgan Chase Library, J. Pierpont Clippings.

228 *"shun the limelight...plague":* See "The Morgan Houses: The Seniors, Their Partners, and Their Aides," *New York Tribune,* April 1, 1913, cited in Carosso Papers, Box 9, Pierpont Morgan Library.

228 *had "not practiced...ritual...suffered far less embarrassment":* Undated clipping.

228 *Tom Lamont was steaming across the Atlantic... "nature and importance of the firm's transactions":* Carosso Papers, courtesy of the Pierpont Morgan Library. A notation in Carosso's handwriting reads, "The full citation for this item is: TW Lamont Papers, File 110–2 (JPM & C.) Baker Library, Harvard Graduate School of Business, Boston."

228 *"classes as enemies...publicity":* See John K. Winkler, "Profiles: Mighty Dealer in Dollars I," *The New Yorker,* February 2, 1929, 23.

228 *Perry Hall proposed... "reconsider our policy of not advertising...":* Fred Whittemore papers, possibly John Young's files.

229 "Alone among the Morgan banks...": Ron Chernow, *The House of Morgan: An American Banking Dynasty and the Rise of Modern Finance* (New York: A Morgan Entrekin Book, Atlantic Monthly Press, 1990), 722.

229 *"Do you want to be on the call?"...action of some sort:* Confidential source, author interview.

230 *"paralyzed the firm... We are Morgan Stanley":* Stephen Roach, author interview.

231 Description of the March 29 meeting from multiple sources who were present.

231 *"Up until March 28...things in the extreme":* Byron Wien, author interview.

232 *"Intrigue Engulfs Morgan Stanley":* See Landon Thomas Jr., "Intrigue Engulfs Morgan Stanley: 2 Executives Out," *New York Times,* March 30, 2005, 1 and C5.

233 CNBC quotations from videotape courtesy of Andrew Merrill.

233 *"...a fair amount of debate...that this wasn't a flight of fancy"... "I probably should have told you this sooner":* Andrew Merrill, author interview.

236 "Letter to the Morgan Stanley Board of Directors," courtesy of the Group of Eight.

237 *Judge Elizabeth T. Maass... "consciousness of guilt...":* See Suzanne Craig, "Age of Discovery: How Morgan Stanley Botched a Big Case," *Wall Street Journal,* May 16, 2005, Internet source.

237   *The* Saturday Night Live *skit: Saturday Night Live*, SNL-Morgan Stan-
       ley, 0:58. This video was widely circulated online.
239   *"biggest shareholder coup in history"*: Michael Martinez, *Associated
       Press*, TK.
239   *"Purcell was hated...ate him alive"*: See James J. Cramer, "Phil Purcell's
       People Problem," *New York Magazine*, June 27, 2005, http://nymag
       .com/nymetro/news/bizfinance/columns/bottomline/12072/.
239   *"It was a merger of patricians and plebeians..."*: Ron Chernow, as
       quoted in Landon Thomas Jr., "Out of the Tar Pits, Into the House
       of Morgan," *New York Times*, April 3, 2005, Sunday Business Sec-
       tion, 4.
239   *"at Morgan Stanley...history matters"*: See Peter Thal Larsen, "Mor-
       gan Stanley's Glory Days Are Gone for Good. The Rebels Will Not
       Undo Purcell's Damage," *Financial Times*, April 4, 2005, 22.
239   *"a so-so credit-card...internal dissension"*: See Michael Thomas, "A Sad
       Wall Street Story Line: Quality Engulfed by Mediocrity," *New York
       Observer*, April 11, 2005, 1.

11: "WHERE'S OUR $30 BILLION?" AND OTHER QUESTIONS

242   *"Bob Greenhill's tried to spin this firm apart...no more them versus us"*:
       Dialogue and description from video of the meeting, courtesy of Mor-
       gan Stanley.
242   *"...killing the competition"*: Ibid.
243   *Purcell organized a dinner..."loyalty oath"*: Recounted to the author by
       multiple confidential sources.
244   *"more properly valued as a stand-alone...asset management business"*:
       See Jed Horowitz, "Purcell: 'I Have Absolute Confidence' in Decisions
       Made,'" *Dow Jones Newswires*, April 4, 2004.
244   *"Some analysts...former executives"..."know all the tricks"*: See Roder-
       ick Boyd, "Morgan Stanley Dissidents Name CEO Choice," *New York
       Sun*, April 6, 2005, http://www.nysun.com/article/11770.
245   *"Phil Purcell has a major people problem...operating units"*: Andrew
       Merrill, as quoted in various newspapers.
245   *"Discover would drop...negatively affected..."*: Brad Hintz, author in-
       terview.
245   Description of London meeting and quotes from video, courtesy of Mor-
       gan Stanley.
246   *"tough under the boards and a decent shooter"*: Confidential source, au-
       thor interview.
246   *Another managing director..."we'll get to the white smoke"*: Confidential
       source, author interview.

246 *"it's over with the board... we are moving on"*: "Another Exec Exits Morgan Stanley. Marks the Sixth Departure of a Key Management Figure at the Investment House in the Last Two Weeks," *CNNMoney.com*, April 8, 2005.

246 *Jack Welch... echoed... "It's over. The board is with him"*: See Shawn McCarthy, "Purcell Bloodied, But Still Standing," *The Globe and Mail* (Toronto), Sympaticomsn.workopolis.com, April 9, 2005.

247 *"Phil was a tough competitor..."*: David Komansky, as quoted in *Financial Times*, April 8, 2005.

247 *"a complex mix... snobbery... not to call them idiots"*: See Michael Skapinker, "What Every Dissident Former Executive Needs to Know," *Financial Times*, April 6, 2005, Internet source.

247 *"according to Vaastu principles"*: See Lavina Melwani, "The High Life," *Little India*, January 2005, http://littleindia.com/january2005/TheHighLife.htm.

248 Description of Merin's "filling station" presentation was recounted to the author by a person who attended the Insights meeting; confidential source.

248 *"To my colleagues at Morgan Stanley... harm our franchise"*: Phil Purcell's internal memorandum, published on Global News today, na.ms.com/portal/site/MorganStanleyToday/index.

249 *"That was a critical error... have stayed at the firm"*: Author interview, confidential source.

249 The Board's letter was published in multiple newspapers.

249 *"united as if they were back on a deal team"*: See Randall Smith, Suzanne Craig, and Ann Davis, "Push to Oust Morgan Stanley CEO Reflects Simmering Culture Clash," *Wall Street Journal*, March 31, 2005, A1.

250 Excerpts from letters and e-mails to the Group of Eight, reprinted by permission of the Group of Eight.

253 *"I want to avoid the emotional issues... heed the call"*: Judson Reis, letter to the board, reprinted with permission.

253 *"What do you guys think you're doing... Just move on"*: Voice mail played for the author by Andrew Merrill.

254 *"People who hold shares... before they give up their votes"*: See Michael Martinez, "Uphill Fight for Morgan Stanley Dissidents," *AP Newswires*, April 8, 2005.

254 *"Scotty was our sacrificial lamb"*: Richard Debs, author interview.

254 *Morgan Stanley's response:* This was published in multiple newspapers.

254 *"It's an edifying spectacle... more internal harmony"*: See Michael Martinez, "MS Dissidents Want New CEO," *AP Newswires*, April 5, 2005.

255 *"Everyone's initial reaction... to succeed"*: Andrew Merrill, author interview.

255 *John Wilson said, "Every day we were sure…locked out":* John Wilson, author interview.

255 *"quite the contrary…abandoning ship":* Richard Debs, author interview.

255 *According to Hintz… "filled the room beyond capacity":* Brad Hintz, author interview.

256 *"Dick never spoke…would have been a Group of Nine":* Jeanne Donovan Fisher, author interview.

256 Details of Bob Scott's plan with the tag "Where's Our $30 Billion?" from his notes, given to the author, courtesy of Robert G. Scott.

259 *"We understand…short on specifics":* This response was published in multiple newspapers.

259 *"The rebels…ousted him from Morgan Stanley":* See *Financial Times* MS, April 6, 2005, Internet source.

259 *As Scott describes the experience… "always in a hurry":* Robert G. Scott, author interview.

259 *"They agreed with a lot we had to say…proxy fight":* Parker Gilbert, author interview.

260 *When Joe Perella returned from England… "than get rid of Phil":* As recounted to the author from multiple confidential sources to whom Perella spoke at the time.

261 *"I'm not sure if mediocrity…governance…plan and vision":* See Michael Martinez, "MS Dissidents Want New CEO," *AP Newswires,* April 5, 2005.

262 *"We are always willing to listen…":* As reported in multiple newspapers.

264 *Karen Scott was about to enter…:* Karen Scott, author interview.

264 *"Gentlemen…very truly yours":* The letter was published in multiple newspapers.

265 *"are considering…advice to the dissidents":* See Katherine Griffiths, "Business Analysis: Where Egos Dare: Wall Street Runs Red in the Battle for Morgan Stanley," *The Independent* (London), April 15, 2005, 62.

265 *"the directors may not have ever seen those clip books":* Andrew Merrill, author interview.

265 *"because of actual or perceived…In all honesty…establishes it":* See Susan Beck, "Recipe for Disaster," *American Lawyer,* April 2006, op cit.

265 *$200 million in "retention bonuses":* Multiple sources, author interviews.

266 *when Joe Perella and Terry Meguid…:* Confidential sources, multiple author interviews.

267 *"business where stature and reputation count for a lot":* See James Politik, David Wells, and Richard Beales (in New York) and Lina Saigol (in London), "Senior Duo Join Exodus from Bank," *Financial Times,* April 14, 2005.

267 *"I found myself uncomfortable…what Phil had done"*: See Avital Louria Hahn, "Banker of the Year: Mr. Relationship," *Investment Dealers Digest* (Thompson Media), January 16, 2006.

268 *"How Much Is Joe Perella's Silence Worth?"*: See Michael Lewis, "How Much Is Joe Perella's Silence Worth?" *Bloomberg.com*, May 27, 2005.

268 *"…to changing the outlook of the board"*: Confidential source, author interview.

268 *"not a very comfortable setting"*: Author interview, confidential source.

269 *"Morgan Stanley never gets an 'F'…better for him to leave"*: Confidential source, author interview.

270 Description of the meeting between Gilbert, Scott, Bernard, and three board members, by Gilbert and Scott. Quotations from transcripts of author interviews with Gilbert and Scott.

12: "I DON'T CARE IF THEY FIRE ME." (AND "I QUIT.")

273 Description of the circumstances surrounding the letter, and quotations from Mary Meeker, Stephen Roach, Byron Wien, Henry McVey, and Ruth Porat are from interviews with the author. Text of the letter reprinted with permissions of Meeker et al.

273 *"Hail Mary"*: See cover story, "Hail Mary," *New York*, January 24, 2000, http://nymag.com/nymetro/news/bizfinance/biz/features/1845/.

274 *"The Human Contrarian" and "Mr. Permabear"*: See Joseph Wiesenthal, "Stephen Roach: The Human Contrarian Datapoint," *The Stalwart.com*, May 23, 2006, http://www.thestalwart.com/the_stalwart/2006/05/digital_rules_b.html.

278 *The board reached a crossroads…*: Confidential sources, author interviews.

278 *"This is what we're going to do"*: Confidential source, author interview.

280 *Bob Scott responded…"failure in Philip Purcell's leadership"*: Bob Scott's response was published in multiple newspapers.

280 *"It is Philip Purcell's board…"*: See Katherine Griffiths, "Morgan Stanley Fails to Silence Rebel Campaign over Purcell," *The Independent* (London), May 2, 2005, Internet source.

280 *Bob Greenhill told the Eight*: Multiple sources, including Group of Eight and others.

13: FALLOUT

281 *"irrational exuberance"*: Term used by Federal Reserve Board Chairman Alan Greenspan to describe the conditions attendant on the technology boom.

281 Description of the Alleghany crisis from Ron Chernow, *The House of Morgan: An American Banking Dynasty and the Rise of Modern Finance*

(New York: A Morgan Entrekin Book/Atlantic Monthly Press, 1990), 413–414 and 309–310.

284 *two of whom had been executives at Dean Witter*: See Gretchen Morgenson, "Who's Watching Your Fund Manager?" *New York Times*, September 14, 2003, Section 3, 1.

284 *"viewed as a nuisance case"*: See Susan Beck, "Recipe for Disaster," *American Lawyer*, April 2006, 88. While many publications reported on the Perelman case as it was unfolding, Susan Beck's long, well-researched article in *American Lawyer* gives a thorough start-to-finish overview, and I have followed her chronology and often relied on her facts. Her interviews with Donald Kempf in particular, including such quotes as "a nuisance case," were helpful and enlightening.

285 *"Mr. Perelman's company...unpacked its tent...appliance graveyard"*: See Max Rottersman, "Perelman and Barkin Show Morgan Stanley the Big Easy," May 2005, www.wallstreetfreethinker.com/video/20050517/msdw_perelman.

286 *"produce all documents...turpitude"*: See Beck, "Recipe for Disaster."

286 *"...didn't seem to have a strong leader"*: Ibid., 135.

286 *"to prove that it didn't know..."*: Ibid., 136.

286 *"We are dealing with...morally bankrupt"*: Ibid., 138.

287 *A Morgan Stanley executive... "What genius..."*: Confidential source, author interview.

287 *"has contumaciously violated...cannot function this way"*: Beck, "Recipe for Disaster," 138.

288 *confided to a journalist...sympathetic to Morgan Stanley*: Confidential source, author interview.

288 *"...Nobody wants to talk to me"*: Confidential source, author interview.

288 Intrade details from Will Leitch, "Executive View: Smart Money Is on Purcell," *Registered Rep*, May 1, 2005. At the time, intrade.com had about 45,000 members. Each contract had a ten-dollar value.

289 *"the mandate to acquire...bank"*: See Carrick Mollenkamp, "Morgan Stanley Asset Manager Tapped for Citigroup Division," *Wall Street Journal*, June 8, 2005, Internet source.

290 *Gridiron Eleven*: Details and quotes from Donald Brennan, William Kneisel, and Robert McCormack.

294 *"Morgan Stanley's White-Shoe Blues"*: See Michael Carroll, "Morgan Stanley's White-Shoe Blues," *Institutional Investor*, May 2005.

294 *"Brahmins at the Gate"*: See Bethany McLean, Andrew Serwer, and Nicholas Varchaver, "Brahmins at the Gate," *Fortune*, May 2005.

295 *"A War Without Winners"*: See Charles Gasparino, "A War Without Winners," *Newsweek*, May 2, 2005.

295 *two-page comic strip, "Morgan v. Stanley v. Morgan Stanley"*: See Peter Arkle and Jon Gertner, *New York Times Magazine*, June 5, 2005.

295 *"In the event that objectionable ... for a minimum of 48 hours"*: "Morgan Stanley Adds Clause So Can Pull Ads," Reuters, May 18, 2005.

296 *"when you have totally lost control ... what it signals"*: See Liz Moyer, "Managing Ads, Not News," *Forbes*, May 23, 2005, Internet source.

296 *"It was a time ... put on the front page ... There's Dad on the phone again"*: Stephen Roach, author interview.

296 *"We took this very seriously ... leaked to the media"*: Mary Meeker, author interview.

296 *"The signers were the first employees ... consequences from the letter"*: See Randall Smith and Ann Davis, "At Morgan Stanley, Some Worry Clash Endangers Culture," *Wall Street Journal*, May 9, 2005, C1.

296 *letter was written "in a positive and constructive spirit"*: Ibid.

297 *"We were taken aback ... "*: Mary Meeker, author interview.

297 *"Being in the paper every day ..."*: "Purcell Backs Morgan Stanley's Path," *Wall Street Journal*, May 10, 2005.

297 *"Everybody walked away with negativity in their souls"*: Richard Bove, quoted in *US Banker,* "Purcell's (Very Public) Predicament," Karen Krebsbach, June 2005.

298 Conversation between Purcell and Roach, and business card anecdote: Stephen Roach, author interview.

299 *Purcell declared ... "what kind of a mind would do that"*: From a video of Purcell's presentation, courtesy of Morgan Stanley.

14: "ANYONE BUT JOHN MACK"

300 *second-quarter earnings per share were down:* The exact number wasn't made public until June 22, 2005; in early June the estimate was that earnings would be down 15 to 20 percent.

301 *"After that they didn't waste any time ... what it was going to look like"*: Confidential source, author interview.

301 *he could take away by $34.7 million ... if he were fired for cause:* See Theo Francis, "Morgan Stanley's Retiring CEO May Leave with $62.3 Million," *Wall Street Journal*, June 14, 2005, A10.

301 Details of Purcell's "platinum parachute" were widely published. Sources include Eric Dash, "The Reward for Leaving," *New York Times*, July 8, 2005, Section C, 1; "Ex-Morgan Stanley Chief to Get Paycheck for Life," *MSNBC.com*, July 7, 2005; and "Fat City: Purcell's Going-Away Purse," *BusinessWeek*, March 13, 2006, 13.

302 *Someone who was there ... "guilt money"*: Confidential source, author interview.

302 *a fee said to be in the $25 million range:* This number was widely believed to be a close approximation of the fee but could not be confirmed.

302 *adamant that the board should not appoint ... exhorted him not to do it*": Author interviews, multiple confidential sources.

303 *"A board should never ... can act vindictively"*: See Ann Davis, "Closing Bell: How Tide Turned Against Purcell in Struggle at Morgan Stanley," *Wall Street Journal*, June 14, 2005, A1.

303 *"I'd heard that he was working on ... we were relentless"*: Anson Beard, author interview.

304 *"I was surprised ... about the way it was working out"*: Parker Gilbert, author interview.

304 *"After the calls ... in choosing a new CEO"*: Robert G. Scott, author interview.

304 Details and quotations from the meeting at which Purcell announced his retirement are taken from the video of the meeting, courtesy of Morgan Stanley.

306 *"Ding Dong! The Wicked Witch Is Dead"*: Recounted to the author by multiple sources. Andy Kessler of the *Wall Street Journal* may have heard the same story. His June 15, 2005, article, "There's No Place Like ... Morgan Stanley," begins, "Ding dong, the witch is dead."

306 *"Phil and the board have independently been considering"*: See "Morgan Chief Quits after 'Unprecedented Attacks. I've Had Enough of Negative Attention,' Says Philip Purcell as He Steps Down," *The Daily Telegraph* (London), June 14, 2005.

307 *"I kind of like him better now that he's out"*: Confidential source, author interview.

307 *"In Business, Tough Guys Finish Last"*: See Joseph Nocera, "In Business, Tough Guys Finish Last," *New York Times*, June 18, 2005, Business/Financial Desk, C1.

307 *"The saddest part ... trumped personal loyalty"*: See David Andelman, "Few Winners from Purcell's Exit," *Forbes.com*, June 13, 2005, http://www.forbes.com/home/management/2005/06/13/morgan_purcell_commentary_cx_daa_0613commentary.html.

307 *"If it's good they make it look bad ..."*: See David Wighton, "Wall Street Fighter Who Fell on His Sword—Interview—Phil Purcell," *Financial Times*, June 14, 2005, 19.

307 *"oozes wounded pride"*: See *Financial Times*, June 13, 2005, http://us.ft.com/ftgateway/superpage.ft?news_id=fto061320050110002400].

307 *"you had a jihad and it wasn't going to stop ... before long"*: See Ann Davis, "Closing Bell: How Tide Turned against Purcell in Struggle at Morgan Stanley," *Wall Street Journal*, June 14, 2005, A1.

308 June 13, 2005, conference call transcript courtesy of Morgan Stanley.

308 *a panel discussion that day, titled "The End of the Imperial CEO"*: See Alan Murray, "Backlash against CEOs Could Go Too Far," *Wall Street Journal*, June 15, 2005, A2.

309   *A person to whom Paulson mentioned . . . got the better of him:* Confidential source, author interview.

309   *"It was over . . . for us to do":* Parker Gilbert, author interview.

310   *"The place went crazy":* Anson Beard, author interview.

311   *"The prescription . . . poor judgment at the top":* See Patricia Sellers, *Fortune* Web site.

311   the importance of *"talent and culture" in the selection process":* See Michael J. Martinez, "Morgan Stanley Benefits from Mack Return," Associated Press, June 27, 2005, as reprinted in nytimes.com.

312   *BlackRock now had a $391 billion asset pool:* See Landon Thomas Jr., "Candidates Emerging as Morgan Seeks Chief," *New York Times*, June 15, 2005, C1.

312   *"Bonds is all about teamwork . . . teams, organization":* Laurence D. Fink, author interview.

312   *"was a tragic story . . . and Dean Witter was" . . . no one could do it better than John Mack:* Laurence D. Fink, author interview.

314   *"John Mack has the culture . . . he can do it":* Eric J. Gleacher, as quoted in Landon Thomas Jr., "Morgan Stanley Is in Talks to Bring Back Ex-President," *New York Times*, June 25, 2005, B1.

314   dinner at the apartment . . . *"I'm going to take it":* Confidential sources, author interviews.

315   *"the ground rules are still in place":* See Thomas, "Morgan Stanley Is in Talks."

315   "I want Perella back": Confidential source, author interview.

315   *"was initially ruled out . . . to make sure he wanted the job":* See Charles Gasparino, "A War Without Winners," *Newsweek*, May 2, 2005, 52.

315   Description of the scene and quotations from the meeting when John Mack's return was announced at Morgan Stanley are from video, courtesy of Morgan Stanley.

318   *"great ending to the book":* See Gasparino, "A War Without Winners."

15: MACK IS BACK

In regard to image, Morgan Stanley asked Leo Burnett Worldwide, the Chicago-based advertising agency that handled the firm's $80 million advertising budget, to participate with other firms in an agency review. Burnett chose to resign the account, citing as the reason "recent changes at Morgan Stanley."

320   *"Few of life's losers land so affluently":* New York Times, "The Wages of Failure on Wall Street."

320   announced an *"Award for Greed":* by Nicholas D. Kristof, *New York Times*, August 14, 2005.

321 *"I don't want anyone to think..."*: Randall Smith and Ann Davis, "Morgan Stanley's Mack Tears Up Own Pay Deal," *Wall Street Journal.com*, July 8, 2005.

322 *"...This would be a wonderful way to live the rest of your life*: Landon Thomas Jr., "Exile from Wall Street," *New York Times*, August 21, 2005, SundayBusiness, 1.

327 *...The Private Wealth Management Division, which served clients who could invest $10 million or more, had fewer advisors in 2005 than in 1997*: Ann Davis, "Morgan Stanley Sees Salvation at Higher End," *Wall Street Journal*, September 14, 2005.

327 *"...That was clearly a first step, and a step I would argue should have been taken in the past"*: Eric Dash, "Discover Card to Stay at Morgan Stanley," *New York Times*, August 18, 2005.

328 *"In April, 2007, chief economist Stephen Roach..."*: "Morgan Stanley Taps Roach as Asia Chairman," Reuters April 23, 2007.

329 *"...a unique, successful franchise...substantial cash flow"*: Liz Moyer, "Mack Refuses to Attack," *Forbes.com*, August 17, 2005.

330 *"...Morgan Stanley and Discover can go their own paths...value for shareholders"*: From transcript of analysts' call by Morgan Stanley.

334 Performance figures supplied by Morgan Stanley, as of end of April 2007.

335 *"You have to give credit to Zoe Cruz for that"*: CNBC transcript, Charles Gasparino, March 21, 2007.

335 *...Morgan Stanley stock showed a 690 percent increase*: Thomas, "Exile from Wall Street."

337 *In the spring of 2007...Old Lane...*: See Eric Dash, *"Citigroup Adds Hedge Fund and Its Leader,"* *New York Times*, April 14, 2007; and also Randall Smith, "Citi's New Matrh: Can Pandit Deal Add to Profit," *Wall Street Journal*, April 14, 2007, B1; quote from Purcell is from Randall Smith's story.

EPILOGUE

347 *the Federal Reserve...agreed to take over $29 billion of Bear's "most toxic assets"*: See Andrew Ross Sorkin "JPM Raises Bid for Bear to $10 a Share," *New York Times*, March 24, 2008.

347 *"to preserve the integrity and viability of the American financial system"*: Ben Bernanke, Testimony, Senate Banking Committee, April 3, 2008.

348 *disgruntled Goldman trader who received $70 million claimed he was worth at least $100 million, and quit in a fit of pique*: E-mail conversation between Arnaud de Borchgrave and the author.

349 *"a failure of execution of a trading strategy rather than a failure of risk management"*: See Randall Smith and Ann Davis, "Subprime Sword Claims Morgan Stanley's Cruz," *Wall Street Journal*, November 30, 2007.

351 *the* New York Times *suggested that she might be the leading candidate to succeed Mack:* See Landon Thomas Jr., "At Morgan Stanley, a New Focus on Succession," *New York Times*, November 9, 2007.

351 *was "one of the best Wall Street poach jobs in the past five years":* See David Weidner, "Mack's Knife Cuts Both Ways," *MarketWatch*, December 4, 2007.

353 *"a rapid shift back to a culture of debate, inter-unit questioning of trading strategy, and sharp discipline":* Guy Moszkowski, "Liquidity reigns, as risk culture is rebuilt," Merrill Lynch, February 21, 2008.

354 *"Nearly Half of Wall Street Bank Profits Are Gone":* See Louise Story, *New York Times*, June 16, 2008.

354 *83,000 financial service employees worldwide had lost their jobs:* See Andrew Ross Sorkin, "On Wall Street, a year of living dangerously," *International Herald Tribune*, June 25, 2008.

355 *"deal-making has all but stopped":* Ibid.

355 *"keep the terms of the deal as far as possible from being influenced by any market movements":* See Heidi Moore, Deal Journal, "How Bad Is it? The Heroic Morgan Stanley Edition," *Wall Street Journal*, February 22, 2008.

355 *"The threat of moral hazard in this case was simply less dire than the threat of financial contagion":* See James Surowieki, "Too Dumb To Fail," *The New Yorker*, March 31, 2008.

356 *"satisfied with how Morgan Stanley navigated the ongoing market turbulence":* Morgan Stanley, First Quarter Earnings Release, March 19, 2008.

356 *"We are impressed with the firm's ability to generate such returns in the face of substantial asset write-downs":* Guy Moszkowski, "Solid qtr. Despite marks, but cautious outlook," Merrill Lynch, March 19, 2008.

356 *"good job" in reducing the firm's mortgage exposures:* See Glenn Schorr, "Strong Quarter, Challenging Outlook," UBS, March 20, 2008.

356 *"The firm is also likely to benefit from recent market dislocations, particularly in prime brokerage":* See Landon Thomas Jr., "Morgan Stanley Gives Wall Street a Brief Lift," *New York Times*, March 20, 2008.

357 *"And we've got to continue moving the share price up":* Morgan Stanley, Firmwide Open Forum, March 20, 2008.

357 *"Stocks off $2.1 trillion this year":* See Adam Shell, *USA Today*, July 1, 2008.

357 *"Everyone else is kind of opening up the kimono . . .":* See Louise Story, "With a Modest Decline in Profit, Goldman Sachs Outshines Rivals Again," *New York Times*, June 18, 2008.

357 *"pretty frigging brutal":* See Susanne Craig and Carrick Mollenkamp, "Still 'Brutal' at Morgan Stanley," *Wall Street Journal*, June 19, 2008.

357   *"Morgan Stanley Reports 58% Decrease in Profit":* See Landon Thomas, *New York Times*, June 19, 2008.

358   *"total return had trailed the S&P Diversified Financial Index by nearly 40 percent" for the preceding five years:* March 3, 2005, letter from the Group of Eight, "Dear Mr. Purcell . . ."

358   *"It only works if people believe in it":* See Andrew Ross Sorkin, "On Wall Street, a year of living dangerously," *International Herald Tribune*, June 25, 2008.

358   *"We'd be Bank of America":* In October, 2007, Bank of America appointed its fourth head of Investment Banking in seven years and cut 3,000 jobs after turning in what a *New York Times* reporter described as "dismal investment banking performance." Earnings were down 32 percent, and profit "plummeted to $100 million from $1.43 billion a year ago." See Eric Dash, "Shake-Up and Job Cuts At Bank of America: Investment Banking Profit Dropped 93%," *New York Times*, October 25, 2007.

ACKNOWLEDGMENTS

Over nearly two years, I interviewed hundreds of people, each of whom made his or her own evaluation, and then sent me along to another source. In nearly every instance, the primary decision as to whether to talk to me was based on concern for the firm. Anson M. Beard Jr., my former brother-in-law, kindly advised other members of the Group of Eight that, while they were dubious about the prospect of a book being written about their campaign, they should at least give me the chance to talk to them. Without that initial introduction, it would have been difficult to earn the trust of a group that, with the exception of three months in 2005, had spent their working lives avoiding publicity of any kind.

Philip Purcell did not answer my requests to interview him, or my offer to submit questions in writing. Mr. Purcell also discouraged others from talking with me and told senior members of the financial services industry that this book was commissioned and paid for by the Group of Eight. That charge is entirely false.

I owe professional and personal gratitude to my agent, Peter Matson of Sterling Lord Literistic, and his supportive assistant, Rebecca Friedman; and to Henry Ferris at William Morrow, who understood why this story was worth telling, and Peter Hubbard, who helped put it between covers.

More than a dozen distinguished and experienced executives in the financial services industry spent hundreds of hours reviewing versions of this manuscript, checking facts, providing background and fine distinctions, creating spreadsheets, and offering technical information.

Any errors, of course, are my own, but these volunteers, none of whom I knew before I began to research this book, have added dimension, accuracy, and warmth to the story.

Members of the Group of Eight submitted to extensive interviews and checked (and corrected) facts. Thanks also to those who turned the "Eight" into "The Gridiron Eleven": Don Brennan, Bill Kneisel, and Bob McCormack. And from Greenhill and Company: Bob Greenhill, Scott Bok, and John Liu. Andrew Merrill was also of great assistance.

Many of my sources were confidential, and I am grateful for their trust. This book owes an incalculable debt to one brilliant executive, whose constant, loyal, skilled, and funny assistance was often offered between 10 P.M. and midnight, via e-mail and telephone.

I am grateful to Robert Baldwin, former chairman of Morgan Stanley, for his generous exposition of Morgan Stanley history, and I admire his contributions to the modern firm.

Jeanne Donovan Fisher spent many hours with me talking about her late husband, Dick Fisher, and provided me with important background information and warm support.

Scott Sipprelle of Copper Arch Capital, the first voice in the campaign to restore Morgan Stanley to its core excellence, gave me additional insight into the structural issues at the firm.

The assistants at "Jurassic Park," who lived through the crisis, kept their spirits up, and their discretion intact, were consistently courteous and helpful. They are Leila Bandy, Margaret Conyak, Joyce O'Reardon, Nancy Nixon, Nancy Novarro, Christine Horrigan, Farah Santoro, and Patricia Schaefer.

With thanks to: Alex Beard and Amy C. Beard; Hillary Beard Schafer and Steven Schafer; Anson H. Beard, Veronica M. Beard, James M. Beard, and Veronica S. Beard. And for the next generation of Beards: Anson, Clarke, Helaina, Landry, Stella, Scarlett, and India; this story is part of their history.

And to: Barton Biggs; Richard Bove; Lee Carpenter Brokaw, with especial thanks for introducing me to Jeanne Fisher; Susan and Allen Butler, with especial thanks for help at North Haven; Donald Callahan; Peter B. Cannell; Kyran Cassidy; Mayree Clark; Rashmi Jolly Dalai, for her thorough and knowledgeable research and friendship;

Sandy Davidson; Larry Fink; Mark Haranzo (in particular for sending me the *American Lawyer* issue); Bob Greenhill; Brad Hintz; Barbara Hogan; Robert Hottenson; Pamela Howard, for graciously putting my interests ahead of her own; Henry King; Lansing Lamont, for his cordial private tour of Sky Farm on North Haven Island; Jeanmarie McFadden; Jane Lancaster; Arthur Martinez; Henry McVey; Mary Meeker; Robert Monks; Charles Morgan; Liza Morse; Tom Nides; Gary Parr; Michael Patterson; Chas Phillips; Dave Phillips; Ruth Porat; Judson Reis; Stephen Roach; Karen Scott; Robert Scully; Glenn Shorr; Edward Foote Ulmann; Lisa Uribe; Byron Wien; Jeff Williams; and Joelle Yudin, for her last-minute rescue missions.

At the J. Pierpont Morgan Library the librarians and staff members were helpful and gracious, even though I was conducting research when the library was closed during renovations, and the archives were stored in temporary quarters. Research at the J. P. Morgan Chase archives was also greatly assisted by a knowledgeable and helpful staff.

The work of the following journalists contributed substantially to the record, and I am grateful for their interesting, nuanced, and accurate reporting.

For in-depth illumination of the Morgans and their firms, the classic biography-cum-histories are:

Jean Strouse, *Morgan: American Financier*, New York: Harper Perennial, 2000.

Ron Chernow, *The House of Morgan: An American Banking Dynasty and the Rise of Modern Finance*, New York: A Morgan Entrekin Book/Atlantic Monthly Press, 1990.

Judge Harold R. Medina wrote a surprisingly readable description of Wall Street circa 1954 in *Wall Street and the Security Markets: Corrected Opinion of Harold R. Medina in the United States of America, Plaintiff v. Henry S. Morgan, Harold Stanley, et al., doing business as Morgan Stanley & Co. et al., Defendants*, filed February 4, 1954; reprint edition: Arno Press, Inc.

For an understanding of Philip Purcell and the Sears culture that influenced him, the invaluable source is Donald R. Katz, *The Big Store: Inside the Crisis and Revolution at Sears*, New York: Penguin Books, 1987.

Judge Harold R. Medina wrote a surprisingly readable description of Wall Street circa 1954 in *Wall Street and the Security Markets: Corrected Opinion of Harold R. Medina in the United States of America, Plaintiff v. Henry S. Morgan, Harold Stanley, et al., doing business as Morgan Stanley & Co. et al., Defendants*, filed February 4, 1954; reprint edition: Arno Press, Inc.

For an understanding of Philip Purcell and the Sears culture that influenced him, the invaluable source is Donald R. Katz, *The Big Store: Inside the Crisis and Revolution at Sears*, New York: Penguin Books, 1987.

INDEX